PARENTAL RIGHTS, BEST INTERESTS AND SIGNIFICANT HARMS

This timely collection brings together philosophical, legal and sociological perspectives on the crucial question of who should make decisions about the fate of a child suffering from a serious illness. In particular, the collection looks at whether the current 'best interests' threshold is the appropriate boundary for legal intervention, or whether it would be more appropriate to adopt the 'risk of significant harm' approach proposed in *Gard*. It explores the roles of parents, doctors and the courts in making decisions on behalf of children, actively drawing on perspectives from the clinic as well as academia and practice. In doing so, it teases out the potential risks of inappropriate state intrusion in parental decision-making, and considers how we might address them.

AF722440

Parental Rights, Best Interests and Significant Harms

*Medical Decision-Making on Behalf of Children Post-*Great Ormond Street Hospital v Gard

Edited by
Imogen Goold
Jonathan Herring
and
Cressida Auckland

• HART •
OXFORD • LONDON • NEW YORK • NEW DELHI • SYDNEY

HART PUBLISHING
Bloomsbury Publishing Plc
Kemp House, Chawley Park, Cumnor Hill, Oxford, OX2 9PH, UK
1385 Broadway, New York, NY 10018, USA
29 Earlsfort Terrace, Dublin 2, Ireland

HART PUBLISHING, the Hart/Stag logo, BLOOMSBURY and the Diana logo are trademarks of Bloomsbury Publishing Plc
First published in Great Britain 2019

First published in hardback, 2019
Paperback edition, 2021

Copyright © The Editors and Contributors severally 2019

The Editors and Contributors have asserted their right under the Copyright, Designs and Patents Act 1988 to be identified as Authors of this work.

All rights reserved. No part of this publication may be reproduced or transmitted in any form or by any means, electronic or mechanical, including photocopying, recording, or any information storage or retrieval system, without prior permission in writing from the publishers.

While every care has been taken to ensure the accuracy of this work, no responsibility for loss or damage occasioned to any person acting or refraining from action as a result of any statement in it can be accepted by the authors, editors or publishers.

All UK Government legislation and other public sector information used in the work is Crown Copyright ©. All House of Lords and House of Commons information used in the work is Parliamentary Copyright ©. This information is reused under the terms of the Open Government Licence v3.0 (http://www. nationalarchives.gov.uk/doc/open-government-licence/version/3) except where otherwise stated.

All Eur-lex material used in the work is © European Union, http://eur-lex.europa.eu/, 1998–2021.

A catalogue record for this book is available from the British Library.

Library of Congress Cataloging-in-Publication Data

Names: Goold, Imogen, editor. | Herring, Jonathan, editor. | Auckland, Cressida, 1992- editor.

Title: Parental rights, best interests and significant harms : medical decision-making on behalf of children post-Great Ormond Street Hospital v Gard / edited by Imogen Goold, Jonathan Herring and Cressida Auckland.

Description: Oxford ; New York : Hart, 2019. | Includes bibliographical references and index.

Identifiers: LCCN 2019030754 (print) | LCCN 2019030755 (ebook) | ISBN 9781509924899 (hardback) | ISBN 9781509924912 (Epub)

Subjects: LCSH: Children with disabilities—Medical care—Law and legislation—Great Britain. | Parent and child (Law)—Great Britain. | Euthanasia—Law and legislation—Great Britain.

Classification: LCC KD3410.E88 .P37 2019 (print) | LCC KD3410.E88 (ebook) | DDC 346.4101/7—dc23

LC record available at https://lccn.loc.gov/2019030754

LC ebook record available at https://lccn.loc.gov/2019030755

ISBN: HB: 978-1-50992-489-9
PB: 978-1-50995-218-2
ePDF: 978-1-50992-490-5
ePub: 978-1-50992-491-2

Typeset by Compuscript Ltd, Shannon

To find out more about our authors and books visit www.hartpublishing.co.uk. Here you will find extracts, author information, details of forthcoming events and the option to sign up for our newsletters.

FOREWORD

VICTORIA BUTLER-COLE QC

Many years ago, I was a postgraduate student at the Centre of Medical Law and Ethics at King's College London. I had never previously studied law, and I recall poring over judgments, analysing their contents, and, more often than not, being highly critical of their reasoning. I remember very clearly reading the following passage in an article by Ian Kennedy and being in complete agreement with his scathing critique of the legal concept of best interests:

> The best interests test may be beloved of family lawyers but a moment's reflection will indicate that although it is said to be a test … it is not really a test at all. Instead, it is a somewhat crude conclusion of social policy. It allows lawyers and the courts to persuade themselves and others that theirs is a principled approach to law. Meanwhile, they engage in what to others is clearly a form of 'ad hocery'. The best interests approach of family law allows the courts to atomise the law, to claim that each case depends on its own facts. The court can then respond intuitively to each case while seeking to legitimate its conclusion by asserting that it is derived from the general principle contained in the best interests formula. In fact, of course, there is no general principle other than the empty rhetoric of best interests; or rather, there is some principle, but the court is not telling. Obviously, the court must be following some principles, otherwise a toss of a coin could decide cases. But these principles, which serve as pointers to what amounts to best interests, are not articulated by the court. Only the conclusion is set out. The opportunity for reasoned analysis and scrutiny is lost.[1]

The challenge to the concept of 'best interests' set down by Kennedy is pursued by the chapters in this volume, and rightly so. Lawyers and judges should think critically about the system in which they are operating, and must be open to the possibility that the way in which decisions are made could be improved. Although Kennedy's criticisms were directed at the substance of those decisions, his points are of equal relevance to the issue addressed in this volume – the basis on which courts should assume the role of decision makers.

There have been formal attempts to identify principles that the courts apply when making decisions about the medical treatment of babies and young children,

[1] I Kennedy, 'Patients, Doctors and Human Rights' in R Blackburn and J Taylor (eds), *Human Rights for the 1990s* (London, Mansell, 1991).

including in particular guidance published by the Royal College of Paediatrics and Child Health in 2006 concerning the withholding and withdrawal of life-sustaining treatment.[2] But, as the cases discussed in this volume demonstrate, dissatisfaction with the role of the courts and the use of the 'best interests' test rumbles on. Various alternative approaches have been proposed in cases over the years, including the test of what a 'reasonable parent' would do, and the imposition of a preliminary threshold of significant harm. The courts have rejected them, focusing on the need to prioritise the child's interests, and implicitly accepting that any dispute about a child's best interests, in the medical sphere, could be the subject of determination by the court.

Difficult decisions about medical treatment, including the continuation or cessation of life-sustaining treatment, are made by doctors and families every day. The vast majority are made without the involvement of the court, though there may well be disagreement, discussion, periods of reflection, and further debate and negotiation before agreement is finally reached. This is entirely unsurprising, considering the emotional context of the decisions that have to be made, the impossibility of perfect predictions about the future course of an illness or disease, and the enormity of the questions that parents are required to confront: can life ever be worse than death? When does the provision of life-sustaining treatment turn into the prolongation of death? If it was right to provide treatment three months ago, last week, yesterday, why is it wrong to provide it tomorrow?

There are no simple answers to such questions, nor perhaps are there right answers and wrong answers. But where disputes cannot be resolved in any other way, the courts have to act as the final arbiter, an individual judge making a decision on a particular day based on the evidence presented at that time.

My view is that switching to a threshold of significant harm would not make any material difference to the judgments made by the courts: doctors tend not to refer disputes to the court unless they have strongly held views that continuing treatment, or failing to provide it, would be completely contrary to their duties to the child. A generous approach to the concept of 'harm' would inevitably be taken in order that such disputes could be resolved – even in cases where a child's ability to experience pain and suffering, and thus to be harmed in the usual sense of the word, was severely compromised or absent.

Even if there is no change to the approach the courts take, either because proposed legislation is not implemented, or because in practice such legislation may not materially alter the judgements reached, the cases discussed in this volume will have an impact. For example:

- It seems likely that health professionals will seek external assistance to resolve disputes at an earlier stage, perhaps using alternative methods such as mediation or the involvement of clinical ethics committees.

[2] *Withholding or Withdrawing Life Sustaining Treatment in Children: A Framework for Practice* (Royal College of Paediatrics and Child Health, 2006).

- It is possible that non-means-tested legal aid will be introduced for parents involved in court proceedings concerning medical treatment disputes.
- Decisions whether to start providing life-sustaining treatment in the context of untreatable degenerative conditions may be taken more carefully. In *An NHS Trust v S & L (A Child) (Withholding Life Sustaining Invasive Treatment)* [2017] EWHC 3619 (Fam), invasive ventilation was not offered other than for a time-limited period and subject to detailed guidelines about its continuation in the absence of improvement, in circumstances where the child's condition was on a downward trajectory.
- If experimental therapies are proposed, those offering them will be invited to obtain full information about the patient before expressing an opinion, and intervention will be pursued more swiftly where the child has a degenerative condition.

Although I now use the phrase 'best interests' almost every day in my professional life, I remain sympathetic to the criticisms made by Ian Kennedy and the need to ensure that words and phrases such as 'best interests' and 'dignity', which can mean everything and nothing, are not relied on to obscure either the values or reasoning being applied. The chapters in this volume are an important contribution to that objective, and to the wider debates generated by the cases of Charlie Gard and Alfie Evans.

CONTENTS

Foreword by Victoria Butler-Cole QC v
List of Contributors xi

Introduction 1
Imogen Goold, Cressida Auckland and Jonathan Herring

1. *Setting the Scene – Supporting and Informing Shared Decision-Making at the Bedside: Avoiding and De-escalating Conflict between Clinicians and Families* 7
Emily Harrop

2. *Evaluating 'Best Interests' as a Threshold for Judicial Intervention in Medical Decision-Making on Behalf of Children* 29
Imogen Goold

3. *Parental Decisions and Court Jurisdiction: Best Interests or Significant Harm?* 49
Rachel Taylor

4. *The Legal Basis of the Court's Jurisdiction to Authorise Medical Treatment of Children* 67
Rob George

5. *In Defence of a Conditional Harm Threshold Test for Paediatric Decision-Making* 85
Dominic Wilkinson

6. *The Harm Threshold: A View from the Clinic* 107
Giles Birchley

7. *Beyond Best Interests: A Question of Professional Conscience?* 137
Jo Bridgeman

8. *Preserving the Therapeutic Alliance: Court Intervention and Experimental Treatment Requests* 153
Sara Fovargue

9. *Futility* 177
Cressida Auckland

10. *Vulnerability and Medical Decisions Concerning Children* *191*
Jonathan Herring

11. *Resolving Disagreements about the Care of Critically Ill Children: Evaluating Existing Processes and Setting the Research Agenda* *207*
Louise Austin and Richard Huxtable

Index *231*

LIST OF CONTRIBUTORS

Cressida Auckland Assistant Professor in Medical Law at the London School of Economics

Louise Austin PhD Candidate in Law, University of Bristol

Giles Birchley Senior Research Associate in Surgical Innovation and Bioethics, University of Bristol

Jo Bridgeman Professor of Healthcare Law and Feminist Ethics, Sussex Law School, University of Sussex

Victoria Butler-Cole QC Barrister, 39 Essex Chambers

Sara Fovargue Reader in Law and Director of Research, Law School, Lancaster University

Rob George Associate Professor of Family Law, University College London; Barrister, Harcourt Chambers, London

Imogen Goold Associate Professor in Law, University in Oxford and Fellow of St Anne's College, University of Oxford

Emily Harrop Interim Medical Director, Helen & Douglas House; Honorary Consultant in Paediatric Palliative Care, Oxford University Hospital Trust

Jonathan Herring Professor of Law, University of Oxford

Richard Huxtable Professor of Medical Ethics and Law, Bristol University

Rachel Taylor Associate Professor in Law, University of Oxford and Tutorial Fellow in Law, Exeter College, Oxford

Dominic Wilkinson Professor of Medical Ethics, Director of Medical Ethics, Oxford Uehiro Centre for Practical Ethics; Consultant Neonatologist, John Radcliffe Hospital

Introduction

IMOGEN GOOLD, CRESSIDA AUCKLAND
AND JONATHAN HERRING [1]

This collection was inspired by the decision of the Court of Appeal in *Great Ormond Street Hospital v Gard* [2017] (the 'Charlie Gard case'). In *Gard*, and in the cases that followed, both the Court of Appeal (and later the Supreme Court in rejecting permission to appeal) affirmed the orthodox position that the threshold for judicial intervention in disputes about medical care of children is the welfare of the child, often referred to as the 'best interests' approach. 'Best interests' is generally used to refer both to the threshold for intervention and as the test applied to determine what should be done once the court is involved. In this volume, we focus solely on the threshold question: when should the court be permitted to make decisions on behalf of very ill children when parents and the medical treating team cannot agree?

In *Gard*, the appellants' case rested in part on the argument that in situations where there is a choice of treatments (the so-called 'Category 2' cases) it should fall to parents, rather than the courts or doctors, to make this choice. Inherent to this view was that there must be some degree of protection of parental discretion in relation to their children. The boundary proposed was that of a 'risk of significant harm', adapted from section 31 of the Children Act 1989 (the so-called threshold criteria that must be satisfied before the court can make a care or supervision order in child protection proceedings). One point made by counsel on behalf of Connie Yates and Chris Gard was that in the absence of such a boundary, the state would otherwise have unfettered power to intervene in parental decisions. Both the Court of Appeal and the Supreme Court rejected this argument. While the position in England and Wales is legally clear, there has been substantial debate in the literature about the appropriate boundaries for judicial power in this context, particularly in the ethics literature. The public debate around the Gard case also revealed that many in the community consider that parents should have the final say about a child's medical care.

[1] We are grateful to the team at Hart Publishing for their help in preparing this collection, particularly to Roberta Bassi for her support and confidence in us throughout the process. Many thanks, too, to all who participated in the very stimulating workshop that preceded this collection, held in Oxford in May 2018. Very many thanks, also, to our excellent research assistants Vassilios Copetinas and Tristan Cummings.

Gard was neither the first case of its kind, nor the last (followed as it was by the Alfie Evans litigation (*Alder Hey NHS Foundation Trust v Evans* [2018] EWHC 308 (Fam)), which raised similar questions, as did the case of Isaiah Haastrup[2]), but it stands out as the case in which a serious challenge was made to the current threshold for judicial intervention in decisions about children's medical care. The case also drew substantial public attention, in part due to the issues around parental authority it raised. Concerns about the erosion of what some regarded as the territory of parental authority, as well as concern for Charlie himself, fuelled an extraordinary public campaign in support of Charlie's parents. At many points in this campaign, it was argued by supporters of the Gard family that it should be for parents, rather than the medical profession or the courts, to have final decision-making authority about a child's health.

It was the combination of this legal challenge and the considerable support for a shift in the law's position that inspired this collection. Both raised the question of whether the law currently draws the threshold for judicial intervention in the right place. It drew attention to the fact that while much of the case-law has focused on applying the test to determine what should be done, there has been comparatively little focus on *when* the court should legitimately intervene. This requires fresh consideration of whether there should be any threshold for court intervention in parental decision-making, and whether the medical context requires a different approach? Where should the line be drawn, and what would be the normative basis of this line? In particular, this collection will look at whether it is appropriate to adopt the 'serious risk of significant harm' approach proposed in *Gard*; the respective roles of parents, doctors and the courts; and the possible risks of inappropriate state intrusion in parental decision-making, and how we might address them.

An important dimension to such analysis must be consideration of what the law should do when public opinion and the law's position seemingly diverge. This is not, in and of itself, a sufficient reason for the law to change. But the substantial levels of concern expressed in some quarters should at least cause us to consider why these objections were raised and whether they are legitimate. We should take these concerns seriously because they go further than disagreement with the law. Rather, they go to a central concern – the appropriate boundary between private, familial decisions and the authority of the state. This goes beyond questions of the limits of parental authority into issues around the right role of the state in relation to the most vulnerable members of society and the extent to which its responsibility to them should trump considerations of familial privacy and parental authority.

It is not only some groups within the public whose views diverge from those of the law. Philosophers and ethicists have weighed in on the debate around parental

[2] *Kings College Hospital NHS Foundation Trust v Ms Thomas, Haastrup and Haastrup* [2018] EWHC 127 (Fam), [2018] 2 FLR 1028.

decision-making, many doing so publicly at the time these cases were in the news.[3] Some criticised taking a court-based approach at all, but some argued for a move to a harm-threshold approach to judicial intervention. These very public statements, plus the popular concern and the direct challenge to orthodoxy brought in *Gard*, therefore make this very much a live question. Further, much of what was written at the time picked up on a debate about moving to a harm threshold that was already live in the ethics and medical law literature. For example, Douglas Diekema, Professor of Pediatrics at the University of Washington School of Medicine, has written extensively on the harm threshold.[4] Lynn Gillam has also offered many sensible insights into the issue via her work on the concept of a 'zone of parental discretion'.[5] The *Gard* case, therefore, brought a question that has been a matter of academic interest into the spotlight and demonstrated precisely why it is a question with which we should actively engage.

This collection addresses this central question of *when* the court should have authority to intervene in medical decision-making on behalf of children. It focuses specifically on non-*Gillick*-competent children, and the withdrawal of treatment. Therefore, it does not concern itself with the issues around children who are competent to consent to treatment (if not to refuse it). It centres on those situations where a court is called upon to intervene in decisions about a child's medical care. This will generally be those situations where the medical team and parents are at loggerheads over what is to be done. But, as evidenced in *Gard*, this may also encompass situations where parents seek to opt for one medical professional's approach over another's. Both the Court of Appeal and the Supreme Court, in *Gard*, took the view that it held the ultimate authority to intervene in such situations once the child's welfare was engaged.[6]

This question is not one that can be easily answered. The court has the authority to intervene via its inherent jurisdiction as well as in situations covered by the Children Act 1989 (the 'Children Act'). Rob George and Rachel Taylor outline the exact position on that jurisdiction from a family law perspective in their chapters, teasing out some of the complexities that arise from the interaction between the

[3] S Boseley, 'US Doctor's Intervention in Charlie Gard Case "Raises Ethical Questions"' *The Guardian* (25 July 2017) www.theguardian.com/uk-news/2017/jul/25/michio-hirano-us-doctor-intervention-charlie-gard-case-raises-ethical-questions (accessed 11 June 2019); J Savulescu and P Singer, 'Charlie Gard: Why Donald Trump and the Pope Are Right' *ABC News* (13 July 2017) www.abc.net.au/news/2017-07-13/charlie-gard-donald-trump-and-the-pope-are-right/8706390; J Savulescu and D Wilkinson, 'Agreement and Disagreement About Experimental Treatment. The Charlie Gard Appeal', blog.practicalethics.ox.ac.uk/2017/05/agreement-and-disagreement-about-experimental-treatment-the-charlie-gard-appeal/ (accessed 11 June 2019).

[4] D Diekema, 'Parental Refusals of Medical Treatment: The Harm Principle as Threshold for State Intervention' (2004) 25 *Philosophy of Medical Research and Practice* 243.

[5] L Gillam, 'The Zone of Parental Discretion: An Ethical Tool for Dealing with Disagreement between Parents and Doctors about Medical Treatment for a Child' (2016) 11 *Clinical Ethics* 1.

[6] *Great Ormond Street Hospital v Yates and Gard* [2017] EWHC 972 (Fam); Lady Hale's explanation of the Supreme Court's decision, as delivered in Court (8 June 2017) www.supremecourt.uk/news/permission-to-appeal-hearing-in-the-matter-of-charlie-gard.html (accessed 11 June 2019).

common law, the Children Act and the Human Rights Act 1998 (HRA). Imogen Goold offers a detailed explanation of the common law foundations for the orthodox position on medical decision-making in her chapter.

Clarity about the legal position is not, however, a sufficient basis on which to determine what the law *should* be in this context. With this in mind, this collection was developed with the explicit intention of drawing on a wide range of relevant perspectives. Hence, the collection includes not only family and medical law academics, but also chapters written by medical professionals directly involved in the clinical care of children. Emily Harrop, Giles Birchley and Dominic Wilkinson all bring insights from their roles as clinicians to their chapters. Harrop presents a deeply moving account of the parental experience in such situations, while Wilkinson and Birchley blend clinical and philosophical analysis in their work. Jonathan Herring's chapter on vulnerability (of parents, children, medics and the judiciary) complements and augments these chapters by offering a unique lens through which to consider the issues (legal and ethical) raised in such cases.

Having such chapters sit neatly and separately beside academic analyses of the issues would be a legitimate but rather unsatisfying approach to the central question considered by this collection. Mindful of this, the editors brought the contributors together early on in the process for a one-day workshop held in Oxford in 2018. Over the course of that day, the clinicians shared perspectives with the legal and philosophical academics, informing and shaping one another's perspectives. We were particularly fortunate to have Victoria Butler-Cole, who acted as Guardian to Charlie Gard in *Gard*, join us for that day to offer a perspective from practice, which proved invaluable, as did the practice experience of Rob George.

In this collection, then, we bring together a variety of backgrounds and a variety of views on where the threshold for judicial intervention is to be drawn. Some, such as Wilkinson and Goold, make the case for moving to some form of harm threshold. Others, such as Taylor, defend the law's current stance.

Other chapters offer additional perspectives. Louise Austin and Richard Huxtable, for example, call for further research into how disputes are being resolved (or not resolved) day-to-day between medical teams and parents, and consequently whether, if at all, we should amend out current mechanisms for addressing these disputes. Cressida Auckland, by contrast, drills down into the difficult and nuanced question of what constitutes 'futility' in the context of withdrawal-of-treatment decisions. Such an analysis is important given the weighty impact the determination that further treatment being deemed 'futile' has in these cases (as seen starkly in *Gard*). Sara Forvague offers an exploration of a particular aspect of these cases – parental requests for experimental treatments. *Gard* is a prime example of the direction of travel in these cases, where the Internet and social media enable parents to research treatments in a manner previously impossible, and also to contact (and be contacted by) those who offer treatments that the medical team has not offered. Jo Bridgman's chapter argues that in such complex cases, medical professionals are not merely applying to court because they consider a particular treatment will not be in the child's 'best interests'. Rather, in cases such as *Gard*, further treatment, in the professional judgement of the medical team involved, was *inimical* to Charlie's interests. Cases of this kind should, she argues, be understood as ones in which the provision of continued treatment is contrary to professional conscience. It is on this basis that the courts should approach the requests of medical professionals to cease treatment.

In determining whether the law should change, we should take account of the spectrum of perspectives on such situations. The law's approach should be both principled and practical. It should account for clinical realities and pay due respect to the professional opinion of those best placed to understand the medical aspects of a child's healthcare situation. But it must also be sensitive to the parents' needs as well as those of the child. We have little doubt that the courts are very much mindful of this, as it is the court that deals with these situations close-in on a daily basis. It is difficult for any regulatory system to balance all the competing needs and demands of those it covers, and the complexity of doing so and walking the line between respecting parental responsibility and protecting those most vulnerable among us is necessarily a difficult question that prompts strong feelings. We hope that the chapters in this collection may offer some valuable assistance in our efforts to answer this question.

1

Setting the Scene – Supporting and Informing Shared Decision-Making at the Bedside

Avoiding and De-escalating Conflict between Clinicians and Families

EMILY HARROP

1. Introduction

Modern paediatric care is practised in an environment where we are seeing increased survival at the extremes of viability, and enticing new therapies that push back the boundaries of possibility. Patients and their families also have unprecedented access to information via Internet searches and support groups on social media. Despite well-publicised advances in medical science, it remains an uncomfortable truth that there are many situations in which we are able to use invasive mechanical technology to keep a child alive, for whom there is yet no prospect of a meaningful 'cure'. The most difficult decisions faced by families, and those healthcare professionals supporting them, tend to arise in this gap between being able to sustain life with aggressive organ support and having a realistic treatment option offering the prospect of a recovery with an acceptable quality of life. The withdrawal of mechanical ventilation in situations considered 'medically futile', where intensive care is likely to represent a burden without realistic benefit, has historically produced the highest number of high-profile cases of conflict, as exemplified by the recent cases of Alfie Evans and Isaiah Haastrup. In addition, the information age has given earlier public access to claims of 'medical breakthroughs', many of which will not yet have been through the usual process of peer review. This leads to the second most significant source of medical conflict: immediate access to novel therapies. This ranges from demands for early access to emerging evidence-based treatments, catalysed by media hyperbole, to requests for the use of molecules not fully tested in man, as is relevant to the case for Charlie Gard.

Fortunately, guidance exists for clinicians[1] about how best to share information to support the making of difficult decisions in partnership with families. There is evidence that early multidisciplinary discussions with careful information-sharing allows effective advance care planning. This in turn reduces the likelihood of significant dispute. Recognisable patterns of behaviour exist among both clinicians and families in the early stages of conflict.[2] Where these are acknowledged and addressed, resources such as impartial second opinions, Patient Advice and Liaison Services (PALS), clinical ethics committees, chaplains and medical mediation specialists can help maintain or reopen channels of communication.[3] Although it will always be necessary for some cases to be put before a court,[4] there is genuine potential for early intervention with a less adversarial approach.[5] In truth, a range of reasonable options are likely to exist in the gap between 'best interests' and 'significant harm', covering many shades of grey rather than a single black and white solution. These are discussed in detail elsewhere in this book.

Most chapters in this book focus on the legal response to these cases. This chapter will take a different perspective, looking at the challenges to professionals and parents before the issue reaches court. It will look at the measures taken by professionals and family members to navigate the complex and challenging ethical issues that arise in current paediatric practice. It should be remembered that the vast majority of cases involving very sick children do not reach courts and it is possible to achieve consensus between family members and medical professionals. This chapter will explain how this is achieved.

First, a detailed understanding of the perspectives of parents will be offered.[6] Second, the chapter considers the perspective of professionals by looking at the scientific advances that have created the options which can generate disputes and the professional guidance they act under. Third, the chapter describes the guidance available to clinicians on identifying early signs of conflict escalation and strategies for early intervention.

[1] V Larcher, F Craig, K Bhogal, D Wilkinson and J Brierley, 'Making Decisions to Limit Treatment in Life-Limiting and Life-Threatening Conditions in Children: A Framework for Practice' (2015) 100 *Archives of Disease in Childhood* 1; General Medical Council (GMC) *Treatment and Care Towards the End of Life: Good Practice in Decision-Making* (London, GMC, 2010); National Institute of Health and Clinical Excellence (NICE) *End of Life Care for Infants, children and Young people with Life-Limiting Conditions: Planning and Management* (London, NICE, 2016) www.nice.org.uk/guidance/ng61.

[2] L Forbat, B Teuten and S Barclay, 'Conflict Escalation in Paediatric Services: Findings from a Qualitative Study' (2015) 100 *Archives of Disease in Childhood* 769.

[3] Larcher et al (n 1); NICE (n 1); GMC (n 1).

[4] Larcher et al (n 1); GMC (n 1).

[5] S Meller and S Barclay, 'Mediation: An Approach to Intractable Disputes Between Parents and Paediatricians' (2011) 96 *Archives of Disease in Childhood* 619.

[6] A Todorovic, 'Palliative Care Is Not Just for Those Who Are Dying' (2016) 353 *British Medical Journal*; P Sidgwick, E Harrop, B Kelly, A Todorovic and D Wilkinson, 'Fifteen Minute Consultation: Perinatal Palliative Care' (2017) 102 *Archives of Disease in Childhood* 114; E Harrop, K Boyce, T Beale and K Brombley, 'Fifteen Minute Consultation: Developing an Advance Care Plan in Partnership with the Child and Family' (2018) 103 *Archives of Disease in Childhood* 282.

2. Setting the Scene from the Parents' Perspective

In the boxes below, the reflections of two bereaved parents are shared in their own words.[7] The clinical cases are very different, but the experiences resonate in many ways. Both situations could very easily have produced damaging conflict. The ways in which this was avoided are illustrated.

Nadia and Ana

Following a diagnosis of a serious fetal heart condition very late in pregnancy, Ana and her partner had been offered a range of 'choices', from the delivery of their baby in a cardiac centre with immediate connection to a heart-lung bypass system, to a late termination of the pregnancy. They felt challenged by the initial 'choices' offered to them, a situation that left them feeling conflicted and bewildered. Without access to multiprofessional specialist care planning, these feelings could easily have turned to anger and resentment, reducing their chances to make a balanced and well-informed decision about Nadia's ongoing care. Interestingly, although a very interventionist approach had been offered at diagnosis, there seemed to be very little optimism for the outcome; something which added to their confusion, as did the apparent lack of a palliative/supportive choice.

The following is an extract from one of the articles subsequently published by Ana:

> 'There is no easy way to say this, but your baby is very, very sick.' I was 37 weeks pregnant, and they had just found our baby had severe dilated cardiomyopathy. The doctor thought she would die within days. Then he sat with us, and they told us that we had to make a choice. We could get in an ambulance and go to Southampton, where I would have a caesarean, [Nadia] would be put on life support, but would likely still die. The alternative path would be to 'put her to sleep' with a needle to the heart, after which her birth would be induced and it would all be over. He suggested injecting potassium in her heart, to be certain that she would not survive terribly impaired. She kicked and squirmed inside me as I tried to wrap my mind around this, stunned with shock. It made no sense to take action. Could we not simply let her die in peace? He said this was not an option. But later – perhaps because I asked – we found palliative care mentioned in the discharge note. And so at our next appointment we were greeted by two paediatricians who wanted to talk to us. They asked us what was going on. It felt natural to tell them our story. They listened intently, and I realised the purpose of this questioning much later: they wanted to get a sense of

[7] Direct quotes from parents who have had to make such decisions about the medical treatment of their children are used, with their permission, to share insight into their thinking. All of these choices were made after extensive involvement of a multidisciplinary team including paediatric palliative care, and in some cases review by a clinical ethics committee. A number of the quotes have already been published elsewhere; where this is the case, references are provided to the full texts

us first. 'What would you like to happen?' I choked up in tears. I hadn't told anyone about my wish to meet her, to hold her while she was dying. They said my wish was common, and a knot of tightness in my chest unravelled. 'And what do you fear most?' I was afraid how this would affect my relationship with my partner. He feared that our son might develop the same heart condition. 'What would you like to know?' What she will look like when she's born, if she's not alive. I desperately needed to know all the details. Both doctors referred to our baby Nadia by name, showing us they knew how real she was to us. One of the doctors said that parents experience this short time spent with their terminally ill infants as meaningful and important. She explained how Nadia would be fed and her pain relief administered. Precise words again. 'Keeping her comfortable', the most common sentence we encountered when enquiring about palliative care, was too vague for me. The doctors were at ease with our tears. In the space of a couple of hours they had transformed what we were going through from something dreadful to something potentially meaningful. She could be a person, a person whom we might not have the chance to meet properly, but a someone nevertheless.

Ana's eloquent reflections give insight into the multitude of emotions that are contained within the decisions to accept or decline aggressive medical intervention in the face of a very poor prognosis. Her desire to meet her baby was a prime concern, but she also understandably worried about the impact of this on her relationship with her partner – highlighting the very real possibility of parents having differing or opposing views, something which can often worsen conflict situations. She wanted to know what her baby would look like and whether it would be a positive experience for her young son to meet his sister. She also needed to understand very practically what Nadia's care would involve. This demonstrates the limitation of an evaluation made purely on the basis of a balance sheet of perceived 'best interests'. In a situation where the unique 'best interests' of an unborn baby are unclear, understanding what the parents most fear, and that for which they still retain hope can be very helpful to finding the way forward and in preventing the emergence of conflict.

Richard and Joseph

Extract from 'Unfathomable Price of Flesh' by Richard GT Gipps (Unpublished Essay and Sketches)

The excerpts below were written by a bereaved father, who had made a carefully considered decision to withhold invasive surgery and airway support, after his one-year-old son suffered life-changing injuries in a car accident, which also killed his partner. Joseph's 'best interests' were very challenging to weigh, with disagreement even among the numerous experienced consultants involved. Decision-making in the face of diverging views both within the treating teams and the family was eventually aided by an ethics committee review within the hospice.

Joseph, who was 14 months old at the time, received varying prognoses at the hospital: at first that he would die, then that he would most likely recover, and then again when he failed to breathe by himself after several attempts, that he would die. Finally, after 17 days in the hospital, I myself turned off his life support. However he then managed to breathe by himself, and we went together to Helen House children's hospice in our home town of Oxford.

Joseph's injuries were all to his brain and spinal cord – a consequence of the sudden jolt of the impact. The principal damage was to his brainstem – that part of the base of the brain which controls animal functions like breathing and swallowing. Because he stopped breathing after the accident he also suffered secondary hypoxic brain damage to his cortex.

Over the weeks and months in the hospice Joseph gradually regained his cortical abilities – he could once again see, hear, point, bang a drum, pick up a toy animal, sit on my lap to read a book. It was astonishing over these few months witnessing him gradually being 'born again' – moving from an insensate and immobile state to one of being able to communicate and play. He could not move his trunk, however, nor maintain a sitting posture without support. Nor could he swallow or vocalise. As a consequence he was fed by a naso-gastric tube; he also learnt a few words of sign language.

As time passed it became clear that, whilst Joseph had made good cortical recovery, his brain stem damage was such that he would need significant operations for him to survive. He would need surgery both so he could in future be fed straight into his stomach and to prevent reflux of material from his stomach into his lungs. He would also need a tracheostomy to aid his breathing. Even with these operations he would still have very significant difficulties with moving, posture, and spasticity. He would require full-time care, and would not be able to enjoy so many of the activities (running, exploring, eating and drinking) that enable a child to play, and eventually to live independently.

Opinions were divided within the medical and nursing professions, and also within the family, about what was the right thing to do for Joseph. One experienced consultant said that he felt that the ethics of Joseph's case were the hardest he had encountered. As for myself, I believed it would be wrong to subject my son to a life of extreme disability, frequent hospitalisation, massive ongoing care needs; to damage his body further to prolong his life; and to put the all-too-easily reached-for consideration 'quality of life' above more fundamental concerns regarding human dignity, integrity and wholeness. As a result, the nurses and I cared for Joseph in the hospice – taking him around the garden, playing with musical instruments and toy farm animals, reading books, going in the spa together, having music, physio and communication therapy, taking trips to nearby farm centres, etc. – and life-prolonging surgery was ruled out. The love and care he and I received from the hospice staff was extraordinary. When Joseph was 19 months old he succumbed to a lung infection; he died whilst I was holding him, quietly, in his room at the hospice.

I have no strong evidence either way, but it is my belief that what most kept me sane was a relentless pursuit of the truth of what had happened. Whereby 'pursuit of the truth' I mean both a quiet ungrasping acknowledgement of the medical facts and,

> more importantly, a willingness to frequently take the ethical temperature of this extreme event, to roll with each punch of the news of Joseph's next prognosis, and to try to keep 'thinking' what had happened in its extremity.
>
> What also kept me sane were the kindnesses of particular others, and I want to write something about this here to urge the importance, for anyone in extreme circumstances, of finding and trusting some such others. People vary in their ability to cope in such events, the simple truth being that it is rare that someone's emotional system – geared up as that system is to enact and support understanding in the midst of our everyday relationships – will be resilient enough to allow their mind to continue to function in the midst of terror, grief and despair. Add to this that those closest to one will often be those themselves most traumatised, and the need for resilient others outside of family and perhaps even of friends will be more apparent still. Very important to me have been the chaplains, psychologists, doctors and nurses I met within the hospital and hospice and who through their capacity to carry on thinking when my own was becoming impaired, restored my mind to its adult functioning – in particular those who were able to listen and reflect back whilst only judiciously offering their own understandings. But I also remember very strikingly the kindness of another parent at the paediatric intensive care unit who, even though I was praying for my own son to be able to die, whilst she prayed for her own to be able to live, could put her arm around me and offer such honest comfort.

Richard talks about the conflict arising within his wider family, and he was also aware of the differing views of clinicians. He describes the benefits of informing himself fully about the twists and turns in his son's medical condition. He also talks about 'taking the ethical temperature' of the situation at regular intervals. The decision to withhold further life-sustaining treatment was very challenging for many of the staff involved. Had the issues not been carefully identified and individually weighed, positions could have become entrenched and the situation could have become much more challenging. This father generously shared his experiences retrospectively with the team developing the Medical Mediation Foundation, and in this way he was able to inform the support offered to future families.

Importantly, Richard and Ana both reflect on their children as being 'a whole being', a 'someone', rather than purely living a life made up of benefits and burdens, equating to an assumed 'quality of life'. They are each very clear about the benefits both of being listened to and of being fully informed about the medical facts of the difficult clinical situations they faced. Both these able and insightful parents describe a situation where their reality was so challenging to accept intellectually that they realised it affected their ability to process information and to 'think' clearly. In each case they were self-aware enough to accept support from a range of professionals. In both cases they reached decisions that fell within the range of reasonable options open to them and maintained good relationships with those caring for them. This provides a window into the inner turmoil of families facing seemingly impossible decisions about the care of their children, and goes some way to explaining how easily these feelings can turn to anger and frustration.

3. National Trends in Paediatric Intensive Care and Long-Term Ventilation

Turning now to the perspective of professionals, it is important to note the technological developments that have taken place in recent years. Although the rate of childhood mortality from all causes in the UK continues to fall, the prevalence of life-limiting illnesses and chronic disease in British children is rising. The most common location for a child's death in hospital is the paediatric intensive care unit (PICU); recent data suggest that an increasing number of these deaths are occurring following an active decision to withdraw life-sustaining treatment.[8] A similar pattern is seen in neonatal intensive care (NICU). National trends in PICU length of stay suggest that children who ultimately do not survive their admission are spending increasingly long periods of time on intensive care before they die.[9] This highlights the rising importance of good mechanisms to support shared decision-making with families, both for the benefit of individual patients and the allocation of scarce resources.

The landscape of modern paediatric care is evolving at a pace such that conditions previously considered 'incurable' or 'invariably fatal' are beginning to develop much less predictable courses. This affects shared decision-making from as early as the prenatal period, when an antenatal diagnosis of a serious anomaly may mean a range of options including in-utero surgery; planned delivery in a specialist centre; or carefully orchestrated palliative care.[10] Experimental treatments for conditions previously fatal in infancy mean that mechanical ventilatory support is more likely to be offered as a bridge to potentially life-lengthening therapies.[11] Long-term ventilation (LTV) is now sufficiently portable that it is sometimes considered appropriate as a 'destination therapy', even when no disease-modifying treatment is possible.[11,12]

Decisions about LTV are therefore increasingly common and present a particular challenge; the question, 'should a particular child receive LTV?' is complex, individual and dynamic. Recent work has been published providing the basis for an ethical framework to guide decisions about ventilation.[13] It must be remembered that LTV is never a curative intervention; it cannot alter static or progressive conditions nor the risks and burdens of comorbidities. Indeed LTV comes with its own burdens; aside from the practical limitations on family life, invasive

[8] A Plunkett and RC Parslow, 'Is it Taking Longer to Die in Paediatric Intensive Care in England and Wales?' (2016) 101 *Archives of Disease in Childhood* 798.

[9] ibid.

[10] See n 7.

[11] S Ray, J Brierley, A Bush, J Fraser, G Halley, E Harrop and L Casanueva, 'Towards Developing an Ethical Framework for Decision-Making in Long-Term Ventilation' (2018) 103 *Archives of Disease in Childhood* 1080.

[12] RS Finkel et al for the ENDEAR Study Group 'Nusinersen versus Sham Control in Infantile-Onset Spinal Muscular Atrophy' (2017) *New England Journal of Medicine* 1723.

[13] ibid.

ventilation also requires regular airway suctioning, which is frequently distressing.[14] The provision of LTV is often most contentious when patients are unable to voice their opinions through disability or developmental age. Physicians should always present an honest account of what life entails for a family caring for a child on LTV. Dealing with uncertainty is a fundamental problem; it is very difficult to assess prognosis and quality of life on an individual basis. The family may have an idealistic, positive outlook of the child's prognosis because he or she has survived previous critical illness. There is also a real risk of physical and emotional depletion for the parents, after long admissions to intensive care, with added challenges in relation to consistency of message from the multiple healthcare teams involved. Thus, conversations around continuing ventilation often occur in an environment ideal for conflict to develop, as is exemplified in the cases of Alfie Evans and Isaiah Haastrup, discussed in detail elsewhere in this volume.

Three Contrasting Choices – The Emerging Role of LTV in Spinal Muscular Atrophy

Spinal muscular atrophy type 1 is an example of a condition where a relatively new treatment exists that modifies the course of the disease. Previously considered likely to be fatal in the first year of life (due to progressive muscle weakness), a treatment now exists which shows promise in slowing the course of the disease.[15] This currently needs to be delivered by injection into the fluid space around the spine, every few weeks, in order to be effective. Some children need mechanical ventilatory support in order to survive long enough to receive the initial course of treatment, or even just to allow them to be stable enough to tolerate the invasive procedure required. This creates a situation where a child may be offered a tracheostomy and LTV in order to access a therapy that is of only potential future benefit to them. The magnitude of the benefit would be unknown, and on current experience, it seems very unlikely that the child would ever regain the ability to breathe unaided. It is likely that the child may need to spend weeks or even months in hospital at the time that ventilation is initiated and access to 'normal family life' is likely to be greatly reduced for the whole family indefinitely. The quality of life achievable for the individual is likely to be somewhat limited in this scenario. In the worst case, ventilation would be instituted for a progressive disease for which the remedy proved ineffective, leading to a 'locked-in' state with no motor activity. The alternative would be to accept supportive care. This would, on average, allow a few months of 'normal baby life' before muscle weakness would cause loss of skills and eventually difficulty in breathing, which would need to be palliated. Both decisions currently comprise reasonable 'best interests' options. The decision is a very personal one; for example, when two families who had made

[14] ibid.
[15] ibid.

opposite decisions happened to visit our hospice at the same time, neither regretted their choice, when faced with the other. Child A was one of three children. Her family valued their access to normal family life, for all their children, above all else. They had been clear from the outset that quality time at home with 'A' was their priority, regardless of the length of her life. It may thus be inferred that they acted in the 'best interests' of all their children. Child B was an only child. One of her parents had given up work in order to care for her full time, and was prepared to bear the principal burden of managing her ventilation. Although 'B' had had a long hospital stay, and her family subsequently struggled to get out of their home very often, her parents were happy with their choice. Prior to the formation of her tracheostomy, the treating teams met her parents to discuss the ethics and the practicalities of LTV. It would be easy to see how conflict could have arisen between the families concerned and their treating teams if their own unique set of priorities and values had not been allowed to inform their decision. In the context of emerging treatments, disagreements between families who want to be afforded time for a 'miracle cure', and professionals who feel expectations are not realistic, are not uncommon and require sensitive handling. In both cases advance care plans were written with the parents soon after diagnosis, and these were informed by the various specialist teams involved. The information about the range of clinical options available was shared openly with them, and the likely 'lived experience' of each option was explained. Those supporting the planning sought to understand what each set of parents valued most, and what they most feared, before guiding them towards their decision. These plans do, however, have to be fluid and allow for the unexpected. A third baby, 'C', with the same condition, collapsed and had to be resuscitated after her second dose of the new treatment. During her subsequent admission to the PICU, it became clear that she had a structurally abnormal MRI brain scan, suggestive of a second diagnosis. Her parents were thus given the chance to re-evaluate their assessment of her potential future quality of life. Following this, 'C' was transferred to the hospice for compassionate withdrawal of life-sustaining treatment. Her parents had decided that the new diagnosis of a 'structurally abnormal brain' tilted the scales of benefits and burdens against considering LTV to enable further doses of the treatment. They reflected positively on their choice, and spent time with their extended family at the hospice. At such times proxy assessments of quality of life are very challenging and need to have the sort of flexibility or 'parallel planning' illustrated in the case of 'C'. The use of an ethical framework-based approach[10] to making these decisions can both provide an equitable approach to the issue and allow for individual family circumstances.

4. National Guidance

As well as the developments in medical science, professionals must follow professional guidance. Recent guidance is available from a number of sources for clinicians in the UK supporting families through decisions to limit treatment.

The Royal College of Paediatrics and Child Health (RCPCH) published 'Making Decisions to Limit Treatment in Life-Limiting and Life-Threatening Conditions in Children: A Framework for Practice' in 2015. This document defines the situations in which it may be permissible to withhold or withdraw life-sustaining treatment as: 'when life is limited in quantity', 'when life is limited in quality' and in the face of 'informed competent refusal of treatment'. The framework would comfortably accommodate the decisions made in all five of the clinical cases discussed above. It specifically recommends early support from sources such as medical second opinions, chaplaincy, clinical ethics committees and PALS, some of which were acknowledged as useful in the parental reflections. Treatments, including palliative care, that are intended to relieve suffering of the child and his/her family produced by illnesses, and their treatments, or by disability are felt ethically justified in all cases.

The General Medical Council (GMC) produced 'Treatment and Care towards the End of Life: Good Practice in Decision Making'[16] in 2010 in order to support the principle that patients need to be able to trust their doctors with their lives and health, particularly as they approach the end of life. A separate section on neonates, children and young people is included, and the involvement of the child or young person in decision-making (appropriate to their level of maturity) is strongly recommended. The document states that parents should be supported to receive all the information required about the child's condition and the options for its treatment, in order to support decision-making, and that the information should be provided in a way in which it is understandable to them. The GMC go on to suggest that when disagreements arise, it is usually possible to resolve them by involving an independent advocate; seeking advice from a more experienced colleague; obtaining a second opinion; by holding a case conference or ethics consultation; or by using medication services. Legal advice is suggested if significant disagreement remains after these options have been exhausted.

Most recently, in 2016 the National Institute for Health and Care excellence (NICE) produced 'End of Life Care for Infants, Children, and Young People with Life-Limiting Conditions: Planning and Management'.[17] This evidence-based, practically focused guideline includes advice on 'information provisions', 'communication' and 'advance care planning', as well as many other aspects of palliative care. It had significant patient and public involvement, including two parent representatives within the committee, a focus group of young people, and many patient support organisations registered as stakeholders. The theme maps shown as Figures 1.1 and 1.2 summarise the published evidence on 'information provision' and 'communication' with the child and family when planning for end-of-life care.

[16] GMC (n 1).
[17] NICE (n 1).

Figure 1.1 Theme map summarising the evidence relating to barriers and facilitators for effective information provision in relation to decisions at the end of life

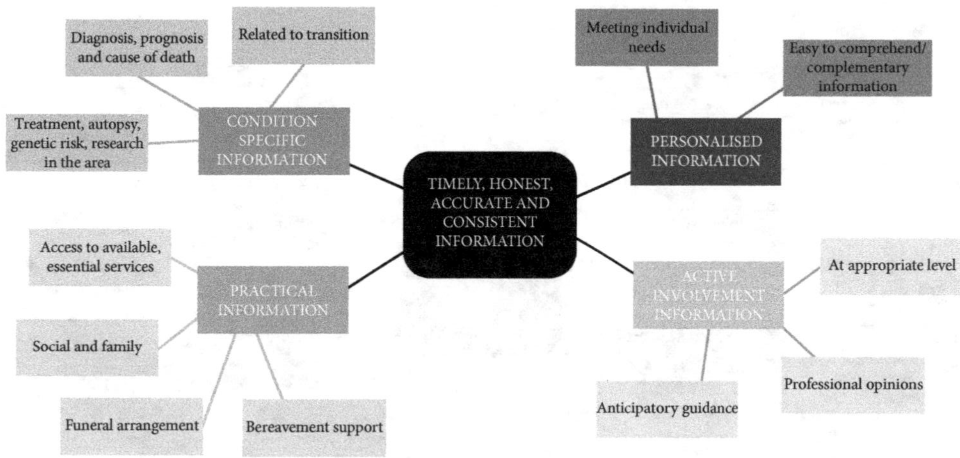

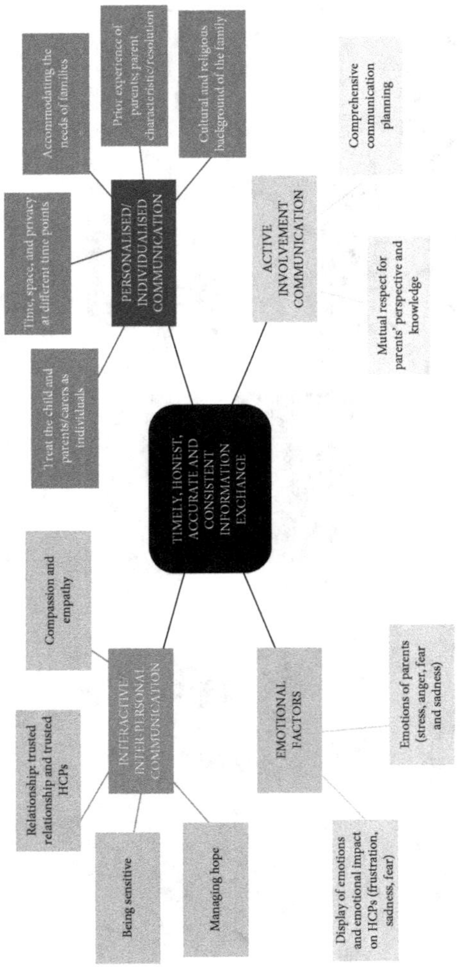

Figure 1.2 Theme map summarising the evidence relating to effective communication, in relation to end-of-life care decision-making

NICE guidance applies the key principles of the RCPCH and GMC guidance at the practical level, in the context of input from service users, offering a framework for planning care, in such a way most likely to avoid conflict.

Some of the most important points of practical guidance are shown in Box 3; when followed, these should significantly reduce the risk of conflict developing.

Practical Guidance

Be alert for signs or situations that suggest that the child or young person or their parents or carers need more information or discussions; for example if:

- They are more anxious or concerned.
- The child or young person's condition deteriorates.
- A significant change to the treatment plan is needed.

When difficult decisions must be made about end-of-life care, give children and young people and their parents or carers enough time and opportunities for discussion.

Think about how best to communicate with each child or young person and their parents or carers:

- When the life-limiting condition is first recognized.
- When reviewing and developing the advance care plan.
- If their condition worsens.
- When they are approaching the end of life.

When a child or young person is likely to die within hours or days, explain to them and their parents or carers:

- Why you think this is likely, and any uncertainties.
- What clinical changes can be expected.
- Whether you think the treatment plan should be changed.

Recognise that children and young people with life-limiting conditions and their parents or carers have a central role in decision-making and care planning.

Explain to children and young people and to their parents or carers that their contribution to decision-making is very important, but that they do not have to make decisions alone and that the multidisciplinary team will be involved as well.

When developing plans for the care of the child or young person with a life-limiting condition, use parallel planning to take account of possible unpredictability in the course of the condition.

Explain to the child and young person and their parents or carers that advance care planning should:

- Help them to be involved in planning their care and give them time to think about their views carefully.
- Help them to understand the life-limiting condition and its management.
- Help them to prepare for possible future difficulties or complications.
- Support continuity of care, for example if there are changes in the professionals involved or in the care setting.

Be aware that discussing the advance care plan can be distressing for children and young people who are approaching the end of life and their parents or carers, and they may:

- Be reluctant to think about end of life.
- Have difficulties discussing end-of-life care with the professionals or with one another.
- Have differences of opinion about the care plan.

When a child or young person is approaching the end of life, discuss with them and their parents or carers and with relevant healthcare professionals:

- Any available treatments that might still be in their best interests.
- Any interventions that they are currently receiving that may no longer be in their best interests.

When withdrawing a treatment from a child or young person who is dying, explain to them and to their parents or carers that it is often difficult to tell if or how this may affect them, or when they will die.

5. Advance Care Planning

The most effective way to record the outcome of the decision-making process is usually in the form of an advance care plan (ACP). This is essentially the record of a discussion between a patient (where possible), their professional caregivers and those close to them about their future care.[18] When performed well, the planning process provides all those involved with a vehicle through which to talk honestly about the future, allowing children and their families to retain autonomy and to influence how they are looked after.[19] The examples below illustrate the positive value to families of making a timely ACP.

Tania is the mother of Imogen, who had severe cerebral palsy, leading to worsening respiratory and gut function. These are her reflections on having written a

[18] Plunkett and Parslow (n 8).
[19] ibid.

detailed ACP, which limited the escalation of certain treatments, and favoured out of hospital care:

> Having the ACP has empowered me as a parent to take control over decisions for my child. I am confident that she will not spend her last moments with men in green jumping on her chest, and if that means her life is potentially a little shorter as a result, I will take that trade. The ACP is not about withholding necessary treatment, but instead about ensuring that when my child dies, she will do so with as much dignity as possible.

Katherine is the mother of Jack, a young man with Tay Sachs disease, who died at the age of seven; she describes the impact of his detailed ACP on the events surrounding his death:

> Jack's ACP ensured the quality of his death and allowed us to concentrate on ensuring the quality of his life. We were not there when he died but when we arrived it was to find all aspects of the ACP being adhered to and this allowed us to deal with other aspects of the trauma.

As illustrated above, an ACP typically covers the concerns and wishes of children and young people about their care, including what should be done, where, how, when and by whom. Importantly, while ACPs also consider what should not be done, it is vitally important that healthcare professionals do not mistakenly believe that an ACP is an automatic statement of intent not to treat. When trust and collaboration between parents or carers and the treating healthcare teams result in a well-written ACP, the child is more likely to receive personalised care and conflict is less likely to arise. Studies in PICUs suggest that almost half of families perceive conflict to have arisen and that the quality of communication is a significant contributor.[20]

6. Identifying the Early Signs of Conflict

Conflict between healthcare staff, patients and families presents a burden to individuals and to healthcare systems, causing burnout, absenteeism and higher staff turnover. Conflict can be defined as a multidimensional construct, involving a process whereby two or more people perceive opposition of another, and a process whereby one's interests, norms and values are opposed by another.[21] In healthcare, such conflict may be 'vertical' between staff and patients, or 'horizontal' between clinicians. As recent high-profile cases (Gard, Evans, Haastrup) have demonstrated, PICUs provide a ripe environment for developing conflict, with a mixture of very sick patients, high mortality, multiple specialities and a frequent need for urgent decisions on complex matters.

A study of the impact of conflict in a UK specialist children's hospital revealed that whilst it was prevalent across paediatrics specialties, some areas such as

[20] GMC (n 1).
[21] ibid.

neonatology and neurology were particularly affected. Nearly 450 hours of healthcare practitioner time was spent over a 24-week study period in managing conflict, and the three most common triggers were felt to be 'communication breakdown', 'disagreements about treatment' and 'unrealistic expectations'.[22] Simply transferring this burden to the court is neither realistic nor desirable. Early intervention to prevent conflict escalation has parallels with the sorts of 'early help' offered in the context of safeguarding children. The aim in both cases is to provide options to support the child and family early in the life of a problem in order to avoid the need for more confrontational approaches that may formally challenge the role of parental decision-making. Second opinions and mediation may be more likely to resolve conflict if offered prior to positions becoming deeply entrenched, as is further examined by Richard Huxtable in chapter 11.

A recent study used semi-structured interviews of staff and parents at the interface of acute and palliative services, in PICUs, NICUs and children's hospices, to describe the stages of a common 'conflict pathway'.[23] Although not all the conflict situations analysed escalated, those that did were found to move through three identifiable stages:

1. *Mild: poor management of relationship with the family.* This early stage included features such as insensitive use of language by clinicians; conflicting messages about prognosis or treatment from the healthcare teams; perceived or genuine errors in treatment of the child (raised by families); and a family having a history of unresolved conflict (effectively sensitising them to disagreements escalating).
2. *Moderate: deterioration of trust.* If left unaddressed, the conflict then escalates to include: repetitive arguments leading to entrenchment (families labelled as 'awkward'); avoidance (not attending meetings, or avoiding discussions); micromanagement (families overmonitor and criticise their child's care); faction building (both sides find others to foster and support their position).
3. *Severe: disintegration of working relationship.* By this stage terms such as 'win' and 'lose' are commonly used to describe the intended outcome. Identifiable features include: the child no longer being the focus ('best interests' are no longer central); conflict takes on a life of its own (and becomes the focus, rather than the child); physical and verbal threats (professional or personal, including threats of going to the media).

Early recognition of these stages can equip healthcare teams to recognize mild or moderate conflict and choose appropriate interventions, to prevent further escalation. Some of these techniques are described below.

[22] L Forbat, C Sayer, P McNamee, E Menson, and S Barclay, 'Conflict in a Paediatric Hospital: A Prospective Mixed-Methods Study' (2016) 101 *Archives of Disease in Childhood* 23.

[23] GMC (n 1).

7. De-escalation Techniques

Conflict-management strategies are not a routine part of clinical training, but research shows that training paediatric staff to recognise the early signs of conflict described above and to apply simple conflict-resolution techniques has the potential to reduce substantially the human and economic costs of conflicts for healthcare providers, healthcare staff, and children/young people and their families.[24] The training would typically include information on what triggers conflict between parents and health professionals and how to spot the warning signs. It can include simulation exercises designed to encourage staff to empathise with patients and families by 'stepping into their shoes' (using parent narratives such as those shared in this chapter) and teach skills to help staff de-escalate conflicts with families.

If conflict persists despite these bedside interventions, seeking a second medical opinion is often helpful, as suggested in both the GMC and RCPCH guidance. This may involve review by a senior colleague, or the involvement of a completely separate medical team. However, it may not always be viewed as completely independent and, should the second opinion be in agreement with the first, it may be seen as collusion between consultants, or even a subtle form of coercion. The option of allowing parents to choose their own second opinion may prove to be a good strategy, as long as the process remains transparent and does not lead to prolonged delays in reaching a decision, or to the use of remote 'experts' without direct knowledge of the case (as seen in the case of Charlie Gard). When the basis of disagreement is a differences in understanding of the medical facts, parents may anyway not believe the medical teams, limiting the benefit of supplementary opinions.

Salient Features of Mediation and Litigation[25]

Table 1.1 Contrasting features of mediation and litigation

Litigation	Mediation
Adversarial	Consensual
Inflexible	Flexible
Backward-looking	Forward-looking
Externally imposed judgement	Mutually agreed solution
Time-consuming	Relatively quick
Very costly	Relatively cheap

Source: S Meller and S Barclay, 'Mediation: An Approach to Intractable Disputes Between Parents and Paediatricians' (2011) 96 *Archives of Disease in Childhood* 619.

[24] L Forbat, J Simons, C Sayer, M Davies and S Barclay, 'Training Paediatric Healthcare Staff in Recognising and Managing Conflict with Patients and Families: Findings from a Survey on Immediate and 6 Month Impact' (2017) 102 *Archives of Disease in Childhood* 250.

[25] Meller and Barclay (n 5).

Consultation with clinical ethics committees about individual cases is also recommended in the published guidance,[26] but convening a quorate committee in a timely enough manner to act proactively can be difficult, and the committee may lack the necessary independence from the hospital trust, in the eyes of the family. If a suitably impartial second opinion and an ethical review do not result in a resolution of the disagreement, it would be usual for doctors to think about approaching the court, which results in entrenchment and a further escalation of already strongly held opinions.

Medical mediation can present a less adversarial option to consider, as suggested by Justice Francis in the case of Charlie Gard. This must take place in a neutral setting and has been defined as 'a flexible process conducted confidentially in which a neutral person actively assists the parties in working towards a negotiated agreement of a dispute or difference, with the parties in ultimate control of the decision to settle and the terms of resolution'.[27] The aim of mediation is not to produce answers but mutually agreed and accepted solutions to deeply held differences of opinion. Mediation can involve families, religious advisers and others who have been recognised as being important in helping to resolve underlying differences of opinion.[28] The key is that all sides are given the opportunity to 'tell their story' to a skilled and impartial third party. A mediator could come from a number of professional backgrounds but requires a knowledge of medical law, a sound understanding of ethics, and access to independent expert medical advice.

In most cases, parents and healthcare teams will come to a consensus, by following the process outlined above. If this is not the case, legal advice from a specialist healthcare lawyer will need to be considered. Although taking legal advice does not necessarily mean that court proceedings will follow, one advantage of initiating such proceedings is that the child will have his/her own appointed representative from the Child and Family Court Advisory Service, thereby ensuring that the child's voice is properly represented.

8. Conclusion

Advances in modern paediatrics mean that children with complex healthcare needs live longer and that the child and family may be faced with an increasingly bewildering array of options falling into the navigable space between 'best

[26] Larcher et al (n 1); GME (n 1).
[27] Meller and Barclay (n 5).
[28] Larcher et al (n 1).

interests' and 'significant harm', as described by Dominic Wilkinson elsewhere in this volume. Both parents and clinicians, however, need to be able to live with the decisions made.[29]

For example, Ana Todorovic reflected, several years after Nadia's death:

> I've come to realise, in the meantime, that the decision itself was the smallest part of the process, psychologically speaking. I spent months and months going over all the details afterwards, adding new bits of information as I learned about Nadia's condition, backing-up and going down different paths mentally, imagining slight changes to what we did and taking them all the way to their conclusion. It was only after I had the feeling that all of these paths were clearly laid out in front of me, that I could really assess whether the decision was sensible. (Luckily, I still think it was.) I suppose what goes on in the doctor's office is a highly condensed version of that, but with more uncertainty.

A recent review focusing on the clinician–parent relationship as the key foundation stone for decision-making for children with life-limiting illnesses[30] outlines the importance of both parties understanding each other's roles in the process. It suggests that parents are likely to see their role as 'advocating' (learning to navigate healthcare systems/dealing with different options for treatment) and 'protecting' (weighing the risks). Clinicians are portrayed both as 'professionals trained to treat' (with the possible inference of preserving life) and 'ethical professionals who will recommend within their realm of expertise what is in the best interest of their patients' (even if this may shorten life). These positions may be both internally conflicting for clinicians and parents, as well as having the potential to create conflict between parties. The review suggests that a mutual understanding of these roles, developed within the parent–clinician relationship, is crucial in preventing the onset of conflict. It is hoped that this chapter gives some insight into the lived experiences of parents and healthcare professionals.

The national guidance available to support the making of such decisions is absolutely consistent on the importance of involving the child and family in the process as early and as completely as is sensitively possible. Furthermore, evidence strongly suggests that children with life-limiting illnesses have a much greater awareness of their own mortality than that attributed to them.[31] Parents and children may seek to protect each other through mutual pretence, but families reflect more positively in bereavement when communication channels have been open.

[29] M Bluebond-Langner, D Hargrave, E Henderson and R Langner, '"I Have to Live with the Decisions I Make": Laying a Foundation for Decision-Making for Children with Life-Limiting Conditions and Life-Threatening Illnesses' (2017) 102 *Archives of Disease in Childhood* 468.

[30] D Wilkinson, S Barclay and J Savulescu, 'Disagreement, Mediation, Arbitration: Resolving Disputes about Medical Treatment' (2018) 391 *Lancet* 2302.

[31] ibid.

This chapter has explored the circumstances in which conflict arises, and how it may be identified, before focusing on early interventions to try to bring about consensus. Figure 1.3 outlines the suggested steps for clinicians.

Figure 1.3 Suggested steps for managing conflict

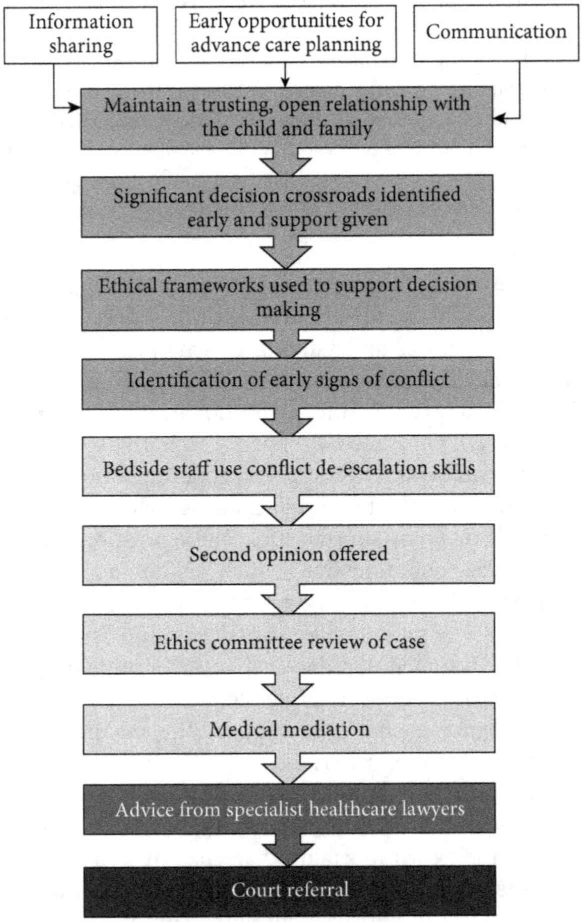

Finally, the RCPCH guidance acknowledges that absolute agreement in decision-making may be neither practical nor achievable, but recognises the obligation to seek as much common ground as possible, whilst accepting that there will be sincerely held differences of opinion.[32] Disagreement is not in itself always a bad thing, because ethically complex decisions – such as those around a child's

[32] Larcher et al (n 1).

treatment towards the end of life – touch on deeply held questions of value on which there can be different reasonable views.[33] Differences of opinion in medicine may be inevitable, but conflict need not necessarily follow.

Ana and Richard both spoke about the importance of considering the '*whole child*' and that their child be viewed as '*a someone*', rather than the output of a formulaic assessment of their '*best interests*' purely on medical grounds. Richard mentioned the importance of not separating the considerations relating to Joseph's body from those relating to his 'soul'.

Some years later, he reflected:

> On that issue of decision-making, I notice that the large Wikipedia entry on 'quality of life', so often used as the reach-for concept in life-and-death healthcare decision-making, doesn't even once mention the matter of human dignity. That, however, was one of the principal elements alive in my mind when I was thinking about Joseph's treatment.

These final thoughts confirm the different approaches to complex decisions between clinicians and families. Healthcare professionals are more likely to use a semi-scientific balancing of individual benefits and burdens, whereas for families the welfare of the whole child (or even the whole family) is likely to be paramount. Although the two approaches may produce a mutually acceptable outcome, there can be the need of much empathy along the way, and differences of opinion may need to be tolerated.

Thus, when we consider reforms of law around decision-making on behalf of very ill children, as many of the chapters in this collection do, it is vital that we fully appreciate the pain and complex emotions experienced by those closest to the child. Consideration of this, as well as issues of law and rights, must inform us so that we develop a sensitive approach to such deeply distressing and difficult situations. The shared reflections of parents who have lived through the experience provide rich insight to those of us seeking to empathise.

The sketches below are an extract from 'The Unfathomable Price of Flesh' by Richard GT Gipps. The difficulties of the choices that he navigated as Joseph's father are clear, as is the extent of his pain.

> flesh
> Your body has no cuts or bruises yet is an open wound.
> Your now so stertorous breath announces you out of sight, pulls me to you, gladdening my heart.
> They ask me, if to keep you alive, I would open this wound further.
> I think now of your mother: her lively eyes, hands, concerns: that so dense texture of her mothering.
> Again and again, the flesh of my mind pulls apart
>
> choice
> To have to choose between your soul and your life.

[33] Wilkinson et al (n 30).

I love you whole, and so that is my answer.
What I can't stand, though is when people say 'I'm sure you chose right."
I mean: how could they know?

grace
His breathing slows and stops.
Ten seconds pass.
Another breath.
Again, ten seconds later, he breathes.
A little blood, trickling from his mouth. Breathes, then … stops.
(As if we might still not have understood that we cannot.)

2

Evaluating 'Best Interests' as a Threshold for Judicial Intervention in Medical Decision-Making on Behalf of Children

IMOGEN GOOLD

1. Introduction

In a series of high-profile cases over the past few years, the English courts have been asked to grapple with a question that had seemed well settled in English law: who should have the final say over a child's medical treatment?[1] Such disputes can arise where parents cannot agree with one another, or where the medical treating team and parents cannot agree. This volume focuses on the latter kind of dispute, which featured in the cases of Charlie Gard, Alfie Evans and Isaiah Haastrup.[2] For the most part, when cases concerning treatment disputes come to court, the question for the court is which course of action is in the child's best interests. This has been the focus of much of the case-law over the past few decades, and the courts have developed a nuanced, considered approach to this question. The question of *when* the courts have the authority to make such a determination has not, however, been regarded as one in need of answer. The threshold for judicial intervention until recently was seemingly uncontroversial, with the court considering itself permitted to take a decision in such matters at the point where the child's welfare is engaged. In *Great Ormond St Hospital v Yates and Gard* (*Gard*),[3] however, this threshold was challenged, and it was argued that in at least some cases the threshold should be such that parents are the final arbiter in decisions about the medical

[1] *Great Ormond Street Hospital v Yates and Gard* [2017] EWHC 972 (Fam) (*Gard*); *Great Ormond Street Hospital for Children NHS Foundation Trust v Yates Court of Appeal (Civil Division)* [2017] EWCA Civ 410 (*Gard 2*); *Alder Hey Children's NHS Foundation Trust v Mr Thomas Evans, Ms Kate James, Alfie Evans (A Child by his Guardian CAFCASS Legal)* [2018] EWHC 308 (Fam) (*Evans*), [2018] 2 FLR 1223; *Kings College Hospital NHS Foundation Trust v Ms Thomas, Haastrup and Haastrup* [2018] EWHC 127 (Fam), [2018] 2 FLR 1028 (*Haastrup*).

[2] ibid.

[3] *Gard* (n 1).

treatment of a child unless there is a serious risk that their decision will result in significant harm to the child. Such a position, echoed in much of the public discourse around the case (and that of *Alder Hey Children's NHS Foundation Trust v Evans*[4] (*Evans*)) as well as the ethics literature, is considered by some as a means to afford greater weight to parental decisions. In particular, Charlie Gard's parents are now pressing for a change in the law to ensure that rather than evaluating best interests, the court should not override parental wishes unless they pose a risk of significant harm to the child.[5]

The debate, then, centres around whether we should retain the low threshold of best interests or engagement with the child's welfare (the orthodoxy), or move to some form of harm threshold. Other chapters in this collection address this debate head on, such as those offered by Giles Birchley[6] and Dominic Wilkinson.[7] I have taken a position on this question elsewhere,[8] and hence in this chapter instead offer some thoughts on how we should approach the question of whether the threshold ought to shift. Rather than arguing for a particular stance, this chapter explains the current threshold's operation and then outlines the various considerations of which we should take account when considering whether to make a change.

The chapter begins by offering a brief background to the orthodox position that remains in place following *Gard* and *Evans*. It then outlines the various reasons for making a change that have been offered, both in *Gard* and also in some of the literature, both legal and ethical. It gives a brief account of the ethical position in favour of an alternative threshold based on risk of harm, before concluding with a number of concerns raised about the implications of such a shift in practice.

The point at which the state may involve itself in our lives necessarily raises fundamental questions about the legitimate bounds of state involvement in citizens' private lives. This is particularly the case in decisions made within families about children, which are often considered private or the purview of parents alone. Certainly, this is the sentiment that animated much of the public discourse.[9]

[4] *Evans* (n 1).

[5] C Burns, 'Charlie Gard's Parents Want "Charlie's Law"' (*BBC News*, June 2018) https://www.bbc.co.uk/news/health-44334306 (accessed 11 June 2019).

[6] G Birchley, 'The Harm Threshold: A View from the Clinic', chapter 6 below.

[7] D Wilkinson, 'In Defence of a Conditional Harm Threshold for Paediatric Decision-Making', chapter 5 below

[8] C Auckland and I Goold, 'Defining the Limits of Parental Authority: Charlie Gard, Best Interests and the Risk of Significant Harm Threshold (casenote)' (2018) *Law Quarterly Review* 37; C Auckland and I Goold, 'Parental Rights, Best Interests and Significant Harms' (2019) 11(2) *Cambridge Law Journal* 287–323.

[9] See, eg: 'Charlie Gard's Parents Refused Permission to Spend His Last Night at Home Before His Life Support Machine Is Switched Off on Friday' (*The Telegraph*, 27 June 2017) www.telegraph.co.uk/news/2017/06/29/charlie-gards-parents-refused-permission-spend-last-night-home (accessed 11 June 2019). Chris Gard, Charlie's father, has himself argued that 'our parental rights have been stripped away' by the court decisions, See M Robinson et al., 'Devastated Parents of Charlie Gard Spend their Last Night With their baby and Blast "Heartless" Doctors for Refusing to Let them Take Him Home to Die Before they Turn Off His Life Support Later Today' (*The Daily Mail*, 30 June 2017) www.dailymail.co.uk/news/article-4653894/Outpouring-grief-worldwide-Baby-Charlie-Gard.html (accessed 11 June 2019).

The Gard family and those who support them are in part taking the position that parental decisions ought to have priority over the views of other interested parties except to the point where a parent's decision puts the child at risk of significant harm. This is, effectively, a demand to push back against state involvement and protect the privacy and authority of parental decisions. When we consider such questions, we cannot frame these merely as questions of parental rights versus the state, however, as they necessarily affect the vulnerable child at the centre of the situation. Therefore, in evaluating the current threshold, this chapter teases out the complexities of how we respect plurality of values in a democratic society while still taking communal responsibility for the protection of the vulnerable amongst us. Before moving on to this analysis, I will briefly explain why the recent cases raise a live question that invites academic attention.

A. Why is it a Live Question?

In a series of high-profile recent cases, the orthodox approach to judicial intervention in disputes between parents and medical teams treating very ill children has come under fire. The cases of Charlie Gard, Alfie Evans and Isaiah Haastrup all involved an application by the treating hospital for life-sustaining treatment to be withdrawn from a seriously ill child. In each, the parents strongly resisted the withdrawal of care. The facts of these cases have been outlined elsewhere in this collection, but a key distinction needs to be drawn out for the purposes of this chapter. In the cases of Alfie Evans and Isaiah Haastrup, the parents wanted a tracheotomy to be performed on the children and for artificial ventilation to be continued. Their hope was to extend their child's lives a little further. Certainly, in *Evans*, there was little expectation of anything but life extension. The relevant question, then, was whether prolonging the life of a heavily brain-damaged and physically disabled child who was likely to die relatively soon was in that child's best interests. Were the potential harms associated with these invasive treatments worth it for that those extra days or weeks of life.

By contrast, in *Gard*, Charlie's parents wanted him to be given an experimental treatment being offered by a physician in the United States. Their hope was that this might both extend his life and improve his condition to some degree. Charlie's treating hospital, Great Ormond Street, argued that it was not in Charlie's best interests to travel to the United States to receive the treatment as there was no real hope of success, and travelling (and the care he would need to do so) was potentially harming.

In all three cases, the court refused to accede to the wishes of the parents, holding that it was not in each child's best interests that they continue to receive life-sustaining care, nor to travel to be given an experimental treatment. Consequently, withdrawal of treatment was authorised in each case as being in the child's best interests. Such cases are far from unique; the courts deal with such requests on a regular basis. Yet, *Gard* (and to a lesser extent *Evans*) have precipitated a highly charged debate over whether the courts were right to intervene and take a decision about each child's care. This derived in part from the media attention the cases attracted, but there is more to it than this. Much of the public concern around *Gard* centred around the rights of parents to make decisions for their children, with many objecting to the role of the state in what some consider to be private, familial decisions. For example, one commenter wrote on social media:

> No matter how skilled the doctors, this was NOT their decision to make, they should have recommended a course of action, of course, but NEVER ever should have they felt they had the right to impose their wishes over those of the parents.[10]

In response to their experience, both Charlie and Alfie's parents are now taking steps to change the law, and their efforts have received a degree of public support. Steven Woolfe MEP announced 'Alfie's Law', aimed at securing legal change to 'restore the rights of parents in such decisions'; while the parents of Charlie Gard have launched a similar initiative, 'Charlie's Law', arguing for a greater voice for parents in such decisions.[11] The latter proposes three core changes to the current system:

1. Ensuring all parties have access to mediation and the input of clinical ethics committees;
2. The provision of independent second opinions to families (and also legal aid); and
3. A shift to 'significant harm threshold', meaning that courts cannot intervene to make decisions on behalf of a child unless the parents' decision poses a serious risk that the child will suffer significant harm as a result.[12]

Thus far, these efforts have been unsuccessful, but as of October 2018, the Parliamentary Under-Secretary of State for the Department of Health and Social Security had agreed to work on possible future steps.[13]

This agitation for change is not itself a sufficient reason to consider changing the law, but the strength of opposition among some members of the community is an indicator that the law may need critical re-evaluation. One of the key reasons we should consider a change in the law, however, is that *Gard* has revealed the full extent of the courts' powers (or its view of its powers) under the inherent jurisdiction, and there are reasons to consider this authority as too wide.[14]

[10] Online comment on 'Charlie Gard's Parents Refused Permission to Spend His Last Night at Home Before His Life Support Machine Is Switched Off on Friday' (*Telegraph*, 27 June 2017). Chris Gard, Charlie's father, has himself argued that 'our parental rights have been stripped away' by the court decisions, see: Robinson et al, 'Devastated parents of Charlie Gard' (2017).

[11] 'MEP Launching Campaign for "Alfie's Law" to Give Parents More Say' (*ITV News*, 26 April 2018) www.itv.com/news/granada/2018-04-26/mep-launching-campaign-for-alfies-law-to-give-parents-more-say (11 June 2019); The Charlie Gard Foundation, 'Charlie's Law' (2018) www.thecharliegardfoundation.org/charlies-law (11 June 2019).

[12] The Charlie Gard Foundation, 'Charlie's Law' (2018).

[13] HL Deb 15 October 2018 vol 793 col 387.

[14] R George, 'The Legal Basis of the Court's Jurisdiction to Authorise Medical Treatment of Children', chapter 4 below.

Further, the justifications given for the courts' expansive power to intervene in those cases highlighted the lack of robust normative justification for the current legal position.[15] Given the cogent and widespread critique of the current position in the ethical and philosophical literature, there is good reason at least to pose the question of whether the orthodox approach is sufficiently justified. We might particularly wonder whether it is justifiable to have a low threshold in the context of medical decisions, when the threshold is higher in the context of family life and care proceedings. There may be good reasons for taking a different approach in different contexts,[16] but this needs greater exploration and discussion. If the current threshold is not sufficiently well justified, we should turn to the secondary question of whether a change should be made. In doing so, we must engage with the deeper concern on which these recent challenges to orthodoxy rest – where should the line be drawn to protect private, parental decisions about children from state intervention (if one should be drawn at all)?

2. Orthodoxy

The courts have made it clear that they have the authority to make medical decisions on behalf of children and affirmed the orthodox position that the threshold for judicial intervention is the welfare of the child, often referred to as the 'best interests' approach (referring to both the threshold and the test applied). In this chapter, I am concerned only with the *threshold* for judicial intervention, that is, what must be the case for the court to have authority to decide on behalf of a child (in lieu of either parents or the treating team). The courts in both *Gard* and *Evans* considered that they had authority to intervene whenever a child's welfare is engaged such that it is possible their best interests may not be met.[17]

The courts' authority to intervene in decisions about a child's medical care has a fairly long history, but despite some minor technical dimensions, the position has remained essentially the same for at least a century. Indeed, Graeme Laurie argues that the courts' inherent jurisdiction to intervene can be seen as grounded in the feudal notion of *parens patriae*, whereby 'the monarch as the ultimate superior' has 'jurisdiction over the very "person" of those who inhabited the land'. As such, he explains, 'the monarch was *parens patriae* – parent of the country' which afforded the monarch 'the right and duty to care for those not able to care for themselves'.[18]

[15] These justifications are outlined below, as is the novel basis of the challenge in the *Gard* case.

[16] A point that Rachel Taylor explores in her chapter, explaining that there are reasons not to take the same approach across different contexts: R Taylor, 'Parental Decisions and Court Jurisdiction: Best Interests or Significant Harm?' in Goold et al (eds) (n 6).

[17] *In the matter of Charlie Gard (Permission to Appeal Hearing)*, Thursday 8 June 2017; *Judgment of the UK Supreme Court in the Case of Charlie Gard*, 19 June 2017, [13].

[18] GT Laurie, 'Parens Patriae Jurisdiction in the Medico-Legal Context: The Vagaries of Judicial Activism' (1999) 3 *Edinburgh Law Review* 95, 95.

The origins of the jurisdiction lie, then, in both the monarch's authority and the vulnerability of those over whom the monarch had power. Like the modern variation (and also like parental authority and responsibility), the monarch has both power and responsibility.

By the mid-19th century, it was made clear in *Re Flynn* that the court had the power to protect children from their parents' decisions where this was 'essential to their safety or to their welfare, in some very serious and important respect'.[19] Although early on this jurisdiction did reflect a sense that parents knew best and so ought to be afforded a substantial degree of leeway, this began to recede. By 1886, the Guardianship of Children Act 1886 had equalised parental rights and made the 'welfare of the child' a statutory factor. A few years later the court's power to intervene was enshrined in the Custody of Children Act 1891 sections 1 and 2, which gave the court the power to interfere with parental rights in the interests of the child. The welfare of the child was considered of paramount importance and was to be understood in its widest sense, according to the court in *In re McGrath (Infants)* in 1893.[20]

This position did not change in any great sense over the following century, and from the 1970s onwards a string of decisions confirmed the ambit and effect of the court's jurisdiction. Lord Justice Waite stated in *Re T* that the Court has the authority to intervene whenever the child's best interests will otherwise not be promoted, and confirmed the welfare basis of this approach.[21]

This does not mean that parents have not been considered to have authority. Far from it. The courts have been at pains to ensure that parents retain power to make decisions for their children in relation to medical care. For example, Lord Scarman said in *Gillick v West Norfolk and Wisbech Area Health Authority* that:

> It is abundantly plain that the law recognises that there is a right and a duty of parents to determine whether or not to seek medical advice in respect of their child, and, having received advice, to give or withhold consent to medical treatment.[22]

Rachel Taylor explains elsewhere in this volume that in a free and diverse society, it is important that courts do not impose 'a particular view as to what is best for children without good reason and clear evidence to support that view', and she outlines how the courts do allow for parental discretion and demonstrate respect for parental decision-making in the approach they take. For example, she cites comments by Baroness Hale in *Williamson* to this effect:

> Children have the right to be properly cared for and brought up so that they can fulfil their potential and play their part in society. The parents have both the primary responsibility and the primary right to do this. The state steps in to regulate the exercise

[19] *In re Flynn* (1848) 2 De G & Sm 457, 474.

[20] *In re McGrath (Infants)* [1893] 1 Ch 143, 148.

[21] *Re T (A Minor) (Wardship: Medical Treatment)* [1997] 1 WLR 242.

[22] *Gillick v West Norfolk and Wisbech Area Health Authority* [1986] AC 112, 184 (Scarman LJ) (*Gillick*).

> of that responsibility in the interests of children and society as a whole. But 'the child is not the child of the state' and it is important in a free society that parents should be allowed a large measure of autonomy in the way in which they discharge their parental responsibilities.[23]

That said, Lord Scarman also made clear that 'the common law has never treated such rights as sovereign or beyond review and control',[24] for as Ward LJ explained in *Re A*, this parental authority 'exist[s] for the performance of their duties and responsibilities to the child' and hence 'must be exercised in the best interests of the child'. Therefore, 'overriding control is vested in the court'.[25] It is therefore clear, and has been for some time, that parents have authority to make medical decisions, subject to that authority being overridden by the courts at the point that welfare concerns are engaged. Fundamentally, however, the orthodox position was made abundantly clear by Lady Hale in *Gard* when she stated: '[P]arents are not entitled to insist upon treatment by anyone which is not in their child's best interests.'[26] Therefore, when in the *Gard*, Justice Francis considered he had jurisdiction to intervene, he was therefore taking very much the orthodox approach to such questions. In supporting his stance, the Court of Appeal and the Supreme Court merely confirmed the status quo, as was also the case in *Evans*.[27]

3. The Challenge

With the law in such a settled state, it would take an unusual fact situation to provide the opportunity for a challenge to be made to the orthodox threshold for intervention. Such facts arose in the *Gard* case, as they offered a situation in which two parents were in agreement, but disagreed with the medical team treating their child. However, unlike other cases, this did not present the kind of impasse that generally gives the courts a basis on which to intervene, as parents cannot demand that an unwilling doctor treat their child, nor may a doctor undertake treatment on the child in the absence of consent from either the parents or the courts. Therefore, disputes come to the courts because the doctors will not or indeed feel they cannot, in good conscience, accede to parental wishes.[28] As a consequence, the court is needed to find a way through the impasse and in such instances,

[23] *R (on the application of Williamson and others) v. Secretary of State for Education and Employment and others* [2005] UKHL 15; [2005] 2 All ER 1, [72]; further discussed below.

[24] *Gillick* (n22), 184 (Scarman LJ).

[25] *Re A (Children)* [2001] 1 Fam 147 (HL); [2001] 2 WLR 480, 178 (Ward LJ).

[26] 'Lady Hale's explanation of the Supreme Court's decision', as delivered in Court (8 June 2017) www.supremecourt.uk/news/permission-to-appeal-hearing-in-the-matter-of-charlie-gard.html (accessed 11 June 2019).

[27] *Great Ormond Street Hospital v Yates and Gard* [2017] EWHC 972 (Fam), [47]–[50].

[28] Jo Bridgeman has rightly demonstrated that many of these cases can be seen as instances of professional conscience: J Bridgeman, 'Beyond Best Interests: A Question of Professional Conscience?', chapter 7 below.

the 'best interests' understanding of the *threshold* makes sense, because someone needs to take a decision on behalf of that child as those involved cannot. This was the situation in almost every case prior to *Gard*, and in these situations an application was made to the court which had to 'arbitrate' between the positions of the two parties and determine what should happen.

The facts of *Gard*, however, did not present such an impasse, and hence raised a novel question about the basis on which (and the point at which) the court could legitimately intervene. Connie Yates and Chris Gard were in disagreement with Great Ormond Street (GOSH) about whether Charlie should receive experimental treatment. GOSH maintained that he should not be given the treatment and was not prepared to do so despite the request made by Charlie's parents. Normally, this would prevent parents from being able to access the treatment, but in *Gard* this was not so because an alternative treating team based in the United States *was* willing to provide the experimental 'nucleoside therapy'. The parents were not trying to force GOSH to treat Charlie; they were merely asking for him to be allowed to be transferred to a different hospital in the United States.

Therefore, there was no need for the court to step in and provide its consent (or a declaration of unlawfulness): treatment had been offered to Charlie, and his parents had consented to him receiving it. Gard and Yates did not need the court to facilitate their wishes being fulfilled.[29] The fundamental question was instead whether GOSH could withdraw treatment from Charlie. This would effectively have prevented him from being taken to the United States. GOSH's application requested that the court make a determination on, amongst other things, whether it was 'lawful, and in Charlie's best interests, for his treating clinicians to provide him with palliative care only' and whether it was 'lawful, and in Charlie's best interests, not to undergo nucleoside therapy provided always that the measures and treatments adopted are the most compatible with maintaining Charlie's dignity'.[30]

As the hospital could not be required to treat Charlie, there was no need to request a determination of whether refusing to treat Charlie was in his best interests. They could legally refuse.[31] This request, however, suggests that they were sufficiently concerned about the impact of the experimental treatment on Charlie's welfare that they felt it necessary to seek a determination that to give it would not have been in Charlie's best interests. This was likely also motivated by a desire to be sure that in withdrawing treatment they were acting appropriately in relation to Charlie. But as we can assume GOSH would not have involved itself in

[29] But GOSH could have made an application to seek court confirmation that it would be lawful to facilitate his removal had they wished to, as it is likely that the hospital would have needed to take steps to enable this. I am grateful to Jonathan Herring for this point.

[30] *Great Ormond Street Hospital for Children NHS Foundation Trust v Yates* [2017] EWHC 972 (Fam), [5].

[31] See: *A Hospital Trust v GM, DK, HK* [2017] EWHC 1710, [23] (Baker J); *King's College Hospital NHS Foundation Trust v MH* [2015] EWHC 1920, [34] (Francis J); *Re J (A Minor) (Child in Care: Medical Treatment)* [1992] 3 WLR 507, 516 (Donaldson MR).

trying to prevent another hospital taking a different approach to a child not in GOSH's care, it was hence also wanting to be sure that it was not required in any sense to *facilitate* Charlie receiving a treatment it felt was not in his best interests. This would in part have been motivated by the duties it, as his treating team, had towards him both in tort and via its human rights obligations to him. In asking for a determination on this matter, it was essentially inviting the court to take a view on this. But in doing so, it opened up the question of whether the court could step into a situation and prevent parents from taking up an offer of treatment from a medical professional.

The question therefore became whether there ought to be a threshold that must be met before the court could interfere in the medical decisions of parents, and if so, what that threshold was. In the Court of Appeal, counsel argued that one could discern, by reading across from the Children Act 1989, and also the Ashya King case, in cases of this kind (what counsel referred to as 'Category 2 cases') the existence of a 'risk of significant harm' threshold.[32] Such a threshold would prevent a court from intervening in a parent's decision about a child's medical care unless that decision exposed the child to a risk of significant harm.

Usually, parents' decisions about *choice* of medical team or hospital are not policed, and they are free to choose between those options available to them. Such choices could, as was the conclusion in *Gard*, mean that a child receives a treatment that is not in his or her best interests. But for the most part, there is the implicit assumption that medical professionals offer treatments that are in a child's interests and if they treat in a way that falls below the *Bolam* standard, they will be negligent.[33] However, the question here was not about the treatment itself, but the parents' liberty to choose it amongst the range of options before them. The decision in *Gard* at all levels was to the effect that they could not choose the option of nucleoside therapy because it was not in Charlie's best interests that he receive it, and therefore the court could legitimately step in to prevent him having the treatment.

In coming to this conclusion, both the Court of Appeal and the Supreme Court (in rejecting the application for leave to appeal) *effectively* dealt with the application as a question of whether they could make a determination on parental *choice* of treatment. They did not do so explicitly, but in being asked to determine whether a treatment that GOSH did not want to administer (and could not be compelled to administer) was not in Charlie's best interests, and then implying that they would prevent his parents moving Charlie to obtain it, they effectively took the view that they could block Gard and Yates from making this choice of treatment. They were able to do so via the orthodox best interests threshold approach, but did not directly engage with the question of whether a threshold currently

[32] See references to *Re Ashya King* [2014] EWHC 2964 (Fam) in *Gard (CA)*, [54]–[82], [96]–[111]. See generally: Taylor (n 16); George (n 14).

[33] *Bolam v Friern Hospital Management Committee* [1957] 1 WLR 583.

exists, or with what that threshold might be. Lady Hale instead simply made clear that parents cannot demand treatment that is not in their child's best interests.[34]

The decisions in *Gard* and *Evans* also made clear how *broadly* the court understands its authority to make decisions once the best interests threshold has been met. Both cases involved questions about whether a child might be taken elsewhere for treatment, raising the issue of whether the court's powers under the inherent jurisdiction extended to issuing an injunction to prevent parents travelling abroad to seek alternative treatment. In *Gard*, McFarlane LJ stated: 'If necessary, and one hopes it that the situation will not arise, such an order would be backed up by an injunction in due course; but, if so, it would be an injunction made by the court.'[35] This situation did not arise in the end in *Gard*, but it was a more pressing question in the end in *Evans*. In that case, Alfie's parents wished to take him to Italy for treatment or at least ongoing life support. In response, Mr Justice Hayden made it was clear that he was refusing the parents' application to 'permit the child's immediate removal to Italy'.[36] The Court of Appeal upheld this decision, and this included rejecting the argument that this breached EU free-movement law. In both decisions, then, the courts were of the view that they had the power to restrain parents from removing children elsewhere for treatment that was not in their best interests. In *Gard*, Lord Justice McFarlane, implied that he would impose an injunction if needed to prevent Charlie's parents moving him to the United States. In doing so, he effectively not only agreed with the application by GOSH that the treatment was not in Charlie's best interests, but also that as a consequence they could legitimately be prevented from accepting an offer of that treatment from another doctor. The limits on parental decisions go beyond merely the court having the power to choose between parent and doctor, and instead prevent parents from accessing the treatment offered by other doctors. The courts also apparently would be prepared to issue injunctions and control the movement of children if need be, even though they did not always explicitly talk in such terms

The necessary logic of these determinations is that the best interests approach is understood as the court having the authority to intervene *wherever* a parent makes a decision that the court considers is not in the best interests of the child if an application that enables them to do so is made. Read in this way, as the decisions in *Gard* and *Evans* support, the threshold in medical decision-making for children under the inherent jurisdiction is potentially very low indeed, yet this is an entirely legitimate interpretation of the best interests threshold, and this is precisely why the *Gard* case is so important – because it reveals the extent of the court's authority to intervene in parental decision-making.

If, as the court suggested in *Gard* and *Evans*, judges can decide upon *any* matter relating to a child's welfare, and intervene wherever they disagree with the parents'

[34] 'Lady Hale's explanation' (n 26).

[35] *Yates & Anor v Great Ormond Street Hospital for Children NHS Foundation Trust & Anor* [2017] EWCA Civ 410, [2017] WLR(D) 391, [117].

[36] *Evans* (n 1), [8].

assessment of the child's best interests, this would be an exceptionally large intrusion by the state into the private decisions of parents. As counsel for Charlie Gard's parents put it before the Supreme Court:

> [I]f the State can, without the highest of justification, intrude into so private an area of human life as a joint parental decision made about one's child's upbringing, the scope for protection against state interference afforded by our most basic constitutional values, as well as by Article 8 ECHR, is considerably eroded.[37]

These cases have rightly sparked both public and academic interest because they make apparent just how low the threshold for judicial intervention is, and how broad the court's power is once it is involved. I have argued elsewhere that the low threshold requires greater justification,[38] and that the law should move to a 'risk of significant harm' threshold before the courts may intervene. In this chapter, I will give an overview of the arguments on both sides of this debate, some of which are explored in more depth by Giles Birchley and Dominic Wilkinson later in this volume. In my view, these arguments fall on the side of moving to a harm threshold, but there is no question that that the issue is a very finely balanced one, with multiple dimensions to it.

4. Objections to a Harm Threshold

A. The Orthodox Approach: Sufficient and Appropriate

There are two strands to this general point. First, one argument for retaining the current approach is that the orthodox approach does already sufficiently account for parental views. The other is that court also already exclude vexatious claims.

On the first argument, as Rachel Taylor points out, while the law read strictly 'appears to allow the court to impose the values of the "reasonable person" to restrict the lawful decisions of parents, simply because a stranger to the decision has raised a question that the court is willing to consider', in fact this kind of 'draconian interference in parental discretion' is already avoided by the attitude the court takes, and in particular the respect it expresses for the importance of parental decisions. She argues that this, rather than a harm threshold, is a better way to permit discretion and scope in parenting while protecting vulnerable children from harmful decisions.[39]

We might also note that clinicians do already take account of parental views well before the court is involved. Giles Birchley makes this point in his chapter, demonstrating from his empirical research as well as that of others that clinicians

[37] *In the matter of Charlie Gard* (n 17).
[38] Auckland and Goold (2019) (n 8).
[39] Taylor (n 16).

generally attempt to balance parental autonomy, parental needs and the best interests of the child when deciding how to treat.[40]

Katie Gollop and Sarah Pope, both of whom appeared in the recent case of *Re R*, which also involved a dispute over a child's care, describe the process of decision-making as one in which 'everyone at the hospital including the lawyers … try hard to facilitate consensus building',[41] rather than one that is adversarial and against the parents.

Although the parents in these cases who have not been allowed to choose for their child as they wish certainly feel disempowered, that in and of itself is not enough to demonstrate that the law as it stands and the processes within hospitals *actually* prevent parents having a sufficient say in the treatment of their children. There is substantial evidence to suggest that parental views are respected to a very great extent in the law and in practice, and so this concern alone is insufficient to support a move to a harm threshold.[42]

On the second point, on vexatious claims, Rachel Taylor argues in this volume that there is no need to import a harm threshold into medical decision-making because the courts already have the mechanism in place to avoid hearing applications with no merit. This is so because an application may only be made where the applicant can demonstrate a genuine interest in the child, regardless of whether the applicant is an individual or a state institution such as an NHS Trust. The courts, she argues, can use this to 'filter out vexatious or unwarranted applications' but it provides 'no substantial hurdle to the applicant with genuine welfare concerns'.[43]

B. Change will be Counter-Productive

In proposing change on the basis of principle, it is right to consider whether that change will produce adverse effects in practice. A number of ways in which a move to a harm threshold might do so have been raised. One concern is that moving to a harm threshold will entail shifting away from an approach that emphasises deciding what is *best for* a child, towards one that explicitly requires the court to demonstrate that is has authority because a parental decision will place that child at risk of harm. Giles Birchley suggests that this involves greater 'evaluative overtones',[44] directing the judge to evaluate the impact of a parent's decision and then determine whether

[40] Birchley (n 6).

[41] K Gollop and S Pope, 'Charlie Gard, Alfie Evans and R (A Child): Why A Medical Treatment Significant Harm Test Would Hinder Not Help' (*The Transparency Project*, 2018) www.transparencyproject.org.uk/charlie-gard-alfie-evans-and-r-a-child-why-a-medical-treatment-significant-harm-test-would-hinder-not-help (11 June 2019).

[42] See further on steps that might be made to improve current processes: L Austin and R Huxtable, 'Resolving Disagreements about the Care of Critically Ill Children: Evaluating Existing Processes and Setting the Research Agenda', chapter 11 below.

[43] Taylor (n 16).

[44] G Birchley, 'The Harm Threshold and Parents' Obligation to Benefit their Children' (2016) *Journal of Medical Ethics* 111, 113.

that decision is likely to harm the child. It would, he rightly suggests, demand that their decision be explicitly characterised as 'harmful', and this could consequently have 'pejorative connotations'.[45] Rather than the court's intervention being framed as a mediation in a conflict between parents and medical practitioners, where the court takes the authoritative view on what is best for the child, the process would necessarily become one in which the court must determine whether the quality of the parents' decision means they can be overridden. The entire process changes by establishing parents as prima facie decision-makers who can then be overridden if they take a decision that is problematic. They have strong initial control but that control is contingent on how it is exercised, and that contingency is determined by the court's view on the risks posed by their decisions. Where parents are, in their own minds, doing everything they can to protect a loved child, such a determination might be particularly harmful. It is clear from Connie Yates' statement when they agreed to withdraw support from Charlie that the way her actions had been characterised by the media and courts had hurt her, and we should be rightly wary of harming parents who are already experiencing such a desperately sad situation. As Gollop and Pope write: 'It's bad enough to have a court finding that what you wanted for your child was not in your child's best interests. It's worse to have a court finding that you have caused your child significant harm.'[46]

Although it may be that in some cases parents will feel this evaluation of their position as a hurtful criticism, it is not clear that parents would necessarily find it any more distressing. However it is framed, a decision to prevent parents having the ultimate say over the treatment of their very ill child is likely to be devastating regardless. The harm derives from the thwarting of their desires, the belief that the alternative decision is one that will harm their child, or fail to save him when he or she could have been saved. This was clearly Connie Yates' view of what happened to Charlie.[47] But if this is so, then the framing of the basis on which the court can intervene will make little real difference, because, however, one phrases it, the essential position is the same – the court's view trumps the parents' view because the court's view (and therefore that of the doctors) is deemed more likely to be what is best for the child (or, conversely, less likely to be harming to the child). Therefore, this argument does not appear sufficient in itself to outweigh the benefits to parents in terms of their enhanced decision-making powers.

C. Change will Make No Practical Difference

An alternative objection is that changing to a harm threshold will make no difference to how these situations play out – in hospitals and in the courts. If this is the

[45] ibid.
[46] Gollop and Pope (n 41).
[47] ibid.

case, then it might be suggested that there is no point in pressing for change. There are two senses in which this might be the case.

First, this is likely to be so because in fact cases rarely, if at all, come to court when there is *not* some risk of harm to the child. In this volume, Birchley and Wilkinson, both of whom work in the medical system and interact with parents in exactly the sorts of situations that arise in these cases, note that medical practitioners do not generally pursue court intervention until they are worried that the child will be harmed by acceding to the parents' wishes.[48] This, in fact, is the very thrust of Jo Bridgeman's analysis of these cases – that they are instances where medics cannot agree to give parents what they want for reasons of professional conscience. They are being asked to do something that is not simply not in the child's best interests, but is in fact something they consider they cannot, morally, do.[49] As Wilkinson comments:

> Paediatricians and general practitioners spend a good deal of time counselling parents and encouraging them to make health care decisions for their children that are likely to promote the child's interests. However, if parents make suboptimal decisions, professionals will usually only seek to override parents if what parents have decided poses a real risk of harming the child.[50]

That harm is generally a key issue is evident, too, from the considerations that the judges examine in their determinations.[51] For example, in *Gard*, the Court of Appeal noted in its conclusion on best interests that: 'It must follow from that unanimous professional and expert evidence, that to move Charlie to America and expose him to treatment over there would be likely to expose him to continued pain, suffering and distress.'[52]

Harm is at issue in most, if not all, of these cases, which given how clinicians tell us they approach these situations, is to be expected. Therefore, it is fair to say that in combination with the discretion already afforded to parents by the courts and the application of a 'reasonable-parent' approach to difference, that a de facto harm threshold is already being applied. A move to an overt one would make no difference in practice. Whether this is a reason to make a shift, however, is therefore necessarily dependent on other considerations.

It may mean that a change in the law is unwarranted. On this analysis, it is more likely to mean that the harm threshold is more in keeping with the actual threshold being applied, both by medical professionals when they refrain from requesting judicial intervention, and by courts when they refuse to override a parent's wishes. Therefore, a move in favour of a harm threshold will not have a

[48] Birchley (n 7); Wilkinson (n 7).
[49] Bridgeman (n 28).
[50] Wilkinson (n 7).
[51] See, eg: *Gard* (HC), [16]–[22]; *Gard* (CA), [49], [97] and [114].
[52] *Gard* (CA), 114.

problematic impact, but it will carry the signalling power of bolstering parental confidence that their wishes will be respected, while offering a clearer line for clinicians to engage with about when to request judicial input. Alternatively, as Gollop, Pope and Taylor suggest, being explicit in response to parents that their decisions are considered harmful may itself be an unnecessarily harsh response for no practical gain (or, as Gollop and Pope argue, with unhelpful impacts). These considerations are examined below.

D. A Harm Threshold will Privilege Parental Views

A core tenet of child law is that the child's welfare takes precedence above other concerns, including parental 'rights'. As Taylor writes: '[T]he law regards the upbringing of children not as a matter of exclusive parental rights, to be defended unless forfeited, but as a collaborative responsibility in which parents take the leading role.'

The move to harm threshold is based on a desire to make parents the primary arbiters of a child's welfare by constraining the courts' power to intervene. This was the view put in *Gard*, and is the justification behind 'Charlie's Law' – that parents should have substantially stronger decisional rights in relation to their children. As Taylor notes, those who support this position can raise 'understandable concerns' that the rejection of this approach in *Gard* 'undermines parental freedom'. But, she argues, the law already recognises the value of parents taking the primary role in determining their child's welfare. This view is borne out in many judicial statements on the nature of the court's jurisdiction and its role in disputes. A harm threshold, Taylor suggests, would effectively carve out a space for parental decisions to be 'immune from challenge'.

One response to this is that the only decisions that would become immune to challenge are precisely those decisions that already are essentially treated in that way. Where parents' decisions fall within what the court considers the range of reasonable parenting, the court does not concern itself, nor do hospitals tend to dispute these decisions. As we saw above, clinicians tend to accede to decisions that fall within this sphere, unless there are reasons to resist doing so.[53] Therefore, currently they are in effect immune, and if the threshold is changed, they will just be more overtly protected. We might also say that a shift would at least make the threshold parents face clearer and more intelligible.

[53] For example, Jonathan Herring suggests that clinicians might care about a parent's *motives*, such that a slightly harmful procedure might be tolerated if the parent thinks it will help and the doctor is less confident of this, but might be resisted by the doctor if the parent wants it purely to make money by selling the child's story, or because the parent is affected by a condition such as Munchausen's syndrome by proxy.

5. In Favour of a Harm Threshold

A. Parents as Prima Facie Decision-Makers

One of the key arguments made in favour of a move to a harm threshold is that it better reflects the parents as the appropriate decision-makers on behalf of their children. This was the basis for much of the anger around the *Gard* and *Evans* cases, and is certainly the position taken by the parents in those cases. Many good reasons for treating parents as prima facie decision-makers for their children can be identified, and this is recognised by the courts as noted above. There are, of course, also many instances where we do not believe this to be the case and the law restricts parents (and children) with this in mind.[54]

One reason is that parents must make a great many choices for their children, and if the state were to police these, it would entail regular invasive monitoring. This would undermine our commitment to respecting privacy and family life in liberal democratic society, and practically, would require vast resources to administer, implement and police.[55]

Another is that in fact many everyday decisions made on behalf of children do not require special skills: most adults can make these decisions relatively well and there is no reason to think that anyone else would likely do better. Therefore, there is little reason to suspect that they need to be policed, or that another party could make these decisions better. Further, the majority of these are trivial decisions that do not, individually, have very large impacts on the child. That some less-optimal choices are made is tolerable, and also allows for differences in parental resources and capacity. These are also best balanced and navigated by parents within the context of the particular family.

Both of these reasons are less likely to hold, however, in the context of medical decisions. In such contexts, the courts *do* have the resources to supervise some of these decisions. Also, the consequences for a child of having or not having treatment may well also be grave. This does not mean parents should immediately yield, because there are other reasons that mean parents ought to retain a degree of authority. One is that parents may be best placed to know what is in their child's interests based on their knowledge of the child's preferences.[56] The parent is also very likely to be motivated largely by care and love for the child, and hence be making a decision aimed at promoting the child's interests. As such, a parent's

[54] Compulsory education, film classifications, smacking and alcohol consumption are all examples. I am grateful to Jonathan Herring for this point.

[55] J Goldstein, 'Medical Care for the Child at Risk on State Supervision of Parental Autonomy' (1977) 86 *Yale Law Journal* 645, 650.

[56] D Diekema, 'Parental Refusals of Medical Treatment: The Harm Principle as Threshold for State Intervention' (2004) 25 *Philosophy of Medical Research and Practice* 243, 244.

decision may be more likely to lead to the option that does, in actuality, benefit the child most where that is a decision of *value* (that is, a decision about how to live one's life and what will make it go well).[57]

Allowing parents a fair degree of latitude in decision-making may also benefit the children in other ways. For example, Goldstein suggests that 'the right of parents to raise their children as they think best, free of coercive intervention, comports as well with each child's biological and psychological need for unthreatened and unbroken continuity of care by his parents'.[58]

Within the medical context, supporting parents as far as possible to be decision-makers is therefore likely to support the familial connections that may be vital to their well-being. Society values the family unit, and as Diekema argues, families *need* to be able to make decisions about themselves with some degree of autonomy and with 'sufficient space and freedom from intrusion from others' to flourish.[59]

There is also the fact that it is parents, along with the child, who will ultimately bear the burdens that flow from the decision. Where, as is almost invariably the case, parents want treatment to continue, it is they who will carry the care burdens that may result. This would seem to be quite a strong reason for them to have a considerable say over what treatment the child receives. As Erica Salter puts it: 'Parents, as the central leaders and bearers of responsibility and accountability for the family, are also generally the central bearers of these decisional consequences.'[60]

Douglas Diekema supports this view with the further point that decisions about a child often affect other family members, and require that parents 'weigh the competing interests … in making a final decision'.[61] Parents are best placed, often, to achieve this balance, and giving them the authority to do so is more likely to support the family unit remaining cohesive.

These reasons do not, of course, hold in all situations. There are parents who make unwise, irrational decisions. There are parents who are not motivated by love and care for their children. But these are the exceptional cases, and are not sufficient, therefore, to speak against a prima facie role for parents as decision-makers who can be displaced. A harm threshold much better reflects this trust, while retaining plenty of space for overriding the decisions of parents where these things are not true – where the parents do not appreciate their child's interests, or are not motivated by care for the child – as the court can still intervene if the consequences seem likely to be unacceptable.

[57] This is in contrast to decisions about medical treatment that are about which treatments are likely to work and so forth, as these rest on the application of specialist knowledge rather than a position about value and experience.

[58] *Bolam* (n 33), 649.

[59] ibid.

[60] E Salter, 'Deciding for a Child. a Comprehensive Analysis of the Best Interest Standard' (2012) 33 *Theoretical Medicine and Bioethics* 179, 181.

[61] 'Lady Hale's explanation' (n 34), 244.

B. Transparency and Reflecting Practice

Above we saw that in many ways, the law and clinicians already operate on the basis of a de facto harm threshold. We might then consider this is a reason not to change the system as it is already accords with the harm threshold, so there is no need to alter the law. To do so would be redundant. However, the fact that this is the practice already, but the law does not reflect actual practice, might also be a good reason to consider change. There may be situations in which it helps for parents to be given a clear message as to why their decision is being overridden. 'Best interests' leaves space for perhaps more dispute, while 'harm' is direct. This, of course, may be harming to the parents if, as noted above, the language is hurtful.

But if this is the threshold point at which clinicians bring in the courts, then we ought to be clear about why that is happening to enable both parties to have a clear, open, honest debate about why someone other than a parent may decide. If a real harm cannot be demonstrated, then it may be clear also that there is not a sufficient reason to override parents' wishes. A best interests approach may obscure the basis for the court making the decision, while harm overtly engages with a parental failure to act in accordance with the welfare of the child. It more accurately reflects the actual position of parents in the law, that is as individuals with *authority* and *responsibilities*, but not rights.

C. Tolerance and Value Decisions

Perhaps the strongest reason, however, to prefer a harm threshold picks up where the clarity and directness point leaves off. There are many hard decisions about a child's care that need to be made, and some of these are on questions where there is space for reasonable disagreement. These will very often be questions of *value*, about what is important in life, about what makes a life go well. In the medical context, a good example is the question of whether length or quality of life is more important. Such a question is often one that challenges the courts in cases of this kind. Indeed, as I have argued elsewhere, the difficult cases that challenge the courts and put pressure on where the right line for intervention lies concern disputes not of fact, but of *value* or *belief*.[62] The courts find these difficult precisely because they test our commitment to respect for plurality of values, pitting our commitment to respect for belief against the communal responsibility for the vulnerable in our society.

If we are really to respect difference and work towards a respectful, pluralistic society, we need to leave space to allow for people to make different decisions

[62] Auckland and Goold (n 8).

about important things. The care of a child is one of these. Some might value more time with their child. Some might think that there are vital features of a good life that others do not value, and these might be intellectual, physical or emotional. A best interests approach does a poor job of cutting through these issues precisely because once we tolerate difference, we have to tolerate the view that there can be more than one 'best' for a person, dependent on what is considered valuable. Where that person cannot speak for themselves, as the children in these cases cannot, then best interests will not help in many cases to yield an answer. A harm threshold, by contrast, does a better (if still imperfect) job by leaving it first to parents to make these decisions of value within the context of their own family, their own values and their knowledge of their child. But it also retains a protective fallback in the form of limiting parental discretion at the point where harm arises. Harm of the vulnerable is the point at which others should step in to protect them; it is the point at which the value determination demands further voices to explore what should be done for the child. We can debate the nature of harm, and we might import notions of dignity and the like into it, but it at least offers a clearer, more effective point at which to override parents.

6. Conclusion

The debate over when the courts can intervene in the decisions made in relation to a child is by its nature highly emotive. Parents in such situations will almost invariably be distressed and fighting for their children. Hospital staff will also be fighting to save this child, but also fighting to do their best to ensure that child is not in needless distress. Courts must step into the middle when relations break down, and when they do so they step into a sphere of life that is otherwise private. We must, therefore, be very careful to ensure the line is clear and appropriate. The debate around where that line should lie is naturally complex, as the chapters in this volume demonstrate. But, on balance, the stronger case lies for the harm threshold.

3

Parental Decisions and Court Jurisdiction: Best Interests or Significant Harm?

RACHEL TAYLOR

1. 'Question of Principle of the Utmost Importance'

At its heart, *Gard* raises an acute dilemma as to the nature of parental authority and the relationship between parental responsibility and the supervisory jurisdiction of the courts. In the Supreme Court, his parents presented the case as raising a 'question of principle of the utmost importance', as yet 'not answered in English law', namely the

> extent to which the state – [including] the court – may legitimately intrude into private and family life in the context of parental decisions … that, but for the court's intervention, parents would be able to make and would be completely free to make in respect of their child.[1]

In order to characterise the problem in this way, the parents' case drew a sharp distinction between two questions raised by the hospital's application.[2] The first question concerned the lawfulness of the proposal by Great Ormond Street (GOSH) to cease providing treatment to Charlie, aside from palliative care. The second concerned the parents' decision to seek alternative treatment and specifically to pursue nucleoside therapy in the United States. The parents accepted that the first question was properly before the court as GOSH was entitled to seek the approval and guidance of the court in discharging its own duties to Charlie.

[1] Richard Gordon QC, leave to appeal hearing Supreme Court, 8 June 2017. Author's transcript of oral submissions, the hearing may be viewed at www.supremecourt.uk/news/permission-to-appeal-hearing-in-the-matter-of-charlie-gard.html.

[2] *Great Ormond Street Hospital for Children NHS Foundation Trust v Yates* [2017] EWCA Civ 410, [2018] 4 WLR 5, [84] (*Yates*).

Nonetheless, the parents argued, this did not give the court jurisdiction to consider the *parents'* decision to seek alternative medical treatment with another medical team. In respect of this question, they argued, GOSH owed no legal duty to Charlie, instead the question was one for his parents under their parental responsibility to Charlie. As Charlie's parents were agreed on the decision to pursue nucleoside therapy, and as their decision would have been lawful, were it not for the courts' intervention, they argued that the court had no jurisdiction to consider the second question unless it would cause Charlie significant harm. For the parents this was an important question of principle because if the court could obtain jurisdiction

> simply by a party approaching the court and raising questions as to what is in the best interests of a child that would erode the whole concept of parental responsibility in fact it would shift the responsibility from parents to the state.[3]

As such, the parents' case raised a fundamental point of principle as to the nature of responsibility for children. From the parents' perspective, if the court's jurisdiction could be invoked without firm and clear limits, parental responsibility would essentially be held on gift from the state, a gift that could be revoked at any point. This would be a decisive shift from recognising parents as having primary responsibility for their children.

This chapter will not consider the detail of the decision in *Gard* itself. Instead it will consider the question raised by the parents in the context of the wider law on parental responsibility and decision-making beyond the medical context. Specifically, the chapter will consider when the courts may legitimately intrude into the, otherwise lawful, decisions of parents and those with parental responsibility. For the purposes of this chapter, the parents' characterisation of their decision to pursue nucleoside therapy as entirely separable from GOSH's duties to Charlie will be accepted.[4] It will be argued that, even on this understanding, the courts were correct as a matter of law to determine Charlie's future on the basis of his best interests and to reject the parents' proposition that courts may only intervene in the mutual decisions of parents in cases of significant harm.[5] Nonetheless, the parents' argument exposes underlying tensions between the roles of parents and the state in the law on decision-making for children.

[3] Richard Gordon QC, (n 1).

[4] Charlie's condition was of such severity that it is doubtful whether this stark distinction between GOSH's responsibility and that of the parents could be sustained. For the parents to implement their decision would require the intimate involvement of GOSH in facilitating Charlie's transfer and sustaining his life until the transfer could take place. In reality, the proposed alternative raised a complex intertwining of the responsibilities of GOSH and the parents. The distinction is accepted for the purposes of this chapter because of the importance of the question raised by the parents and because in other cases parents may be in a position to put their proposed plans into practice without active involvement from others with duty to the child.

[5] The Court of Appeal in *Gard* considered that the parents' proposed treatment may reach the significant harm threshold, there was, however, no formal finding on this point.

2. The Nature and Limits of Parental Responsibility

To consider the parents' argument further it is first necessary to define the rights and responsibilities of parents. In both domestic and international law parental rights are subsumed into the broader concept of parental responsibility.[6] There is, however, ambiguity as to the nature and limits of parental responsibility. As John Eekelaar has observed, parental responsibility 'can represent two ideas: one, that parents must behave dutifully towards their children; the other, that responsibility for child care belongs to parents, not the state'.[7] Both of these meanings can be found in the Children Act 1989 and in the UN Convention on the Rights of the Child (CRC).[8] Each of these propositions is important and the fault-line between them is at the heart of many of the most difficult questions of child law, including that in *Gard*. The tension is particularly acute where the parents' sincere view as to what is best for their child conflicts with that held by the majority in society or by professionals involved with the child. Charlie's parents sought to resolve this tension by arguing that the mere fact that the court disagreed with the parents' view was insufficient to permit the court to overrule them, instead the court could only intervene if the parents' decision would cause significant harm. To evaluate this argument, we must first consider the two meanings of parental responsibility in more detail.

The first important principle of parental responsibility is that the parental role is one of responsibility to children rather than proprietary rights over them. This understanding of the parental role was reflected in the 20th-century legislation and case-law that firmly established the primacy of the welfare of the child in judicial decisions concerning their upbringing.[9] This fundamental principle is also recognised as a right and guiding principle of international children's rights law in the CRC.[10] Although the Children Act 1989 states that courts must apply the welfare principle when making decisions concerning children's upbringing, its application to parents is less clear; there is no domestic equivalent to Article 18 CRC, directing *parents* to consider the child's best interests in decision-making. Nonetheless, the drafting of the Children Act 1989[11] was intended to reflect the approach to parental authority found in the seminal decision of the House of Lords in *Gillick v West Norfolk and Wisbech Area Health Authority*.[12] In *Gillick*, the House of Lords considered that parental authority was derived from duties towards children and

[6] *Children Act 1989* s3(1).

[7] J Eekelaar, 'Parental Responsibility: State of Nature or Nature of the State?' (1991) 13 *Journal of Social Welfare and Family Law* 37.

[8] *Convention on the Rights of the Child* Article 18(1): 'Parents … have the primary responsibility for the upbringing and development of the child. The best interests of the child will be their basic concern'.

[9] See, eg: *J v. C* [1970] AC 668. The modern law is found in *Children Act 1989* s1(1).

[10] *Convention on the Rights of the Child* Article 3.

[11] Law Commission, *Review of Child Law, Guardianship and Custody* (Law Com No 172, 1988), [2.4].

[12] *Gillick v. West Norfolk and Wisbech Area Health Authority* [1986] AC 112 (*Gillick*).

that those duties defined the scope of that authority. In this way, the interests of children provided both the normative justification for parental authority and the limits on its acceptable use. This point was expressed by Lord Fraser:

> [P]arental rights to control a child do not exist for the benefit of the parent. They exist for the benefit of the child and they are justified only in so far as they enable the parent to perform his duties towards the child, and towards other children in the family.[13]

Lord Scarman emphasised the role of welfare in providing the limits of that parental authority:

> [W]hen a court has before it a question as to the care and upbringing of a child it must treat the welfare of the child as the paramount consideration in determining the order to be made. There is here a principle which limits and governs the exercise of parental rights of custody, care and control. It is a principle perfectly consistent with the law's recognition of the parent as the natural guardian of the child: but it is also a warning that parental right must be exercised in accordance with the welfare principle and can be challenged, even overridden, if it be not.[14]

The implication of this approach is that a parent who exercises parental decision-making in a manner that does not further the interests of the child is acting outside of the proper scope of their authority and is vulnerable to court intervention to restrain that excess. This is an important principle and vital to establishing the child as a person with their own rights and interests recognised and protected in law.

The second important principle of parental responsibility is that responsibility for children's upbringing lies primarily with parents rather than with the state. Reasonable people will frequently disagree on what is best for children; the fact that parents are obliged to exercise their authority in line with children's best interests does not often yield a single right answer to a particular decision. Instead, parents are generally granted a broad discretion to exercise their responsibilities as they see fit, for example in naming, educating, feeding and disciplining their children. There are many good reasons for giving parents this zone of discretion. Children have an interest in being able to trust that important decisions about their lives will be made by those adults who have an intimate and caring relationship with them and who are able to respond to them as an individual.[15] If parents are to make decisions that respond to their child's individual needs and interests, they will need sufficient discretion and choice to be able to do so. More pragmatically, care for children places heavy demands on the time and resources of most parents. The reality for many parents is that they may have to compromise in some of the decisions that they make for their children in order to meet the competing interests of other family members and to balance demands on their resources.

[13] ibid, 170; see also: ibid, 184 (Scarman LJ); ibid, 200 (Wilberforce LJ).

[14] ibid, 184.

[15] Failure to involve a parent in important decisions may sometimes amount to a breach of the child's rights: *Glass v UK* [2004] 1 FLR 1019.

Parents often need flexibility in order to meet all of these responsibilities in practice. There are also important considerations of freedom and diversity: in a free society, the state should be cautious in imposing a particular view as to what is best for children without good reason and clear evidence to support that view.[16] This point was recognized by Baroness Hale in her well-known explanation of the law in *Williamson*:

> Children have the right to be properly cared for and brought up so that they can fulfil their potential and play their part in society. Their parents have both the primary responsibility and the primary right to do this. The state steps in to regulate the exercise of that responsibility in the interests of children and society as a whole. But 'the child is not the child of the state' and it is important in a free society that parents should be allowed a large measure of autonomy in the way in which they discharge their parental responsibilities.[17]

The challenge for the law is how to accommodate these two important aspects of parental responsibility: recognising the primary role of parents whilst also requiring that they protect the interests of their children. As Baroness Hale observes, although parents have the primary role, the state also has a legitimate role in regulating parental decisions in the interests of children and society. The CRC similarly recognises that responsibility for children is collective: the primary role of parents is not an exclusive role, instead children and parents require the support of the state and wider community. This means that the state has important obligations to assist parents and provide the conditions for children to thrive.[18] Further, whereas the CRC requires states to respect 'the rights, responsibilities and duties of parents',[19] the parental role is to be exercised 'in a manner consistent with the evolving capacities of the child' and by guiding the child in the exercise of their rights. In this way, both domestic and international law recognise the importance of the primary parental role, but also the legitimacy of state intervention to protect children. As a result, the broad zone of parental discretion is circumscribed by legal obligations and restrictions such as the duty to ensure that the child receives a suitable education. A further important limit is found in the 'significant harm' test that must be passed before the court can make a compulsory child protection order through which the state can obtain control of the child's upbringing.[20] The test means that some children will be left with parents who are not acting in their best interests, indeed with parents who are causing them harm, provided that that

[16] See also: I Goold, 'Evaluating Best Interests as a Threshold for Judicial Intervention' in I Goold, J Herring and C Auckland (eds), *Parental Rights, Best Interests and Significant Harms: Medical Decision-Making on Behalf of Children Post-Great Ormond Street Hospital v Gard* (Oxford, Hart, Forthcoming).

[17] *R (on the application of Williamson and others) v. Secretary of State for Education and Employment and others* [2005] UKHL 15; [2005] 2 All ER 1, [72]; further discussed below.

[18] See, eg: *Convention on the Rights of the Child* Article 27, the obligation to assist parents in providing the conditions of living necessary for the child's development.

[19] *Convention on the Rights of the Child* Article 5.

[20] *Children Act 1989* s31, the welfare principle also applies. A similar test in s100(4) applies to an application by a local authority to invoke the court's inherent jurisdiction.

harm is not 'significant'. Mr Justice Hedley's oft-quoted observations in *Re L* make this clear:

> [S]ociety must be willing to tolerate very diverse standards of parenting, including the eccentric, the barely adequate and the inconsistent. It follows too that children will inevitably have both very different experiences of parenting and very unequal consequences flowing from it. It means that some children will experience disadvantage and harm, while others flourish in atmospheres of loving security and emotional stability. These are the consequences of our fallible humanity and it is not the provenance of the state to spare children all the consequences of defective parenting. In any event, it simply could not be done.[21]

This dictum was relied upon by Charlie's parents in the Court of Appeal as a statement of principle in support of the proposition that it is the significant harm test, rather than welfare, that provides the legitimate point at which the state may intervene in the mutual decisions of parents.[22] To assess this argument it is first necessary to consider the role of welfare in judicial control of parental decision-making.

3. Welfare and Parental Disputes

Education provides a good example of this broad but limited parental discretion. Parents are obliged to provide their children with a suitable, efficient and full-time education[23] but have considerable freedom in how they do so. This means that parents, at least to the extent that they have the resources and opportunity to do so, can choose the form of education that best suits their child and family, whether that is religious or secular, single-sex or mixed, selective or comprehensive, at school or at home. If parents disagree on how to discharge their mutual duties and take the dispute to court, the court will decide on the basis of its own assessment of the child's welfare.[24] In so doing, the court will usually be choosing from a range of reasonable and lawful options that the parents may otherwise have chosen, and may well impose a solution with which at least one of the parents profoundly disagrees.

A good example of such a parental dispute can be seen in *Re G (Children)*,[25] which concerned the future education of five children, boys and girls between the ages of 3 and 11, whose parents had separated following their mother's decision to leave the ultra-orthodox Jewish Chareidi community in which they had all been brought up. The mother wished to enrol the children in coeducational Modern Orthodox schools to give them the educational opportunities and future career

[21] *Re: L (Care: Threshold Criteria)* [2007] 1 F.L.R. 2050, [50].
[22] *Yates* (n 2), [65].
[23] *Education Act 1996* s7.
[24] *Children Act* 1989 s1(1).
[25] *Re G (Children)* [2012] EWCA Civ 1233; [2012] 3 FCR 524.

prospects that were not available in their current Chareidi schools. The father wished to continue their current education in order to maintain the children's relationships with family and peers and equip them for life within the religious community. The options put forward by each parent were intimately connected to their respective religious beliefs and conceptions of the purposes of education. The court was clear that its role was not to determine which parent was correct but to assess the child's welfare from the standpoint of the 'generally accepted standards' of the 'reasonable' parent in modern society. As this 'reasonable parent' would value equality of opportunity, aspiration and bringing the child to the cusp of adulthood with the maximum opportunity to pursue their own vision of the good life, the court found in favour of the mother's proposed schools. In doing so it was careful to emphasise that the only reason that the state was involved in the decision was because the parents had brought their disagreement to the court.[26] There was no suggestion that the education favoured by the father would cause the children 'significant harm' that would warrant state intervention through care proceedings: parents who jointly decide to educate their children in Chareidi schools are free to do so.

As *Re G* makes clear, the welfare principle does not provide a purely objective test; instead it frequently depends on the values and assumptions by which it is assessed. Given that fact, the imposition of the court's values and assumptions requires justification. If the court's jurisdiction is invoked in a dispute between parents, each of whom has a duty to act to further the welfare of the child, the normative basis for the court's intervention is readily found in the parental decision to bring the dispute before the court. The court can only resolve that dispute by giving an authoritative determination of the child's welfare, the basis on which the parents are each obliged to carry out their responsibilities to their children. Similarly, parents who are not in dispute might seek the court's determination of the best course of action for the child when faced with a difficult decision that they feel unable to take for themselves.[27] The same normative basis can be found in relation to disputes between parents and those non-parents, such as healthcare professionals, who also owe duties to act in the child's best interests[28] and may seek the guidance of the court if they cannot agree on how those duties should be discharged.

The court's intervention is more difficult to justify if there is no dispute between duty-holders but instead a third party seeks to intervene in their decision.

[26] ibid, [90]–[94].

[27] See, eg: the case reported in 'Judge Rules to Allow Severely Ill 11 Month Old to 'Die Peacefully'' (*the Guardian*, 13th Dec 2018) in which it appears that the parents did not object to the proposed withdrawal of treatment but did not wish to take the decision that would lead to their daughter's death themselves. The case does not yet appear to have been reported. I am grateful to Jonathan Herring for drawing this to my attention.

[28] This was the basis on which the court was entitled to resolve the dispute between GOSH and Charlie's parents as to how GOSH should discharge *its* duties to Charlie i.e. the first question identified above.

Take, for example, a person who is sincerely concerned that neighbouring children are being educated in a school that teaches a narrow religious curriculum such as that favoured by the father in *Re G*. Should the court permit the concerned neighbour to argue that the children's welfare would be better served by an alternative school that encouraged aspiration, equality of opportunity and secular achievement despite the fact that the children's parents were united and otherwise acting within the law? One might argue that parents who exercise their responsibility in a manner that is inconsistent with the vision of welfare favoured by the court are failing in their duty and that this would justify court intervention to maximise the interests of the child. There are, however, strong reasons to reject such an approach. To hold parents who are acting jointly and lawfully to the 'generally accepted standards' of 'reasonable parents' would amount to an oppressive imposition of majority values, rendering the decisions of all parents who did not subscribe to those values suspect and justifying draconian intervention in the freedoms of minority groups. If such intervention is warranted, it is better imposed through the general law where it will be subject to democratic scrutiny and will apply to all children, rather through ad hoc intervention. To hold parents to those standards through third-party litigation would make a mockery of the educational choices granted to parents in existing legislation. Such an approach would also undermine the second understanding of parental responsibility: the primacy of the parental role. Finally, it is quite clear that the law does not regard the courts as the sole arbiters of welfare or even as the best forum for determining children's interests. Reform of family law has long been directed at removing disputes from the judicial arena and instead encouraging parents to make their own agreements without recourse to the courts. This is also evident from the judicial approach to applications for consent orders embodying agreements between parents. In such cases the court is obliged to apply the welfare principle but will do so by checking that the agreement falls within the broad range of reasonable understandings of the child's welfare, rather than by conducting a full judicial assessment.[29] There are a range of strong reasons for shielding lawful and mutual parental decisions from judicial intervention on the basis of welfare.

The example of the busybody neighbour may seem fanciful; it might be hoped that there are few individuals with the resources and inclination to seek to intervene in the lives of others in such a manner. Nonetheless, the argument made on behalf of the parents in *Gard* effectively cast GOSH in a similar guise. On their analysis of the case, GOSH had no legitimate role in the decision to seek alternative treatment with a different medical team and was merely a third party seeking to intervene in the mutual and lawful decision of the parents. The question that Charlie's parents raised was therefore an important one. Few parents can be confident that all of their decisions would survive unscathed if subject to a forensic analysis against a judicially determined welfare standard. Parents routinely make decisions

[29] *AI v MT* [2013] EWHC 100 (Fam), [27]–[32] provides an interesting example of this approach.

that do not maximise their child's interests but are 'good enough' in the context of the needs, resources and wishes of all members of the family. In reality, much of parenting occurs within the gap between causing significant harm and maximising welfare. The 'question of principle' raised by Charlie's parents effectively asked how the law applied to parents within this gap: can parents be confident that they are immune from judicial intervention if they are acting jointly, within the law and without risking significant harm?[30]

4. Parenting 'In the Gap': Jurisdiction and the Children Act

Charlie's parents sought to find the answer to their question of principle by imposing firm limits on the jurisdiction of the court to reflect words of Baker J in *Re King*:

> [I]t is a fundamental principle of family law in this jurisdiction that responsibility for making decisions about a child rest [*sic*] with his parents. In most cases, the parents are the best people to make decisions about a child and the state – whether it be the court, or any other public authority – has no business interfering with the exercise of parental responsibility unless the child is suffering or is likely to suffer significant harm as a result of the care given to the child not being what it would be reasonable to expect a parent to give.[31]

This dictum captures the general principle of the primacy of the parental role and describes the ordinary experience of most parents. It is, however, not intended as a complete statement of the law and it would be a fallacy to treat it as such. Although the law generally operates to inhibit unwarranted intervention in family life, the court retains a protective jurisdiction that is not dependent on significant harm or parental disagreement. This is evident from considering the circumstances in which the Children Act 1989 permits judicial intervention in the exercise of parental responsibility.

The Children Act 1989 provides the framework by which parental responsibility is allocated and the primary means by which a court can supervise its exercise. The most serious form of intervention is through its compulsory child protection provisions, the gateway to which is found in the significant harm test described above.[32] Outside of these provisions, judicial intervention is primarily through section 8, which gives the court the power to make orders concerning the child's living and contact arrangements and to control the exercise of parental responsibility through specific issue and prohibited steps orders.[33] The welfare principle

[30] See generally: Goold (n 16).

[31] *Re Ashya King* [2014] EWHC 2964 (fam); [2014] 2 FLR 855.

[32] *Children Act 1989* s31.

[33] Discussed in more detail in R George, 'The Legal Basis of the Court's Jurisdiction to Authorise Medical Treatment of Children' in Goold et al (eds) (n 16).

provides the test by which a court is to decide any case brought under section 8. The Act imposes rules on who can apply for an order to limit the excessive intervention in family life that might be wielded through specific issue and prohibited steps orders.[34] These rules draw a clear distinction between parents and others with parental responsibility, who are entitled to apply for an order, and those without parental responsibility, who must obtain the leave of the court before they do so.[35] This sharp distinction can be seen as reflecting the justification considered above: those with legal responsibility to act in the child's welfare are entitled to bring disputes to the court to determine how that duty should be discharged; those who do not must show good cause before they may question the decisions of parents. The leave requirement is not, however, intended to pose a substantial hurdle to those who raise genuine concerns. An applicant for leave need not demonstrate that there is any likelihood of harm to the child or that the application will further the child's welfare. Instead the court has a discretion to grant leave having considered a number of factors, including the applicant's connection to the child and whether the application is likely to cause harmful disruption to the child's life.[36] Applications for leave are not restricted to individuals, they may also be made by institutions, including state authorities such local authorities[37] and NHS Trusts. Indeed, in *Gard* GOSH obtained leave to apply for a specific issue order in addition to its application under the inherent jurisdiction.[38] The threshold for third parties to challenge the decisions of parents is therefore not significant harm but the far lower threshold of leave, even if that party is a public authority.

Courts also have the jurisdiction to make section 8 orders to further the welfare of the child in any family proceedings, regardless of whether an application to do so has been made.[39] For example, in a recent dispute between a known sperm donor and the child's parents, the judge considered that the child would benefit from contact with the donor's parents and ordered that such contact take place, despite the fact that they had not sought that order and the child's parents opposed their involvement. The Court of Appeal rejected the parents' argument that this undermined the system of leave and refused to restrict the court's power to further the child's welfare through section 8 orders.[40] The power for the court to make orders of its own volition is an important aspect of the court's protective

[34] HL Deb on the Children Bill 6 December 1988, *Hansard*, col 491, (MacKay LC).

[35] *Children Act 1989* s10(2) and (4).

[36] *Children Act 1989* s10(9).

[37] There are additional restrictions on local authority applications to prevent applications that circumvent the child protection process: *Children Act 1989* s9(5)(b).

[38] In *JM (A Child)* [2015] EWHC 2832 (Fam) (*JM*); [2016] 2 FLR 235 (Mostyn J), reaffirmed that specific issue orders provided the appropriate route for the resolution of disputes between parents and healthcare professions over children's medical treatment. For procedural reasons, the court recommended that serious cases, especially those involving deprivation of liberty, should be pursued through both the inherent jurisdiction and section 8, see esp. paras 25–28. This was the route followed by GOSH in making their application in *Gard*.

[39] *Children Act 1989* s10(1)(b).

[40] *Re G (A Child)* [2018] EWCA Civ 305, [21].

jurisdiction concerning children. This power would have permitted the court in *Gard* to restrict the parents' decision to pursue alternative treatment, regardless of whether that issue had been raised by GOSH.

There is nothing in the Children Act 1989 to suggest that the jurisdiction of the court is limited in the manner proposed on behalf of Charlie Gard's parents. Instead the Act facilitates the court's use of its protective jurisdiction in order to protect the welfare of the child. The significant harm test is not the boundary that demarcates legitimate court intervention into mutual parental decisions; instead it is the boundary that must be crossed to allow ongoing state involvement in the life of the child, and particularly to allow local authorities to obtain ongoing discretionary authority over the child's life through a care order. This may, however, appear a rather fine distinction to parents seeking to resist state intervention in the treatment of their terminally ill child. As Mostyn J noted in *JM (A Child)*,[41] section 8 was primarily drafted to address parental disputes rather than cases in which the state sought to impose medical treatment against the wishes of the child's parents. Nonetheless, the balance between the two aspects of parental responsibility comes not through restrictions on the jurisdiction of the court but through judicial restraint and sensitivity to the important role of parents in securing their children's welfare. This self-restraint takes on even greater importance in cases involving the court's inherent jurisdiction.

5. The Inherent Jurisdiction

The application in *Gard* was primarily brought under the inherent jurisdiction. The powers of the court under the inherent jurisdiction are far broader than those contained in the Children Act, extending beyond control of parental responsibility and granting the court powers that are not available to parents. The breadth of the inherent jurisdiction derives from its origins, as Lord Donaldson MR explained in *Re R*: 'This jurisdiction is not derivative from the parents' rights and responsibilities but derives from, or is, the delegated performance of the duties of the Crown to protect its subjects and particularly children who are the generations of the future.'[42]

The jurisdiction is often described as 'theoretically limitless'[43] and in the memorable words of a seminal article on the subject as 'so amorphous and ubiquitous and so pervasive in its operation that it seems to defy challenge to determine its quality and establish its limits'.[44] These characteristics mean that

[41] *JM* (n 38), [25]. This case is discussed further by George (n 33).

[42] *Re R (A Minor) (Wardship: Consent to Treatment)* [1992] Fam 11, 25. As this dicta makes clear, the inherent jurisdiction is not limited to the protection of children and also extends to adults who require its protection.

[43] ibid.

[44] IH Jacob, 'The Inherent Jurisdiction of the Court' (1970) 23 *Current Legal Problems* 23.

the inherent jurisdiction provides an extraordinarily useful means of dealing with difficult and new problems for which there is no adequate existing legislative solution and through which the court can intervene to protect children in ways that would not otherwise be possible. The jurisdiction has, for example, been used to protect children from being taken abroad to join terrorist groups[45] and from sexual exploitation.[46] Broad as the inherent jurisdiction is, it is not a 'lawless void'[47] permitting complete free rein in the name of improving child welfare. One important limitation on the jurisdiction is that it is residual, in that it may not be invoked in circumstances where there is already a statutory route to achieve the protection in question.[48] Further, the ability of local authorities to invoke the jurisdiction is specifically limited by statute to prevent it from being used to circumvent the Children Act 1989 procedure.[49] Local authorities may only apply under the inherent jurisdiction if they obtain leave, which they may only do if they are able to show that there are reasonable grounds to believe that the child is likely to suffer significant harm if the jurisdiction is not exercised.[50] Although at first sight this might appear to support the parents in *Gard* in their argument that the significant harm test provides the boundary of court intervention in parental decisions, other applicants are not so constrained and may apply if they have a 'genuine interest in the child' with no need to obtain leave or demonstrate risk of harm. This allows the court to consider applications from a broad range of people who need not have any relationship or legal duty to the child. For example, in *Re D (A Minor) (Wardship: Sterilisation)*[51] an educational psychologist successfully challenged the decision of a mother and her doctors to sterilise an 11-year-old child with significant learning disabilities. The case is a good example of the court intervening in the medical decisions of parents at the behest of third parties in order to promote the welfare of the child, without the need to first overcome the significant harm test that formed the basis of the parents' argument in *Gard*.

The inherent jurisdiction remains a breathtakingly broad route to extensive intervention and control of children's lives on the basis of the court's interpretation of best interests. Parents who find their decisions challenged under the jurisdiction might be forgiven for thinking that the law does indeed regard the child as the child of the state, despite Baroness Hale's assurances to the contrary. The courts are aware of the need for restraint in deploying these powers. The question of when those powers might be used to prevent parents from seeking

[45] *Re M (Children) (Wardship: (Jurisdiction and Powers)* [2015] EWHC 1433 (Fam), [2016] 1 FLR 1055.

[46] *Redbridge London Borough Council v A* [2015] EWHC 2140 (Fam), [2015] 3 WLR 1617.

[47] ibid, [36].

[48] Practice direction 12D 1.1. The limitations on the use of the inherent jurisdiction are discussed in more detail by George (n 33).

[49] *Children Act 1989* s100(2).

[50] *Children Act 1989* s100(3) and (4).

[51] *Re D (A Minor) (Wardship: Sterilisation)* [1976] Fam 185.

experimental treatment for their child is an important one and one that appears to becoming more common as parents are able to seek out treatments and make connections abroad via the Internet.[52] The argument that the court should only permit intervention in such cases if significant harm is shown is, however, clearly unsupported by current law. The inherent jurisdiction is a protective jurisdiction that is routinely and invariably deployed on the basis of the 'best interests' test. As each of the courts in *Gard* agreed, there was simply no authority for the argument that a significant harm test should apply. To the extent that the court had the freedom to choose to introduce further self-restraint in the cases that it would receive under the jurisdiction, there was little to commend the use of significant harm as the means of doing so. The legislative choice to use significant harm as a threshold for local authority applications but not for other parties would seem to be clear indication that Parliament did not intended to impose that limit on the jurisdiction. Further, such a test would be inconsistent with the approach of the Children Act 1989 which, as we have seen, reserves significant harm for the threshold at which local authorities might acquire ongoing discretionary authority over the life of the child. Given that cases routinely combine applications under the Children Act and the inherent jurisdiction,[53] it would be undesirable to apply substantially different tests in those applications, particularly as limitations placed on the use of the inherent jurisdiction could usually be circumvented through the application under the Children Act.[54]

A further reason for rejecting the significant harm test is that it would be unnecessarily cruel and combative to require loving and sincere parents to defend themselves against a test based on harm unless required to do so. Court proceedings over a child's medical treatment almost inevitably indicate that the relationship between the parents and healthcare professionals has already seriously broken down. The significant harm test is unlikely to be conducive to salvaging that vital relationship, particularly as the test also provides the gateway to coercive action by the state through child protection proceedings and so raises the spectre of the parents being further excluded from their child's care. Any legal process should aim, so far as it is possible to do so, to recognise the importance of partnership between parents and others caring for the child in striving to find the best outcome for the child.[55]

[52] A development considered in more detail in: S Fovargue, 'Preserving the Therapeutic Alliance: Court Intervention and Experimental Treatment Requests' in Goold et al (eds) (n 16).

[53] As discussed in more detail in: George (n 33).

[54] The cases in which the Children Act is not available are primarily concerned with children who are already subject to a care order. Children Act 1989 s9(1) prevents the court from making a specific issue order in such cases. It is difficult to see why applications to treat these children should be subject to an additional test of significant harm when compared to children in a similar position who are not under a care order.

[55] For further consideration of establishing this partnership in practice, see: E Harrop, 'Setting the Scene – Supporting and Informing Shared Decision Making at the Bedside: Avoiding and De-escalating Conflict between Clinicians and Families' in Goold et al (eds) (n 16).

6. Children's Welfare and Valuing Parents

The discussion so far has demonstrated that the jurisdiction of the court to intervene in mutual parental decisions is not limited to cases of significant harm. Instead, the court retains a broad protective jurisdiction over children's welfare both in statute and the inherent jurisdiction. For third parties, other than local authorities seeking ongoing involvement in the child's life, there are minimal procedural barriers to invoking that jurisdiction, meaning that a sincere applicant who raises a genuine concern is likely to be heard by the court. This conclusion may be alarming to parents, who might object that to allow the court's jurisdiction to be invoked at the behest of a third party undermines their role and, as was argued in *Gard*, shifts responsibility for children from parents to the state. This argument is particularly important given the malleability of the meaning of welfare discussed above. The current law appears to allow the court to impose the values of the 'reasonable person' to restrict the lawful decisions of parents, simply because a stranger to the decision has raised a question that the court is willing to consider. This would permit draconian interference in parental discretion, particularly if the court's jurisdiction were invoked by an institution of the state, such as an NHS Trust, with far greater access to resources than the parents. These are genuine concerns but the answer to them is found not in the limits of the courts' jurisdiction, but in the courts' respect for the importance of parental decisions.

The role of the courts might be more easily justified if a clearer distinction were drawn between those cases in which there is a dispute between duty-holders, such as parents, and those in which a third party seeks to intervene. The duty to act in the child's best interests provides both the legal justification for parental authority and the limits on its acceptable use. The same reasoning also applies to other duty-holders such as health professionals. Although there may be a spectrum of reasonable and lawful interpretations of the child's welfare in any one case, in a case brought by duty-holders, the court must give an authoritative assessment of the impact of the decision on the child's welfare in order to give the parties clarity on the basis on which they should discharge their responsibilities to the child. In cases of third-party intervention in parental decisions the justification for the court's intervention is different. The court has a residual role and may intervene to prevent parents from acting outside of the proper scope of their authority. But parents have the primary responsibility for their children and a wide discretion in discharging that responsibility. Provided that parents are acting within the broad spectrum of reasonable and lawful approaches to their child's welfare, the court has no need to intervene merely because it, or a third party, would prefer a different interpretation.

This distinction is not clearly articulated in the case-law, perhaps because there are relatively few cases in which the mutual decisions of parents are challenged. It does, however, provide a good explanation for the way in which the courts approach welfare in those cases that do come before them. The case of Ashya King,[56] relied upon by the parents in *Gard*, is one such example. In that case the parents wished to pursue a relatively new form of proton therapy to treat their son's brain tumour and had raised funds to do so, the treating medical team had advised the use of conventional radiotherapy but by the time the case came to court did not oppose the parents' plan. Despite the fact that there was no active dispute, the court was involved because Ashya had been made a ward of court in the midst of previous uncertainty as to his whereabouts and safety. As a result, court approval was required for Ashya to travel for treatment in Prague and that approval could only be given on the basis of Ashya's welfare. Rather than considering the evidence and making an entirely independent analysis of that welfare as would be the case in resolving a dispute, Baker J found that 'there was no reason to stand in the way of the parents' proposal'.[57] Contrasting the case with those where parents sought a 'wholly unreasonable course of treatment', Baker J justified his approach on the basis that: 'Both courses are reasonable and it is the parents who bear the heavy responsibility of making the decision. It is no business of this court, or any other public authority, to interfere with their decision.'[58]

In this way, the court's own obligation to act in Ashya's best interests was discharged by recognising the parents' primary responsibility and respecting their reasonable decision on his welfare. A similar approach can be seen in *BC v EF*.[59] This case had started as a parental dispute over vaccination, and the court had found that it would be in the children's best interests to be vaccinated as the father wished. Unusually, after the conclusion of the case the father changed his mind and the parents sought to vary the order whereas the children's guardian sought to have it enforced. Despite the finding that vaccination was in the children's best interests, the court declined to enforce the order, deciding that it was now a matter for the parents' joint responsibility. These cases illustrate the reluctance of the court to intervene in the joint decisions of parents as to the welfare of their child. Although the test for the court remains the welfare principle, rather than the reasonableness of the parents,[60] the court will decline to intervene if the parents are jointly committed to a reasonable understanding of the child's welfare.

Respect for the importance of the parental role can also be seen in cases in which there is a conflict between parents and third-party duty-holders. This is well illustrated by the developing case-law on local authority decision-making for children in care. A care order grants parental responsibility to the local authority

[56] *Re King* [2014] EWHC 2964 (Fam); [2014] 2 FLR 855.
[57] ibid, [34].
[58] ibid.
[59] *BC v EF (Parental Responsibility: Immunisation)* [2017] EWFC 49. With thanks to Jonathan Herring for drawing this case to my attention.
[60] *Re T (A Minor)* [1997] 1 WLR 242.

that obtains it[61] and although parents retain their parental responsibility, the local authority is granted the power to determine the way in which the parents may exercise that responsibility.[62] This appears to give clear statutory authority to the local authority to impose its will over that of parents on almost all decisions, provided that it is acting to promote the child's welfare. Nonetheless, the courts have stressed that for important decisions all of those with parental responsibility should be able to contribute to the decision and that disagreements should be referred to the court, rather than by relying on the controlling position granted to local authorities in the Children Act. Hence, for example, in *Re C (Children) (Child in Care: Choice of Forename)*[63] a local authority wished to prevent a mother from naming her twin children Cyanide and Preacher. The local authority had an interim care order which gave them ostensible power to prevent her from doing so, but the fundamental importance of naming children meant that the approval of the court had to be sought, particularly as to overrule the mother without judicial oversight would engage her rights under Article 8 of the European Convention on Human Rights (ECHR). Similarly, local authorities have been required to obtain judicial approval in disagreements with parents over vaccination[64] and medical treatment of children in care.[65] These illustrate two important points. First, the court encourages collaboration in protecting the welfare of the child rather than merely relying on the technical hierarchy of decision-making authority on the face of the statute.[66] Second, the parental role is considered to be of great importance, even in cases where there has been a risk of significant harm, both because the parent is often best placed to know the child and because the parent–child relationship is protected through Article 8 ECHR.[67]

The importance of parents' responsibility for their children is recognised in law not by hard barriers to prevent judicial intervention but by careful respect for the relationship between parents and children in determining children's welfare. It is in this way that the tension between the two meanings of parental responsibility, identified at the start of this chapter, is best reconciled by the courts.

[61] *Children Act 1989* s33(3)(a). This responsibility is subject to a small number of statutory restrictions primarily concerned with safeguarding the fundamental elements of the child's identity and connection to family: *Children Act 1989* s33(6)–(8).

[62] *Children Act 1989* s33(3)(b), s33(4) imposes the condition that this control may only be imposed to the extent necessary to safeguard or promote the child's welfare.

[63] *Re C (Children)* [2016] EWCA Civ 374; [2016] 3 WLR 1557.

[64] *London Borough of Barnet v SL* [2017] EWHC 125 (Fam), [49].

[65] Re *Jake (A Child)* [2015] EWHC 2442 (Fam); [2016] 2 FCR 118. see also: *Re AB* [2018] EWFC 3 in which the application for a care order was withdrawn with the approval of the court, which made it clear that it would usually be inappropriate and ineffective for a local authority to apply for a care order for the purpose of consenting to medical treatment against the wishes of parents esp. at para. 24.

[66] A similar point may be made in relation to disputes between parents on medical treatment. Despite the fact that the consent of one parent appears to be sufficient in statute, disputes in serious cases may require court authorisation rather than relying on technical parental responsibility: *An NHS Trust v SR* [2012] EWHC 3842.

[67] Goold (n 16).

7. Conclusion

This chapter has considered the question asked by the parents in *Gard* as to when the state, especially the courts, may legitimately intrude onto the mutual and otherwise lawful decisions of parents concerning their children. The parents sought to find the answer to that question in imposing limits on the courts' jurisdiction through the test of significant harm. This argument was rightly rejected at each stage of the judicial process: the significant harm test is reserved in legislation for situations in which local authorities seek to obtain ongoing discretionary authority to intervene in the life of the child. Outside of that specific situation, the court will resolve cases concerning the child's upbringing through the welfare principle, with no additional need to demonstrate harm. The limit of this jurisdiction is found in the need for the applicant to obtain leave or to demonstrate genuine interest in the child, regardless of whether the applicant is an individual or a state institution such as an NHS Trust. It is through these mechanisms that the court may filter out vexatious or unwarranted applications, but they provide no substantial hurdle to the applicant with genuine welfare concerns. This answer may surprise many parents, whose ordinary experience is that they are free to act as they wish provided that they do so within the law and without risking significant harm to the child. Fundamentally, however, the law regards the upbringing of children not as a matter of exclusive parental rights, to be defended unless forfeited, but as a collaborative responsibility in which parents take the leading role. The argument in *Gard* sought to make parents the sole arbiters of their child's welfare within firm boundaries designed to limit judicial oversight. That argument challenged the foundations of child law and was justifiably rejected by each court that considered it. There are understandable concerns that this rejection undermines parental freedom but the law recognizes that value by emphasizing the primary role of parents in determining their child's welfare rather than by carving out decisions in which parents are immune from challenge. The court will rarely intervene if the parents jointly adopt a reasonable interpretation of their child's welfare. The tragedy in *Gard* was there was no viable treatment that offered a reasonable alternative in Charlie's interests despite the strenuous efforts of his sincere and loving parents.

4

The Legal Basis of the Court's Jurisdiction to Authorise Medical Treatment of Children

ROB GEORGE*

As the default holders of parental responsibility,[1] parents are charged with making decisions about their children's upbringing. The scope of parental responsibility[2] includes authorising or refusing to authorise medically approved[3] treatment, and without consent no doctor can provide treatment without putting him- or herself at legal risk.[4]

Three situations can make that general position more complex. One is that the child in question has sufficient maturity and understanding to make the decision for him- or herself; in such cases, the law provides – controversially – that a doctor may treat so long as *either* the parent or the competent child has given informed consent, even if the other objects to the treatment.[5] The second situation is that there is a genuine emergency, and it is not possible to contact the parents in the available time; here, the law allows a doctor to provide life-saving treatment without consent on the basis of 'necessity'.[6] The final situation is where a child is in the care of a local authority following care proceedings, such that the local authority

* I am grateful to John Eekelaar, Peter Harris, Victoria Butler-Cole and the editors for comments on drafts of this chapter. The views expressed and any errors are mine alone.

[1] Children Act 1989, s 3. See further J Bridgeman, 'Beyond Best Interests: A Question of Professional Conscience?', chapter 7 below. All statutory references are to the Children Act unless otherwise stated.

[2] Parental responsibility is defined in s 3 only in broad terms, but its scope includes medical decision-making: see, eg, S Gilmore, 'The Limits of Parental Responsibility' in R Probert, S Gilmore and J Herring (eds), *Responsible Parents and Parental Responsibility* (Oxford, Hart Publishing, 2014).

[3] Neither parents, patients, nor the courts have the power to require a doctor to provide treatment which he or she does not consider medically appropriate: *Aintree University Hospitals NHS Foundation Trust v James* [2013] UKSC 67, [18].

[4] Criminal and tortious consequences would follow, in addition to the repercussions at a professional level.

[5] *Gillick v West Norfolk and Wisbech AHA* [1986] AC 112 (HL); *Re R (Wardship: Consent to Treatment)* [1992] Fam 11 (CA).

[6] *Re R (Wardship: Consent to Treatment)* [1992] Fam 11 (CA).

has parental responsibility for the child and may determine the extent to which the parents are able to exercise their parental responsibility for the child.[7]

Both in the general case and in these specific examples, situations arise where the approach favoured by the medical professionals differs from the approach favoured by the child's parents and/or the child him- or herself.[8] Where the parent (or child) seeks treatment that the doctor does not consider appropriate, the parent's only choice is to seek another doctor who will treat in the way the parent wishes; no doctor can be required to provide treatment against his or her medical opinion,[9] and even if another doctor will provide treatment, the original treating doctor could seek court declarations as to whether that treatment was in the child's best interests. Conversely, if the parent opposes treatment that the doctor thinks is in the patient's best interests, the doctor will require a court declaration in support before treatment can be given.

This chapter explores the court's legal basis for determining such disputes. With one or two notable exceptions,[10] the courts almost invariably conclude that treatment proposed by medical professionals should be authorised;[11] but what is the legal basis of their decisions?

The court is clear that it has jurisdiction to determine cases such as this;[12] what is less clear is what the legal basis for its ensuing decisions should be. There are essentially two options for the court. One is to rely on its statutory powers under the Children Act 1989; the other is to turn to the High Court's inherent jurisdiction. Both were sought in the Gard case, in line with authority,[13] but questions remain as to whether both applications are really needed.[14] This chapter will explore this issue, setting out the argument in the following stages.

The first part will establish the nature and uses of the inherent jurisdiction in the context of children's medical treatment. This will show that the court uses the inherent jurisdiction for a number of purposes, including the authorisation of treatment, declarations of capacity, and declarations in relation to children being deprived of their liberty for the purpose of treatment.

The second part of the chapter will consider the scope of the Children Act, setting out in particular the potential utility of orders under section 8 of that

[7] S 33(3).

[8] Local authorities have been told that they 'will usually be ill-advised to rely upon [their] parental responsibility under section 33(3)(a) of the 1989 Act as entitling it to authorise medical treatment opposed by parents who also have parental responsibility': *Re AB (A Child)* [2018] EWFC 3, [24(iii)].

[9] *Aintree University Hospitals NHS Foundation Trust v James* [2013] UKSC 67, [18].

[10] *Re T (Wardship: Medical Treatment)* [1997] 1 WLR 242 (CA)

[11] J Bridgeman, 'The Provision of Healthcare to Young and Dependent Children: The Principles, Concepts, and Utility of the Children Act 1989' (2017) 25 *Medical Law Review* 363, 375.

[12] This was a major argument at the Court of Appeal hearing in *Yates and Gard v GOSH* [2017] EWCA Civ 410

[13] *Re JM (A Child) (Medical Treatment)* [2015] EWHC 2832 (Fam), [2016] 2 FLR 235, discussed below.

[14] In refusing permission to appeal, the Supreme Court noted that both applications had been made and commented that that 'applications such as this are provided for by statute', thereby raising, but not addressing, the question of why the inherent jurisdiction was required as well.

legislation and the limitations on the uses of the inherent jurisdiction which were introduced by the Act. I will argue that orders under the Children Act can cover the range of situations which arise in relation to children's medical treatment in most circumstances.

The final part of the chapter considers the issue of deprivation of liberty in more detail, since this is an area where it is less clear whether the inherent jurisdiction is required or not. However, I argue that it is not. Consequently, I suggest that the courts are drawing on the inherent jurisdiction in circumstances where it is not necessary because there is a statutory scheme which adequately addresses the issue of the medical treatment of children. I argue that this is an inappropriate use of the inherent jurisdiction, running contrary to one of the core restrictions on the use of those powers.

1. The Inherent Jurisdiction

The inherent jurisdiction of the High Court is a phrase used to mean many things. The first point is to disambiguate two distinct uses of the phrase *the inherent jurisdiction*:

> 'it can be both a basis for exercising jurisdiction and the source of the power to make orders, as opposed to having recourse, say, to the powers under the Children Act 1989.'[15]

Our interest is in the inherent jurisdiction as a source of the power to make orders, effectively as an alternative to statutory powers, where the court has already established that it has a basis for exercising jurisdiction.[16]

Even used in this more limited way, the inherent jurisdiction, so called, might be best understood as a number of jurisdictions merged together under one broad label. What appears to tie them together is that, other than an occasional tweak[17] or confirmation of the jurisdiction from Parliament,[18] the basis of these jurisdictions lies outside statute.[19] Three areas usually taken to be part of the inherent jurisdiction are of relevance.

The first is the High Court's inherent power to make declarations of lawfulness.[20] Such a declaration states that a previous or proposed course of action would, or

[15] *Re J (1996 Hague Convention) (Morocco)* [2015] EWCA Civ 329, [75] (Black LJ), reversed on other grounds [2015] UKSC 70.

[16] Prior to the UK's departure from the EU, the Brussels IIA Regulation (2201/2003) governed jurisdiction in matters to do with parental responsibility, with the child's habitual residence providing the primary basis. It is expected that similar rules will apply after Brexit, governed by an amended Family Law Act 1986. The inherent jurisdiction can be used as a source of jurisdiction in this sense only in exceptional cases that are not relevant to the issues discussed in this chapter: see *Re B (A Child)* [2016] UKSC 4, [2016] AC 202.

[17] See, eg: Senior Courts Act 1981, s 41.

[18] ibid, s 19(2).

[19] *Re HJ (A Child)* [2013] EWHC 1867 (Fam), [10].

[20] See, eg, *N v A Clinical Commissioning Group* [2017] UKSC 22, [23]. Although declarations of lawfulness are invariably said to be made under the inherent jurisdiction, that is doubtful: *Chapman v*

would not, be lawful; the declaration changes nothing: 'All that the court is being asked to do is to declare that, had a course of action been taken without resort to the court, it would have been lawful anyway.'[21]

The second form of inherent jurisdiction order that may be relevant is injunctive relief, which can also be sought from the High Court. The purpose of such an injunction is generally to preserve the status quo pending determination of the main issues, such as in *Re S*.[22]

Third, but most significantly, in cases concerning children[23] the court may also invoke its *parens patriae* jurisdiction. The *parens patriae* jurisdiction stems from the Crown's power to protect its subjects, and has a somewhat opaque history.[24] The best-known use of the inherent jurisdiction in this sense is in *wardship*, although that is merely a 'convenient machinery' to operate the broader jurisdiction and its use is not essential.[25] When used, wardship comes with significant automatic consequences. It places the court in the position of the child's parent, and indeed the court's parental powers displace those of the parents (or anyone else who holds parental responsibility); no significant decision may be made in relation to the child's life without the court's consent, and in making any decision the court acts as the judicial 'reasonable parent' in assessing the child's welfare or best interests.[26] Orders made under the inherent jurisdiction in relation to children are usually, although not always,[27] decisions about a child's upbringing and so section 1 of the Children Act applies to make the child's welfare the court's paramount consideration.

Whether involving wardship or not, the *parens patriae* jurisdiction in relation to children is referred to almost invariably simply as 'the inherent jurisdiction' in modern authorities, but previously had various names.[28] Whatever terminology is

Michaelson [1909] 1 Ch 238 (CA), 243. The jurisdiction to grant a declaration *where no consequential remedy was sought* was granted to the Court of Chancery by s 50 of the Court of Chancery Procedure Act 1850, and extended to all divisions of the newly created High Court by s 24 of the Judicature Act 1873; its continued existence is reflected in r 40.20 of the Civil Procedure Rules 1998.

[21] *Re F (Mental Patient: Sterilisation)* [1990] 2 AC 1 (CA), at 20 (Donaldson MR) and similarly at 42 (Butler-Sloss LJ); see also *An NHS Trust v Y* [2018] UKSC 46, citing *R (Burke) v General Medical Council* [2005] EWCA Civ 1003, [80]: 'The true position is that the court does not "authorise" treatment that would otherwise be unlawful. The court makes a declaration as to whether or not proposed treatment, or the withdrawal of treatment, will be lawful.'

[22] *Re S (Hospital Patient: Court's Jurisdiction)* [1995] Fam 26 (HC), 35–36

[23] The *parens patriae* jurisdiction previously applied also to adults who lack mental capacity, but in this context the jurisdiction has quite a different history, both in its origins and more recently. This issue is beyond the scope of this chapter, but see *Re F (Mental Patient: Sterilisation)* [1990] 2 AC 1 (HL) and *Re SA (Vulnerable Adult with Capacity: Marriage)* [2005] EWHC 2942 (Fam), [2006] 1 FLR 867.

[24] J Seymour, 'Parens Patriae and Wardship Powers: Their Nature and Origin' (1994) 14 *OJLS* 159.

[25] *Re L (An Infant)* [1968] P 119 (CA); N Lowe and R White, *Wards of Court*, 2nd edn (London, Barry Rose, 1986), para 1.5.

[26] *J v C* [1970] AC 688 (HL).

[27] For example, decisions about publicity in relation to a child fall outside this generalisation: see *Re Z (Identification: Restrictions on Publicity)* [1997] Fam 1 (CA).

[28] Alongside *parens patriae jurisdiction*, common earlier terms included *paternal jurisdiction*, *prerogative jurisdiction*, and *protective jurisdiction*. The term *inherent jurisdiction* barely features in the Law Commission's seminal paper, *Wards of Court* (Working Paper No 101, 1987).

favoured, the scope of the jurisdiction is vast – indeed, 'theoretically limitless'.[29] As the High Court recently explained:

> Under its inherent jurisdiction, the court may make any order or determine any issue in respect of a child. However, whilst the jurisdiction of the court under the inherent jurisdiction is theoretically unlimited, there are, in fact, far-reaching limitations on the exercise of the jurisdiction.[30]

The full extent of these limitations is not relevant to this chapter – nor, indeed, clearly established – but one of the key limitations is central to my argument, namely the so-called 'principle in *Attorney-General v De Keyser's Hotel*'.[31] This case was about the Crown's prerogative powers in relation to the requisitioning of property in wartime, but the general principle is of broader application, and is this: where Parliament has legislated in an area that was previously within the scope of the prerogative so as to provide limitations or conditions on the exercise of an equivalent power, it is not open to the Crown to continue to rely on the prerogative.[32]

Put another way, the inherent jurisdiction cannot be deployed to circumvent the provisions of an Act of Parliament. Such circumvention might be direct, by doing something under the inherent jurisdiction which is inconsistent with statute, or indirect, by 'interven[ing] on the merits in an area of concern entrusted by Parliament to another public authority'.[33] Some legislation contains specific restrictions on the use of the inherent jurisdiction,[34] and more generally the jurisdiction cannot be used to ride roughshod over a statutory scheme;[35] it is a jurisdiction that fills the gaps, not one that allows the court to ignore a statute.[36] In *Re T (Child: Representation)*, Waite LJ said this:

> The scheme of the Children Act 1989 is to establish a statutory code for both the private and public law field. … The courts' undoubted discretion to allow wardship proceedings to go forward in a suitable case is subject to their clear duty, in loyalty to the scheme and purpose of the Children Act legislation, to permit recourse to wardship only when it becomes apparent to the judge in any particular case that the question which the court is determining in regard to the minor's upbringing or property cannot be resolved under the statutory procedures in Part II of the Act in a way which secures the best interests of the child; or where the minor's person is in a state of jeopardy from which he can only be protected by giving him the status of a ward of court; or where the court's functions need to be secured from the effects, potentially

[29] *Re W (Consent to Medical Treatment)* [1993] 1 FLR 1 (CA), 12.
[30] *HB v A Local Authority and the Local Government Association* [2017] EWHC 524 (Fam), [50].
[31] *Attorney-General v De Keyser's Royal Hotel Limited* [1920] AC 508 (HL).
[32] ibid, 526 (Lord Dunedin), 538 (Lord Atkinson) and 575 (Lord Parmoor).
[33] *Re W (A Minor) (Wardship: Jurisdiction)* [1985] AC 791 (HL), 797. See also the important discussion in *Re A Ward of Court* [2017] EWHC 1022 (Fam).
[34] S 100 is the best example.
[35] *Richards v Richards* [1984] AC 174 (HL); see also Law Commission (n 28), [2.23].
[36] *A v Liverpool City Council* [1982] AC 363 (HL); *DL v A Local Authority* [2012] EWCA Civ 253, [61].

> injurious to the child, of external influences (intrusive publicity for example) and it is decided that conferring on the child the status of a ward will prove a more effective deterrent than the ordinary sanctions of contempt of court which already protect all family proceedings.[37]

In theory, anyone with a genuine interest in the matter being brought before the court may make an application under the inherent jurisdiction, subject to two caveats. The first is the general restriction in Practice Direction 12D that applications under the inherent jurisdiction should be made only where the outcome sought cannot be achieved by the making of order under the Children Act. The second applies to local authority applicants; they require specific leave to bring any application under the inherent jurisdiction, and the leave may be granted only when the outcome sought could not be achieved by orders under the Children Act for which the local authority could apply, and there is reasonable cause to believe that the child would suffer significant harm if the inherent jurisdiction were not used.[38]

It is therefore imperative properly to determine the scope of the relevant statutory powers and whether a 'gap', so called, is in fact an omission where the legislation does not address the issue, as opposed to a deliberate policy choice by Parliament not to provide a remedy.[39] Clearly in the context of the medical treatment of minors it is not realistic to suggest that there would be no remedy to a dispute, so the question becomes more focused on whether the available statutory remedies are deficient. In order to address that, we need to understand the scope of the statutory scheme under the Children Act relevant to medical decision-making.

2. The Children Act

The answer is that the Children Act 1989 addresses the situation in a number of relevant provisions. The Act places the primary responsibility for children's upbringing on holders of what is termed 'parental responsibility' (which is usually vested in both parents in the first instance).[40] Where there are issues in relation to how aspects of parental responsibility should be exercised, the Children Act provides for a range of orders that the court can make in private law disputes between parents or others concerned with the child's upbringing, in effect allowing the court to regulate how parental responsibility is exercised. In doing so, the court will act according to the welfare principle,[41] and will only make orders where

[37] *Re T (Child: Representation)* [1994] Fam 49 (CA), 59–60.

[38] S 100.

[39] *Re W (A Minor) (Wardship: Jurisdiction)* [1985] AC 791 (HL), 802 (Lord Scarman). However: 'It may be possible to recognise the difference between a hole in a blanket, which needs to be patched, and a hole in Swiss cheese, which is part of the fabric and virtue of the cheese itself, but it is difficult to describe it in legislative language': Law Commission (n 28), [4.17].

[40] Ss 3 and 4. For more detail, see: Bridgeman (n 1); Bridgeman (n 11), 379–81.

[41] S 1(1).

doing so is better for the child than making no orders at all.[42] Although parents are usually the parties involved in such litigation, the Act allows anyone with a sufficient interest in the child – such as a hospital or a local authority – to apply for such orders, subject to a requirement of obtaining leave.[43] The orders that regulate such disputes are found in section 8; they are generically termed 'section 8 orders', and the two relevant ones are defined in the Act as follows:

> 'a prohibited steps order' means an order that no step which could be taken by a parent in meeting his parental responsibility for a child, and which is of a kind specified in the order, shall be taken by any person without the consent of the court;
>
> 'a specific issue order' means an order giving directions for the purpose of determining a specific question which has arisen, or which may arise, in connection with any aspect of parental responsibility for a child.

In effect, a *prohibited steps order* (PSO) determines that a course of action which a parent could have undertaken in the exercise of their parental responsibility shall not be done (for example, a baby boy shall not be circumcised[44]), whereas a *specific issue order* (SIO) provides that something which a parent could have authorised within their parental responsibility shall be done (for example, a child shall receive an immunisation[45]).

Section 9 contains a number of important restrictions on the making of section 8 orders, and some of them need to be highlighted. Section 9(1) prevents the making of SIOs or PSOs in respect of a child who is in local authority care under a care order or interim care order. Section 9(6) and (7) prevent the making of any section 8 order after the child has reached the age of 16, or which continues in effect after the child is 16, unless the circumstances are exceptional.

The statutory framework of the Children Act therefore provides that the parents have the primary responsibility for the upbringing of their children, and that the court has powers under section 8 to regulate the exercise of particular aspects of parental responsibility where there is a dispute. In deciding such a dispute, the child's welfare is the court's paramount consideration, and anyone with a suitable interest in the matter may make an application so long as they first obtain leave. The Act has priority over applications under the inherent jurisdiction, in that the latter may be made only if the outcome sought cannot be achieved by way of orders under the Act.[46]

[42] S 1(5).

[43] S 10.

[44] eg, *Re J (Child's Religious Upbringing and Circumcision)* [2000] 1 FLR 571 (CA).

[45] eg, *Re C (Welfare of Child: Immunisation)* [2003] EWHC 1376. The scope of this power is important to note – it is to do what a parent could have done, and so does not enable the court to order third parties to take positive steps that go beyond what a parent could require.

[46] Practice Direction 12D – Inherent Jurisdiction (Including Wardship) Proceedings, para 1.1. This is, in effect, a reflection of the rule in *Attorney-General v De Keyser's Hotel* [1920] AC 508 (HL), discussed above.

3. The Scope of the Children Act in Medical Cases

The court in the Gard case faced applications under both the Act and the inherent jurisdiction, with little clarity as to which was used in the making of the orders. Authority establishes that both applications should be made,[47] but the question is whether that is really necessary and if so why. Put another way, the question is whether the legislative scheme of the Children Act 1989 is adequate to allow all relevant orders to be made in the case of contested medical decision-making about a child.

As Stephen Gilmore has noted, the statutory history of SIOs and PSOs reveals limited information.[48] However, one point of potential relevance to this discussion comes from Lord Mackay LC at the Children Bill's Second Reading, when he said: '[I]f there is a dispute about a particular matter – for example, where the child should go to school, or *whether he should have a serious medical operation* – the court can make a specific issue order settling the matter.'[49]

From the wording of the Act, the principal limitation on the scope of an SIO would appear to be that there is a 'question' relating to an aspect of parental responsibility;[50] similarly, a PSO is limited to steps 'which could be taken by a parent' in the exercise of parental responsibility. The scope of parental responsibility itself is, of course, wide,[51] and as a general proposition clearly includes consenting to the medical treatment of a child, including (as Lord Mackay LC said) serious medical treatment. The question might be, therefore, whether it extends to *all* medical treatment of a child, or whether there is a category of medical decision-making that is *beyond* what has been termed in other contexts the 'zone' of parental responsibility.[52]

In Australia, the High Court has ruled that the sterilisation of a child requires court approval because it is part of a category of 'special cases' which are beyond the scope of parental authority to sanction because of the seriousness of their consequences and the significant risk of making the wrong decision.[53] Quite what lies within this category of 'special cases' is unclear, as nothing other than sterilisation seems to have been identified.[54]

[47] *Re JM (A Child) (Medical Treatment)* [2015] EWHC 2832 (Fam), [2016] 2 FLR 235.

[48] S Gilmore, 'The Nature, Scope, and Use of the Specific Issue Order' (2004) *Child and Family Law Quarterly* 367.

[49] *Hansard, Lords Debates*, vol 502, col 491 (6 December 1988), emphasis added. See also J Mackay, 'Perceptions of the Children Bill and Beyond' (1989) 139 *New Law Journal* 505, 506.

[50] Gilmore (n 48).

[51] Lord Justice McFarlane, 'Making Parental Responsibility Work' [2014] Fam Law 1264, 1270.

[52] *Re D (A Child) (Residence Order: Deprivation of Liberty)* [2017] EWCA Civ 1695, [78].

[53] *Secretary, Department of Health and Community Services v JWB (Marion's Case)* [1992] HCA 15, (1992) 106 ALR 385, but note the strong dissents from Brennan, Deane and McHugh JJ who considered that parents were able to authorise the sterilisation of a minor when that procedure was medically justified.

[54] The court previously included the authorisation of treatment for gender dysphoria, but it was removed by *Re Kelvin* [2017] FamFAFC 258.

The position in England is different. In *Re B (A Minor) (Wardship: Sterilisation)*,[55] Lord Templeman suggested that any proposed sterilisation of a minor required the consent of a High Court Judge, and could not be lawfully done on the basis of parental consent.[56] However, that view was not endorsed by the rest of the House, and no guidance was offered (as was by the Australian courts) as to what would differentiate sterilisation from any other serious medical procedure so as to require court authorisation. Later cases do not appear to have accepted Lord Templeman's approach, and the House of Lords in *Re F (Mental Patient: Sterilisation)* took the broader approach of describing a court application – there, in the context of adult patients who lack capacity – as merely 'a matter of good practice',[57] albeit strongly encouraged,[58] and not legally required.[59] The Supreme Court in *An NHS Trust v Y* has made clear – this time in the context of an adult in a persistent vegetative state – that an application to the court for a declaration is not always required.[60] Consistently with this approach, guidance to medical professionals suggests that court applications are primarily appropriate only where parents disagree with medical opinion or are unable to give valid consent themselves,[61] reflecting cautious safeguarding against criminal or tortious liability, rather than any positive legal requirement that prompts court applications to be made regarding serious medical treatment.

Where a court order is required, in both the sterilisation context[62] and beyond, there is clear authority to the effect that in a children case a section 8 order can indeed be used to grant the requisite authorisation for medical treatment.[63] Inevitably, it was not long after the Children Act came into force that the issue fell to be determined. In *Re R (A Minor) (Blood Transfusion)*,[64] Booth J was faced with an application brought by a local authority in respect of a young girl who was considered by medical professionals treating her to require blood transfusions; her parents were Jehovah's Witnesses and opposed the transfusions on religious grounds. The local authority took the view that, other than in relation to this aspect of medical treatment, there was no problem with the parents' care of the girl.

[55] *In Re B (A Minor) (Wardship: Sterilisation)* [1988] AC 199 (HL).

[56] ibid, 205.

[57] *Re F (Mental Patient Sterilisation)* [1990] 2 AC 1 (HL), 56 (Lord Brandon); this is also the language used in Practice Note (Official Solicitor: Declaratory Proceedings: *Medical and Welfare Decisions for Adults Who Lack Capacity)* [2006] 2 FLR 373, [6].

[58] ibid, 52 (Lord Bridge), 70 (Lord Griffiths), 79 and 83 (Lord Goff).

[59] *An NHS Trust v Y* [2018] UKSC 46, [12].

[60] ibid.

[61] See, eg, V Larcher, F Craig, K Bhogal, D Wilkinson and J Brierley, 'Making Decisions to Limit Treatment in Life-Limiting and Life-Threatening Conditions in Children: A Framework for Practice' (2015) 100 *Archives of Disease in Childhood*, Suppl 2.

[62] *Re HG (Specific Issue Order: Sterilisation)* [1993] 1 FLR 587 (Peter Singer QC).

[63] See generally Gilmore (n 48), 380 and the cases cited therein.

[64] *R A Minor* [1993] 2 FLR 757 (HC).

Re R stands for the proposition that an SIO can be made to address the issue of contested medical treatment of a child, as between the parents and a third party (here, a local authority). As Booth J put it:

> In the present case I am in no doubt that the application is well-founded under s 8 of the Act. The result which the local authority wishes to achieve, namely, the court's authorisation for the use of blood products, can clearly be achieved by the means of such an order. There is no need for the court otherwise to intervene to safeguard the little girl, so that I am satisfied that it is unnecessary and inappropriate for the court to exercise its inherent jurisdiction.[65]

Similarly, in *Re HG (Specific Issue Order: Sterilisation)*,[66] the High Court made an SIO relating to the sterilisation of a 17-year-old girl. Conversely, the court has made PSOs which prevent a child from undergoing surgery or receiving blood transfusions.[67]

It is notable that all of the decisions cited in relation to this issue stem from High Court rulings in the immediate aftermath of the implementation of the Children Act. Despite being reported, those cases then more or less disappear into history and are not cited in the later authorities, although they are referenced in some texts as examples of the uses of SIOs.[68] This is notable because it begs the question: why, after the court initially held the Children Act to be adequate to address medical treatment disputes, do the later cases revert to using the inherent jurisdiction?

There is virtually no discussion of this issue in the case-law. The only more recent engagement with these authorities came from Mostyn J in *Re JM (A Child) (Medical Treatment)*,[69] where his Lordship took the view that an application under section 8 was the appropriate way for the main issue – namely, the authorisation of medical treatment – to be addressed, although with the inherent jurisdiction also potentially required for some subsidiary aspects of these cases.[70] Consequently, my argument is that where the court resorts to its inherent jurisdiction to make the primary orders which authorise (or forbid) medical treatment of minors, it is doing so unnecessarily – the Children Act allows such orders to be made, and therefore the Act should be used.

A. Potential Limitations of Section 8 Orders

Re JM and the early 1990s cases it cites represent a small minority of the decisions in this area; Mostyn J's decision clearly came as a surprise to some, and was far

[65] ibid, 760. See also the consent order made in *MM (Medical Treatment)* [2000] 1 FLR 224 (HC).

[66] *Re HG (Specific Issue Order: Sterilisation)* [1993] 1 FLR 587 (HC).

[67] *Re S (A Minor) (Medical Treatment)* [1993] 1 FLR 376 (HC). Cf *Re W (A Minor) (Medical Treatment: Court's Jurisdiction)* [1993] Fam 64 (CA).

[68] See, eg, R White, P Carr and N Lowe, *The Children Act in Practice* (Oxford, Butterworths, 2002) 164.

[69] *Re JM (A Child)* [2015] EWHC 2832 (Fam), [2016] 2 FLR 235.

[70] ibid, [24].

from uncontroversial. For example, the leading family law text for practitioners, the *Family Court Practice 2018*, gives *Re JM* rather short shrift:

> In most serious medical treatment cases a declaration is sought that the treatment proposed is in the best interests of the child and for authorisation for the treatment to be given or withdrawn. This can only be granted by the High Court. Where a child is in care, the local authority cannot apply for a specific issue order. The nature of the issues that arise is not within the scope of a s 8 order. It also does not take into account: the delay that this procedure would entail; the need for the child's interests to be independently considered by being made a party to the proceedings and for the child to be represented; the hurdles that would have to be overcome to obtain legal funding and representation for the child; and the fact that the case would have to be dealt with by a judge of the Family Division, thus requiring a transfer to the High Court.[71]

Leaving the declaration point to one side for a moment, it is convenient to consider the other criticisms made here first.

i. Children in Care

It is right that where a child is the subject of a care order, the court cannot make an SIO or a PSO.[72] The basis for this limitation is best explained as a matter of policy: a local authority which has a child in its care has gained parental responsibility for that child, and the local authority's parental responsibility, although limited in some ways,[73] can 'trump' the parental responsibility of the parents.[74] Consequently, it can be suggested that Parliament envisaged that there could not be disputes about any aspect of parental responsibility in relation to a child in local authority care, because the local authority had been given the power to make such decisions irrespective of the agreement or otherwise of other holders of parental responsibility. In the context of serious medical decisions, however, that has not been the approach taken in recent case-law. Sir James Munby P has suggested that, whatever the technical position might be, the local authority would be unwise to seek to rely on its parental responsibility to override parental decisions about medical treatment, not least because of the risks of a breach of Article 8 rights.[75]

If a care order is already in place, and if the local authority's parental responsibility cannot be used to authorise the treatment, section 9(1) prevents the making of an SIO and the court may have to fall back on the inherent jurisdiction.[76] The reason why the local authority cannot – or, at least, should not – use its parental responsibility to sanction serious medical treatment under a care order would seem to be twofold.[77] First, the Article 8 rights to respect for private and family life

[71] *The Family Court Practice 2018* (Bristol, Jordans, 2018) 1546.
[72] S 9(1).
[73] S 33(6) and (7).
[74] S 33(3)(b).
[75] *Re AB (A Child)* [2018] EWFC 3, [24(iii)].
[76] By analogy, see *Re C (Child in Care: Choice of Forename)* [2016] EWCA Civ 374.
[77] ibid, [76].

of the child and of the parents probably militate against a state body being able to make significant decisions for the child without court oversight. Secondly, in a case where there was scope for reasonable disagreement with the proposed course of treatment, the parents' only recourse would be to seek discharge of the care order. That might not be appropriate, but there would be no other way within the ambit of the Children Act for the local authority's decision to be challenged.[78]

However, since the local authority should not be using the vehicle of a care order specifically to intervene in medical decision-making,[79] then the difficulty around the court's inability to make an SIO or a PSO arises only in that minority of cases where a child who is already in care for other reasons then requires serious medical treatment. In that case, the inherent jurisdiction may well be required, because of the section 9(1) restriction. However, in the more common case where a local authority becomes concerned about the medical treatment of a child who is not otherwise in care, there seems to be no reason why a section 8 order cannot be used.[80]

ii. Other Criticisms of Re JM

The issue of legal aid funding is a real one, although whether that in itself justifies the use of the inherent jurisdiction if there is otherwise a valid statutory route seems doubtful on a principled basis, even though as matter of practicality it may be justifiable.

The other criticisms made by the *Family Court Practice* do not appear well-founded. First, where delay is a concern because the matter is urgent, there is no reason why an application for a section 8 order cannot be made in the Urgent Applications Court at the High Court just as well as an application under the inherent jurisdiction can be, so it is not clear why there would be delay.[81] Second, making a child a party to proceedings is no more or less difficult under the Children Act than under the inherent jurisdiction – indeed, both are governed by the same rules and principles.[82] Third, the application could clearly be issued in the Family Court, but in the Royal Courts of Justice and therefore automatically before a High Court Judge sitting in the Family Court; the issue of transfer, if required, is therefore a technicality rather than any kind of practical hurdle.

4. The Need for Declarations

So far, the implication of this argument is that, except in relation to a child in care, no recourse to the inherent jurisdiction is required. However, the first point in the

[78] It might be possible for injunctive relief under s 8 of the Human Rights Act 1998 to be sought: see, by analogy, *Re DE (A Child)* [2014] EWFC 6.

[79] *Re AB (A Child)* [2018] EWFC 3.

[80] *Re R (A Minor) (Blood Transfusion)* [1993] 2 FLR 757 (HC).

[81] The court office at the Royal Courts of Justice can accept C100 applications, which are used to apply for s 8 orders, so long as the issues raised justify allocation to a High Court judge.

[82] FPR 2010 r 16.2 and Practice Direction 16A.

critique of the *Family Court Practice* relates to declarations, and in *Re JM* Mostyn J identifies the possibility that a High Court declaration may be required:

> [I]t is questionable whether the Family Court has the power to grant final declaratory relief, which may well be the principal relief (or a component of such relief) which is sought. This is because CPR r 40.20, whereby the court is given explicit power to make 'binding declarations whether or not any other remedy is claimed' is not replicated in the FPR (although, strangely, there is a power in FPR 2010, r 20.2(1)(b) to make an interim declaration). In a serious medical case the declaratory relief sought may concern the authorisation of a deprivation of liberty. That cannot be ordered within a specific issue direction.[83]

The answer to this apparent difficulty for Mostyn J was that an applicant should seek *both* an order under section 8 *and* a declaration under the inherent jurisdiction.

As noted previously, the nature of a declaration under the inherent jurisdiction is, in one sense, straightforward – it *declares* a person's legal rights or status, or it declares whether a course of action, past or proposed, was or would be lawful; however, it does nothing to *change* the legal position.[84]

It is true that declarations are sought as a matter of course, but what is their function?[85] One is simply to determine the substantive issue – a declaration that it is or is not in the child's best interests for treatment to be withdrawn, or whatever the issue is. That kind of declaration seems to encompass exactly the territory which we have seen can be addressed with a section 8 order. The court may also be asked to make declarations as to the child's lack of capacity, although whether that is actually required for a child under the age of 16 is not clear, since the law presumes that the child is not competent to make such decisions in any event, and even when the child is competent the court has long asserted its right to override the child's decision.[86] A final potential use of the declaration is to authorise a deprivation of liberty of a child.

In the context of medical decision-making, whether relating to children or to adults, the sole criterion for the courts in determining whether to grant such a declaration is the best interests of the patient, taken in their widest sense.[87] That, of course, is also the sole criterion for determining whether to make an SIO or a PSO,[88] and in that context is also required to be interpreted in its widest sense.[89] The intellectual process and relevant considerations to the granting of a declaration or the making of a section 8 order appear, therefore, to be the same. The question, then, is whether a High Court declaration adds anything that the section 8 order does not.

[83] *Re JM (A Child) (Medical Treatment)* [2015] EWHC 2832 (Fam), [2016] 2 FLR 235, [26].

[84] See n 21.

[85] See generally *An NHS Trust v Y* [2018] UKSC 46, discussing declarations in the context of an adult patient in a persistent vegetative state.

[86] *Re R (Wardship: Consent to Treatment)* [1992] Fam 11 (CA).

[87] See, eg, *Re F (Mental Patient: Sterilisation)* [1990] 2 AC 1 (HL) at 56 (Lord Brandon) and 79 (Lord Goff).

[88] Children Act 1989, s 1(1).

[89] *Re G (Education: Religious Upbringing)* [2012] EWCA Civ 1233, [2013] 1 FLR 677.

A deprivation of liberty for the purposes of Article 5 ECHR has three limbs or elements,[90] summarised by the Supreme Court as follows: '(a) the objective component of confinement in a particular restricted place for a not negligible length of time; (b) the subjective component of lack of valid consent; and (c) the attribution of responsibility to the state'.[91]

With a child under the age of 16,[92] questions around any deprivation of liberty for Article 5 purposes appear to arise only where the parents (or, if *Gillick* competent, the child him- or herself) are not only in dispute with the hospital about the proposed course of treatment, but in fact do not consent to the child remaining in the hospital's care at all.

Where the parents consent to their child remaining in hospital, even if they dispute the course of treatment to be given, then the authorities establish that this will not amount to be a deprivation of liberty as the child's position is properly regulated by the parents' exercise of their parental responsibility; so long as there is parental consent to the child's being in hospital, this will remove any breach of Article 5 ECHR due to component 2 of *Storck* not being satisfied.[93] (If a child is in local authority care, the local authority may not use its parental responsibility to authorise the deprivation of liberty; parental consent might still suffice, but ordinarily a court order will be required in such circumstances.[94])

Even then, there is some doubt that all cases would involve an Article 5 deprivation of liberty. The confinement of 'young' and 'very young' children is seen as being typical of the experience of most children that age; a baby is rarely left unsupervised, but this does not amount to 'confinement' within *Storck* component 1. Whether the child is at home, in a nursery or in a hospital makes little difference. The case-law appears to start to draw a significant distinction in early adolescence, at 11 or 12 years of age.[95] However, even a child over this age is unlikely to be 'confined' for the purposes of *Storck* component 1 if their 'confinement' is in a hospital as a result of a medical condition that would require anyone to be hospitalised.[96] Consequently, whereas Mostyn J suggests that applications of this nature will normally include an application for a declaration authorising a deprivation of liberty, it is not clear that in the majority of cases that would be necessary.

[90] *Storck v Germany* (app no 61603/00) (2005) ECHR 406.

[91] *P (by his Litigation Friend, the Official Solicitor) v Cheshire West and Chester Council* [2014] UKSC 19, [2014] AC 896, [37].

[92] Or, indeed, a child aged 16 or 17 if they are not *Gillick* competent: see *Re D (A Child) (Residence Order: Deprivation of Liberty)* [2017] EWCA Civ 1695, [144], but note that this case was heard in the Supreme Court in October 2018, with judgment pending at time of writing.

[93] *P (by his Litigation Friend, the Official Solicitor) v Cheshire West and Chester Council* [2014] UKSC 19, [2014] AC 896, [54] (Lady Hale) and [72] (Lord Neuberger); *Re D (A Child) (Deprivation of Liberty)* [2015] EWHC 922 (Fam), [2016] 1 FLR 142, [55]–[57], approved by *Re D (A Child) (Residence Order: Deprivation of Liberty)* [2017] EWCA Civ 1695, [103].

[94] *Re AB (A Child) (Deprivation of Liberty: Consent)* [2015] EWHC 3125 (Fam), [2016] 1 WLR 1160, [29], approved by *Re D (A Child) (Residence Order: Deprivation of Liberty)* [2017] EWCA Civ 1695, [109]–[112].

[95] *Re A-F (Children)* [2018] EWHC 138 (Fam), [43].

[96] *R (Ferreira) v HM Coroner for Inner South London* [2017] EWCA Civ 31, [88]–[90], citing *Austin v UK* (2012) 55 EHRR 359, [59]; *Evans and James v Alder Hey Children's NHS Foundation Trust (No 2)*

Moreover, if the issue is that the parents in a particular case do not, in fact, consent to their child remaining in the hospital's care, but if they did so consent that would amount to valid consent so as to authorise the deprivation of liberty, that appears to show that the issue falls within the ambit of parental responsibility. If that is so, it is not clear why a section 8 order cannot be used to authorise a deprivation of liberty of a child, by the making of an SIO that the child be held at the medical facility. The legal test to be applied to the making of such an order is the welfare principle in section 1 of the Children Act.

The court sometimes also issues injunctions in relation to medical treatment, such as a non-removal injunction.[97] From the reported cases, such cases appear to be made in the context of adult patients only, as it is difficult to see any objection to a PSO being made to the same effect when the patient in question is a child.[98]

However, it is notable that the President of the Family Division has said, in terms, that the placement of a child in such a way as amounts to 'confinement' within the terms of Article 5, but falling outside the scope of section 25 of the Children Act which allows for 'secure accommodation' orders to be made in certain limited circumstances, can be authorised only by the High Court under its inherent jurisdiction.[99] No authority is cited in support of this proposition, and working from first principles as set out above it is difficult to identify any difficulty with the section 8 order approach. Here, some analogy with the authorisation of a deprivation of liberty for an adult under the Mental Capacity Act 2005 may be of value.

The 2005 Act provides that it does not authorise any person (referred to as 'D' in the Act) to deprive any other person (referred to as 'P') of his or her liberty,[100] but that P may be deprived of their liberty in certain circumstances, including if D 'is giving effect to a relevant decision of the court'.[101] This 'relevant decision' is defined specifically as 'a decision made by an order under s 16(2)(a) in relation to a matter concerning P's personal welfare',[102] or the deprivation may be authorised under Schedule A1 of the Act in relation to hospital and care home residents.

Taking the section 16 route first, the relevant provision there provides:

> (2) The court may–
>
> (a) by making an order, make the decision or decisions on P's behalf in relation to the matter or matters, or
>
> (b) appoint a person (a 'deputy') to make decisions on P's behalf in relation to the matter or matters.

[2018] EWCA Civ 805, [60]–[62]; the same point is made by the Supreme Court in refusing permission to appeal in *Re Alfie Evans (No 2)*, 20 April 2018, [12].

[97] See, eg, *Re S (Hospital Patient: Court's Jurisdiction)* [1995] Fam 26 (HC).

[98] Such orders are used regularly in other contexts.

[99] *Re A-F (Children)* [2018] EWHC 138 (Fam), [26].

[100] Mental Capacity Act 2005, s 4A(1).

[101] ibid, s 4A(3).

[102] ibid, s 4A(4).

The making of any order under these provisions is subject to the Act's general principles in section 1 and to the best interests standard in section 4. Ultimately, however, taking into account the factors specified in those sections, the decision of the Court of Protection leads to an order under section 16(2)(a), the key determinative consideration being the best interests of P. This is the court's general power to make orders to protect and promote the welfare and best interests of adults subject to the Act's scheme, in much the same way that section 8 orders under the Children Act provide the general powers in relation to children.[103]

Schedule A1 provides for authorisation of the deprivation of liberty of P to be provided by the managing authority of a hospital or care home. These provisions apply only to persons aged 18 or over,[104] and there is no equivalent provision for children in statute. The closest equivalent provision is section 25 of the Children Act 1989 which allows the court (but not any other body) to authorise a child to be detained in secure accommodation when certain conditions are satisfied. Paragraph 7 of the Children (Secure Accommodation) Regulations 1991 makes clear that section 25 applies to children accommodated by health authorities as well as local authorities. However, the conditions for the making of such an order are strict: the child must (i) be being looked after by a local authority and (ii) either have a history of absconding and be likely to suffer significant harm if he absconds again, or be likely to injure himself or another if not kept in secure accommodation. These conditions are unlikely to apply to children in need of serious medical treatment (although they could in relation to an older child who abjectly opposed treatment and was liable to try to leave hospital to avoid treatment).[105]

Consequently, it would appear that for adults Parliament has provided a specific statutory route to the authorisation of a deprivation of liberty by the Court of Protection, and that route involves a standard type of order which can be used to address any aspect of the person's personal welfare. There is no equivalent order for children, but the Children Act provides standard orders for addressing disputes about the welfare of children in section 8, in the form of child arrangements orders (not applicable here), SIOs and PSOs, all of which are made under the umbrella of the welfare principle which makes the child's welfare the court's paramount consideration. The two orders, under section 16(2)(a) of the Mental Capacity Act and under section 8 of the Children Act, appear to be cut from the same cloth,

[103] The analogy is not exact, since under the Mental Capacity Act 2005 the court is taking a decision on behalf of P because of P's incapacity in relation to that decision, whereas under the Children Act 1989 the court is taking the decision in relation to the child and, in a sense, takes the place of the parent in doing so.

[104] Mental Capacity Act 2005, Sched A1, para 13.

[105] One example is in relation to older children with anorexia nervosa, where the court has previously used its inherent jurisdiction to authorise their forced detention at medical facilities and subsequent treatment: see, eg, *Re W (Medical Treatment: Court's Jurisdiction)* [1993] Fam 64 (CA); *Re C (Medical Treatment: Court's Jurisdiction)* [1997] 2 FLR 180 (Wall J). Whether recourse to the inherent jurisdiction is justified in such cases is beyond the scope of this chapter, but is open to question on the same basic argument as is set out in relation to medical treatment generally.

and it is difficult to see why a section 8 order could not be used to authorise the deprivation of liberty of a child if such an order was in the child's best interests.

5. Conclusions

This chapter has sought to explore the reasons for the ongoing use of the High Court's non-statutory powers in relation to the medical treatment of children. From the analysis offered, serious questions have arisen about the justification for the court's reliance on its inherent jurisdiction, whether in the form of *parens patriae* or of declarations. It is argued that the Children Act provides remedies which can be used in this context perfectly well in the vast majority of cases and, that being so, it is inappropriate for the court to continue to rely on its inherent jurisdiction.

The focus of this chapter has been on the technical legal position, which opens it up to challenge from those who would say that, particularly in the context of children's medical treatment, the technicality is less important than whether all parties have been heard and the right result has been achieved.[106] However, as Bridgeman has argued in more detail, there are potentially significant differences of approach and outcome.[107] One particular issue which she raises is that the reliance on the inherent jurisdiction allows an undue focus on the competing claims of parents and of healthcare professionals, which she argues can distract attention from the child concerned, particularly regarding children's independent rights under the UN Convention on the Rights of the Child 1989[108] – a concern that can be seen played out in the Gard case, where the main arguments in the Court of Appeal and Supreme Court were about parental rights.

As Bridgeman concludes, the potential uses of the Children Act in this context have not yet been properly realised by the courts.[109] A large part of the reason for this is that the judges have not fully engaged with the potential of the Act because of their default position of relying on their inherent jurisdiction. Although that may be an easy option, and (given the theoretically unlimited powers of the inherent jurisdiction) removes any question about whether the orders required by the particular situation are conceptually possible, the Act and its Practice Directions demand that the courts resort to the inherent jurisdiction only where the Act is inadequate to the task. It is far from clear that it is inadequate in the context of medical decision-making for children.

[106] cf *R v Portsmouth Hospitals NHS Trust, ex parte Glass* [1999] 2 FLR 905, 910.
[107] Bridgeman (n 11), esp 391 onwards.
[108] ibid, 392.
[109] ibid, 396.

5

In Defence of a Conditional Harm Threshold Test for Paediatric Decision-Making

DOMINIC WILKINSON

The case of Charlie Gard raises a number of serious ethical questions, including how a child's best interests should be assessed, the role of parents in decision-making for a child, the appropriateness of trying untested experimental treatment in a seriously ill child, and the allocation of limited healthcare resources. Elsewhere, I have reviewed these questions in some detail and explored the implications for future disputes over medical treatment for children.[1] In this chapter, I will focus on one of the questions that arose in the Gard case and was also raised in the subsequent case of Alfie Evans. If there is disagreement between parents and health professionals about treatment for a child, should courts overrule parents on the basis of an assessment of what would be *best* for the child, or only if what the parents propose would be *harmful* for the child? I will largely focus on the ethical question (and leave the more specific legal questions to other commentators in this volume).[2] I outline the ethical case for using a harm threshold test rather than a best interests test, identifying a set of cases where these tests may yield different decisions. I respond to a series of counterarguments against the use of harm thresholds. In the last part of the chapter, I propose a compromise, a conditional harm threshold test that would apply only if there is a question of preventing parents from pursuing treatment that other health professionals are offering to provide. I explore the implications of this test for a set of challenging cases similar to the Gard/Evans cases, setting out two different alternatives for evaluating the harm of prolonging life in children with absent consciousness.

[1] D Wilkinson and J Savulescu, *Ethics, Conflict and Medical Treatment for Children: From Disagreement to Dissensus* (Edinburgh, Elsevier, 2018).

[2] I Goold, 'Evaluating Best Interests as a Threshold for Judicial Intervention', chapter 2 above.

1. Harm or Best Interests in the Case of Charlie Gard?

In the Gard case, part of the first legal appeal focused on when courts may override parental wishes. The High Court had previously heard evidence about the risks and benefits of prolonging life-sustaining treatment (and seeking experimental therapy) for Charlie Gard. Justice Francis had cited the previous case of Wyatt, noting that 'the intellectual milestones for the judge in a case such as the present are, therefore, simple, although the ultimate decision will frequently be extremely difficult. The judge must decide what is in the child's best interests.'[3] Justice Francis concluded that it would be in Charlie's best interests to withdraw treatment and allow him to die.

However, Charlie's parents argued in the Court of Appeal that this was the wrong standard to apply. Their lawyers claimed that:

> [T]he court may not interfere with a decision by parents in the exercise of their parental rights and responsibilities with regard to their child's medical treatment, save where *there is a risk the parents' proposed course of action may cause significant harm* [emphasis added].[4]

One of the arguments that the legal team drew on in support of this claim made an analogy with the legal approach to placing children in care. The UK Children Act 1989 sets out when public authorities can remove a child from their parents. Social services in the UK can obtain a court order only if 'the court is satisfied that the child concerned is suffering or is likely to suffer significant harm, and that the harm, or likelihood of harm, is attributable to parental care or the child being beyond parental control'.[5]

But if the 'harm threshold' is the standard for the state intervening in parental everyday decisions – why shouldn't that also apply to medical decisions? The legal team representing Charlie's parents suggested that in cases where parents have an alternative viable treatment option to that proposed by doctors, the test should not be whether one of these is 'better'. Instead, the parents' wishes should be overridden only if their preferred treatment plan would be significantly harmful.

That was the argument put to the Court of Appeal. The judges in that court ultimately rejected it. As a point of law in the UK, medical treatment cases *are* treated differently from decisions about when local authorities can take over the care of a child. In the case of Alfie Evans, the Supreme Court reached a similar conclusion.[6]

That still leaves the ethical question unanswered – *should* we use the harm threshold for deciding when parents' wishes about medical treatment should be

[3] *Portsmouth NHS Trust v Wyatt* [2005] 1 FLR 21.

[4] *Yates and Anor v Great Ormond Street Hospital for Children NHS Foundation Trust & Anor (Rev 1)* [2017] EWCA Civ 410 (*Yates*), [54].

[5] Children Act 1989, s 31.

[6] *In the matter of Alfie Evans* [2018] UKSC Permission to appeal determination 20 March.

respected or refused? If we think the answer to that is right, it may be that the law should change.

2. Definitions, Distinction

In order to be clear about what is at stake, it would be useful to clarify the two different ways of resolving disputes about medical treatment between doctors and parents.

- *Best interests test:* A decision should be reached based on an assessment of which course of action would promote the best interests of the child. Parents' wishes about treatment should be followed only if they are consistent with the child's best interests
- *Harm threshold test*: A decision should be reached based on an assessment of whether the default decision-maker's chosen course of action would be harmful. Parents' wishes should ordinarily be respected, unless what they are requesting will cause the child to suffer or is likely to cause the child to suffer significant harm.

One important issue, if a harm threshold is employed, is what would count as a sufficient magnitude of harm, or a sufficient chance of harm, for intervention to be justified. Different accounts of the harm threshold employ different language. For example, the Children Act refers to 'significant harm'. Diekema refers to a 'significant risk of serious preventable harm'.[7] For this chapter, I will employ the language used in the Children Act, but will largely set aside what level of harm this refers to.

There are two different settings in which disputes may occur. Parents may be refusing a recommended course of treatment for the child. Alternatively, they may be requesting or demanding that treatment be provided or continued for their child. Important ethical differences between these two types of conflict will become apparent.

3. Three Ethical Arguments in Defence of the Harm Threshold

Although the Gard case is the first court case in the UK (to my knowledge) where the issue of harm thresholds has been raised directly, there has been active debate

[7] DS Diekema, 'Parental Refusals of Medical Treatment: The Harm Principle as Threshold for State Intervention' (2004) 25 *Theoretical Medicine and Bioethics* 243.

over the best interests test within bioethics for more than two decades.[8] There is wide agreement that 'best interests' represents a laudable *goal* for decision-making about children. The United Nations Declaration on the Rights of the Child states the child's best interests should be a 'primary consideration' when decisions are made about them.[9] However, it seems more problematic to use best interests as a *threshold* for deciding whether courts should overrule parents.[10] Here are three reasons for this concern.

A. Moral Uncertainty

Critics of the best interests standard have argued that it is unknowable or 'vague'.[11] This points to the difficulty in many cases of knowing what, exactly, would be best for a child. When it comes to a decision about medical treatment (should it or shouldn't it be provided), the best interests test appears to imply that there is a simple yes or no answer to the question. If treatment is in a child's best interests, it should be provided; if it isn't in the child's best interests, it shouldn't (Figure 5.1).

That answer, however, appears hopelessly simplistic when we reflect on the typical cases where medical treatment is under dispute. Cases of conflict have often arisen over life-sustaining treatment for a child. They are often situations where parents wish for treatment to continue, but health professionals believe that this offers no benefit to the child (and may be harmful). The assessment of best interests in such cases involves weighing up the benefits of life (including an assessment of the quality of a child's life) against the harms of invasive medical treatment. This is a profoundly difficult assessment to make, partly because of uncertainty about what might lie ahead for the child. Yet, the difficulty also arises from the fundamentally value-laden nature of the decision. Even if a child's future quality of life were known with certainty, even if we could predict accurately the amount of pain/pleasure they would experience, the ethical difficulty would remain.[12] How much weight should we give to different benefits or harms?

[8] LM Kopelman, 'The Best-Interests Standard as Threshold, Ideal, and Standard of Reasonableness' (1997) 22 *Journal of Medicine and Philosophy*; Diekema (n 7); R McDougall, C Delany and L Gillam (eds), *When Doctors and Parents Disagree: Ethics Paediatrics and the Zone of Parental Discretion* (Sydney, Federation Press, 2016); RJ McDougall and L Notini, 'Overriding Parents' Medical Decisions for Their Children: A Systematic Review of Normative Literature' (2014) 40 *Journal of Medical Ethics* 448; JC Bester, 'The Harm Principle Cannot Replace the Best Interest Standard: Problems with Using the Harm Principle for Medical Decision Making for Children' (2018) 18 *American Journal of Bioethics* 9; G Birchley, 'Harm Is All You Need? Best Interests and Disputes about Parental Decision-Making' (2016) 42 *Journal of Medical Ethics* 111; R Dresser, 'Standards for Family Decisions: Replacing Best Interests with Harm Prevention' (2003) 3 *American Journal of Bioethics* 54.

[9] D Archard, 'Children's Rights' (2008) *Stanford Encyclopedia of Philosophy*, https://plato.stanford.edu/entries/rights-children/.

[10] Diekema (n 7).

[11] RM Veatch, 'Abandoning Informed Consent' (1995) 25 *Hastings Centre Report* 5; H Brody and WG Bartholome, 'In the Best Interests of' (1988) 18 *Hastings Centre Report* 37; Kopelman (n 8).

[12] D Wilkinson, *Death or Disability? The Carmentis Machine and Treatment Decisions for Critically Ill Children* (Oxford, Oxford University Press, 2013).

Figure 5.1 The best interests test

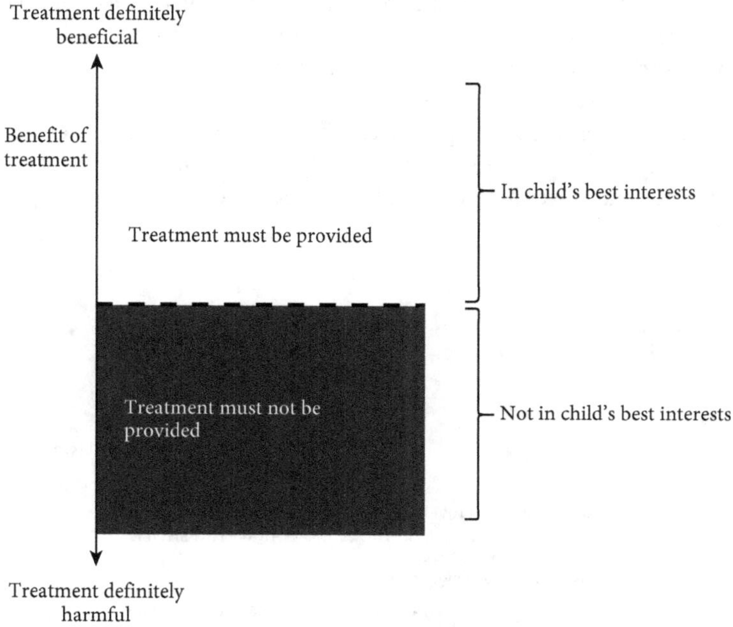

How should we weigh up the benefit of continued existence (for example, in a state of minimal consciousness) against the discomfort of medical treatment? These are questions of substantial moral uncertainty, on which there can be a range of different reasonable viewpoints.[13]

The challenge for the best interests test in the setting of moral uncertainty is that there can be, and often are, competing views about what would be best for the child. In that setting, it seems a problem for courts to be tasking themselves with identifying a single 'best' course of action.

Moral uncertainty does not always undermine decisions made on the basis of best interests for a child. There are some cases that are clear-cut. For example, paradigm cases include parental refusal of a blood transfusion for a child (for example, because of their religious belief), or parental requests for mutilating female circumcision. In those instances, there is not genuine moral uncertainty about the benefits and harms of the requested treatment. There is not reasonable disagreement about the pros and cons of intervening in such instances.

Clear cases (such as parental refusal of a transfusion) do sometimes reach the court. However, perhaps predictably, the most contentious cases are not so

[13] Wilkinson and Savulescu (n 1).

clear (Figure 5.2). The cases where moral uncertainty raises problems are those where the benefits or harms of treatment are relatively small or uncertain. Table 5.1 identifies a set of possible cases of this type. Case A (transfusion) and F (infibulation) are clear cases, whereas cases B–E are ones where there is more uncertainty. It is relevant that the benefits/harms are relatively small in magnitude in these cases. That is because there is more scope for reasonable disagreement about the balance of benefits and burdens. Others may reasonably reach a different conclusion about whether treatment is overall in the interests of the child.

Figure 5.2 Harm thresholds

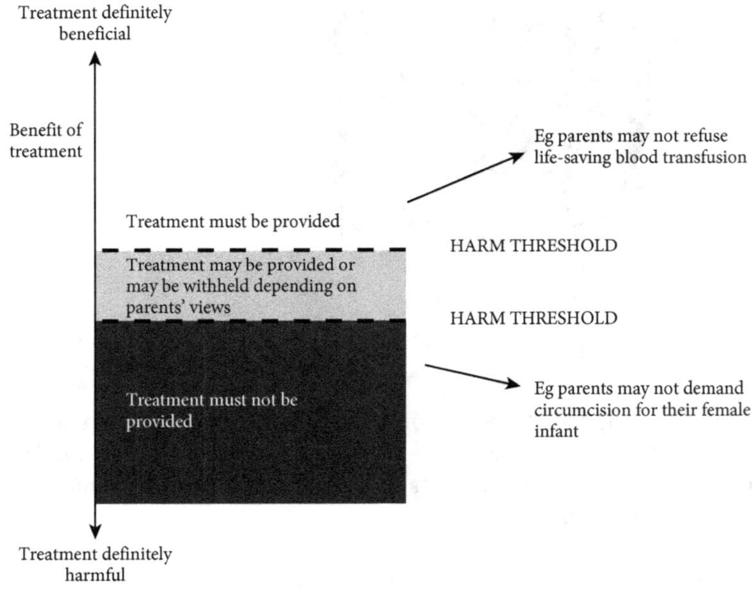

Table 5.1 The spectrum of decisions. Rows highlighted in grey are those where there is plausibly moral uncertainty about providing treatment. Case X appears in multiple rows as, depending how the harms and benefits of treatment are evaluated, it may be considered to fit into several different categories (see text)

	Example	
Refusal of medical treatment where benefit is certain and significant	A.	Blood transfusion in a child following trauma (parents are Jehovah's Witnesses)
Refusal of medical treatment where benefit is certain, but is small	B.	Immunisation against a common childhood illness (chance of severe complications is very small)

(continued)

Table 5.1 ***(Continued)***

		Example
Refusal of medical treatment where benefit is uncertain	C.	Life-prolonging treatment in a newborn with severe brain injury[14] (X. Prolonged life-sustaining treatment – absent consciousness)
Request for medical treatment without benefit	D.	Complementary medicine (no scientific evidence to substantiate, but risks negligible) (X. Prolonged life-sustaining treatment – absent consciousness)
Request for medical treatment where harm is certain, but is small Request for medical treatment where harm is uncertain	E.	Male circumcision. Minimal forms of female circumcision[15] (X. Prolonged life-sustaining treatment – absent consciousness)
Request for medical treatment where harm is certain and significant	F.	Infibulation (X. Prolonged life-sustaining treatment – absent consciousness)

B. Value of Parental Freedom

If there is genuine moral uncertainty about whether a proposed course of action is in the best interests of a child, whose view should be followed? One intuitive response to that question is that parents' wishes should usually be respected.

There are several reasons to give weight to parents' interests and views in decision-making.[16] One reason is that the interests of the child and those of parents often overlap and are interdependent. Parents may be in a unique epistemic position to assess the interests of the child – they may be in a better position than the health professionals to assess the child's quality of life and predict their ability to cope with treatment.[17] Beyond that, though, we usually think that it is good for parents to have significant latitude in deciding how to bring up their child. After the child, they are the ones likely to be most affected by those decisions. Parents may seek guidance and advice in how to raise their children. It is, though, a necessary part of parenthood for parents to make ethical evaluations and choices.

Parental freedom to make decisions for and about their children is closely linked to respect for individual autonomy. However, parents' freedom to decide

[14] D Wilkinson, 'A Life Worth Giving: The Threshold for Permissible Withdrawal of Treatment from Disabled Newborn Infants' (2010) 11 *American Journal of Bioethics* 20.

[15] DS Davis, 'Ritual Genital Cutting of Female Minors' (2010) 125 *Pediatrics* 1088.

[16] D Wilkinson, 'How Much Weight Should We Give to Parental Interests in Decisions About Life Support for Newborn Infants?' (2010) 20 *Monash Bioethical Review* 13.1.

[17] ibid.

about treatment for their children is more constrained than their freedom to decide about their own health. That constraint is the important concern to avoid causing harm to the child. Yet, if parents' decision about medical treatment for a child would *not* cause significant harm to the child, what business is it of doctors, or of the state to intervene?[18]

C. Consistency

Finally, the harm threshold should apply to legal disputes about medical treatment as a matter of simple ethical consistency. This is the threshold that applies elsewhere in life and in medicine.[19]

As already noted, the harm threshold is used in cases where there are decisions about taking a child into care. Children will only be removed from their parents if remaining with the parents would pose a significant risk of serious harm. More generally, though, parents make a wide range of decisions that are suboptimal. Whether deciding what to feed their children, what school to send them to, how much screen-time they should be permitted, or what activities or interests to encourage or support, parents constantly fail to maximise their children's interests. That reflects, in part, the fallibility of parents. Parents do not always know what would be best, or (even when they know better) make the right choices. It reflects, too, the necessary conflict between the interests of family members. When parents have more than one child, there are often decisions that may be better for one child, but worse for another. There is simply no way to maximise all of their interests. Moreover, the interests of children compete with those of parents. Optimal choices for children may require very substantial sacrifice of the parents' own wellbeing. How much sacrifice must parents make? We do not usually think that the state should interfere whenever parents fail to optimise the child's wellbeing.

In medical decisions, it isn't usually thought that doctors' views about treatment should always predominate and that parents' wishes should be ignored. Paediatricians and general practitioners spend a good deal of time counselling parents and encouraging them to make healthcare decisions for their children that are likely to promote the child's interests. However, if parents make suboptimal decisions, professionals will usually only seek to override parents if what parents have

[18] Similar points are raised in this current volume in the chapters by Goold (n 1) and R Taylor, 'Parental Decisions and Court Jurisdiction: Best Interests or Significant Harm?', chapter 3 above.

[19] Taylor (n 18) argues that the law is not inconsistent in its use of these thresholds. The courts apply the harm threshold to situations where local authorities are seeking 'ongoing state involvement in the life of the child … [and] ongoing discretional authority over the child's life'. In contrast, for specific decisions, the court can make decisions on the basis of the welfare of the child under its 'inherent jurisdiction', or under s 8 of the Children Act. My argument here is not that the law is inconsistent, or being applied inconsistently – rather that there is ethical inconsistency in overruling parents' decisions about medical treatment if they are not in the child's best interests, but only overruling other decisions (around education, diet, religious practice, etc) if they would be significantly harmful.

decided poses a real risk of harming the child. Table 5.1 indicates some examples where, in fact, parents may not be making decisions in the best interests of a child, but those decisions are usually respected. In practice, in cases such as B–E, treatments/interventions are sometimes provided and sometimes not provided, largely on the basis of parents' wishes. For example, it is not in a child's interests to receive a complementary medicine that has no scientific or medical basis and offers no plausible benefit. However, so long as there is no reason to think that it would be harmful, such treatments are commonly given to children, and health professionals do not oppose this. It is in a child's interests to be immunised, to have vitamin K prophylaxis or to have newborn screening tests. Yet, health professionals do not normally invoke child protection proceedings if parents refuse these interventions.[20] Although paediatricians are often discomfited and disquieted when parents decline their recommendations, they do not seek to impose their own views for the reasons already highlighted: there is often some degree of moral uncertainty about how to weigh up the risks and benefits of treatments; there is clear social value in allowing parents (within reason) broad discretion to make decisions about their children; there would be significant harm, both to children and to families, and substantial costs (in time and resources) if legal mechanisms were employed to enforce mandatory treatment against parental opposition.

4. Counterarguments to the Harm Threshold

A. No Difference

Some critics of the harm threshold argue that it is unnecessary to seek any change in the threshold for intervention because harm is already incorporated into the best interests test as it is applied by courts.[21] On this view, a change in the threshold would make no difference. In the Gard case, it was suggested in the Court of Appeal that a decision based on harm would have been identical to the decision that was made on the basis of best interests.

> [T]he judge was not invited to consider the law in the way that it is now put before this court, let alone to consider the existence of 'Category 2' cases with the need to establish a threshold for significant harm. … It is clear, in my view, that if the judge had been invited to form a conclusion on whether Charlie was or was not suffering significant harm currently, that finding would have been made.[22]

[20] Giles Birchley's empirical research, described in his chapter, supports the notion that something like a harm threshold is, in fact, employed by clinicians in deciding whether to respect, or oppose parental wishes about treatment. G Birchley, 'Parental Decisions and Court Jurisdiction: Best Interests or Significant Harm?', chapter 6 below.

[21] C Foster, 'Harm: As Indeterminate as "Best Interests", but Useful for Triage' (2016) 42 *Journal of Medical Ethics* 121; TM Pope, 'The Best Interest Standard for Health Care Decision Making: Definition and Defense' (2018) 18 *American Journal of Bioethics* 36.

[22] *Yates* (n 4) para 114.

One way of understanding this argument is conceptual. Harms and benefits can be seen as opposite sides of a coin. If an intervention would be in someone's interests, it would be harmful to withhold that intervention. Conversely, if it would be harmful to provide a particular treatment, it would be in the patient's best interests not to do this.

However, on conceptual grounds this seems to be a mistake. First, harms are typically understood as a thwarting or a setback in someone's interests.[23] That is different from failing to promote or enhance an interest. (Compared with a neutral reference point, one makes the child worse, the other fails to make them better.) Second, harms and benefits are often thought to be asymmetric. The claim (consistent with many people's intuitions) is that it is *worse* to harm than to fail to benefit.[24] This necessarily implies that failure to benefit does not always constitute harm. Third, the harm threshold (but not the best interests test) includes an assessment of the magnitude of change for the child. There must be *significant* harm. It might be in a child's best interests to have a second helping of supper (because, for example, they are still hungry and desire it) – but it seems to be a quite different claim to suggest that they would be harmed by not having an additional serving.

It is worth pointing out that the fact that best interests and harm *converge* in some cases does not prove that the two tests are coterminous. Although it is *not* the case that withholding treatment that is in the child's interests is necessarily a significant harm, the opposite does hold. *If* a particular course of action would pose a significant risk of serious harm, it must be the case that this would not be in the child's best interests. It may be that in many cases of disputed treatment that come before the courts, the harm threshold has been crossed. If so, the same decision would be justified using either the harm threshold test or the best interests test. Yet that does not prove that in *all* cases the two tests would reach identical conclusions.[25]

As highlighted above in section 3.A, it seems too simplistic to claim that treatment must be either in or against a child's interests. Given moral uncertainty, there are situations where it may or may not be in the child's interests to provide treatment.

Furthermore, where the benefits or harms of treatment are small, there are clear cases where a determination of the child's best interests and assessment of significant harm diverge. One example is that of routine immunisation. There have been some cases that have come before the court where those with parental authority

[23] J Feinberg, *The Moral Limits of the Criminal Law: Harm to Others* (Oxford, Oxford University Press, 1984).

[24] D Alm, 'Deontological Restrictions and the Good/Bad Asymmetry' (2009) 6 *Journal of Moral Philosophy* 464; FM Kamm, *Intricate Ethics: Rights, Responsibilities, and Permissible Harm* (Oxford, Oxford University Press, 2009), 17; D Benatar, *Better Never to Have Been: The Harm of Coming into Existence* (Oxford, Clarendon Press, 2006).

[25] I will return in section 5 to specifically discuss the question of whether applying a form of harm threshold test to the Gard and Evans cases would have led to a different decision.

have disagreed about whether their child should be immunised.[26] In those cases, the courts have consistently concluded that immunisation *would* be in the child's interests.[27] However, it does not seem at all likely that a court would (in a situation where parents are in agreement) conclude that refusal of a routine childhood immunisation constitutes significant harm. It seems highly unlikely that a court would (in the absence of other, more clearly harmful behaviour) authorise immunisation against the parents' wishes.

B. Harm (to Children, to Families)

A second potential objection to the harm threshold is that this would be damaging to both children and families. For example, it could be claimed that use of the harm threshold test rather than the best interests test would threaten the wellbeing of children, allowing their interests to be compromised for the sake of the interests of parents or other family members. (We might imagine, for example, that parents do not wish a child to have surgery because it would interfere with their professional career.) Yet the harm threshold, *by definition*, does not permit children to receive (or be denied) treatment where that would be harmful to them. It does not mean that the interests of the child are ignored; where treatment is clearly in the interests of the child, it must be provided. Furthermore, as noted in section 3.C above, the harm threshold already applies to parental care of children in most circumstances and to most medical decisions. That is not thought to constitute a breach of children's rights.

The harm threshold might be damaging in a different way if it led to families (in cases of disputed medical treatment) being treated as though they seek to deliberately harm their children.[28] For example, if a court decided that the course of action favoured by parents represented a significant harm to the child, would that mean that the family's care of other children would be examined by social services, or their children would be removed from their care?

Barristers Katie Gollop and Sarah Pope have advanced this argument against a harm threshold, drawing on a case of disputed treatment for a child where a local authority had applied a significant harm test and taken a child protection approach.[29] When a mother disagreed with health professionals about provision

[26] *Re SL (Permission to Vaccinate)* [2017] EWHC 125 (Fam); *B (A Child: Immunisation)* [2018] EWFC 56.

[27] R English, 'Should Courts Order Vaccination against Parents' Wishes?' (8 February 2017) www.ukhumanrightsblog.com/2017/02/08/should-courts-order-vaccination-against-parents-wishes/ (accessed 12 December 2018).

[28] Birchley (n 20); Taylor (n 18).

[29] K Gollop and S Pope, 'Charlie Gard, Alfie Evans and R (A Child): Why a Medical Treatment Significant Harm Test Would Hinder not Help' (22 May 2018) www.transparencyproject.org.uk/charlie-gard-alfie-evans-and-r-a-child-why-a-medical-treatment-significant-harm-test-would-hinder-not-help/.

of antibiotics for her severely disabled daughter, the local authority obtained an interim care order, and 'used every occasion on which R's mother had not accepted medical advice to build its case on significant harm'.[30] The child was placed in residential care, with restricted access from her mother, over a period of six months while a final hearing was awaited.

If families were to be stigmatised, scrutinised or unfairly treated as a consequence of using the harm threshold for treatment decisions, this would unquestionably be of concern. However, it is worth pointing out that this sort of problem depends entirely on how a harm threshold test is applied to medical treatment decisions. There is nothing intrinsic in the test itself that means that families would be so treated, and some reason to think that they wouldn't.

The Children Act stipulates a presumption (unless shown otherwise) that involvement of parents in the life of the child will further the child's welfare (section 2A). The courts aim to make orders that will cause the least disruption to the child's life. Where parents have requested a treatment, and a court has found that this treatment should not be provided (because it would be harmful), there is no reason to think that it would be in the child's best interests to be removed from the parents' care. This would certainly not count as being the least disruptive course for the child.

Secondly, it is the case at present in UK law that the harm threshold test is primarily invoked in situations where there is concern that the child should be removed from the parents' care. That means that local authorities, health professionals and the courts currently focus on whether remaining in the parents' custody would pose a risk to the child. If the test were to be applied, however, to *specific* medical treatment issues, there would be a different focus of enquiry. The question would be on whether the treatment (or refusal of it) poses a risk of significant harm – not whether the *parents* pose a risk of significant harm. For that reason, such an enquiry need not be inquisitorial, stigmatising,[31] and contrary to the ideal of seeking consensus between professionals and parents in the way that Gollop and Pope fear.

C. Indeterminacy

One counter-argument to the harm threshold has been that the concept of harm is just as vague and indeterminate as 'best interests'.[32] If it is difficult to work out

[30] ibid.

[31] One separate argument against a harm threshold is that the language of 'harm' is itself stigmatising or damaging to parents. Birchley (n 20); Gollop and Pope (n 29). It is an open empirical question whether parents would find it more difficult or just as difficult to come to terms with a court decision that continued life-sustaining treatment for their child is 'significantly harmful' rather than 'not in their best interests'. Gollop and Pope note that '[p]erhaps no linguistic usage or avoidance helps, when the person who is yours to care for is taken away from you against your will' (I would add – 'or when a loved child is allowed to die when you had desperately hoped that they would survive').

[32] Birchley (n 20); Bester (n 9).

whether it would be best to continue or to withdraw life-prolonging treatment in a seriously ill child, it may also be difficult to decide if it would be harmful to do this. The harm threshold incorporates an assessment of the magnitude of harm ('significant'). Yet, there is then a challenge in determining how to define or determine the significance of a putative harm.[33]

However, although the harm threshold may be vague, there is no reason to think that it is any more vague that the best interests test.[34] Indeterminacy would not provide an argument against the harm threshold – merely undermine one possible argument in its favour. If the harm threshold were only being used in place of the best interests test because of its putative ease of use, or because the best interests were 'vague' – these objections would be particularly important. However, as noted above, there are several arguments in favour of the harm threshold that do not depend on it being clear or determinate (consistency, the importance of respecting parents' wishes, moral uncertainty).

D. Requiring Professionals to Provide Treatment against Better Judgement

In cases that have come to the court (including *Gard* and *Evans*), paediatricians have felt strongly that life-prolonging treatment should be withdrawn because it was not in the child's best interests. However, if the harm threshold had been applied by the court, it is possible that the court would have concluded that treatment did not constitute a significant harm to the child.[35] What should happen then?

Should professionals be compelled to treat the child against their considered view of what would be helpful for the child? That may, understandably, lead to significant moral distress. Courts have traditionally been loath to impose on health professionals an obligation to provide medical treatment. (For example, a court order may provide permission to withdraw treatment, although professionals are

[33] J Savulescu, J Everett, DJC Wilkinson and T Nair, 'Settling for Second Best: When Should Doctors Agree to Parental Demands for Suboptimal Medical Treatment?' (2017) 43 *Journal of Medical Ethics* 831; L Gillam, 'The Zone of Parental Discretion: An Ethical Tool for Dealing with Disagreement between Parents and Doctors about Medical Treatment for a Child' (2015) 11 *Clinical Ethics* 1. As noted in section 2, it is beyond the scope of this chapter to set out where exactly the harm threshold should be drawn. In my co-authored book on the Gard case, I set out a process (the dissensus framework) that might be employed to determine whether the course of action pursued by parents should be permitted. Wilkinson and Savulescu (n 1).

[34] Shah, Rosenberg and Diekema have argued that although the harm threshold remains vague, it is *less vague* than best interests. SK Shah, AR Rosenberg and DS Diekema, 'Charlie Gard and the Limits of the Harm Principle – Reply' (2018) 172 *Journal of the American Medical Association Pediatrics* 301.

[35] Shah and coauthors argued in the wake of the Gard case, that the Harm Threshold, correctly applied to that case, would have permitted treatment SK Shah, AR Rosenberg and DS Diekema, 'Charlie Gard and the Limits of Best Interests' (2017) 171 *Journal of the American Medical Association Pediatrics* 937. I will return shortly to assess this specific question in more detail.

not obliged to do so.) Professionals may feel that continuing treatment would be contrary to their professional role, and conscientiously object to providing the treatment.[36] Furthermore, a requirement to continue treatment in such cases could lead to harm in other ways, even if it wouldn't risk significant harm to the child. Requests for suboptimal treatment may harm other children through consuming limited medical resources.[37] I have elsewhere highlighted the significance of resource limitations in judgements about futility in intensive care.[38] In my book on the Gard case, I outline the importance of separating out consideration of limited resources in treatment disputes.[39] Even if treatment would not be harmful to the child, it would be wrong to continue to provide that treatment if that would thereby mean that other children were unable to access intensive care.

5. The Conditional Harm Threshold

I have defended the idea that the harm threshold provides the correct normative test for overruling parents' decisions about medical treatment for a child. Yet, there is still an important role for the best interests test in relation to medical treatment for children. That is, firstly, because some situations cannot be resolved by invoking the concept of harm. Table 5.2 illustrates situations where it would be ethically inappropriate to invoke a harm threshold. In those situations, decisions must be based on a consideration of what would be best for the child. For example, in situations where parents are in conflict about treatment for a child, it is not possible to apply a harm threshold.

Second, the *ideal* is for the child's interests to guide decision-making and for those making decisions to make the best available choice for the child. The best interests test is what parents and health professionals *should* apply in order to reach decisions about treatment. Doctors should recommend courses of action that would be best for the child, and discourage choices that would be suboptimal.

Thirdly, as argued above, it would be ethically problematic for doctors to be required to provide treatment that they believe would not be in a child's best interests, or would be contrary to the interests of other patients.

For these reasons, it may be appropriate for the default legal test to remain best interests. However, this could be supplemented by a harm threshold in some specific situations. In the following sections I will set out both when a harm threshold should be applied, and what the implications might be.

[36] D Wilkinson, 'Conscientious Non-Objection in Intensive Care' (2017) 26 *Cambridge Quaterley of Healthcare Ethics* 132. The courts in the UK have usually, in disputed treatment cases, indicated that they will not (and are unable to) take into account these sorts of issues.

[37] Savulescu et al (n 33).

[38] D Wilkinson, P Stavros and J Savulescu, 'Expensive Care? Resource-Based Thresholds for Potentially Inappropriate Treatment in Intensive Care' (2018) 35 *Monash Bioethics Review* 2.

[39] Wilkinson and Savulescu (n 1).

Table 5.2 Situations where a harm threshold test cannot apply to medical decisions

a. Absent decision-maker	Where both parents (and anyone else with parental responsibility) are incapacitated or absent, and a decision needs to be made. The court may need to make a decision on behalf of the child (or appoint a surrogate to do this).
b. Conflict between parents	Those with parental responsibility to make decisions on behalf of a child are unable to reach agreement
c. Conflict between health professionals	Health professionals are in conflict about what would be best for a child, and parents are unable to decide.
d. Health professional/parental uncertainty	Health professionals are uncertain about whether a particular course of action would be best for a child (or legal) and have sought a court determination.

A. Refusal of Treatment

Where parents are declining medical treatment that health professionals believe would be in the best interests of the child, parents may enact their refusal by not presenting the child to medical care or by removing the child from a healthcare environment. Consider the following example:

> *Refusal:* A newborn infant is born following a normal delivery and an uncomplicated pregnancy. The infant is due to be discharged home, but one of the midwives calls the paediatric team as the parents have declined prophylaxis with vitamin K. (Intramuscular vitamin K injections are provided to newborns to prevent a rare life-threatening complication – haemorrhagic disease of the newborn.) Should the doctor seek a court order to compel vitamin K prophylaxis?

In *Refusal*, the parents are declining a routine intervention that is part of normal newborn care. The paediatricians may try to persuade the parents that their child should have the injection. There is good reason to think that this would be in the best interests of the child. However, if the parents continue to refuse, they may decide to leave the hospital. For the child to receive the vitamin K, the doctors would need to restrain the parents from leaving hospital, or remove the child from the parents' care. That would be possible, but would be require making an urgent application to the court for an Interim Care Order.[40] The legal threshold for care proceedings would be the harm threshold. (In my personal experience of such cases, social workers or hospital lawyers would almost certainly not pursue a court

[40] This was what happened in the case of Ashya King, a five-year old boy with a brain tumour, whose parents did not wish him to have conventional radiotherapy (they sought a new treatment – proton beam therapy). When his parents removed him from Southampton Hospital, the local authority filed an application in the High Court to make him a ward of court, on the basis that he was at significant risk of harm. *In the matter of Ashya King (A child)* [2014] EWHC 2964.

order unless there was good reason to fear significant harm from the refusal of treatment.)

Because parents can simply remove the child from a place of treatment, in cases of parental refusal of treatment, a dispute about treatment would already be likely to involve the harm threshold if health professionals seek court intervention. There would be no need for a supplementary test.

B. Demands for Treatment

Where parents are demanding medical treatment, the ethical considerations are slightly different. For a health professional to withhold the treatment would not involve physically restraining the parents or removing the child from the child's care. Moreover, as highlighted above, it would be problematic if the harm threshold meant that professionals felt compelled to provide treatment that they feel is of no or minimal benefit to the child. That would potentially be harmful to other children – by consuming limited resources. Consider the following case:

> *Provision:* An infant is born following a normal delivery and an uncomplicated pregnancy. The child's parents have been reading about haemorrhagic disease of the newborn and had a friend whose baby tragically died from this complication despite normal preventative measures.[41] They have accepted routine vitamin K for their child; however, they are requesting the paediatrician to take blood for a full set of coagulation studies on their child, and to give their child an additional intramuscular dose of vitamin K at 4 weeks of age, in order to reduce even further the risk of this complication.[42] Should the paediatrician provide the treatment?

In *Provision*, the paediatrician may believe that what the parents are requesting is not in the child's best interests. There is no reason to think that the child is at increased risk of this rare condition (notwithstanding the parents' concern). The downsides of what the parents are requesting are relatively small (an extra blood test and an extra injection), but the benefits of doing so seem negligible.[43] However, even if what the parents are requesting does not constitute a significant harm, it does not seem that the paediatrician should be obliged to do what the parents are asking. The paediatrician may be mindful that it would constitute a waste of limited medical resources to be performing a blood test and providing a medication without any reason to think that these would be of benefit. In this case,

[41] VH Flood, FC Galderisi, SR Lowas, A Kendrick and LK Boshkov, 'Hemorrhagic Disease of the Newborn Despite Vitamin K Prophylaxis at Birth' (2008) 50 *Pediatric Blood & Cancer* 1075.

[42] MS Elalfy, IA Elagouza, FA Ibrahim, SK AbdElmessieh and M Gadallah, 'Intracranial Haemorrhage Is Linked to Late Onset Vitamin K Deficiency in Infants Aged 2–24 Weeks' (2014) 103 *Acta Paediatrica* e273.

[43] One estimate puts the risk of vitamin K deficiency bleeding in infants who have received the standard prophylaxis as <1 in a million; AW McNinch and JH Tripp, 'Haemorrhagic Disease of the Newborn in the British Isles: Two Year Prospective Study' (1991) 303 *British Medical Journal* 1105.

the resource implications of providing the treatment are small – the cost of these interventions is pretty minimal. However, in other cases (for example, in intensive-care cases), provision of treatments that have no evidence of benefit would clearly have significant resource implications. Furthermore, allowing, as a general principle, parents to demand medical treatments that have no scientific evidence to support benefit, would have enormous implications for a publicly funded healthcare system. We might consider, though, a variation of the case where the situation is different.

> *Preventing Provision:* An infant is born following a normal delivery and an uncomplicated pregnancy. The child's parents wish the child to have an additional blood test and injection because of their fear of haemorrhagic disease of the newborn. The paediatrician refuses to offer this intervention, and parents leave the consultation dissatisfied. Subsequently, the paediatrician learns that the child's GP has agreed. Should the paediatrician seek court intervention to prevent the GP from performing the blood test/giving the additional injection?

In *Preventing Provision*, the paediatrician would not be refusing to provide treatment, but would be seeking to limit the parents' freedom to access treatment (as well as impacting on the freedom of the other healthcare provider).

Perhaps the GP is aware of evidence that the paediatrician has not considered? The paediatrician may have reason to reconsider her views about the child's best interests. However, even if the paediatrician is right that these interventions are not in the child's interests, it seems a further step is required to justify intervening. The harm threshold (in a more restricted form) should apply to cases such as *Preventing Provision*.

Since it applies only to cases where additional conditions apply, I have denoted it the conditional harm threshold.

> *Conditional harm threshold test:* A decision to prevent parents from accessing a particular treatment option should be based on an assessment of whether the chosen course of action would be harmful. Where the following conditions apply, parents' wishes should ordinarily be respected, unless what they are requesting will cause the child to suffer or is likely to cause the child to suffer significant harm:
>
> i. The parents are requesting provision or continuation of a medical treatment for the child.
> ii. The child's health professionals do not support that treatment.
> iii. Other suitably qualified health professionals are prepared to provide that treatment and any ongoing care necessary (including if necessary, transfer of the child to another health facility).[44]

[44] As noted at the start of this chapter, my focus here is largely on ethics rather than law. I set aside for those with legal expertise whether a conditional harm threshold would require a change to the Children Act. One possibility is that no change would be required. Parents could request and arrange transfer of their child's care to another health professional. If a health care team wished to prevent this, they could seek a care order (using the harm threshold).

The conditional harm threshold restricts parents from seeking medical treatment in cases such as *Preventing Provision*. It is similar to the test that the Gard parents' lawyers had argued should apply in their case. It would not require health professionals to provide treatment that would be contrary to their professional judgement or would harm other patients. It would sanction courts overriding parents on the same basis as court intervention in other parental decisions.

C. Implications of the Conditional Harm Threshold – Prolonged Unconsciousness

I have elsewhere (with Julian Savulescu) explored in detail when treatment requested by parents would or would not cross the harm threshold.[45] In particular, we defend the importance of reasonable disagreement in establishing the moral uncertainty that underpins parental discretion over treatment. If there is reasonable disagreement about whether treatment would be in a child's best interests, parents' views should be decisive. In that work, we set out some characteristics that would help identify whether disagreement is reasonable or unreasonable.

For the final part of this chapter, however, I wish to focus on a distinctive type of situation where disagreement may occur. If a child has a severe disorder of their brain such that they are unconscious and have no prospect of recovering consciousness, is it a significant harm to prolong their life?

In Table 5.1, I refer to this situation as condition X: 'Prolonged life-sustaining treatment – absent consciousness'. This includes children in a persistent vegetative state, and closely related conditions (for example, a minimally conscious state). It is important, because this state (or a variation of it) was potentially the situation of the children in all three of the recent UK disputed cases (Gard, Haastrup, Evans). It is also ethically contentious because it is difficult to evaluate the putative harm of treatment in condition X. In Table 5.1, I indicate that there are four possible views about such cases. Treatment might be regarded as offering an uncertain benefit (since it prolongs life in the absence of consciousness), as offering zero benefit (since the child has no experience and no conscious interests), as offering uncertain harm (since the child might experience pain or discomfort), or offering certain harm (since it extends the dying process, risks causing suffering, and does not benefit the child). There are two possible ways that the conditional harm threshold might impact on future cases involving condition X.

i. No Significant Harm

One response to condition X is to suggest that treatment in such cases would offer uncertain benefit or harm. If the child truly is completely unconscious, he/she

[45] Wilkinson and Savulescu (n 1).

would not suffer pain or discomfort; however, neither would they ever experience any conscious benefit from continuing to live. That might support a view that treatment would be neither beneficial, nor harmful. However, the neuroscientific literature from adults in persistent vegetative state points to the challenge in distinguishing between patients with completely absent consciousness and those with some minimal level of consciousness.[46] A child in a condition like those of Alfie Evans or Charlie Gard might experience intermittent pain or discomfort, might have some awareness of their parents' presence, or might experience none at all.

Given such a state, it appears unclear whether it would be in the child's best interests to prolong their life. It would be permissible to withdraw life-prolonging treatment and allow the child to die, and health professionals may also decline to provide treatment on the basis that they do not consider it to be in the child's best interests. However, if parents have identified alternative health professionals who are prepared to provide treatment, the conditional harm threshold would, on this view, allow parents to pursue that treatment.

On this understanding of condition X, the best interests test and the conditional harm threshold test would diverge. Treatment would be withdrawn if courts assess best interests, but may be permitted if they apply a conditional harm threshold and the family are able to find another health provider willing to continue treatment.

ii. Significant Harm

However, it is not inevitable that the conditional harm threshold would permit treatment in condition X. As noted above, in the Court of Appeal, Justice MacFarlane indicated his belief that the initial judge (Justice Francis) would have regarded continued treatment (and experimental treatment) for Charlie Gard as being harmful.

There are two different ways of substantiating such a claim. The first would be to focus on the possibility of significant physical discomfort without corresponding benefit. That claim would depend on the child's specific circumstances. Intensive care and the forms of life-prolonging treatment that are often under dispute cause children to experience pain. For example, children who are dependent on mechanical ventilation require regular suctioning of tracheal secretions (which is potentially painful) and experience intermittent sensations of dyspnoea or choking. There are ways of alleviating those symptoms for patients in the short term, but it is more challenging to do this over a prolonged period, and it is likely that even with the best symptom management that children with condition X

[46] MM Monti et al, 'Willful Modulation of Brain Activity in Disorders of Consciousness' (2010) 362 *New England Journal of Medicine* 579; RM Gibson et al, 'Somatosensory Attention Identifies Both Overt and Covert Awareness in Disorders of Consciousness' (2016) 80 *Annals of Neurology* 412. To my knowledge, there have been no studies investigating covert consciousness in children with brain disorders

(if they are capable of perceiving anything at all) would experience some pain and discomfort. If there is a low magnitude of benefit from prolonging life, or there is a low probability of benefit, most children kept alive in such circumstances may be harmed. On that basis, I argued, at the time of the Gard case (and based on evidence as presented to the court) that it would be harmful to pursue experimental treatment.[47] This argument would be strongest in cases where there is evidence that a child is experiencing pain/discomfort, or there is good reason to suspect that they are. (Children with severe brain injury, or who are paralysed, may be unable to manifest usual signs of distress.)

The second justification for claiming that it would be a significant harm to keep a child alive with condition X is that this would compromise the child's wellbeing even if it did not lead to physical suffering. For example, it may be regarded as bad to prolong a child's dying phase if there is no realistic prospect of them recovering, or of gaining benefit from continued life. Alternatively, reference might be made to the child's dignity. The claim would be that it is undignified to prolong life artificially (for example, with mechanical ventilation or other invasive medical treatment) if the child has no capacity for conscious awareness.

There is some reference to non-subjective harms of this sort in the Gard and Evans cases. Justice Hayden rejected an argument that Alfie Evan's life lacked dignity. Nevertheless, he held that continuing treatment might compromise that value: 'He requires peace, quiet and privacy in order that he may conclude his life, as he has lived it, with dignity. … The continued provision of ventilation, in circumstances which I am persuaded is futile, now compromises Alfie's future dignity.'[48]

In an earlier case of a child with severe hypoxic brain injury (as well as underlying physical disability), Justice Macdonald made it clear how he understood the concept of dignity: '[W]hen it is recognised that life is ending, for many the concept of dignity becomes encapsulated by the idea of a "peaceful" or "good" death.'[49]

The courts may, therefore, regard it as a significant harm to prolong life in future cases of disputed treatment in condition X.[50] Such a determination would be consistent with the approach that UK courts have taken to end-of-life decisions in children with severe brain injury. I have elsewhere noted, however, that this line of argument is also challenging to defend because of the contested and conflicting accounts of what 'dignity' means at the end of life.[51]

[47] D Wilkinson, 'Beyond Resources: Denying Parental Requests for Futile Treatment' (2017) 389 *Lancet* 1866.

[48] *Alder Hey Children's NHS Foundation Trust v Evans & Anor* [2018] EWHC 308 (Fam), paras 62, 66.

[49] Kings College and MH [2015] EWHC 1920 (Fam) para 70.

[50] In the seminal case relating to treatment of an adult with absent consciousness – the case of Tony Bland – it was argued that it was a damage to his dignity to prolong his life by artificial means. *Airedale NHS Trust v Bland* [1993] AC 789.

[51] Wilkinson and Savulescu (n 1), 34–35.

6. Conclusions

The ethical and legal challenges raised by cases such as those of Charlie Gard or Alfie Evans are vexing and profound. They relate to the role of parents in decision-making for a child, the role of the state in overruling parents, and the role of courts in arbitrating disputes. There are conflicting interests at stake – the interests of parents, the interests of the child, the interests of wider society. And there are, inevitably, conflicting views about what would be best for the child. Any response to those challenges involves compromises, and will mean that some views are respected whereas others cannot be.

In this chapter, I have argued that as a general ethical principle, parents' views about medical decisions for their children should be respected, unless their choices would risk significant harm for their child. That does not dismiss the importance of 'best interests'. Health professionals and parents should continue to seek treatment that would be in a child's best interests. There is no obligation for health professionals to provide treatment that they reasonably judge to be not in the child's best interests, or an unjust use of limited medical resources. The best interests test may be applied by courts in cases where there is conflict between those with parental responsibility, or health professionals are uncertain which course to pursue. Where treatment is judged not to be in a child's best interests, health professionals may be given permission by the court to withdraw or withhold it.

I have articulated a form of compromise, a restricted role for the harm threshold in disputes about medical treatment: this should be applied in situations where health professionals or others wish to prevent parents from pursing treatment that other professionals are prepared to provide. In such cases, the harm threshold is the correct normative threshold for overruling parents. However, the implications of such a test will depend on how courts understand harm. In some of the most difficult cases, those relating to children with severe disorders of consciousness, the effect of the test will depend on an evaluation of the value of dying well, and the disvalue of possible suffering.

6

The Harm Threshold: A View from the Clinic

GILES BIRCHLEY

1. Introduction

It is a well-known legal trope that difficult cases make a bad basis for policy.[1] One such difficult case is that of Charlie Gard,[2] a high-profile disagreement between the parents and doctors of a critically ill infant with mitochondrial disease whose parents asserted it was in his best interests to receive an innovative treatment. In this chapter I shall argue that *Gard* proves no exception to this observation. 'Charlie's Law', drafted with the support of Charlie's parents, 'proposes to clarify the law around "best interests" and ensure families going through … difficult times are properly supported'.[3] Inter alia 'Charlie's Law' seeks to strengthen parental rights by preventing legal interference with parental decisions about their child's best interests unless the decision causes significant harm to the child – a so-called 'harm threshold'. The move would bring medical decisions into line with social decisions about children, for example those about education, religion or diet.[4] 'Charlie's Law' has support within Parliament and, while yet to influence the law, retains significant momentum.

The harm threshold has significant support in bioethics.[5] Its proponents claim numerous motivations, several of which are outlined in detail in this volume by

[1] M Brazier, 'Hard Cases Make Bad Law?' (1997) 23 *Journal of Medical Ethics* 341.

[2] The case went through multiple stages of appeal: *Great Ormond Street Hospital v Yates, Gard and Gard* [2017] EWHC 972 (Fam) (*Gard 1*); *Yates and Gard v Great Ormond Street Hospital for Children NHS Foundation Trust and Gard* [2017] EWCA Civ 410, [2018] 4 WLR 5 (*Gard 2*); *In the matter of Charlie Gard*, Supreme Court, 8 June 2017 (*Gard 3*); *Judgment of the UK Supreme Court in the Case of Charlie Gard*, 19 June 2017 (*Gard 4*); *Gard and others v the UK* (application no 39793/17) ECHR (*Gard 5*). An application to the European Court of Human Rights was rejected as 'inadmissible'.

[3] The Charlie Gard Foundation, 'Charlie's Law' (2018) www.thecharliegardfoundation.org/charlies-law/.

[4] R Taylor, 'Parental Decisions and Court Jurisdiction: Best Interests or Significant Harm?', chapter 3 above.

[5] F Schoeman, 'Parental Discretion and Children's Rights: Background and Implications for Medical Decision Making' (1985) 10 *Journal of Medicine and Philosophy* 45; R Dresser, 'Standards for Family

Dominic Wilkinson.[6] These arguments assert the following: (1) we allow suboptimality in other areas of parental decision-making. Therefore the absence of a harm threshold in medical law amounts to an unjustifiable inconsistency both with the way the law considers other types of parental decisions and with the usual catholic approach to parental decisions in medical practice; (2) the best interests test is too vague to deal with complex, value-laden decisions where benefits and harms are marginal and uncertain; and (3) parents have fundamental rights to autonomy. These are underpinned by the fact that parents have an epistemically privileged view of the welfare of their child and are most affected by any decisions that are made about their child. Although parental autonomy rights are not unrestricted, they should be constrained by the harm threshold rather than a test of best interests.

These arguments can be characterised as a rights claim on behalf of parents: that 'parental autonomy' is infringed by lack of a harm threshold in medical law. The arguments contain a mixture of normative and empirical claims, so my discussion is divided into two parts. The first part (A) investigates the empirical basis of the claim about parental decision-making in medical practice. It uses an analysis of interviews that reveal some thresholds of decision-making that are volunteered by parents and healthcare professionals in discussions about non-treatment decisions in paediatric intensive care. A number of thresholds occur. Although these suggest that a complex range of factors are considered, the dominant threshold adopted by parents is that a decision is best for the child, whereas the dominant threshold for clinicians is that a decision is best for the family. This indicates that healthcare professionals' approaches are indeed sensitive to the rights of parents. To some extent this bears out the analysis of clinical decision-making offered by proponents of the harm threshold. In the second part of the discussion (B), I take issue with the normative conclusion that this clinical picture means we ought to support the introduction of a harm threshold into medical law. I argue that a harm threshold is largely unmotivated because the current system of decision-making patently does consider the rights of parents as well as children. Although this may not be a good fit for some interpretations of the best interests standard, I suggest that this discord may arise from fundamental differences between clinical and legal decision-making. Proponents of the harm threshold may

Decisions: Replacing Best Interests with Harm Prevention' (2003) 3 *American Journal of Bioethics*, 54; S Diekema, 'Parental Refusals of Medical Treatment: The Harm Principle as Threshold for State Intervention' (2004) 25 *Theoretical Medicine and Bioethics* 243; RJ McDougall, 'Indeterminacy and the Normative Basis of the Harm Threshold for Overriding Parental Decisions: A Response to Birchley' (2016) 42 *Journal of Medical Ethics* 119; SK Shah, AR Rosenberg and DS Diekema, 'Charlie Gard and the Limits of Best Interests' (2017) 171 *Journal of the American Medical Association Pediatrics* 937; JP Winters, 'When Parents Refuse: Resolving Entrenched Disagreements Between Parents and Clinicians in Situations of Uncertainty and Complexity' (2018) 18 *American Journal of Bioethics* 20; D Wilkinson and J Savulescu, *Ethics, Conflict and Medical Treatment for Children: From Disagreement to Dissensus* (Edinburgh, Elsevier, 2019).

[6] D Wilkinson, 'In Defence of a Conditional Harm Threshold Test for Paediatric Decision-Making', chapter 5 above.

nevertheless be motivated simply by the desire to make medical law consistent with public law. I argue that there are differences in the level of certainty in clinical and social outcomes, that imply we need significantly more caution when making social welfare decisions. I also note that there may be unintended consequences from the adoption of the harm threshold that may impinge on the rights of parents and increase conflict in the healthcare arena. Finally, I argue that the very characterisation of arguments for parental rights as being about liberty is incorrect. Although I accept that the best interests test may be in need of reform, I deny that the harm threshold is the answer.

2. The Harm Threshold as a Current Issue

The case of Charlie Gard has excited interest in the harm threshold. Charlie Gard was a critically ill infant with a mitochondrial illness whose parents wished him to receive an experimental treatment, nucleoside therapy, offered by Professor Michael Hirano, a US neurologist. Professor Hirano had published a case series of 18 children with a related, but distinct, genetic illness. The research suggested that the treatment had a positive effect on that condition. The treatment was a dietary supplement, and thus involved minimal risks. Charlie's hospital initially agreed to a trial of the treatment having established (because the therapy could not reverse brain damage) that Charlie's brain was undamaged. However, before treatment was begun, Charlie did sustain severe brain damage, after suffering almost three weeks of persistent subclinical seizures (meaning that he was having continuous epileptic fits with no outward clinical signs). The damage was evidenced by severely abnormal electroencephalography (EEG) scans of his brain's electrical activity. His doctors and a second opinion from a specialist team from Barcelona agreed that further treatment would prolong Charlie's life without offering any hope of recovery, and thus further treatment would not in his best interests. While accepting that he was extremely ill, Charlie's parents did not accept that his condition was beyond help, and, importantly, did not accept that the EEG scans were accurate (because Charlie was receiving a sedative). Encouraged by Professor Hirano, who had not seen the scans, they continued to demand access to nucleoside therapy, for which they now proposed to take Charlie to the United States. The treating hospital sought, and obtained, a legal declaration that treatment was not in Charlie's best interests. The parents appealed, seeking to identify a precedent that, in respect of treatment offered by

> expert physicians in a reputable hospital … the court may not interfere with a decision by parents in the exercise of their parental rights and responsibilities with regard to their child's medical treatment, save where there is a risk the parents' proposed course of action may cause significant harm.[7]

[7] *In the Matter of Charles Gard* [2017] EWCA Civ 410, [54].

Although the courts rejected this argument, these proposals suggested a fundamental revision of the workings of private law under the Children Act 1989.

The overarching international framework is that decisions about children should be made in their 'best interests'. This principle is found in Article 3.1 of the 1989 United Nations Convention on the Rights of the Child, and in England and Wales is reflected in the language of section 1(1) of the Children Act 1989[8] as well as a large volume of case-law. Pertaining to public law, section 31(2) of the Act provides that any proposal to intervene with the living arrangements of children by local authorities (the lowest tier of English government, tasked inter alia with child protection) should first pass a 'harm threshold'. The upshot of this public law threshold is that only if a child is at risk of significant harm can a care or supervision order be made, an order that will be based on the best interests of that child.[9] This is broadly founded on a principle that the courts should avoid removing children from parents whose parenting is merely mediocre (or simply unusual), since to act otherwise would amount to social engineering.[10] In this context, the harm threshold is designed to ensure that only parenting that is seriously substandard merits state intervention.[11] Since the local authority is not usually a party in medical decisions (although there are exceptions),[12] the harm threshold does not generally apply to medical decision-making.[13] Instead, interventions by healthcare professionals fall under the Children Act's private law provisions for interventions by private parties with an interest in the child's welfare. Private applications do not require a harm threshold to be satisfied, in part because they fall under section 3(5) of the Act, which permits anyone caring for a child to 'do what is reasonable in all the circumstances of the case for the purpose of safeguarding or promoting the child's welfare'.[14] However, given both the powerful legal apparatus that a hospital can bring to bear in a dispute between doctors and parents about the best interests of medical treatment, and the connection of healthcare provision in England to

[8] For a more detailed descriptions of the workings of the Children Act, see R George 'The Legal Basis of the Court's Jurisdiction to Authorise Medical Treatment of Children', chapter 4 above.

[9] Of course, the Local Authority can make decisions about what educational support, social work intervention and so on may be needed without crossing the threshold, and with parental consent all kinds of intervention are possible.

[10] See, eg, *B (A Child)* [2013] UKSC 33, [180]; the Children Act 1989 was widely viewed to mark a break from the legal approach lasting from the Poor Law Amendment Act 1889, where powers to remove children for their welfare were first introduced, until the Children Act 1975, which sanctioned permanent Local Authority care automatically for any child who had been removed from their family for more than three years. These approaches disproportionately affected the poor and are now usually held to either be inspired by, or result in, social engineering.

[11] I Goold, 'Evaluating Best Interests as a Threshold for Judicial Intervention', chapter 2 above, presents reasons for not intervening too readily in parental decisions.

[12] See, eg, *Re R (A Child)* [2018] EWFC 28; I will discuss these in section 2.

[13] Although NHS bodies must still seek leave, see Taylor (n 4).

[14] J Bridgeman, 'The Provision of Healthcare to Young and Dependent Children: The Principles, Concepts, and Utility of the Children Act 1989' (2017) 25 *Medical Law Review* 363.

the state due to the function and governance of the NHS, it is unsurprising that some consider hospitals as the apparatus of the state.[15] This was nowhere more true than in the eyes of the family of Charlie Gard and their supporters.[16]

These supporters have kept up the momentum for legal change. Although Charlie died after his treatment was eventually withdrawn, Charlie's parents have proposed a raft of legal changes they call 'Charlie's Law'. They argue these will reduce conflict between hospitals and families. These changes have three central features: (1) to provide parties access to mediation and clinical ethics committees; (2) to provide parents access to independent second opinions and legal aid; and (3) to strengthen parental rights by introducing a 'harm threshold' for court involvement.[17] The proposals have some parliamentary support: having introduced amendments to the Mental Capacity (amendment) Bill based on the first proposal,[18] Lord MacKay is reported as saying: 'I hope will be the first small step toward realising Charlie's Law.'[19] Although these amendments were withdrawn at committee stage, the Parliamentary Under-Secretary of State for the Department of Health and Social Security undertook to work on these issues with interested parties.[20] This suggests there is still significant impetus for statutory changes that may introduce a harm threshold into medical law.

3. The Harm Threshold in Bioethics

Bioethical arguments for the harm threshold claim to have historical and philosophical roots in JS Mill's harm principle: 'The only purpose for which power can be rightfully exercised over any member of a civilised community, against his will, is to prevent harm to others.'[21] Mill claimed that such a principle would protect individuality,[22] which he characterised as the source of both happiness,[23] personal

[15] See, eg, *Great Ormond Street Hospital for Children NHS Foundation Trust v Yates and others* [2017] EWHC 1909 (Fam), [17] (Francis J); J Bridgeman, 'A Threshold of Significant Harm (f)or a Viable Alternative Therapeutic Option?' (2018) 44 *Journal of Medical Ethics* 466.

[16] L Johnson, 'Charlie Gard "Is Being Held Prisoner by the NHS" – Family Spokesman Blasts Authorities' *Daily Express* (16 July 2017) www.express.co.uk/news/uk/829104/Charlie-Gard-update-latest-parents-condition-story-NHS.

[17] Charlie Gard Foundation (n 3).

[18] Mental Capacity (amendment) HL Bill, 4 September 2018, 117-I(a) publications.parliament.uk/pa/bills/lbill/2017-2019/0117/18117-I(a).pdf

[19] S Greenhill, 'No Other Family Should Be Put Through Our Heartbreak: Charlie Gard's Parents Fight for "Charlie's Law" that Would Allow Parents of Sick Children to Move Them to a Different Hospital if They Disagree with Doctors' *Daily Mail* (5 September 2018) www.dailymail.co.uk/news/article-6136369/Charlie-Gards-parents-vowed-boys-death-make-difference.

[20] HL Deb vol 793 col 387 (15 October 2018).

[21] JS Mill, *On Liberty* [1859] (New York, Dover Publications, 2002) 8.

[22] ibid, 46.

[23] ibid, 47.

growth and human genius.[24] His doctrine remains a central tenet of liberal philosophy. We should note that, in variance to contemporary supporters of the harm threshold, Mill argued that parenting decisions were separate from the exercise of liberty. In Mill's view, parental autonomy was an exercise of power rather than of liberty,[25] and he did not believe that the harm principle should protect parental choices from the interference of the community. Yet such a view depends on a recognition that children's best interests can be legitimately determined by persons other than their parents. A significant constituency of contemporary bioethicists are sceptical of this view – citing, as Wilkinson does in this volume, the uncertainty about what is good in a pluralist society and the deep familiarity between parent and child.[26] A number have voiced support for the harm threshold.[27] Of these, Douglas Diekema offers the most developed theoretical explanation, which is both widely cited[28] and largely unrevised[29] since. Therein Diekema argues that judgements of best interests should be mediated by the harm standard. Only if a parental refusal of treatment poses a serious risk of significant harm to their child should doctors invoke the power of the state to override that refusal

[24] ibid, 53.

[25] Mill argued that 'it is in the case of children, that misapplied notions of liberty are a real obstacle to the fulfilment by the State of its duties. One would think that a man's children were supposed to be literally, rather than metaphorically, a part of himself, so jealous is opinion of the smallest interference of law with his absolute and exclusive control over them; more jealous than of almost any interference with his own freedom of action: so much less do the generality of mankind value liberty than power' (ibid, 88–89). Mill's resistance to parental rights has not been shared by the more libertarian wing of contemporary liberalism. Such a view, as popularised by thinkers such as Robert Nozick (eg R Nozick, *Anarchy, State and Utopia* (New York, Basic Books, 1977) 167). can be placed within the context of a wider project to minimise the state to a bare 'night-watchman' that implicitly sees family affairs as voluntary, and therefore private and inviolable. It is within such a political philosophy that we might cast the case for the harm threshold as it appears in bioethics.

[26] Wilkinson (n 6).

[27] ibid.

[28] Diekema is cited almost everywhere the harm threshold is advocated, and I am unaware of any attempt to finesse or reappraise his theory. The theoretical characterisation of the harm threshold is usually light. For example, the analysis in the context of the Gard case by Wilkinson and Savelescu is typical in this respect. These authors define the harm threshold as a prohibition on parents making a decision if their child is likely to suffer significant harm as a result, cite Diekema and claim they follow JS Mill. See D Wilkinson and J Savulescu, 'After Charlie Gard: Ethically Ensuring Access to Innovative Treatment' (2017) 390 *Lancet* 540.

[29] In his 2004 article Diekema identifies harm with the concept of basic interest without further definition. In his 2011 article, he expands on this definition somewhat, quoting several other authors to offer a list including 'interference with interests necessary for more ultimate goals such as physical health and vigor, integrity and normal functioning of one's body, absence of absorbing pain and suffering, or grotesque disfigurement, minimal intellectual acuity, and emotional stability. … loss of health or some other major interest, deprivation of basic needs, and deprivation of future opportunities or freedoms … death'. Diekema's later work has also clarified ambiguities relating to the status of the best-interests standard: he asserts that best interests should govern the types of advice that doctors give parents, the decisions of judges when parents cannot agree between themselves and, ideally, should guide parental decisions. The latter notwithstanding, parental decisions should only be subject to state intervention if they pose a serious risk of significant harm. See S Diekema, 'Revisiting the Best Interest Standard: Uses and Misuses' (2017) 22 *Journal of Clinical Ethics* 128.

or preference.[30] Advocates of the harm threshold have stated they intend these arguments to form a basis for reshaping the law so that the approach found in law pertaining to custody and residence of children is mirrored in medical law.[31]

Justifications for this theory make a number of common assertions. Typical is the recent iteration proposed by Wilkinson and Savulescu,[32] who argue that: parents are commonly allowed to make imperfect choices, so this should follow for medical treatment;[33] it is often not clear what is best when making decisions for children, and this follows for deciding between medical treatments;[34] parents know the child best and will express family values that are valid proxies of the child's current or future values;[35] parents will bear a significant burden of any decision that is made;[36] medical and judicial practice generally approximates the level of discretion offered by the harm threshold;[37] there is something potentially dangerous about the operation of the current legal standard, since it raises the possibility of untoward damage to the interests of parents.[38] Of the latter, Wilkinson and Savulescu suggest legal precedent may be to blame, whereas Diekema asserts that the lack of clarity about the best interests test[39] may lead decision-makers to challenge decisions that are legitimately within the bounds of parental discretion.[40] Numerous advocates of the harm threshold have also argued that the harm threshold is clearer and more actionable than best interests.[41] A further common assertion is that the harm threshold correctly ensures that discussion is focused on whether intervention in a parental decision is justified, rather than on which option is best for the child.[42]

Together with the focus on the concept of 'parental autonomy', the latter apparently identifies the harm threshold with a claim that parental rights should be strengthened. This seems compatible with the assertions made on behalf of the Gard family during that case. It is nevertheless true that advocates of the harm threshold often use the term 'parental autonomy' rather than 'parental rights'.[43] This indicates a preference that the harm threshold is seen as the extension of liberal democratic principles to confer a limited privacy right for parents. Although the use of 'autonomy' in this context is perhaps a questionable characterisation of

[30] Shah, Rosenberg and Diekema (n 5).
[31] Diekema (n 29).
[32] Wilkinson and Savulescu (n 5).
[33] ibid, 14.
[34] ibid.
[35] ibid, 89.
[36] ibid, 91.
[37] ibid, 93.
[38] ibid.
[39] See Wilkinson (n 6) for a similar argument.
[40] Diekema (n 5).
[41] See eg, L Gillam, 'The Zone of Parental Discretion: An Ethical Tool for Dealing with Disagreement between Parents and Doctors about Medical Treatment for a Child' (2016) 11 *Clinical Ethics* 1.
[42] McDougall, but also see others in n 5.
[43] Wilkinson and Savulescu (n 28).

parental *authority*,[44] I shall nevertheless use this preferred terminology to avoid misunderstanding.

Taken together, I suggest these arguments for the harm threshold seem to make the following claims:

1) Parental autonomy is ethically justified and commonly allowed.
2) In practice, the harm threshold governs decision-making in medicine.
3) The lack of formal legal basis for (2) risks both parental autonomy being infringed, and the law being inconsistent.
4) (3) is caused by the current operation of the best interests standard.
5) The optimal remedy to (3) is to adopt the harm threshold.

For now, I shall not dwell on parental autonomy to any great extent, other than to observe two things: first, the harm threshold argues that parents are the best people to identify the child's welfare, but does not dispute the basic assumption that parental rights should be based on advancing children's welfare. Without further argument, I suggest advancing children's welfare should be the motivation for any policy in this area.[45] Second, even if we accept the harm threshold is a justifiable approach to advancing children's welfare in some situations, it may not be similarly justified in other situations such as parental medical decision-making.[46] I will offer arguments for this latter claim in due course, as well as making a more general normative critique of the harm threshold. First, however, I wish to engage with the argument that something akin to the harm threshold is used in clinical practice. In doing so I will use empirical data to illustrate the complexity of clinical decision-making practice.

A. Investigating Empirical Claims with a View from the Clinic

In an attempt to gauge the situation in clinical practice, an analysis of interviews with parents and clinicians (doctors, nurses and clinical ethics committee

[44] The term 'parental autonomy' has a long history of underwriting parental rights claims in bioethics. For example, Schoeman argues that parents should have autonomy because the question of what is good parenting is not amenable to expertise, while Ross asserts constrained parental autonomy on the basis that children are not full Kantian persons. Nevertheless, it is not an altogether coherent concept as commitment to parental autonomy raises conflicts with children's autonomy: the more we extend autonomy to parents by lowering the bar of parental competence, the more we allow parents to disvalue their children's autonomy even where their decision-making ability exceeds the same bar of competence. However, such problems do not immediately apply in the case of very young children. See Schoeman (n 5); LF Ross, *Children, Families, and Health Care Decision-Making* (Oxford, Oxford University Press, 1998).

[45] I have examined elsewhere the difficulties in making a non-welfare-based argument based on property, observing that it seems to collapse ultimately into an argument against harm. See G Birchley, 'Charlie Gard and the Weight of Parental Rights to Seek Experimental Treatment' (2018) 44 *Journal of Medical Ethics* 448. For the sorts of reasons commonly given for why parents might be thought to have prima facie have authority, see Goold (n 11) and Wilkinson (n 6).

[46] Further discussion of the latter point is contained in Taylor (n 6).

members) who had experience of making decisions in the 'best interests' of sick children in intensive care was undertaken.[47] Somewhat unsurprisingly, the interviews contained few instances of the word 'harm'. Nevertheless, the interviews did contain numerous, usually spontaneous, discussions of thresholds of (non)treatment. Because some of these thresholds alighted on the role of parents, they nevertheless seemed useful in adding more detail to the picture of practice that is presented in discussions of the harm threshold. From these we can broadly appraise how closely decision-making in the clinic resembles the harm threshold.

i. Themes

Interviews and information about the study were focused on what the 'best interests' of children might imply. Perhaps due to this framing, despite participants being given space to talk freely, the word 'harm' was mentioned only seven times in over 50 hours of interviews. Where the word 'harm' occurred, there was little pattern to the way it was used. For example: a clinical ethicist remarked that patients could be caused harm by overtreatment; a parent remarked that sometimes it was necessary to risk doing harm to treat a child; another parent remarked that an incorrect diagnosis had not caused any harm. The word harm was applied to both physical harms and, potentially, to more holistic understandings of harm. This absence of the word harm from discussions perhaps signals that the way decision-making was framed by the term 'best interests' meant that concepts of harm did not spring into participants minds; that harm was very rarely a justificatory focus for a decision (presumably we intend our actions to benefit rather than be harmful or merely be harmless); or that other terms are more often used as proxies for the word harm, for example 'pain and suffering' (which I discuss later). The topic may be worthy of investigation in future studies that focus more specifically on harm.

[47] The data is drawn from the 'Best Interests in Paediatric Intensive Care' (BIPIC) project, a doctoral fellowship funded by the Wellcome Trust (grant WT097725R). The data was collected in 2014 via 39 semistructured interviews with 45 clinicians and parents who had experience of making decisions about critically ill children in one of three English paediatric intensive care units (PICUs). Participants had a variety of different experiences, for example, some parents had been bereaved, whereas others had a child who recovered. The characteristics of parents and clinicians are described in the appendix. Interviews discussed the participants' experiences of making decisions in the 'best interests' of critically ill children. Interviews had three broad stages; they began by asking participants to give an account of a situation where they had to make potentially life-or-death decisions. For parents this often involved a detailed narrative of how their child became sick, how decisions were made about treatment and how the parent felt about the outcome. A second stage asked the participant to reflect on some of the dilemmas encountered in treating children (eg who should make a final decision if there were differences between parental and medical views). A final stage considered understandings of common terminology such as 'best interests' and 'quality of life'. Although the focus of the study was on 'best interests', the first and second stages in particular offered accounts of decision-making that had not sharply focused on any theoretical account. A reanalysis of this portion of the data was undertaken in the final quarter of 2017, with a particular focus on what the results could tell us about the harm threshold.

ii. Minor Thresholds of (Non)Treatment

More informatively, a number of thresholds of (non)treatment were also discussed. Although not always having a direct bearing on my later argument, I include them here to remind us that clinical decision-making is complex, and poses challenges to attempts to theorise approaches such as best interests and the harm threshold. Decision-makers bring a plurality of views, some of which may aid, and some pose difficulties, to agreeing decisions in practice.

The first four thresholds were mentioned by only a few participants, whereas a further four occurred more widely.[48] Importantly, these thresholds occurred in an early portion of the interview where participants were asked to give narratives of their own experiences of decision-making for children, so they were usually offered spontaneously. It was not always clear if participants advocated a threshold; rather these were thoughts expressed aloud. Sometimes participants made later, contradictory statements, or mentioned more than one threshold. What the data most clearly illustrate is that these ideas entered the decision-making approaches of some participants. To paraphrase Anspach,[49] they were part of the decision-making 'ecology'.

The four less frequently mentioned thresholds were 'child's body deciding', 'life at any cost', 'cost of treatment' and 'happiness'. 'Child's body deciding' was mentioned by two participants. This threshold viewed the child's survival or death, with or despite full intensive care, as an expression of the child's will that was worthy of respect. It was exemplified by a father in interview P40 saying:

> [M]y philosophy started to change and it was actually more about, you know, we've got to start listening to his body. And that's what began to drive our decisions towards the end, wasn't it? that we would support him as long as his body kept fighting.

Bearing in mind the children being discussed were less than four years old (and hence unlikely to have expressed complex antecedent wishes) and fully anaesthetised (so did not talk or express feelings clearly), this threshold had little to do with taking the views of a child into account. Nor is the death of the child on full intensive care in any way a 'natural' death. Children in this situation die despite being connected to ventilators and being given powerful medicines that help the heart to function. Instead, this threshold seemed to be a way of shifting the vast burden of making a decision about a child's treatment away from any of those who had real agency in the situation. This response does not seem uncommon in other types of medical decision-making, for example in legal decisions to withdraw medical feeding from adults in a minimally conscious state.[50]

[48] Given this was a non-randomised study, numbers need not be significant.

[49] R Anspach, 'Prognostic Conflict in Life-and-Death Decisions: The Organization as an Ecology of Knowledge' (1987) 28 *Journal of Health and Social Behavior* 215.

[50] G Birchley, '"… What God and the Angels Know of Us?" Character, Autonomy, and Best Interests in Minimally Conscious State' (2018) 26 *Medical Law Review* 392.

Several participants discussed 'life at any cost' as a potential threshold, although only one (a parent, P55) sustained vehemently pro-life views (others merely recognised that 'life at any cost' was a possibility), and she later expressed some doubts in the case of terminal illness. Before this point, she expressed the view was that there should be no threshold of non-treatment, besides death: 'a person's life, you know, it's priceless'.

Such views are relatively rare, but the diversity of beliefs encountered in medical treatment decisions, and the fact that they may be tied to particular, strongly held religious beliefs, mean that they feature relatively frequently as a reported basis of parental objections to non-treatment.[51]

Three participants (a member of a clinical ethics committee, a doctor and a parent) cited economic reasons as a potential threshold. Significantly, while advancing economic considerations, none considered the 'cost of treatment' to be sufficient in its own right to be a threshold of non-treatment. The threshold is exemplified by this quote from parent P64:

> You could be fighting so much to get that child to survive, which is another two to three weeks. … But in those two weeks of fighting and trying, there could have been another four or five children that could have used that medication, used that time, and they could have all been fine.

The small numbers of participants suggesting this threshold may reflect a reluctance to discuss resource constraints as a basis for non-treatment. This may be more acute in a state-funded health system such as the NHS, where costs are communalised.

Finally, in 'happiness', five participants (two nurses, two members of clinical ethics committees and one parent) considered that the child's potential to be happy presents a threshold of non-treatment. A quote from clinical ethics committee member E33: '[If I were in their shoes] actually I want some pleasure in life in some way, shape or form, whatever it is I do that gives me pleasure.'

In some ways it is curious that happiness did not feature more as a spontaneous threshold – the briefest sweep of the media suggests that the desire to raise happy children is keenly felt in society at large.[52] However, happiness is both fleeting and difficult to measure. As Rawls notes, there is no happiness metric.[53] Moreover, given the discomforts associated with intensive care, happiness would be a high bar for decisions to continue the treatment of critically ill children.

More broadly, the themes 'child's body deciding', 'life at any cost', 'cost of treatment' and 'happiness' suggest the wide range of potential thresholds that any putative standard, be it best interests or the harm threshold, may need to navigate

[51] J Brierley, J Linthicum and A Petros, 'Should Religious Beliefs Be Allowed to Stonewall a Secular Approach to Withdrawing and Withholding Treatment in Children?' (2013) 39 *Journal of Medical Ethics* 573.

[52] See, eg, M Lamb, '7 Secrets to Raising a Happy Child', *Parents* website, www.parents.com/toddlers-preschoolers/development/fear/raising-happy-children/.

[53] J Rawls, *A Theory of Justice* [1971], rev edn (Cambridge, MA, Harvard University Press 1999) 486.

in contested decisions. Some themes present severe difficulties to either standard: attention to costs of treatment suggests challenges to any child-facing (rather than public-facing) standard such as the best interests test. Whether being (un)happy, or pursuing life at any cost is a significant harm or a benefit does not seem readily apparent, perhaps indicating that a harm threshold is unlikely to reduce conflicts in the clinic in the way the Gard Foundation hopes. 'Child's body deciding' is redolent of the difficulties even deeply committed parents may experience when taking responsibility for fatal decisions about their child, whatever the guiding standard.

Although these four thresholds were spontaneously voiced relatively rarely across the interviews, four further thresholds were more widely distributed. These were 'minimising pain and suffering', 'quasi-quality of life', 'best for the child' and 'best for the family'. These seem to have a more direct bearing on the use of something approaching the harm threshold in medical practice.

iii. Major Thresholds of (Non)Treatment

The larger number of participants discussing major thresholds allows for an interesting breakdown of which groups of participants found particular thresholds significant enough to spontaneously mention them. A full breakdown of this information is given in table 6.1.

Table 6.1 Spontaneous thresholds of (non)treatment

Threshold	Clinical ethics	Doctor	Nurse	Parent	Total
Child's body deciding	0	1	0	1	2
Life at any cost	1	0	0	2	3
Cost of treatment	1	1	0	1	3
Happiness	2	0	2	1	5
Pain and suffering	3	4	1	5	13
Quasi-quality of life	3	2	5	4	14
Best for the child	6	2	1	11	21
Best for the family	2	6	7	5	20

In total 13 participants spontaneously mentioned a 'minimising pain and suffering' threshold of (non)treatment. Those volunteering this threshold saw the avoidance or minimisation of discomfort as an imperative. As one doctor (D50) said: 'I suppose where I come from is that there's worse things in life than death. So living a life that is full of pain and discomfort isn't – isn't appropriate, so there is worse than dying.' Another participant, this time a mother (P42), recollected of her dying child: 'I wanted him to be out of pain, and I wanted him to be as comfortable as he could, no matter what was going on.'

Scholars asserting the harm threshold often give pain (or its absence) as one example of harm (or its absence).[54] To this extent, the frequency of the threshold of pain and suffering seems to confirm that the rare instances of the actual word 'harm' belie fairly common use of such a threshold by both clinicians and parents. However, as the quote from the doctor (D50) shows, pain may not be the only potentially harmful consideration, and there is inherent questionability of what is taken to be a harm or a benefit. Moreover, it is potentially surprising that pain and suffering is not more universally cited (other thresholds were cited more), because pain and suffering are so commonplace in intensive care. We can surmise that pain and suffering are not always seen as harm. Most intensive care interventions are uncomfortable and many are painful, especially as there are difficulties with maintaining anaesthesia over periods extending to days and weeks. The overall effect is that there is a clinical difficulty in preventing suffering in intensive care. Therapies are frequently a trade-off between short-term pain and long-term recovery. Thus, pain has limitations as an indicator of (non)treatment. Given pain is easily equated to harm, this might indicate potential complications for the harm threshold, at least in critical care environments and other settings where trade-offs between suffering and recovery are common (such as oncology).

A similar number of participants (14) used quasi-quality of life thresholds. These posited that certain abilities and/or experiences characterised a life that was worth living. For example, one experienced nurse (N29) suggested:

> You can keep somebody alive on machines, but if they can't communicate, if they can't feel, touch, if they can't be cuddled, if they can't smile or if they can't feed, if they can't do any of those things, then they might be alive but actually do they have any niceness in their life, do they have any quality?

And one parent (P58) said:

> [I]f my child had got to the stage where they were going to be fully dependent in terms of they couldn't feed themselves, um they could not begin to even lead any kind of independent sort of life, you know, they're gonna need 24 hour every day help, constant help … and they're pretty much not able to do anything, that's not the kind of life that I could imagine would be a good one.

As these examples indicate, there was not necessarily agreement between the quasi-quality-of-life measures used by participants. A wide variety of different thresholds and language was used, for example 'flourishing' (an ethics committee member in E28), 'brain-damaged and not able to use their limbs' (a parent in P40) and 'indicat[ing] wants … enjoy[ing] food' (a doctor in D52). The huge difficulties in successfully determining quality-of-life measures that are both objectively and

[54] For example: Diekema (n 5); T Nair et al, 'Settling for Second Best: When Should Doctors Agree to Parental Demands for Suboptimal Medical Treatment?' (2017) 43 *Journal of Medical Ethics* 831; R Gillon, 'Why Charlie Gard's Parents Should Have Been the Decision-Makers about Their Son's Best Interests'(2018) 44 *Journal of Medical Ethics* 462.

subjectively agreeable are well documented.[55] It is important to note that, although the thresholds reported here were spontaneously reported, the later stages of these interviews elicited participants views on quality of life as a concept. This indicated that many participants perceived these difficulties in 'quality of life' as a quantitative concept, even if they accepted that it could house useful qualitative considerations. As one parent (P62) said: '[Quality of life is] questionable, isn't it? It's questionable. But I would still use it.'

The most frequently mentioned threshold was what is 'best for the child'. It was mentioned by 21 participants, a majority made up of parents and clinical ethics committee members. This threshold emphasised that the welfare of the child was the goal of any decision, without necessarily defining the goal further. For example, one ethics committee member (E32) described a case involving a dying child that had been referred to the committee where an intervention had been proposed due to the distress of the child's parents: '[W]e were very clear that that was not acceptable to treat for the parents; you had to be doing it in the best interests of the baby that you're talking about at the time.'

Although sometimes clearly motivated by a legalistic understanding of 'best interests', such cases were frequently nuanced. In the example above, E32 discussed at length how the parent and the child's interests are difficult to extricate. A poignant example of this came from one mother's (P59) contemplation of the looming death of their (severely chronically ill) daughter:

> We're gonna get to the point one day where we're gonna [say] enough is enough, [child's name] – it's gonna come, you know … how much can you actually put a child through? You can't – you know, we're not the one that – we're not the ones that are laid there on that – on that bed, on a ventilator … there is only so much you can put a kid through. And I think it is, a lot of it's selfishness … you are just thinking of you at the time, aren't you really? 'Cos you're like, 'I don't wanna lose her. I don't want her to – to go and I don't want her to die.

The nuanced nature of the discussion is a powerful refutation of the possibility that, motivated by both a knowledge of the law and the topic of research, participants suggesting a threshold based what is best for the child were offered an answer that they felt the interviewer wanted to hear (what is technically known as a 'satisficing' response). Indeed, the discussion by the mother above seems to lay bare the struggle many parents are likely to feel between powerful emotional drives to avoid the pain of losing their child, and the perception that doing so would not be what is best for their child. Overall, participants who offered this response felt that a threshold of what was best for the child was both practically and emotionally demanding (for which parents often expressed the need for guidance and support) but normatively the correct approach.

It is interesting to note that very few doctors or nurses spontaneously volunteered a threshold based on what was best for the child. This may simply mean

[55] G Bognar, 'The Concept of Quality of Life' (2005) 31 *Social Theory and Practice* 561.

that doctors and nurses used more nuanced accounts – a sizeable cluster (five out of seven) nurses used quasi-quality-of-life thresholds. Yet there were no similar correlations except among the 20 participants who volunteered a threshold of (non)treatment based on what was 'best for the family'. The relative popularity of the latter among doctors (half the doctor participants) and nurses (all nurse participants) potentially bears out the assertion by advocates of the harm threshold that clinicians use a family-facing approach that ill matches the best interests test.[56] This is because the threshold allowed limited trades against a child's well-being to secure a parental benefit. For example, one doctor (D47) described a situation where treatment continued to be given to allow parents come to terms with their child's death:

> [W]e were carrying on infusions and we didn't stop then, I suppose that is primarily to protect, to help the parents with the situation. We never thought that – well I never thought that he was going to recover enough to have the [definitive treatment] at that point, so yes you could argue that we continued because the parents wanted it. … we had kept him um fairly sedated and on the same treatment as he was before, I don't think we were extending his burden much more. … But you could argue, yes, 12 hours of intensive care wasn't in his best interests.

Another clinician, a nurse (N37), recalling a case where treatment was given that the healthcare team thought was 'futile', said:

> I'd say it wasn't wrong [to give the treatment], because we had to do what was – the family wanted to carry on. And there was quite intense discussions at the time, and we agreed in the end that it was, well we'd go for what the family wanted, and then after [an agreed time] stop, or review.

Thus, an uneasy balance was struck between a primary duty toward (as participants saw it) satisfying the wishes of the family, and attempting to minimise deleterious effect on the child.[57] This viewpoint is apparent in similar studies,[58] which suggests it is a frequent feature in the ecology of paediatric medical decision-making. Indeed, an increasing appreciation of children's rights[59] in the legal steer has gone hand in hand with the growth of a shared decision-making approach, where the judiciary accepts that medical decisions are usually a private matter between parents and doctors.[60]

To summarise, when discussing their experiences of making decisions for children, participants spontaneously volunteered a range of decision-making

[56] *Gard* (n 7).

[57] See generally: J Bridgman, 'Beyond Best Interests: A Question of Professional Conscience?', chapter 7 below.

[58] MA de Vos et al, 'Talking with Parents about End-of-life Decisions for Their Children' 135 *Pediatrics* 465.

[59] J Read and L Clements, 'Demonstrably Awful: The Right to Life and the Selective Non-Treatment of Disabled Babies and Young Children' 31 *Journal of Law and Society* 482.

[60] G Birchley, 'Deciding Together? Best Interests and Shared Decision-Making in Paediatric Intensive Care' (2014) 22 *Health Care Analysis, Journal of Health Philosophy and Policy* 203.

thresholds – indeed, only 3 of 39 interviews did not include a spontaneously mentioned threshold at this stage in the interview. These data should give some sense of the types of argument that inform the thinking of decision-makers in the clinic. These indicate that decision-making is extremely nuanced – indeed, factors may challenge any standard that claims to focus on the experience of the child, which both best interests and harm aim, in their own ways, to do. The data also indicate the plurality of different views around, for example, quality of life, which suggests that any standard or threshold would struggle to clarify its objectives. Pain and suffering were a relatively frequent threshold of non-treatment that is perhaps totemic of 'harm'. However, the commonplaceness of this type of harm in intensive care perhaps belies the usefulness of harm simpliciter, at least in the most arduous clinical environments. More comfort for the harm threshold may be derived from the most predominant thresholds. These were focused on either the welfare of the child ('best for the child') or the welfare of the child's parents ('best for the family'). Arguably, the introduction of a harm threshold is about advancing parental autonomy. Although these data indicate considerable nuance, potentially the fact that support for the 'best for the family' threshold of (non)treatment is concentrated among clinicians could be read to offer empirical support for the claim that a harm threshold is commonly used by clinicians in practice.[61] A threshold consistent with one view of the best interests standard (as a maximisation of what is best) was also popular, but it was concentrated particularly among parents rather than clinicians. Once again, this is not necessarily inconsistent with harm threshold: the harm threshold's advocates argue that parental decisions generally aim at what is best for their child.[62]

Yet the arguable empirical reasonableness of claims made on behalf of a harm threshold are only one part of the story. In the second part of this discussion I shall dispute some of the normative arguments made on behalf of a harm threshold. I suggest that parental autonomy is generally respected, indicating that the harm threshold may not be needed; that there may be valid differences in legal and clinical decision-making; that there are also differences in assessing welfare in clinical and social situations that speak against legal consistency; and that there may be unintended effects arising from the harm threshold. Ultimately, I suggest that, although the best interests standard is clearly problematic, these problems are not best solved by adopting the harm threshold.

B. Disputing Normative Arguments for the Harm Threshold

The status of parents as partners in shared decision-making is decided law and embedded in medical practice. Even in patient – doctor encounters, shared

[61] Diekema (n 5); Wilkinson and Savulescu (n 28).
[62] See, eg, Diekema (n 29).

decision-making has always been an ambiguous concept, potentially supporting a variety of types of relationship and approaches.[63] These problems are more acute in situations where decision-making is shared with proxies of the patient.[64] Where that patient is a child, bioethicists have gravitated toward a threshold approach to clarify these ambiguities, with thresholds based on harm,[65] reasonableness[66] and basic interests[67] (many of which overlap on detail). Some assert that such thresholds cannot satisfactorily work under the best interests test. They claim the best interests test does not consider important factors in decision-making, holding parents up to impossible standards and denying the essential interconnectedness of the interests of parents and children.[68] Others dispute this characterisation, and argue the best interests test allows a broad and flexible assessment of the interests at stake.[69] A final argument, that to an extent runs besides these debates, is that a harm threshold is more consistent with practice[70] or other parts of the law.[71] This debate raises a number of questions: does the current operation of the best interests test indicate inflexibility, such that stronger protections of parental autonomy are needed in medical decisions? Should the law adopt a harm threshold because it is more consistent with practice? If so, what would be the impact of a harm threshold on practice?

Decisions made in practice have been subject to some, although I believe insufficient, study, which has tended to concentrate on non-treatment rather than routine issues. There are historical instances of doctors acceding to parental requests of this nature.[72] Yet Anspach's[73] study of end-of-life decisions in US neonatal intensive care in the late 1980s, and McHaffie's lengthy interview study with UK parents of neonates in the late 1990s, suggested parents more often experienced

[63] L Sandman and C Munthe, 'Shared Decision Making, Paternalism and Patient Choice' (2010) 18 *Health Care Analysis* 60; C Charles, A Gafni and T Whelan, 'Shared Decision-Making in the Medical Encounter: What Does It Mean? (or it Takes at least Two to Tango)' (1997) 44 *Social Science & Medicine* 681.

[64] Birchley (n 60).

[65] Winters (n 5); Rosenberg and Diekema (n 5).

[66] JC Bester, 'The Harm Principle Cannot Replace the Best Interest Standard: Problems with Using the Harm Principle for Medical Decision Making for Children' (2018) 18 *American Journal of Bioethics* 9; LM Kopelman, 'Disputes over Moral Standards Guiding Treatments for Imperiled Infants' (2009) 33 *Seminars in Perinatology* 372; Diekema (n 5).

[67] A Buchanan and D Brock, *Deciding for Others* (Cambridge, Cambridge University Press, 1990); Diekema (n 5).

[68] D Wilkinson and T Nair, 'Harm Isn't All You Need: Parental Discretion and Medical Decisions for a Child' (2015) 42 *Journal of Medical Ethics* 116.

[69] JC Bester, 'The Best Interest Standard and Children: Clarifying a Concept and Responding to its Critics' (2019) 45 *Journal of Medical Ethics* 117; LM Kopelman, 'The Best-Interests Standard as Threshold, Ideal, and Standard of Reasonableness' (1997) 22 *Journal of Medicine and Philosophy* 271.

[70] Diekema (n 29).

[71] Wilkinson and Savulescu (n 28).

[72] Indeed, the most notorious of these instances, *R v Arthur [1981]* 12 BMLR 1, shows neither parent nor doctor is a cast-iron guarantor of the welfare of children in such private decisions.

[73] R Anspach, *Deciding Who Lives: Fateful Choices in the Intensive-Care Nursery* (Berkeley, CA, University of California Press, 1993).

insensitivity and disempowerment.[74] On the other hand, perhaps indicating an evolution of practice, contemporary studies suggest that clinicians allow a latitude of parental discretion.[75] In some cases this is clearly intended to benefit a parent rather than a child – for example, delaying withdrawal of treatment to allow parents to come to their own appreciation of physiological realities. Such a view of practice is, unsurprisingly, not shared by parents who have failed to convince a court that their view is in the child's best interests. Charlie Gard's mother suggests that the ameliorative measures proposed in 'Charlie's Law' would bring 'a much-needed balance that we passionately feel has been absent to date'.[76] Yet, without belittling these sincere feelings, I must observe that Charlie Gard's case did not contain the features of a system that systemically fails to seek a balance between parental autonomy and claims about children's welfare:[77] Charlie's clinicians consulted an ethics committee about plans for long-term ventilation. They spent several months seeking expert opinions to check there was wider clinical agreement about withdrawal of treatment once they had reached that view. Although the case became associated with value conflict about seeking miraculous cures, this assessment sits uncomfortably with the facts of the case. These suggest it was an inability of Charlie's parents to accept the expert interpretation of the EEG scan as empirical evidence of brain damage that lay at the heart of the dispute. Once evidentially accepted, the brain damage indicated the impossibility of the sort of benefit Charlie's parents sought. Continuing treatment in these circumstances needed to be balanced against the very real depredations of intensive care: modern anaesthetics are limited in the duration that they can prevent pain and anxiety.[78]

[74] HE McHaffie, *Crucial Decisions at the Beginning of Life: Parents' Experiences of Treatment Withdrawal from Infants* (London, Radcliffe Medical Press, 2001).

[75] de Vos et al (n 58); G Birchley, R Gooberman-Hill, Z Deans, J Fraser and R Huxtable, '"Best Interests" in Paediatric Intensive Care: An Empirical Ethics Study' (2017) 102 *Archives of Disease in Childhood* 930.; this latitude of discretion is not unlimited. In both these studies it is clear that the choice parents have at the end of life is starkly one of continued intensive care while their child continues to deteriorate, and non-treatment. A study by Shaw et al. illustrates that relaying such a situation as a choice, rather than a fait accompli, reduces disagreement and increases parental acceptance. See: C Shaw, E Stokoe, K Gallagher, N Aladangady and N Marlow, 'Parental involvement in neonatal critical care decision-making' (2016) 38 Sociology of health & illness 1217. How real this choice is, is questionable, as some parents related in interviews reported in Birchley et al. (2017), above.

[76] Greenhill (n 19).

[77] Per *GOSH v Yates* [2017] EWHC 972, as concerns about Charlie's quality of life grew, advice was sought from an ethics committee who advised not to offer a tracheostomy (that would facilitate long-term ventilation). Once a clinical consensus had been reached that Charlie would not benefit from further treatment, three months passed, during which numerous second opinions were sought to ensure that the clinical facts were correct and the implications agreed, before an application to the court was made to resolve the disagreement. It could still be argued that these interventions were insufficient compromise as they aimed primarily to persuade Charlie's parents, rather than accommodate their view. Yet given the extremely polarised positions of the parties, a delay while the medical evidence was scrutinised seems the only possible compromise.

[78] ME Cunningham and AM Vogel, 'Analgesia, Sedation, and Delirium in Pediatric Surgical Critical Care' (2019) 28 *Seminars in Pediatric Surgery* 33; EM Boyle and KJS Anand, 'Sedation, Analgesia and Neuromuscular Blockade in the Neonatal ICU' in P Rimensberger (ed), *Pediatric and Neonatal Mechanical Ventilation* (New York, Springer, 2015).

The severe psychological scars experienced by adult patients[79] and children[80] after experiencing intensive care of the sort Charlie Gard received lead paediatricians commonly to liken the experience of intensive care to torture.[81] It is unclear if Charlie's doctors could have more satisfactorily balanced the rights of his parents to seek months of further intensive care with scant chance of the cure they sought, with a duty to ensure that the view of Charlie's welfare most closely underwritten by robust physiological findings and research evidence was protected. In this case, and more generally, the empirical picture suggests that parents are frequently given discretion. Widespread disregard of parental autonomy is not obviously apparent.

If the operation of the best interests test does not result in practice that routinely disregards parental autonomy, it may still be unhelpful since it fails to indicate that such practice is legitimate. Scholars may therefore make the argument that the harm threshold better concurs with the way decisions are made in practice. They may suggest we should close this gap to avoid misunderstandings[82] or legal fictions,[83] or simply in the name of consistency.[84] As I note above, the claim about practice appears prima facie plausible: clinicians arguably see a fair balance between the interests of the parents and the interests of their child as an implicit part of a good decision. Yet it is simplistic to simply see this as a manifestation of clinical acceptance of parental autonomy. I have argued elsewhere[85] that clinicians' attempts to balance the needs of children and parents is apparently motivated by a desire to fairly balance the immediate needs of a child with the potentially devastating long-term impacts of a mishandled bereavement.[86] This is hardly a laissez-faire approach to parental autonomy, and fits neither the best interests standard nor the harm threshold very perfectly. How the law should respond to this inconsistency raises serious questions about the purpose of law in this area. To translate clinical behaviour into a legal prescription ignores potential differences between the legal and clinical decision-making.[87] As Cave and Nottingham[88] have argued, a clinical assessment of best interests takes place against constantly changing

[79] K Chahraoui et al, 'Psychological Experience of Patients 3 Months After a Stay in the Intensive Care Unit: A Descriptive and Qualitative Study' (2015) 30 *Journal of Critical Care* 599.

[80] LP Nelson and JI Gold, 'Posttraumatic Stress Disorder in Children and Their Parents Following Admission to the Pediatric Intensive Care Unit: A Review' (2012) 13 *Pediatric Critical Care Medicine* 338.

[81] GA Pearson, 'Intensive Care: Because We Can or Because We Should?' (2018) 103 *Archives of Disease in Childhood* 527.

[82] Diekema (n 29).

[83] SK Shah, 'Does Research with Children Violate the Best Interests Standard? An Empirical and Conceptual Analysis'(2013) 8 *Northwestern Journal of Law and Social Policy* 121.

[84] Wilkinson and Savulescu (n 28).

[85] G Birchley et al (n 75); G Birchley, 'The Harm Principle and the Best Interests Standard: Are Aspirational or Minimal Standards the Key?' (2018) 18 *American Journal of Bioethics* 32.

[86] To simply view this behaviour as misguided paternalism seems to ignore a quite fundamental expectation that a doctor should be motivated by a conscientious care for their patients.

[87] See Taylor (n 4).

[88] E Cave and E Nottingham, 'Who Knows Best (Interests)? The Case of Charlie Gard' (2017) 26 *Medical Law Review* 500.

dynamics where failures to compromise incur penalties including increased burdens to the patient, heightened scrutiny of the decision-makers and expended resources, whereas a court decision can only judge whether the declaration sought is supported by the evidence submitted.[89] If this is the case, unless harm is a less discretionary judgement than is best interests (and the limited evidence suggests that this is unlikely to be the case),[90] it is likely than a gap between legal and clinical decision-making will remain. It is also unclear how the harm threshold would operate when determining medical welfare. Some have expressed concerns that, far from bulwarking parental autonomy, the very ambiguity of harm will reduce, rather than reinforce, the ability of parents to offer their view of the good of the child.[91] The harm threshold is already used in child protection cases where a question about where a child lives is raised. Some cases, such as *Re AB* [2018] EWFC 3 and *Re R (A Child)* [2018] EWFC 28, involve a combination of residency and medical issues. These are able to give direct examples of how the harm threshold is employed if it becomes the key boundary demarcating the limits of parental discretion. These cases show that the orders granted under the harm threshold can curtail parental views whenever they disagree with medical opinion, with scant regard for the wider considerations, such as social relationships and spiritual beliefs that are central to the current approach assessment of best interests. In *Re AB*, the parents of a life-limited child being cared for at home, failed to give the prescribed doses of rescue medication for his painful dystonic episodes because they believed the dosage was excessive and would kill the child. In the first decision the judge decided that the failure of the parents to give the medication as prescribed amounted to a harm. On appeal, and in the light of expert evidence that the current arrangements were working, Munby J made a more sensitive and holistic judgement in favour of the parents. Not all cases reach appeal, as *Re R* shows. In that case a mother opposed life-saving treatment of her profoundly disabled child because, in variance to her doctors, she felt the child's quality of life was too poor. Despite the mother's eventual compliance, the case was judged to breach the threshold of harm. The child was placed in residential care while the mother had ongoing psychotherapy. As Gollop and Pope comment, such cases demonstrate the possibility that the harm threshold may have a chilling effect upon parental autonomy.[92]

[89] ibid, 11.

[90] G Birchley, 'Harm Is All You Need? Best Interests and Disputes about Parental Decision-making' (2016) 42 *Journal of Medical Ethics* 111.

[91] Bester (n 66).

[92] K Gollop and S Pope, 'Charlie Gard, Alfie Evans and R (A Child): Why a Medical Treatment Significant Harm Test Would Hinder Not Help' (2018) www.transparencyproject.org.uk/charlie-gard-alfie-evans-and-r-a-child-why-a-medical-treatment-significant-harm-test-would-hinder-not-help/; An opposing view to Gollop and Pope's arguments is provided in C Auckland and I Goold, 'Parental Rights, Best Interests and Significant Harms: Who Should Have the Final Say over a Child's Medical Care?' (2019) The Cambridge Law Journal 1

Part of the problem in both these instances is the definitionally problematic nature of both harm and best interests. As I indicated at the conclusion of section 3A, it is unclear where the border lies between harmful and beneficial treatment. Treatments such as intensive care and oncology involve inflicting both limited (pain, discomfort, fear, upset) and sustained (sterility, heart problems, lung problems, psychological dysfunction) harms on children, in an attempt to benefit them overall. Moreover, some treatments, just do not fall into a straightforward harm/benefit dichotomy. Demanding unnecessary antibiotics, or refusing a vaccine, for example, may neither significantly harm, nor benefit a child, although they may have harms and benefits to the wider community. In most cases, harm does not any better specify where the line for court intervention should be drawn than best interests.[93]

This notwithstanding, because the harm threshold is used within social welfare, some have argued that the harm threshold will bring a more consistent approach to social and medical welfare.[94] Yet we should question whether such consistency is desirable. Rather than asking for parity between medical and social standards about children, we might ask why standards of decision-making for children should differ from standards of decision-making for any other incompetent person. Like other forms of care, parenting involves compromise and dutiful sacrifice of our heartfelt aims and life plans. The broad acceptance of welfare as a basis of parental rights suggests that good parenting is fittingly signalled by a system that overtly prioritises what is best for children. The harm threshold seems to break the link with the necessity to act with a child's welfare in mind. The reasons for breaking this link in social welfare are both historical and expedient. The historical welfarist project of removing children from predominantly poor parents in order to improve children's welfare, was, even on its own terms, a scandalous failure.[95] Social intervention struggles with the strict limits to the resources provided by the state for social welfare provision. A concurrent lack of effective social interventions mean, unfortunately, outcomes for many children raised outside families are mediocre.[96] For these reasons social intervention remains a last-ditch activity. Without the resources[97] and (perhaps) the know-how, we cannot be confident that changing a child's living arrangements will produce significant benefit. So long as these factors remain in place, this uncertainty suggests the precautionary approach emphasised by the harm threshold is justified in social welfare.

A survey of the same reasons – resources and confidence in outcomes – suggests decisions about medical welfare are quite different. The totality of current

[93] Birchley (n 90).

[94] Wilkinson and Savulescu (n 28).

[95] P Bean and J Melville, *Lost Children of the Empire* (Abingdon, Routledge, 2018).

[96] P Roy, M Rutter and A Pickles, 'Institutional Care: Risk from Family Background or Pattern of Rearing?' (2000) 41 *Journal of Child Psychology and Psychiatry* 139; A Goemans, M van Geel and P Vedder, 'Over Three Decades of Longitudinal Research on the Development of Foster Children: A Meta-Analysis' (2015) 42 *Child Abuse and Neglect* 121.

[97] Or at least the political will to provide them.

levels of social care and healthcare spending are similar, but the social care spending is spread much more thinly.[98] Investments in children's healthcare dwarf the resources that are available for children in care. Moreover, we can have far more confidence when trying to predict the likely outcomes of healthcare interventions. Huge investments continue to be made in research to better understand the risks and benefits inherent in medical decisions. Although there are numerous areas where better evidence is required, the situation is constantly improving. On top of this, quantitative, basis for medical intervention, clinicians will accumulate a wealth of qualitative knowledge that they can bring to bear to make informed judgements on the basis of their close familiarity with the situations they encounter. Importantly, to recognise this difference in social and medical judgements is not to make an unguarded plea for medical paternalism. There are numerous features of human judgement that suggest that decision-making is fallible, especially where values are at stake.[99] Nor are we necessarily able, as some suggest, to disentangle the dense web of facts and values in order to permit an authoritative evaluation of facts on the basis of value.[100] Without deeply engaging in the complex philosophical and epistemic issues involved in claims of fact–value separation (it would be difficult to do so briefly), we can note that a naïve separation between facts and values is far from universally accepted among philosophers and bioethicists.[101] These challenges to reasoning are why a shared decision-making approach is desirable, particularly one that goes beyond the parent – doctor dyad and brings a plurality of views. Yet this approach should be focused on ensuring that the child's welfare is as well served as possible under the circumstances, even if this means taking an alternative view to that of the parents about what is good for their child. Attending to the child's overall good will usually mean a need

[98] See E Kelly et al, *Public Spending on Children in England: 2000 to 2020* (2018) www.childrenscommissioner.gov.uk/wp-content/uploads/2018/06/Public-Spending-on-Children-in-England-CCO-JUNE-2018.pdf; NHS Digital, 'Hospital Admissions Hit Record High as Population Ages' (NHS, 2016) www.digital.nhs.uk/news-and-events/news-archive/2016-news-archive/hospital-admissions-hit-record-high-as-population-ages; Office for National Statistics, *Households below Average Income: 1994/95 to 2016/17* (2018) www.gov.uk/government/statistics/households-below-average-income-199495-to-201617

[99] Experimental psychology suggests that moral reasoning closely maps people's immediate emotional reactions. Although the ability to use reasoned argument plays an important part in moral deliberation, reasoning generally seeks to evidence that confirms, and fails to seek evidence that challenges, these emotional reactions. Indeed, in experiments where participants' initial emotional reactions are manipulated to produce unfounded moral objections, a significant minority of these participants adhere to their initial emotional reactions even when presented with strong arguments to the contrary. See G Harman, K Mason and W Sinnot-Armstrong, 'Moral Reasoning' in J Doris (ed), *The Moral Psychology Handbook* (Oxford, Oxford University Press, 2010).

[100] See, eg, Wilkinson and Savulescu (n 5).

[101] See, eg, H Putnam, 'Beyond the Fact–Value Dichotomy' (1982) 14 *Crítica: Revista Hispanoamericana de Filosofía* 3; AM Hedgecoe, 'Critical Bioethics: Beyond the Social Science Critique of Applied Ethics' (2004) 18 *Bioethics* 120; R De Vries and B Gordijn, 'Empirical Ethics and its Alleged Meta-Ethical Fallacies' (2009) 23 *Bioethics* 193; J McMillan, 'Empirical Bioethics and the Fact Value Distinction' in J Ives, M Dunn and A Cribb (eds), *Empirical Bioethics: Theoretical and Practical Perspectives* (Cambridge, Cambridge University Press, 2017).

to maintain clinical dialogue with the parents, and, on balance, this may entail some degree of suboptimisation of treatment goal. Yet at no point should it mean simple capitulation to obviously poor parental judgements. Although the authority or otherwise of expert decisions requires an account of legitimate political authority[102] that shall not be discussed here, the nature and extent of knowledge about medicine clearly distinguishes medical decisions from decisions about parenting style, involvement in contact sports or a host of other social decisions that are commonly considered by proponents of the harm threshold.[103]

We might argue that such concerns do not matter. The empirical data in section 3A, above, indicate that the best interests standard does not align strongly to actual decision-making. If the practical approach to decision-making is necessarily different from the law, then the harm threshold might essentially mean that business is carried on as usual. In this scenario the harm threshold would be part of the law's role of signalling the boundaries of acceptable behaviour to the wider public. It would signal that society values and, except in exceptional cases, protects parental autonomy as a means to advance the welfare of children. Yet it is worth noting that the use of the harm threshold in determining the social welfare of children is by no means unproblematic, as the regular drip of appalling cases where children die as a result of their parents' mistreatment attests. In most of these cases, members of the public, social workers, teachers or doctors note the signs of neglect or abuse but the harm threshold signals that they should be wary of taking these concerns further. Signals are important, and we should take serious stock of the failures of social welfare in this regard.

I have so far considered whether there is a strong case for the harm threshold in current clinical practice and whether we might want to introduce a more consistent approach to social and medical welfare. But this might not be the end of the story. Recently, some have argued that a harm threshold will require greater attention to resource limitations. Before I conclude, I would like to consider the potential for unintended consequences of adopting the harm threshold.

One of the motivations of the harm threshold as it is seen within Charlie's Law is to reduce conflict.[104] Some have also suggested that the harm threshold may enjoy public support,[105] and if this were so,[106] it might also indicate that the adoption

[102] D Estlund, *Democratic Authority: A Philosophical Framework* (Princeton, NJ, Princeton University Press, 2008).

[103] Wilkinson and Nair (n 68).

[104] Charlie Gard Foundation (n 3).

[105] T Nair, J Savulescu, J Everett and D Wilkinson conducted an online survey of the views of 178 visitors to a US crowdsourcing website. They found almost 60% of participants were willing to support a hypothetical parental demand for a substitute treatment that increased the risk of their child's death by 4%. The authors concluded that the harm threshold is more representative of public opinion, and that, given the weight of bioethical commentators supportive of the harm threshold, the harm threshold should therefore be adopted – albeit with a lower-risk threshold than that supported in the survey. See: T Nair, J Savulescu, J Everett and D Wilkinson, 'Settling for Second Best: When Should Doctors Agree to Parental Demands for Suboptimal Medical Treatment?' (2017) 43 *Journal of Medical Ethics* 831.

[106] There is some reason to question the representativeness of these findings: crowdsourced samples are not representative of general populations, and thus any claim that Nair et al's research offers a

of the harm threshold would reduce instances of conflict in paediatric healthcare. However, the harm threshold may have the unintended effect of bringing deeper conflicts about resource limitation to the fore, at least in the United Kingdom. Medical decisions in the United Kingdom are capable of commanding extensive levels of resources irrespective of ability to pay. Healthcare spending on the range of therapies that are offered by local commissioners is putatively allocated on the basis of the individual need. In other words, whether an individual child receives a therapy for 5 days or 50 will be determined clinically rather than by any limit of individual funding. In practice, widespread shared decision-making means that need is determined between a parent and a doctor. Resource limitations, as we saw in the empirical data in section 3A, may be a consideration, but they are rarely an explicit one. Resources that might be available to parents and doctors in individual cases, although not unlimited, are extremely extensive nevertheless. Under a putative harm threshold, the clinical recommendation against a treatment that is harmless, but of no particular benefit, must take a back seat to parental demand for a treatment. For a costly but harmless treatment, very large amounts of resource may be thus be concentrated on meeting that parental demand with little clinical justification.

Advocates of the harm threshold have been alert to this problem, and suggest a central role for resource limitation. Wilkinson and Savulescu[107] spend considerable energies arguing that it is financial resources, rather than best interests, that should demarcate the limit on children's treatment. Whatever its ethical merits, there is a practical problem to this solution: making decisions to limit treatment solely on the basis of resources is extremely unpopular with the British public.[108] The apparent political toxicity of this strategy is highlighted by reviewing the outcome of attempts at fair resource allocation by the National Institute for Health and Care Excellence (NICE). NICE decisions have been undermined by both public campaigns (often bankrolled by companies with a financial interest in overturning NICE's decision)[109] and government policy.[110] The overall impression is that an era of bald resource allocation ushered in by a harm threshold would be a significantly more divisive way to demarcate the limits of treatment than the current system that gives weight to clinical expertise. Indeed, it is likely that, under

balanced view of public attitudes is suspect. See J Chandler and D Shapiro, 'Conducting Clinical Research Using Crowdsourced Convenience Samples' (2016) 12 *Annual Review of Clinical Psychology* 53.

[107] Wilkinson and Savulescu (n 5).

[108] H McKenna, *Are We Expecting Too Much from the NHS?* (2018) www.health.org.uk/sites/default/files/NHS-70-Are-we-expecting-too-much-from-the-NHS.pdf.

[109] M Wood, 'Depoliticisation, Resilience and the Herceptin Post-Code Lottery Crisis: Holding Back the Tide' (2015) 17 *British Journal of Politics and International Relations* 644.

[110] V Kirkbride, 'Health Economics: Decisions and Choices at the End of Life' in L Hagger and S Woods (eds), *A Good Death? Law and Ethics in Practice* (Farnham, Ashgate Publishing, 2013).

a harm threshold, health and governmental authorities will come under significant public pressure to raise or remove caps to resources in high-profile cases. Without a major change in public and political attitudes to health rationing, the harm threshold seems to raise potential for significant conflicts in this area.[111]

For children, for parents or for society at large, it is clear that there are significant risks to adopting a harm threshold. There are good reasons to be dissatisfied with the opacity of the best interests test, and it is correct to investigate apparent inconsistencies in the law as well as the significant concerns raised by supporters of Charlie Gard's parents. Although the harm threshold usefully focuses attention on these areas, it is not the answer to the apparent deficiencies in the current approach. Without a specification of the harms it intends to limit, it will not bring transparency. It is true, it could bring a veneer of consistency to social and medical decision-making – but to what end if the factors involved in these decisions are fundamentally different? It seems likely that any conflict ameliorated by the harm threshold will redouble in other areas. Nevertheless, it is true that a systematic revision of healthcare decision-making is timely. A central concern should be our approach to power relations in decision-making.[112] To this extent, as JS Mill recognised,[113] questions of parental autonomy (as well as medical authority) are questions of the power of each party over a child, rather than questions of individual liberty. Most apparently agree that the welfare of the child who is the recipient of a decision is central. Welfare must be contingent on facts rather than fictions. Yet, given the very amorphous nature of welfare when facts are in short supply, any approach that concentrates power with a parent, a doctor or any other party risks failing to take account of important perspectives. What is needed is some way of diffusing power among a plurality of stakeholders to increase the perspectives consulted in a decision. Shared decision-making is a good start, yet risks excluding consideration of the child.[114] Developing better approaches remains contingent on improving our understanding of the interaction between policy and practice in children's healthcare. Academics are fond of stating that 'more research is needed'. As there is clearly a dearth of empirical research into practice, and, importantly, into a range of practice settings to capture more everyday experiences, on this occasion the adage seems especially apt. These issues are simply too important to make policy without a sound empirical basis.

[111] Although the harm threshold might threaten the current way that socialised healthcare is organised in the UK, there is clearly a constituency for which this is an acceptable price, or even a goal. For example, groups that are highly critical of the NHS as an institution played a vocal role in the campaign to continue the active treatment of Charlie Gard. See R Hurley, 'How a Fight for Charlie Gard Became a Fight Against the State' (2017) 358 *British Medical Journal* 3675.

[112] M Quigley, 'Best Interests, the Power of the Medical Profession, and the Power of the Judiciary' (2008) 16 *Health Care Analysis* 233.

[113] See n 25.

[114] Birchley (n 60).

4. Conclusion

There is a peak of interest in the harm threshold following the Charlie Gard case. In this chapter I have sought to consider the harm threshold through the prism of decision-making in a clinical setting. These show the breadth of considerations that decision-makers take into account. Proponents of a harm threshold are likely to take succour from findings that suggest features of the harm threshold are in operation in practice. Yet, for reasons I have outlined in my analysis, I believe the picture is rather more complicated. The broader literature seems to indicate that, rather than simply allowing parents autonomy so long as their decisions are not harmful, clinicians try to steer a path that balances benefits and harms to both the child in their care, and to the child's parents. True, this fits the conventional account of the best interests test rather poorly. Yet it is no better a fit to the harm threshold. Of course, this is unlikely to convince those who argue that there are nevertheless strong normative reasons to support the harm threshold: to some of these scholars, the case of Charlie Gard was emblematic of a wider abuse of parental autonomy. To others the desire for consistency in the law is offended by the differing clinical and social standards by which children's welfare is judged by the law. Still others, including some of the authors of chapters in this book, offer a normative justification based on a supposed parental right to autonomy.

I have argued that parental autonomy is not widely abused in contemporary healthcare. In the case of Charlie Gard, parental objections were met, not with clinical obduracy, but a willingness to seek other opinions and make sustained attempts to overcome misunderstandings, albeit within lines that were drawn by the clinical evidence about Charlie's medical welfare. What we know of the wider empirical picture indicates that parental wishes are usually treated with sympathy and respect. Moreover, the nature of clinical and legal interventions is quite different. The differences between this clinical picture and the apparent intent of the legal test of best interests should therefore not necessarily inspire changes in the law. Nor should the inconsistency between the social and clinical standards of welfare intervention necessarily be undesirable. Differences between the apparent political willingness to pay for medical interventions, and the much greater knowledge of the efficacy of medical interventions compared to social ones, markedly reduces the degree of uncertainty about the impact of clinical decisions. This reduces the degree of caution with which we should otherwise approach decisions that seek the best for a child. Although it is possible that adopting the harm threshold could ultimately have minimal effects on decision-making in practice, it is equally possible that a switch to the harm threshold signal would involve radical changes. These may involve unintended consequences to parental autonomy, since the harm threshold may invite a much more clinically dominated approach to welfare than the current system. It may also open decision-making up to greater conflicts, since limits in resources would play a much more overt part in limiting children's treatment. New approaches to decision-making are needed, but liberal welfare should be based on pluralised decisions, rather than concentrating power in one group or another. Even if best interests is not the perfect standard by which to express such ideals, the harm threshold does not advance the process of reform.

Appendix

Table A.1 Parent characteristics

ID[1]	Present at interview	Age of child	Admission type	Length of admission[2]	LLC[3]	Outcome of admission[4]
P40	Both parents	<1 month	Emergency	>1 month	Yes	Ongoing ill-health
P41	Both parents	<1 month	Emergency	>1 month	Yes	Death
P42	Mother and relative	1–12 months	Emergency	<2 weeks	Yes	Death
P45	Both parents	1–4 years	Emergency	2–4 weeks	No	Ongoing ill-health
P55	Mother	1–4 years	Emergency	2–4 weeks	No	Recovery
P56	Both parents	1–12 months	Elective	<2 weeks	No	Recovery
P58	Mother	1–4 years	Emergency	<2 weeks	No	Ongoing ill-health
P59	Both parents	1–4 years	Emergency	<2 weeks	Yes	Ongoing ill-health
P60	Mother	<1 month	Emergency	2–4 weeks	No	Recovery
P61	Mother	1–4 years	Emergency	<2 weeks	No	Ongoing ill-health
P62	Mother	1–4 years	Elective	<2 weeks	No	Recovery
P63	Mother and friend	1–4 years	Elective	<2 weeks	No	Recovery
P64	Mother	<1 month	Emergency	<2 weeks	No	Recovery
P65	Both parents	1–12 months	Emergency	<2 weeks	No	Recovery

[1]Participant identifier.
[2]Period of time given to aid anonymity.
[3]Life-limiting condition, as categorised by R Hain and M Devins, 'Directory of Life-Limiting conditions v1.3' (Together for Short Lives/University of South Wales, 2014), https://www.togetherforshortlives.org.uk/resource/directory-life-limiting-conditions/ (accessed 13 June 2019).
[4]Recovery is where child leaves the PICU with an improvement in their pre-admission baseline health; ongoing ill-health is where the child leaves the PICU with a deficit to their baseline health.

Table A.2 Clinician characteristics

ID	Designation[1]	Years of experience of PICU decisions
D27	Trainee	5–10
E28	Chaplain (clinical ethics committee)	3–5[2]
N29	Senior nurse	>10
D30	Consultant	10–20
N31	Staff nurse	5–10
E32	Doctor (clinical ethics committee)	3–5
E33	Nurse (clinical ethics committee)	3–5
D34	Consultant	10–20
N35	Staff nurse	<5
E36	Doctor (clinical ethics committee)	<3
N37	Staff nurse	<5
N38	Staff nurse	<5
E39	Lay member (clinical ethics committee)	3–5
N43	Staff nurse	5–10
D44	Consultant	>20
D46	Consultant	10–20
D47	Trainee	5–10
N48	Senior nurse	>10
D49	Consultant	10–20
D50	Trainee	<5
E51	Doctor (clinical ethics committee)	3–5
D52	Consultant	10–20
E53	Lay member (clinical ethics committee)	3–5
N54	Senior nurse	5–10
D57	Trainee	<5

[1]Doctors were either intensive care consultants or 'trainees'; experienced doctors below consultant level who were receiving training in paediatric intensive care. Nurses from Agenda for Change band 6 and above were classified as senior nurses. Ethics committee members are identified by profession rather than seniority.
[2]Participant could not recall actual length of service.

Study methodology

Participants were approached with a letter from an intensive care consultant (in the case of parents) or by email from a manager or a direct approach by the author in the case of clinicians. Participants were invited to respond to the author and those who did were given an opportunity to discuss the study and decide if they wished to take part. Before interview, participants gave written, informed consent. With participants' permission, interviews were audio-recorded and transcribed, before being analysed using the thematic method. This analysis took place in the first instance in 2014–2015, where it informed several papers.[115] Permission to conduct the research was granted by the Plymouth and Southwest Research Ethics Committee (approval reference 12/SW/0210).

[115] G Birchley, 'You Don't Need Proof When You've Got Instinct! Gut Feelings and Some Limits to Parental Authority' in R Huxtable and RT Meulen (eds), *The Voices and Rooms of European Bioethics* (London, Routledge, 2015); G Birchley and R Huxtable, 'Critical Decisions for Critically Ill Infants: Principles, Processes, Problems' in C Stanton, T Hervey, A Farrell and A Mullock (eds), *Pioneering Healthcare Law: Essays in Honour of the Work of Margaret Brazier* (London, Routledge, 2016); Birchley et al (n 75) 930–35.

7

Beyond Best Interests: A Question of Professional Conscience?

JO BRIDGEMAN

1. Introduction

The litigation surrounding the future medical treatment of Charlie Gard confirmed, if there ever was any doubt, that the principle by which such cases are to be determined is the best interests of the child. Although best interests is undoubtedly the principle applied by parents and clinicians deciding together upon a child's medical treatment and by the court in disputes, I argue that Charlie's case, as with other cases in the recent body of case-law, was not a disagreement over Charlie's best interests. I argue that questions about Charlie's future medical treatment were referred to court not because continued ventilation was, in the professional opinion of the treating clinicians not in Charlie's *best* interests but, beyond that, was in their professional judgement *inimical* to his interests and, I argue, should be understood in terms of the provision of continued treatment being *contrary* to professional conscience.

In cases concerning the withholding or withdrawal of life-sustaining treatment from a child, contrary to the view of the child's parents as to what is in their child's best interests, there is a further principle, beyond best interests. Originating in the judgment of Lord Donaldson MR in *Re J*,[1] this principle is that neither the court nor parents can require clinicians to treat contrary to their professional judgement. This is cited in judgments concerned with the withdrawal or withholding of life-sustaining treatment but its meaning has not been examined in detail in the case-law, with the exception of the early judgments of Lord Donaldson MR and Hedley J in *Wyatt*.[2] The purpose of this chapter is to consider what is meant by professional judgement in this context and what effect it has in practice in terms of the circumstances in which NHS Trusts refer decisions about the future medical treatment of a child to court and the consequences

[1] *Re J (A Minor) (Wardship: Medical Treatment)* [1991] Fam 33 (*Re J*).
[2] *Re Wyatt* [2005] EWHC 2293 (*Wyatt*).

for the subsequent best interests determination. In practice decisions about the continuation of life-sustaining treatment[3] are often only referred to court where the clinicians, supported by second opinions and in accordance with professional guidance have reached the limits of what is professionally conscionable. This shift in practice, to greater accommodation of parental wishes with regard to their child's treatment, is consistent with the shift in medical law to greater respect for patient autonomy and for the responsibility of the patient for decisions about his or her treatment. Furthermore, it serves to demonstrate that not only the decision of the child's parents, in the exercise of their parental responsibility, but also that of the child's clinicians, informed by their professional conscience, is driven by caring concern for the child.

This chapter first considers the concepts of professional judgement and professional conscience. Consideration is then given to *Re J*, from which the principle that neither the court nor parents can require practitioners to treat contrary to their professional judgement originates, and the case of *Wyatt* in which Hedley J developed the concept of professional conscience. I then examine the case-law to demonstrate that although the concept may have originated as a professional judgement of the child's best interests in accordance with a competent body of professional opinion, many of the recent cases could be understood as examples of clinicians considering that not only is continued treatment not in the best interests of the child but is against the interests of the child and, as such, is contrary to their professional conscience. I demonstrate how this could be a way of understanding the case of Charlie Gard. I argue that appreciating that clinicians are seeking a ruling from the court because they have reached the limits of what they consider conscionable is important for understanding this body of case-law but more fundamentally important for parents in such cases to understand why the clinicians caring for their child can no longer treat as they wish.

2. Professional Judgement and Professional Conscience

Robin Downie and Jane Macnaughton have explained that a judgement is 'an assertion made with some evidence, or for a good reason, in a context of uncertainty'.[4] A professional judgement is one made in a professional context in which 'the uncertainty derives from the professional context and the evidence

[3] This chapter is therefore not concerned with applications to court for withholding or withdrawal of life-sustaining treatment from children in local authority care whose parents may not have the capacity to make the decision or who do not have a clear view as to their child's best interests: eg *In re Jake (A Child)* [2015] EWHC 2442.

[4] R Downie and J Macnaughton, 'In Defence of Professional Judgement' (2013) 15 *Advances in Psychiatric Treatment* 322, 322.

or relevant considerations are acquired by means of professional knowledge and skills'.[5] Professional judgement must be exercised in accordance with a competent body of professional opinion that is 'capable of withstanding logical analysis'[6] given the risks and benefits, and accord with the values of the profession as detailed in *Good Medical Practice*.[7] Diagnosis, identification of treatment options, assessment of which of the available options is clinically best, and treatment that is in the overall best interests of the child are thus professional judgements, informed by medical knowledge, experience, and critical reflection in the context of uncertainty about the efficacy of treatment and other relevant factors such as the extent to which the child experiences pain and suffering. The conclusion that there are no further treatments that can benefit the child, that continued treatment is 'futile', is a professional judgement.

In the vast majority of cases, the medical treatment of a child is provided through a partnership in which professionals, exercising their professional judgement, work together with parents, in the exercise of their parental responsibility, to identify the medical treatment that is in the best interests of the child.[8] Clinicians may, in the exercise of their professional judgement, be prepared to try a therapy even though they do not consider it to be clinically best for the child or in the best interests of the child,[9] accommodating parental wishes as far as 'professional judgement and conscience' allows.[10] Giles Birchley, in his chapter, gives examples of clinicians offering treatments perceived to be for the benefit of the parents rather than the child or delaying withdrawal of life-sustaining treatment to give parents time to come to terms with the situation.[11]

However, there are limits beyond which clinicians will not wish to go in the administration of therapies or interventions to a child which, I argue, should be understood in terms of professional conscience. As Jonathan Montgomery has observed, the 'law expects health professionals to have, and act upon, consciences'.[12] Giles Birchley has argued 'conscience has an important part to play in the delivery of health care', as he observed, we would not want practitioners to lack a conscience.[13] Although much of the academic literature is concerned with moral conscience – for example, individual moral judgements affecting the

[5] ibid.

[6] *Bolitho v City and Hackney Health Authority* [1998] AC 232.

[7] GMC, *Good Medical Practice*, www.gmc-uk.org/ethical-guidance/ethical-guidance-for-doctors/good-medical-practice.

[8] *Re J* (n 1) (Lord Donaldson MR).

[9] Harm, rather than best interests, as a threshold is considered by G Birchley, 'The Harm Threshold: A View from the Clinic', chapter 6 above and D Wilkinson, 'In Defence of a Conditional Harm Threshold Test for Paediatric Decision-Making', chapter 5 above.

[10] *Wyatt* (n 2), [41].

[11] See Birchley (n 9).

[12] J Montgomery, 'Conscientious Objection: Personal and Professional Ethics in the Public Square' (2015) 23 *Medical Law Review* 200, 200.

[13] G Birchley, 'A Clear Case for Conscience in Healthcare Practice' (2012) 38 *Journal of Medical Ethics* 13, 13.

involvement of practitioners in, for example, the termination of pregnancy[14] or assisted suicide[15] – I am here concerned with professional conscience. Although moral values are an inevitable aspect of professional conscience, I am referring to a professional, and not a personal, conclusion. As Stephen Smith has argued, not all conscience claims are generalisable rules, they also arise where the provision of treatment which the professional does not have a general objection to, for example, mechanical ventilation, can no longer be provided with good conscience because, for example, it is sustaining the life of a child who has no conscious interaction and no ability to breathe independently, for whom there is no treatment and no prospect of recovery.[16] I employ Stephen Smith's three requirements for a claim to conscience, namely that the decision is based upon moral values, is owned by the individual and relates to the individual's own conduct.[17] The exercise of professional conscience involves technical expertise as well as moral choices[18] tested against professional guidance and the opinions of professional colleagues.[19] Importantly, it should be understood as a caring judgement. A conscientious decision involves individual moral choices leading the individual to act in a way that they strongly and sincerely believe is not morally wrong.[20] As Smith explains, decisions based upon conscience need not be based upon a set of rules, although they do need to be explained in general terms. As such, a view that the point has been reached that continued treatment is contrary to conscience may not have been predicted but reasons for that position must be given. Further, it is an individual decision, with which others may disagree, and as such is not 'correct' but a matter of judgement.[21] In the context of withdrawing or withholding life-sustaining treatment from a child, I argue, an individual professional judgement must be supported by the views of others, but that does not preclude disagreement. Practitioners, Giles Birchley has argued, should be encouraged to listen to their consciences although they must also be prepared for them to be subjected to challenge.[22]

[14] Abortion Act 1967, s 4 provides for conscientious objection to participation in treatment. Considered by S Fovargue and M Neal, 'In Good Conscience: Conscience-Based Exemptions and Proper Medical Treatment' (2015) 23 *Medical Law Review* 221; S McGuinness and M Thomson, 'Medicine and Abortion Law: Complicating the Reforming Profession' (2015) 23 *Medical Law Review* 177; Montgomery (n 12).

[15] R Huxtable and A Mullock, 'Voices of Discontent? Conscience, Compromise and Assisted Dying' (2015) 23 *Medical Law Review* 242.

[16] *Re A (A Child)* [2016] EWCA Civ 759.

[17] S Smith, 'Individualised Claims of Conscience, Clinical Judgement and Best Interests' (2018) 26 *Health Care Analysis* 81, 84.

[18] Montgomery (n 12).

[19] Dominic Wilkinson has argued that clinicians should provide treatment that is legally and professionally accepted despite a personal belief that this is morally wrong: D Wilkinson, 'Conscientious Non-Objection in Intensive Care' (2017) 26 *Cambridge Quarterly of Healthcare Ethics* 132.

[20] S Smith, 'A Bridge too Far: Individualised Claims of Conscience' (2015) 23 *Medical Law Review* 283, 286–87.

[21] Smith (n 17), 84.

[22] Birchley (n 13).

3. Professional Conscience in Children's Medical Treatment

In reaching his judgment following the hearing in April 2017 Francis J applied the established framework for judicial determination of the best interests of the child to the evidence presented on behalf of Charlie's parents, Guardian and GOSH.[23] Francis J did not cite the principle which originated in the obiter comments of Lord Donaldson MR in *Re J (1990)*,[24] that neither the court, nor parents, can require clinicians to treat contrary to their professional[25] judgement.[26] Lord Donaldson continued to say that parents cannot insist on treatment, and doctors can refuse to administer treatment which they consider to be 'medically contra-indicated or for some other reason is a treatment which they could not *conscientiously administer* [emphasis added]'.[27] As demonstrated below, given the more recent cases, it would be more accurate to use the terminology employed by Hedley J in *Wyatt* that clinicians cannot be required to treat contrary to their professional conscience.

Charlotte Wyatt had a range of medical problems, as a result of her premature birth at 26 weeks gestation, including chronic respiratory and kidney problems and profound brain damage. A year after the Trust had successfully applied for a declaration that ventilation would not be in Charlotte's best interests if she suffered a respiratory arrest and given improvement in her condition, Charlotte's parents applied for a discharge of the declaration whilst the Trust made a 'novel' application for authority, in the event of an irreconcilable disagreement about her treatment, for decisions to be made by her doctors.[28] The relationship between her parents and the hospital had become volatile and acrimonious; her parents had made complaints to the police about Charlotte's care and were only permitted to visit her accompanied by security.[29] Hedley J discharged the declaration which had the effect of returning responsibility to consent to the provision or withholding of ventilation to Charlotte's parents. In these circumstances, Hedley J was concerned to explain clearly the nature and limits of the legal and professional duties doctors owe to their child patient. Hedley J stressed that where the patient

[23] *GOSH v Yates & Gard* [2017] EWHC 972, [35]–[43].

[24] *Re J* (n 1).

[25] *King's College Hospital NHS Foundation Trust v MH* [2015] EWHC 1920 (*King's College Hospital*), [34] 'It is important to note that the court has no power to *require* doctors to carry out a medical procedure against their own professional judgement'; *GOSH v NO & KK & MK* [2017] EWHC 241, [23] quoting *MH* rather than *Re J* (n 1); *A Local Authority and An NHS Trust v MC & FC & C* [2017] EWHC 370, [42]; *King's College NHS Trust v Thomas & Haastrup* [2018] EWHC 127, [1]; *An NHS Trust v A & B & C* [2018] EWHC 2750, [30] quoting *MH* rather than *Re J*.

[26] Baker J expressed the principle as 'Importantly, therefore, the courts cannot compel a doctor to act in a way that he considers to be contrary to the patient, although it may of course be the case that another doctor would take a different view.' *An Hospital Trust v GM, DK, HK* [2017] EWHC 1710, [22].

[27] *Re J* (n 1), 41 (Lord Donaldson MR), repeated as part of his ratio in *Re J (A Minor) (Child in Care: Medical Treatment)* [1992] 3 WLR 507 (*Re J No2*), 516.

[28] *Wyatt* (n 2), [14].

[29] ibid, [17]–[26].

lacks competence the doctor's duty is to act in the patient's best interests and to work in partnership with the child's parents,[30] accommodating parental wishes where to do so is not an 'affront to the clinician's conscience'.[31] Hedley J delineated four categories in which disagreement may arise between parents and clinicians about a child's medical treatment:

> (i) Where a doctor advocated treatment which parents resisted (eg a blood transfusion) and a failure to administer such treatment would be an affront to that doctor's conscience;
> (ii) Where a doctor advocated treatment which the parents resisted on grounds that, whilst reasonable, were contrary to the clinician's view;
> (iii) Where parents wanted treatment, which the clinician could not advise, but the giving of which would not be an affront to conscience; and
> (iv) Where the treatment requested would be an affront to conscience.[32]

The judge observed that the majority of disagreements fall into the middle two categories and that all the clinicians giving evidence to the court agreed that 'in those circumstances they would, in the last resort, accommodate the views of the parents; and that is as it should be'.[33] But Hedley J continued, quoting *Re J (1992)*, to state that professionals cannot be required to act contrary to their professional conscience.[34] Acting according to professional conscience was, Hedley J explained, an 'intellectual' process in which the doctor must take account of all the circumstances, professional guidance and second opinions, to conclude what is in the patient's best interests and consider whether there is a 'reasonable basis' for the provision of the treatment even if he is inclined against it.[35] The judge explained that professional conscience is more of an intuitive than rational confirmation of the intellectual conclusion and 'honed by experience of patients, exposure to the practice of colleagues, and the ethos of his work'.[36] Hedley J tentatively concluded that:

> [W]here a clinician concludes that a requested treatment is inimical to the best interests of the patient, and that his professional conscience, intuition or hunch, confirms that view he may refuse to act and cannot be compelled to do so, though he should not prevent another from so acting, should that clinician feel able so to do.[37]

Hedley J was not referring to the legal duty to act in accordance with a competent body of professional opinion, or the professional duty to act in the best interests of the child as in the majority of cases where treatment decisions are reached by doctors and parents working in partnership. He was referring to circumstances in which the professional judgement is not only that the treatment is not in the best interests of the patient but that it is 'inimical' to the best interests of the patient

[30] ibid, [29].
[31] ibid, [30].
[32] Ibid, [30].
[33] ibid, [31].
[34] ibid, [32].
[35] ibid, [34].
[36] ibid, [35].
[37] ibid, [36].

and further contrary to professional conscience. Although Hedley J used the term 'professional conscience', it is clear from his exposition of the concept that he was referring to the discharge of professional duties rather than a process of examining individual or personal conscience. As Sara Forvargue and Mary Neal have argued, Hedley J was not here referring to a 'general right of conscience'.[38] It is clear from his exposition that Hedley J was contemplating *individual professional* judgements[39] rather than *personal* judgements upon the medical treatment of a child. The judge was not considering 'predictable' 'generalisable rules' such as a conscientious objection to the termination of pregnancy but 'practices which the doctor does not usually object to but does so in *this* instance on *these* facts'.[40] What Hedley J seemed to be contemplating in *Re Wyatt* was a professional judgement of the limits of what is acceptable in the provision of treatment or medical intervention given the current diagnosis and prognosis, second opinions and professional guidance. Hedley J was, I argue, invoking a concept of 'conscientious professional discretion'.[41] As such it might be what Stephen Smith has argued is 'a 'bridge too far', so that treatment previously provided has now become 'objectionable',[42] or the child's condition deteriorated so that what may have once been in the child's best interests or whilst not the best option within the range of acceptable options or something that it is acceptable to do at parental request has crossed a line and become unconscionable. Inevitably, it is also the case that the provision of treatment or continued treatment is not in the child's best interests. Clinicians may also use terms such as futile or unethical.[43] But, I argue, the benefit of understanding the decision in terms of professional conscience it to understand that a professional judgement has been reached, supported by independent opinion, that to be asked to continue to treat is to be asked to do something they consider to be professionally wrong. I now turn to consider the case-law, which I argue demonstrates a shift from professional judgement about a child's best interests to the limits of what is professionally conscionable.

4. Ending Life-Sustaining Medical Treatment: From Professional Judgement to Professional Conscience?

In *Re J (1990)* there was 'no real difference of opinion' between J's parents and clinicians but the decision as to J's future medical treatment was a matter for the

[38] Fovargue and Neal (n 14), 225; such as statutory provisions providing for conscience-based exemptions to provide specific services such as those in relation to abortion or assisted reproduction, Abortion Act 1967, s 4; Human Fertilisation and Embryology Act 1990, s 38.

[39] Smith (n 17), 83.

[40] Smith (n 20), 284.

[41] Montgomery (n 12), 201.

[42] Smith (n 20), 284.

[43] Futility was defined by Francis J in *GOSH v Yates & Gard* [2017] EWHC 972 as of 'no effect but may well cause pain, suffering and distress' [49] and as 'pointless or of no effective benefit' [93]; *Alder Hey Children's NHS Foundation Trust v Evans* [2018] EWHC 308, [51].

court as J was, for unrelated reasons, a ward of court.[44] The question was whether it was in J's best interests to be ventilated in the event of a crisis where this would enable him to survive a life-threatening event but further compromise his quality of life. The application of the principle that neither parent nor the court can require clinicians to treat contrary to their professional judgement had the consequence that the professional judgement of the child's best interests prevailed.[45] In *Re C*, as the unanimous evidence of the doctors was that reventilation was not in C's best interests, the court could not make an order which would require the clinicians to 'undertake a course of treatment which they are unwilling to do'.[46] Cazalet J in *A National Health Service Trust v D* stated that the court could not require clinicians to treat contrary to their clinical judgement of the best interests of the child but emphasised that clinicians were at liberty to reassess *D* upon admission and provide ventilation if appropriate.[47] Counsel for the Trust, parents and Official Solicitor in *Royal Wolverhampton Hospital NHS Trust v B* were agreed that the court cannot order treatment overriding the clinical judgement of the child's doctors.[48]

This too was the application of the principle in respect of the future treatment of Charlotte Wyatt. In the first application to court in October 2004 when Charlotte was one year old, the view of her clinicians was that she would suffer a fatal respiratory infection over the winter. Although it was agreed that she should be maintained in her present condition, medical opinion was unanimous that in the event of respiratory infection it was not in her best interests to ventilate her. Hedley J considered the dispute to fall into the third category of cases he identified (above), in that all medical experts were agreed that it was not in Charlotte's best interests to reventilate but that an elective tracheostomy or initial ventilation was not an affront to their professional conscience.[49] Making the declaration, Hedley J emphasised that it was permissive and, consequently, it would be lawful to withhold ventilation but the clinicians should act according to their clinical judgement of Charlotte's best interests.

A year later, Hedley J summed up the evidence before the court which was that, apart from Dr G, all were agreed that Charlotte should be provided with all treatment other than invasive intensive care. If she survived mechanical ventilation it would in all likelihood cause a significant deterioration in her condition from which she was unlikely to recover but it was doubtful whether she would

[44] *Re J* (n 1).

[45] In *An NHS Trust v MB* [2006] EWHC 507, Bodey J stated his conclusion that continued ventilation was in MB's best interests in the widest sense but that applying the principle that a judge has no 'right or power' 'to require doctors to carry out a positive medical intervention against their own judgment' [54], he did not make a declaration to that effect, [90].

[46] *Re C (a minor) (medical treatment)* [1998] 1 FLR 384.

[47] *A National Health Service Trust v D* [2000] 2 FLR 677.

[48] *Royal Wolverhampton Hospital NHS Trust v B* [2000] 2 FCR 76.

[49] *Portsmouth NHS Trust v Wyatt & Wyatt, Southampton NHS Trust Intervening* [2004] EWHC 2247, [18].

survive and so ventilation would deny her a 'peaceful death'.[50] Concluding that it was not in Charlotte's best interests to die while receiving futile, aggressive, treatment, Hedley J noted:

> Dr H and Dr A came close to saying that such treatment would be inconsistent with professional conscience. Others, like Dr F and Dr I, did not go that far but expressed firm views that such treatment would not accord with her best interests.[51]

However, a careful reading of the more recent cases demonstrates a greater willingness on the part of clinicians to continue to treat at the request of parents only seeking a declaration of the court where continued treatment is, in professional judgement, not only not in the best interests of the child but, in the professional judgement of clinicians antithetical to the interests of the child[52] and, as such, could be considered to be contrary to professional conscience in the sense detailed by Hedley J in *Wyatt*. As such, they have reached the limits of what is possible and permissible. For example, *An NHS Trust v W and X* concerned 11-year-old X who had, three months earlier, contracted a virus that compromised his heart functioning. He was admitted to hospital with end-stage heart failure and was fitted with devices as a temporary measure prior to a heart transplant, for which there were long waiting lists. X's lung functioning was deteriorating, caused in part by a blood clot around his left lung, his chest had to be kept open (increasing

[50] *Wyatt v Portsmouth NHS Trust and Wyatt (By her Guardian) (No 3)* [2005] EWHC 693, [15].

[51] ibid, [16].

[52] *Royal Wolverhampton Hospital NHS Trust v B* [2000] 2 FCR 76, chronic lung disease which was 'necessarily non-reversible, and that to offer her intensive support would only delay the inevitable'; *Re L (Medical Treatment: Benefit)* [2004] EWHC 2713, incurable genetic condition, any treatment merely palliative; *Re OT* [2009] EWHC 633, [71], mitochondrial condition, 'Future treatment is futile and will only escalate his suffering'; *Re RB* [2010] 1 FLR 946, inherited muscular disorder caused by genetic defect, congenital myasthenic syndrome, 'the prospect of effective treatment … which would involve both identifying the defective gene and relying upon the development of a new pharmaceutical, must be many years down the line' [5]; *NHS Trust v Baby X and others* [2012] EWHC 2188, cardiac arrest resulting in catastrophic brain damage rendering him profoundly unconscious with no spontaneous purposeful movement so that there was 'no chance of recovery and no purpose in treatment' [20]; *An NHS Foundation Trust v AB and CD and EF* [2014] EWHC 1031, untreatable incurable neurodevelopmental disorder; *King's College Hospital NHS Foundation Trust v T, V, and ZT* [2014] EWHC 3315, the judge referred to the 'unanimous opinion of the five treating consultants that continued treatment serves no purpose and confers no benefit on the baby' who had irreversible brain damage [23]. A second opinion from a consultant neonatologist, in December 2013, expressed the opinion that 'the baby had suffered catastrophic brain damage, which rendered him unable to move or to breathe for himself without hope of survival without invasive ventilation' [8]. Ten months later, when Russell J made declarations that it was lawful to withdraw ventilation, there had been no improvement only deterioration and there was no prospect of improvement; *Central Manchester University Hospitals NHS Foundation Trust v A and others* [2015] EWHC 2828, children were 'artificially surviving', their condition was irreversible and could only deteriorate further [25] such that 'prolongation of the treatment not only futile but unjustifiable' [18]; *An Hospital Trust v GM, DK, HK* [2017] EWHC 1710, nothing to be gained from further neurosurgical intervention, no prospect of any recovery, condition will continue to deteriorate and baby will not survive long [21]. The unanimous medical evidence before the court in the case of Isaiah Haastrup was that ventilation would sustain his life but there was no therapy or treatment available and, due to the severity of his brain damage, there no prospect of recovery or improvement, *King's College NHS Trust v Thomas & Haastrup* [2018] EWHC 127.

the risk of infection), his kidney function was deteriorating, his muscles were wasting, his skin was breaking down. He had to be given the maximum dosage of ketamine to make any procedure, such as turning, tolerable. Due to these complications, X was no longer suitable for a transplant. The Trust sought a declaration that it was not unlawful to withdraw the devices which were keeping him alive. His surgeon's evidence was that they had

> left no stone unturned in their attempts to treat this young boy and have nothing left to offer that can achieve a promising future. In my opinion, we are lengthening X's suffering without any chance of success; this is as futile as it can get.[53]

Bodey J concluded that the 'evidence points all one way';[54] that 'the limits of what is technically feasible' had been reached,[55] X was in extreme pain and the devices were merely prolonging an inevitable death.

In *An NHS Trust v A & B & C*, having unsuccessfully tried eight medications in an attempt to control C's seizures which daily required bagging and regularly required cardiopulmonary resuscitation (CPR), graphically described in the judgment, the clinicians responsible for his care, supported by second opinions, had reached the conclusion that there was no treatment available which could restore his health or improve his condition. The medical evidence was that the continued use of bagging and CPR after the trial of the 'final option' medication had proved unsuccessful was merely delaying an inevitable death. Russell J noted, 'There can be little doubt that the discomfort felt by the medical professionals reflects their reluctance to continually inflict pain and distress to C.'[56] To do so when there was no treatment they could offer to improve his condition and when death was inevitable was contrary to his interests and, it could be argued, the professional conscience of those responsible for his medical care.

In *GOSH v NO & KK & MK*,[57] Great Ormond Street Hospital sought a declaration of the court that it would not be in the best interests of eight-month-old MK, who had been diagnosed prior to birth with a heart condition which carried a high risk of mortality, to have further aggressive treatment but that care should be reoriented to palliative care. MK had undergone heart surgery, but due to complications it had not been possible to perform the necessary second-stage operation. At a meeting of her treating team it had been agreed that there were no further surgical options available, a view shared by clinicians at Evelina and Birmingham Children's Hospital. Russell J noted that: 'All the medical opinion is that MK is not in a clinical position to receive any further surgical treatment.'[58] There was no medical or nursing evidence or opinion before the court supporting the continuation of active treatment. For the Trust it was argued that to administer

[53] *An NHS Trust v W and X* [2015] EWHC 2778, [16].
[54] ibid, [26].
[55] ibid, [17].
[56] *An NHS Trust v A & B & C* [2018] EWHC 2750, [44].
[57] *GOSH v NO & KK & MK* [2017] EWHC 241.
[58] ibid, [8].

'further painful and invasive medical interventions in circumstances where her death is both imminent and inevitable will confer on her no medical benefit, cause her unnecessary pain, suffering and distress and would not be in her best interests'.[59] The judge concluded that MK was 'dying and nothing can be done to reverse that process' and that the ventilation and CPR her parents wanted her to have would cause her suffering but only 'delay her death by a very short time'.[60] Although the case appears to be one of a disagreement about the best interests of a child for whom there was no active treatment, for her clinicians to put her to the risk of anaesthesia and consequent sedation for ventilation or to carry out CPR on a child who had had two heart operations could be seen as not only not in her best interests but inimical to her best interests and unconscionable. The evidence before MacDonald J in *King's College Hospital NHS Foundation Trust v MH* was that to intubate and provide artificial ventilation to seven-year-old Y who had spinal muscular atrophy type 1 and showed no evidence of cognitive activity following cardiorespiratory arrest would not 'alter her prognosis' but would lead to 'an unquantifiable period of time having her life artificially maintained on an intensive care unit' from which she would never leave.[61]

With evident distress, in his evidence the treating clinician in *Re A* told the court:

> This is the first time in my twenty-seven years I'm coming here and it is prolonging a suffering and we are here. It was not an easy decision for the whole team to come here. I mean, we thought long and hard. It is not only the 8 paediatric intensive consultants, it is 80–100 odd nurses, it is the neurology team, the neurosurgery team, it is the physiotherapists. Everything together, we decided that it is not in A's best interest to continue this type of intensive care to keep him alive. He is not benefiting from any of this and that is why we're here, so that deferring it, and for us, we think that it is inhuman to keep A-a suffering like that. That's why we're here.[62]

This position was articulated on behalf of the Trust in *An NHS Trust v AB*:

> Miss Powell explained to the court that the medical team have now reached the stage where they would decline to treat AB as it would be unethical so to do. When asked by my Lord, McCombe LJ, whether that was the same as a best interest test, she said that it was not. What it represented, she told the court, was that we have now reached a state of affairs where the clinicians have come to the view that AB's clinical condition is such that life preserving treatment is so contrary to her best interest that it would be inimical to their respective Hippocratic oaths to treat her and would therefore be unethical.[63]

[59] ibid, [15].

[60] ibid, [43].

[61] *King's College Hospital* (n 25), [22], urgent out-of-hours telephone hearing. Final orders were made the following week by which time the father was no longer opposed to the application but did not want to make the decision, *King's College Hospital NHS Foundation Trust v Y & MH* [2015] EWHC 1966.

[62] *Re A (A Child)* [2016] EWCA Civ 759, [17], ventilation was keeping alive A who had catastrophic injuries following an accident which meant he could not feel anything below his neck, did not respond to noise, had no sign of awareness of his surroundings, was minimally conscious and had no spontaneous respiratory effort [6].

[63] *An NHS Trust v AB* [2016] EWCA Civ 899, [23].

In the case of Alfie Evans,[64] Hayden J considered at length the medical evidence of those responsible for his care at Alder Hey, the second opinions secured by the Trust and from the parents' expert, and the views of clinicians from Rome and Munich who were prepared to accept him as a patient. Although he had at that time no diagnosis, his clinicians were of the opinion that there were 'no more tests which can now sensibly be undertaken',[65] and there was no medical treatment available to him. The medical evidence was that his brain had been irrecoverably devastated by a progressive, ultimately fatal neurodegenerative condition such that continued ventilation sustained his life but there was no prospect of any recovery of his brain function. As judgements about professional conscience are individual judgements, although ones that needs to be supported by other professionals, where it is not contrary to the conscience of another professional to treat a transfer should be arranged if it is safe to do so.[66] The clinicians in Rome and Munich did not have a different opinion about Alfie's prognosis or treatment options but rather upon the management of his end-of-life care. The hospital in Rome was prepared to offer long-term ventilation and feeding by nasogastric tube, the German doctor to provide home ventilation and training for his parents in its use. As Hayden J observed this distinction was a matter of personal belief not professional judgement.[67] Further, his clinician considered that transfer risked sudden and undignified death and where that was proposed for 'treatment' which would be of no benefit, '[a]s treating doctors we cannot in *good conscience* agree that by simply transferring Alfie to another hospital (to continue prolonged treatment which is of no benefit to Alfie) that we are acting first and foremost in Alfie's best interests [emphasis added]'.[68]

5. Professional Conscience in the Care of Charlie Gard

Charlie's life had been sustained by mechanical ventilation while the doctors at Great Ormond Street Hospital explored all therapeutic options, including nucleoside bypass therapy. Initially prepared to try nucleoside bypass therapy, as it had not been tested or used in patients with Charlie's condition,[69] they prepared an application to their Clinical Ethics Committee. Before this application could be made, Charlie suffered seizures that his treating doctors considered caused him irreversible brain damage. In these changed circumstances, his clinicians in the

[64] *Alder Hey Children's NHS Foundation Trust v Evans* [2018] EWHC 308.

[65] ibid, [59]. His condition GABA-transaminase deficiency was diagnosed post-mortem.

[66] *Re J No2* (n 27), 518.

[67] *Alder Hey Children's NHS Foundation Trust v Evans* [2018] EWHC 308, [44].

[68] *In the Matter of E* [2018] EWCA Civ 550, [22].

[69] For an analysis of the role of the courts in cases of experimental treatment, see S Fovargue, 'Preserving the Therapeutic Alliance: Court Intervention and Experimental Treatment Requests', chapter 8 below.

exercise of their professional judgement believed that it was no longer in Charlie's best interests to try the therapy. His clinicians considered that trial of the therapy was futile and consequently, as it was agreed that his 'present quality of life is one that is not worth sustaining',[70] it was in his best interests for ventilation to be withdrawn. Charlie's parents disagreed. In the exercise of their parental responsibility, Charlie's parents reached a considered decision that continued ventilation to enable a trial of nucleoside bypass therapy was in Charlie's best interests and that the therapy offered a chance which Charlie should be given. Charlie's parents thus disagreed with his clinicians' judgements about best interests, futility and the ethics of trial of the therapy.

Charlie's clinicians reached a conclusion about his best interests after considering all the circumstances, that is, his diagnosis and prognosis, and their professional judgement that the therapy would be of no benefit. In multidisciplinary meetings they reviewed the evidence from the US doctor. They secured second opinions from St Mary's, Southampton, Newcastle upon Tyne NHS Foundation Trust and the independent expert for the parents from Southampton General to test whether there was a reasonable basis for trial of the therapy informed by the practice of colleagues. Withdrawal of ventilation was in accordance with the Royal College of Paediatrics and Child Health good-practice framework.[71] On the basis of this evidence, trial of the therapy and consequently continued ventilation for that purpose was not in Charlie's best interests, nor was it within the range of acceptable options, or an option to which they could accede to at parental request. Given that their professional judgement was that Charlie had no spontaneous respiration, no purposeful response, was not capable of spontaneous movement, his condition was deteriorating, irreversible and the invasive procedures necessary to sustain his life were probably causing him pain and suffering,[72] to continue with those life-sustaining procedures could be seen to be antithetical to his interests.

Considering whether to grant a further stay of the declaration to enable the European Court of Human Rights to consider the parents' application, Lady Hale observed that it was lawful for the clinicians to continue to provide ventilation and artificial nutrition and hydration. However, following the conclusion of Francis J that it was not in Charlie's best interests, his clinicians felt that it was 'professionally wrong' to continue to act 'otherwise' and 'contrary' to his best interests.[73] Although this was in the context of the determination by Francis J of Charlie's best interests, the judge had confirmed their professional judgement of Charlie's best interests. I argue that they had reached the point where they could

[70] *GOSH v Yates & Gard* [2017] EWHC 972, [48].

[71] RCPCH framework for good medical practice, V Larcher, F Craig, K Bhogal, D Wilkinson and J Brierley, 'Making Decisions to Limit Treatment in Life-limiting and Life-threatening Conditions in Children: a Framework for Practice' (2015) 100 *Archives of Disease in Childhood* 1.

[72] *GOSH v Yates & Gard* [2017] EWHC 972, [58], [88], [114].

[73] *In the matter of Charlie Gard (Permission to Appeal Hearing)*, 19 June 2017, www.supremecourt.uk/news/latest-judgment-in-the-matter-of-charlie-gard.html, [15] [17].

no longer, in all good conscience, participate in the provision of ventilation to maintain his life at the point at which, unable to persuade his parents, the Trust applied to court for the court to exercise its inherent jurisdiction. I argue that Charlie's case could and should be understood as only being referred to court when his clinicians believed that continued ventilation for the provision of a therapy that in their professional judgement was futile was not only not in Charlie's best interests but, furthermore, was 'professionally wrong'[74] was 'otherwise', perhaps 'inimical', to his best interests. To do so would be causing harm to a child in their care, which was contrary to their conscience.

6. Why is Consideration of Professional Conscience Significant in Children's Medical Treatment Cases?

Best interests, long-established and recently confirmed by the Supreme Court in Charlie's case as the principle by which judges determine disputes between professionals and parents as to whether it is lawful to continue to treat a child, has proven resistant to challenge. However, it has not been the purpose of this chapter to do so.

The purpose of this chapter has been to identify a shift in the circumstances in which cases are being brought to court for authority to withhold or withdraw life-sustaining treatment from a child.[75] Analysis of the early case-law demonstrates that court authority was sought when clinicians wanted to treat in accordance with their professional judgement as to a child's best interests. Now, the majority of cases are brought to court only when the responsible clinicians have reached the conclusion that to provide the treatment the parents have requested is contrary to the interests of the child and continued treatment is contrary to their professional conscience. If, as the wealth of academic literature reflecting upon changes in the doctor–adult patient relationship and its legal regulation argues,[76] patients

[74] *In the matter of Charlie Gard (Permission to Appeal Hearing)*, 8 June 2017, www.supremecourt.uk/news/permission-to-appeal-hearing-in-the-matter-of-charlie-gard.html, [15].

[75] J Brierley, J Linthicum and A Petros, 'Should Religious Beliefs Be Allowed to Stonewall a Secular Approach to Withdrawing and Withholding Treatment in Children?' (2013) 39 *Journal of Medical Ethics* 573, identify steps taken to resolve disagreements including discussions with the multidisciplinary team, assistance of religious leaders, ethical reviews, second opinions and the Patient Advice and Liaison Service.

[76] With *Montgomery* being understood by many commentators as a continuation of the trajectory in which the law has been travelling towards recognition of patient autonomy: R Heywood and J Miola, 'The Changing Face of Pre-operative Medical Disclosure: Placing the Patient at the Heart of the Matter' (2017) *LQR* 296; JM Laing, 'Delivering Informed Consent Post-Montgomery: Implications for Medical Practice and Professionalism' (2017) 2 *Tottel's Journal of Professional Negligence* 128. Although Jonathan Montgomery and Elsa Montgomery argued that the principle of respect for patient autonomy was only upheld by failing to respect the choices and characteristics of the patient: J Montgomery and E Montgomery, 'Montgomery on Informed Consent: An Inexpert Decision' (2016) 42 *Journal of Medical Ethics* 89.

are regarded not as passive recipients of care but as autonomous decision-makers, rights-holders and increasingly 'consumers exercising choices',[77] in the context of the medical treatment of children, it is parents who are claiming rights and making choices. Parents, like the patients recognised in *Montgomery*, are able to secure information about symptoms, investigations, treatment options, risks and side-effects via the Internet and from patient support groups and other sources of information. Like adult patients, parents are 'capable of understanding that medical treatment is uncertain of success and may involve risks, accepting responsibility for the taking of risks affecting their [children's] lives, and living with the consequences of their choices'.[78] But choices can only be made from the options available, which may include those that clinicians consider not to be in the best interests of the child but those they are prepared to provide. But a change in circumstances can mean that what was once an acceptable option has become an affront to professional conscience.

The best interests of the child is a titanic principle that is inured to erosion in either courtroom or practice. Stephen Smith has argued that where claims to conscience are at issue the reasons the doctor cannot provide the requested treatment become wrapped up within the best interests assessment,[79] as they did in Charlie's case. The Court of Appeal in *Wyatt*, and the appeal courts in *Gard* rejecting the arguments for a threshold of significant harm, emphasised that when the matter has been referred to court

> the forensic debate should, in our judgment, be unfettered by any potentially contentious glosses on the best interests test which are likely either inappropriately to shift the focus of the debate, or to restrict the broad exercise of the judicial discretion involved in balancing the multifarious factors in the case.[80]

In practice, however, the move seems to be to the position set out by Hedley J in *Re Wyatt*, that the clinician

> does not take orders from the family any more than he gives them. He acts in what he sees as the best interests of the child: no more and no less. In so doing, however, parental wishes should be accommodated as far as professional judgement and conscience will permit, but no further. It is vital that that is understood by all.[81]

The significance for understanding the limits of the professional judgement of conscience in the future care of a seriously ill or dying child is threefold. First, it would enable a better understanding as to why, in cases referred to court, judges usually agree with the child's clinicians rather than parents. This is not out of deference to the medical profession or that the clinicians are better placed than parents

[77] *Montgomery v Lanarkshire Health Board* [2015] UKSC 11, [75].
[78] ibid, [81].
[79] Smith (n 20).
[80] *Re Wyatt (a child) (medical treatment: continuation of order)* [2005] EWCA Civ 1181, [86].
[81] *Re Wyatt* [2005] EWHC 2293, [40].

to decide what is in the best interests of the child 'in the widest possible sense', but because continued provision of treatment has gone beyond the limits of what is professionally conscionable. Secondly, explanation as to why the clinicians cannot agree to the treatment parents want for their child may serve to assist parents to understand that the limits of what is possible have been reached and prevent the need for court intervention. Thirdly, decisions to end life-sustaining medical interventions on a seriously ill child will always be extremely difficult, and where they follow disagreement with the responsible clinicians and the decision of a court, they will inevitably be extremely distressing. It is important to appreciate that this conclusion results from the demonstration by clinicians that they have reached the limits of the professionally possible and permissible in their professional judgement of care for the child, not a competing view of what is best.

8

Preserving the Therapeutic Alliance: Court Intervention and Experimental Treatment Requests

SARA FOVARGUE*

1. Introduction

The court cases relating to Charlie Gard[1] received much attention within the United Kingdom and beyond.[2] The key issue in the cases was the parents' right to request experimental treatment for their child.[3] One commentator on the cases suggested that:

> A time-limited trial of treatment in accordance with the parents' request might have avoided conflict, preserved the therapeutic alliance and built trust. Moral distress might have been minimised, and the resort to the courts have been unnecessary. Under these circumstances, an appropriate transfer to palliative care might have been accepted as one of the agreed goals of treatment.[4]

* Many thanks to Margot Brazier, Jo Bridgeman, José Miola, John Murphy and Suzanne Ost for their comments on earlier drafts, and to the participants at the 'Parental Decision-Making' workshop at St Anne's College, Oxford University, 24 May 2018, where I presented a version of this chapter.

[1] *Great Ormond Street Hospital v Yates, Gard and Gard* [2017] EWHC 972 (Fam) (*Gard 1*); *Yates and Gard v Great Ormond Street Hospital for Children NHS Foundation Trust and Gard* [2017] EWCA Civ 410, [2018] 4 WLR 5 (*Gard 2*); *In the matter of Charlie Gard*, Supreme Court, 8 June 2017 (*Gard 3*); *Judgment of the UK Supreme Court in the Case of Charlie Gard*, 19 June 2017 (*Gard 4*); *Gard and others v the UK* (application no. 39793/17) ECHR (*Gard 5*); *Great Ormond Street Hospital v Yates, Gard and Gard* [2017] EWHC 1909 (Fam) (*Gard 6*).

[2] See, eg, 'Charlie Gard', *The Guardian*, www.theguardian.com/uk-news/charlie-gard; C Auckland and I Goold, 'Defining the Limits of Parental Authority: Charlie Gard, Best Interests and Risk of Significant Harm Threshold' (2018) 134 *LQR* 37; K Seema and JD Shah, 'Charlie Gard and the Limits of Best Interests' (2017) 171 *Journal of American Medical Association Pediatrics* 937; A Norman, 'Charlie Gard and the Magical Mantra of Best Interests', *The Small Places* (4 July 2017) thesmallplaces.wordpress.com/2017/07/04/guest-post-charlie-gard-and-the-magical-mantra-of-best-interests/.

[3] For a discussion of parents' rights and responsibilities in this regard, see J Bridgeman, 'Parental Responsibility, Professional Conscience and the Protection of the Court?', chapter 7 above.

[4] H Gold, 'When Best Interests Are Not Good Enough' (2017) 53 *Journal of Paediatrics and Child Health* 1143, 1144. Similar comments about offering a time-limited trial were made in D Wilkinson and

The idea that simply acceding to parental requests (demands?) is an appropriate response when parents and treating teams disagree can be questioned in many cases, but where the 'treatment' is experimental and has not been tested on a human being,[5] such a proposition raises a number of issues. Indeed, Vic Larcher and others have called for 'a principled, consistent, fair and transparent response to the increasing demand for innovative treatment on a compassionate basis'.[6] I argue that this should be in the form of the court as the final decision-maker where parents and treating teams cannot agree about the use of experimental treatment.

The court should play such a role because of three interconnected and overlapping concepts, namely religious-based faith, hope and trust. These are linked to and are variations of faith, and are identifiable in cases that involve parents and medical treatment. These variations of faith can, I suggest, interact to such an extent that parents' ability to decide whether to proceed with experimental treatment can be questioned. Although similar concerns about the quality of consent can be raised in other situations, the nature and status of experimental treatment exacerbates these concerns. I thus argue that the court has an important role to play in bringing clarity to this complex and complicated situation. Where experimental treatment may be available for a child, and the parents and treating team cannot agree on its use, then once other avenues of reaching agreement have failed,[7] there are compelling reasons for the court to be the ultimate decision-maker.[8] Although there may be good reasons for the court to be involved in other cases, even if parents and the treating team agree (such as those relating to sterilisation), the reasons for court involvement are more compelling when there is no such agreement and the proposed treatment is experimental. In this chapter, I am concerned with how, if at all, we should regulate parental requests for experimental treatment when parents and the treating team cannot agree. This question often gets lost in a sea of broader considerations and discussions of best interests; however, some cases in which this issue is salient reach the courts for one of at least two reasons: either because we currently lack appropriate legal and ethical frameworks to consider these matters, or because existing frameworks are inconsistently applied.

J Savulescu, 'After Charlie Gard: Ethically Ensuring Access to Innovative Treatment' (2017) 390 *Lancet* 540; but see their slightly different view in D Wilkinson and J Savulescu, 'Hard Lessons: Learning from the Charlie Gard Case' (2018) 44 *Journal of Medical Ethics* 438.

[5] For discussion of the meaning of experimental treatment, see section 3 below.

[6] V Larcher, H Turnham, J Brierley, 'Medical Innovation in a Children's Hospital: "Diseases Desperate Grown by Desperate Appliance Are Relieved, or Not at All"' (2018) 32 *Bioethics* 36, 42.

[7] For discussions on ways to avoid, de-escalate and resolve disagreements between parents and treating teams, see L Austin and R Huxtable, 'Resolving Disagreements About the Care of Critically Ill Children: Evaluating Existing Processes and Setting the Research Agenda', chapter 11 below and E Harrop, 'Supporting and Informing Shared Decision Making at the Bedside in the Context of Paediatric Palliative Care: Avoiding, De-escalating and Resolving Conflict Between Clinicians and Families', chapter 1 above.

[8] For a discussion of the legal basis for court involvement in the health context, see R George, 'The Legal Basis of the Court's Jurisdiction to Authorise Medical Treatment of Children', chapter 4 above.

In the next section, I highlight how the three variations of faith are in evidence in the reported cases to show how they may affect parental decision-making, especially in the context of experimental treatments. I then set out how experimental treatment is and could be defined, and how it is currently regulated, before explaining the courts' role in considering requests for experimental treatment. My argument is that where experimental treatment is a possibility and parents and the treating team disagree as to its appropriate use, there is a role for the court *because of* what is at issue.

2. Three Interconnected Variations of Faith and their Role in Parental Decision-Making

A. Religious-Based Faith

'Faith' has many meanings and aspects, and the term is most commonly used in relation to religious-based faith. This type of faith may be the basis for rejecting medical advice, as in *Haastrup* and in *Evans* (withdrawal-of-treatment cases),[9] and it may be both powerful and strong. For example, in *An NHS Trust v Child B and Mr & Mrs B*, B required a blood transfusion following a burn, but his parents' religious faith prevented them from agreeing to it. Molan J said that:

> [T]hey love B dearly. They also want the best medical treatment for him. But, [B's father] explained, *they are devout Jehovah's Witnesses and as a result cannot accept blood being provided to B.* … They are raising B in the faith and cannot agree to and oppose treatment which includes the transfusion of blood [emphasis added].[10]

Religious-based faith can be used, misused, abused or manipulated, as it perhaps was by some of Alfie Evans' supporters and other commentators.[11] Indeed, when parents are asked to make decisions regarding the use of experimental, or even other, treatment, they may be more open to the influence of others who seek to appropriate the case to meet their own ends or objectives, be they religious or otherwise. There is thus a sense that parents in this position need to be cared for, even protected, to minimise this possibility.

[9] *Alder Hey Children's NHS Foundation Trust v Evans, James and Evans* [2018] EWHC 308 (Fam), [51] (*Evans 1*); *King's College Hospital NHS Foundation Trust v Thomas, Haastrup and Haastrup* [2018] EWHC 127 (Fam), [54] (*Haastrup*). See also *An NHS Trust v MB* [2006] EWHC 507 (Fam) (*MB*).

[10] *An NHS Trust v Child B and Mr & Mrs B* [2014] EWHC 3486 (Fam), [13].

[11] See, eg, Erasmus, 'The Pope's Role in the Plight of Alfie Evans Was Regrettable', *The Economist* (29 April 2018); TI Burton, 'The Controversy Surrounding the Death of British Toddler Alfie Evans, Explained', *Vox* (28 April 2018) www.vox.com/policy-and-politics/2018/4/27/17286168/alfie-evans-toddler-uk-explained; G Hinsliff, 'Alfie Evans' Parents Needed Help. The Vultures Came Instead', *The Guardian* (26 April 2018); K Sheridan, 'Kathy Sheridan: Battle Over Life of Alfie Evans a Lesson for Us All – Religious Exploitation of Toddler's Short Life Serves as Warning Ahead of Vote on Eighth Amendment', *Irish Times* (2 May 2018).

Religious-based faith may also ground requests for experimental treatment, as well as refusals of such treatment, as occurred in *The NHS Trust v A*.[12] In this case, the only effective treatment was a stem-cell (bone marrow) transplant, which was described by the parents' counsel as 'an experimental procedure' because of the limited number of transplants that had been performed worldwide to those with the same condition as A,[13] and by Holman J as 'pioneering and evolving, but even in such patients it is certainly not so experimental as to be treating A as a proverbial "guinea pig"'.[14] A stem-cell transplant for someone with A's condition had a 50:50 'prospect of effecting a lasting cure so [A] then has a normal life expectancy',[15] but her parents did not want her to receive the treatment because A had 'already greatly suffered', they did not expect her to be in the 50 per cent cured by the transplant and so she would die anyway, they wanted to minimise her suffering and prolong her current quality of life as long as possible, and 'finally, but they stress it is a quite separate consideration, they have a faith that God will or may yet cure her'.[16]

Evidence that religious-based faith can influence parental decision-making, and also combine with hope, can be found in this case. For example, in her written evidence A's mother said that: 'I am a Christian and both me and my husband have faith and hope that God can heal our daughter and *our conviction is that He will heal her* [original emphasis].'[17] In court, she said: 'We strongly believe that God has the ability to heal her. We hope fervently that He will do so. Our belief in a miracle gives us the ability to make decisions for her quality of life, even if short term.'[18] Furthermore, her father said: 'You can only believe. I don't know whether He will do it or not. He may heal A.'[19] At the same time, A's mother and father both emphasised that their faith in God was 'complementary to their trust in doctors', with her father saying 'I do believe in doctors', and her mother that 'I do believe that God works through the medical profession'.[20] Religious-based faith can thus combine with the hope that the medical profession will find an answer to the problem.

B. Hope

Hope is also a complex concept,[21] and in the research context it has been suggested that it may be 'a possible factor within [the therapeutic misconception]', and that where it is the reason that parents have agreed to their child being involved in

[12] *The NHS Trust v A* [2007] EWHC 1696 (Fam).
[13] ibid, [53], [54].
[14] ibid, [55] (Holman J).
[15] ibid, [1] (Holman J).
[16] ibid, [37] (Holman J).
[17] ibid, [31] (Holman J).
[18] ibid, [31] (Holman J).
[19] ibid, [32] (Holman J).
[20] ibid, [33] (Holman J).
[21] A Samson et al, 'The Lived Experience of Hope Among Parents of a Child with Duchenne Muscular Dystrophy: Perceiving the Human Being Beyond the Illness' (2009) 5 *Chronic Illness* 103.

research, it can 'feed a serious misconception'.[22] At the same time, though, there is 'the potential for parents to believe that they are being … denied hope', and hope may have 'a role in helping individuals to cope with existential challenges, including the ability of a parent to cope with their child's life-limiting disease'.[23]

Hope may engender comparable responses in the treatment context, and it may combine with parents' understandable desire to do all they can to help their child so that they hope that established or experimental treatment *will* succeed, regardless of the medical evidence or lack thereof. Parents may similarly feel that they must not 'give up' on their child, and must 'fight as hard as possible' for them as that is their job and their moral duty, especially in situations where they may feel that they have no control and/or no other options.[24] This can mean that it becomes hard to say 'stop', as doing so means defeat, giving up, failure. This was explicitly acknowledged in *Evans* where it was said that Alfie's father believed that 'the hospital [was] giving up on Alfie', implying that this was not something that he was prepared to do.[25] In *Gard*, Francis J said that: '*Understandably*, Charlie's parents have *grasped that possibility* [of nucleoside therapy]. They have done all that they could possibly have done. They have very publicly raised funds. What parents would not do the same? [emphasis added]'.[26] It thus becomes easy for parents to believe that only parents who do not love their children enough would behave in any other way, because parents will do anything they can if it might, as they hope, help their child. Again, this was recognised in *Gard* by MacFarlane LJ in the Court of Appeal.[27]

Hope can, however, lead to parents grasping at straws, not accepting the opinions of experts that do not match those hopes (and this might foster distrust in those experts),[28] and undertaking a (global) search for other experts who support their view.[29] Simon Mellor and Sarah Barclay have raised concerns about this form of 'doctor shopping',[30] and MacDonald J cautioned against it in *Haastrup*:

> It would be extremely unfortunate if the standard response to applications of this nature was to become one of scouring the world for medical experts who simply take the view

[22] S Woods, LE Hagger and P McCormack, 'Therapeutic Misconception: Hope, Trust and Misconception in Paediatric Research' (2014) 22 *Health Care Analysis* 3, 16. Also, see V Shilling and B Young, 'How Do Parents Experience Being Asked to Enter a Child in a Randomised Controlled Trial?' (2009) 10 *BioMed Central Medical Ethics* 1, 7.

[23] Woods et al, ibid.

[24] See further: J Bridgeman, '"Leaving No Stone Unturned": Contesting the Medical Care of a Seriously Ill Child' (2017) 29 *Child and Family Law Quarterly* 63. Also, Shilling and Young (n 22), 7.

[25] *Evans 1* (n 9), [10].

[26] *Gard 1* (n 1), [16]. Similarly, see *Evans 1* (n 9), [37] (Hayden J), and *E (A Child)* [2018] EWCA Civ 550, [37] (King LJ) (*Evans 2*).

[27] *Gard 2* (n 1), [112].

[28] See K Kavanaugh, TT Moro and TA Savage, 'How Nurses Assist Parents Regarding Life Support Decisions for Extremely Premature Infants' (2010) 39 *Journal of Obstetric, Gynaecologic and Neonatal Nursing* 147.

[29] eg, experts from Spain, the UK and the US were involved in *Gard*; from Germany, Poland and the UK in *Haastrup*; and from Germany, Italy, Poland and the UK in *Evans*.

[30] S Mellor and S Barclay, 'Mediation: An Approach to Intractable Disputes Between Parents and Paediatricians' (2011) 96 *Archives of Disease in Childhood* 619, 619.

> that the medical, moral or ethical approach to these issues in their jurisdiction, or in their own practice is preferable to the medical, moral or ethical approach in this jurisdiction. This is particularly so where parents in the situation these parents find themselves in are understandably desperate to grasp any apparent life raft in the storm that is engulfing them.[31]

A quick search of the Internet will uncover numerous stories of parents striving to 'fight' and to 'leave no stone unturned' in terms of possible treatments, experts to support their use, and raising funds to pay for any treatments.[32] There are examples of this in court cases relating to experimental treatment too (such as Jaymee Bowen and Jonathan Simms),[33] as well as cases relating to alternative treatment (Neon Roberts).[34] And, as Jo Bridgeman has highlighted, Ashya King's case is:

> [o]ne example of the lengths to which parents will go to in order to secure what they believe to be best for their child. Researching alternative treatments, securing second opinions, finding a treatment centre offering innovative or experimental treatment, travelling to another country, selling belongings or otherwise raising funds for treatment, even risking imprisonment.[35]

While it has been judicially acknowledged that it is important for parents to know that they have done all they can to help their child,[36] it is must also be recognised that hope can be false or 'forlorn',[37] and that it can lead to parents deluding themselves as to medical possibilities, especially with regard to experimental treatment.[38] Such delusions may foster and flourish where trust in medicine, or health professionals, has been challenged or even eroded.

C. Trust

Religious-based faith and/or hope may link to (or lead to) trust (or mistrust) in God, or in the health profession itself, or in individual health professionals, or in a combination thereof. Trust is clearly integral to the therapeutic alliance and

[31] *Haastrup* (n 9), [83].

[32] See, eg, 'A Matter of Life and Death: Ont Mother Desperate to Fund Treatment for Son', *CTV News* (3 February 2018) www.ctvnews.ca/health/a-matter-of-life-and-death-ont-mother-desperate-to-fund-treatment-for-son-1.3788085/; 'Bubs' Treatment Costs', *gofundme*, www.gofundme.com/bubs039-treatment-costs.

[33] *R v Cambridge Health Authority, ex parte B* [1995] 1 WLR 898, CA (*ex parte B*); *Simms v Simms* [2002] EWHC 2743 (Fam) (*Simms*).

[34] *An NHS Trust v SR* [2012] EWHC 3842 (Fam) (*SR*).

[35] J Bridgeman, 'Misunderstandings, Threats, and Fears, of the Law in Conflicts over Children's Healthcare: *In the matter of Ashya King* [2014] EWHC 2964' (2015) 23 *Medical Law Review* 477, 489. The case report can be found at *Portsmouth City Council v King and King* [2014] EWHC 2964 (Fam) (*King*).

[36] *Haastrup* (n 9), [114] (MacDonald J); *MB* (n 8), [108] (Holman J).

[37] *Kings College Hospital NHS Foundation Trust v Y and MH* [2015] EWHC 1966 (Fam), [43] (MacDonald J) (*Y and MH*).

[38] This was noted in a non-experimental treatment case: *MB* (n 9), [42], [45]–[46] (Holman J).

whereas it may once have been the case that trust in health professionals was rarely questioned, this is not always so today and trust in the health profession or professionals may be tested by a number of matters, including the fact that the internet has made it easier to learn of experimental treatments. Research undertaken by parents was noted in the *Haastrup* and *Evans* cases,[39] and in *Gard* Francis J said that:

> The parents in this case have done what any parent would do for their child. They have searched far and wide for the possibility of a cure or, if a cure is not available, treatment that would prolong life or even slightly improve the condition.[40]

There is a long history of parents searching for new 'treatments',[41] and once the *possibility* of an experimental treatment is raised, it is easy to see how the promise of it can take hold – *because of* parental faith (in God, science and/or medicine) and parents' understandable hope for a cure. Problems or tensions in this context may be further heightened where, as in *Gard*,[42] parents are willing to privately fund experimental treatments, which may have very small chances of success, as this reinforces their view that they should be *entitled* to use them.[43] Indeed, one of the key moments in the timeline of *Gard* seems to be when, because of a deterioration in his condition,[44] Charlie's parents were informed that his treating teams agreed that using nucleoside therapy would be 'futile and only prolong Charlie's suffering'.[45] Providing nucleoside therapy was now believed to be 'potentially painful but incapable of achieving anything positive for him',[46] but Charlie's parents still wanted to use it. From this point onwards, there seems to have been a serious and significant divergence in the therapeutic alliance,[47] and this divergence may have been intensified by the fact that an expert made it clear that 'were Charlie in the

[39] *Gard 1* (n 1), [70]–[75]; *Haastrup* (n 9), [13]; *Evans 1* (n 9), [18], [39]–[40].

[40] *Gard 1* (n 1), [70]. The lengths parents may go to save their child are discussed further below.

[41] See, eg, *ex parte B* (n 33); *Simms* (n 33); *SR* (n 34); *King* (n 35); *B v D and the Ministry of Defence* [2017] EWCOP 15.

[42] See especially 'Charlie Gard #charlie's fight', *gofundme*, uk.gofundme.com/please-help-to-save-charlies-life.

[43] Despite Francis J refuting the idea that the refusal to use nucleoside therapy was based on financial rather than medical considerations (*Gard 1* (n 1), [80]–[81]), the link between the cost of and finance for the treatment and its use was highlighted by, eg, Gold (n 4); R Truog, 'The United Kingdom Sets Limits on Experimental Treatments: The Case of Charlie Gard' (2017) 318 *Journal of the American Medical Association* 1001; D Wilkinson, 'Beyond Resources: Denying Parental Requests for Futile Treatment' (2017) 389 *Lancet* 1866.

[44] *Gard 1* (n 1), [17], [82]–[83].

[45] This information was relayed at a 'most significant meeting': *Gard 1* (n 1), [83].

[46] *Gard 1* (n 1), [17].

[47] Similar divergence can be found in, eg, *Evans 1* (n 9) [10]. In contrast, given the circumstances of Isaiah Haastrup's birth, it is questionable whether there was ever a therapeutic alliance in that case: *Haastrup* (n 9), [18]–[19]. Furthermore, it is clear that trust (an essential part of the therapeutic alliance) was absent from the outset: [20]–[21]. The idea of key moments in cases and a divergence in the therapeutic alliance can be found in other cases, including *Re TM* [2013] EWHC 4103 (Fam), [10]–[12].

United States, he would treat him if the parents so desired and could pay for it'.[48] Charlie's parents were thus faced with experts, who they were supposed to trust, telling them two diametrically opposed 'facts'. Such differences in opinion and approach can irrevocably undermine trust between parents and treating teams, and the dynamics of the therapeutic alliance may change so that what may once have been seen as a relationship directed towards a common goal shifts into one of conflict. The hospital bed may then become a battle zone.[49]

The very fact that an experimental treatment exists, and that there appears to be a responsible health professional prepared to provide it,[50] may also tap into the trust, hope and faith that parents have in medical developments and the profession as a whole. Indeed, where an experimental treatment offers a possibility that chimes with their own desires and hopes as parents, it is not surprising that they want to pursue that chance. Nevertheless, it is important to recognise that not only may parental views 'be coloured by emotion or sentiment',[51] but also that with experimental treatment parents are being asked to make a decision on the basis of limited medical knowledge – both theirs and more generally. Although this may often be the situation with experimental treatment, if trust in the treating team has been tested or challenged, perhaps because there is someone else who states that they are willing to provide that treatment, then any information may be (too easily) dismissed or ignored – especially if it does not fit with what the parents want to hear. Decision-making may, therefore, be affected by the situation that parents and their child are in (with no or limited alternatives available), and experimental treatments 'may be accepted *because* they provide hope in the face of an otherwise bleak outcome [emphasis added]'.[52] Given this, it is essential that trust in such treatments *and* those providing them are well placed.

Trust in health professionals may, however, be tested by the behaviour of and interactions between health professionals, parents and others. This can result in, for example, trust in those conveying the information being displaced or (mis) placed in others who promise much, perhaps because of the power of hope and the parental desire to do everything to save a child. For example, Charlie's parents did not accept that his condition was as reported by those caring for him,[53] and they suggested that not only was Charlie allowed to have seizures without being

[48] *Gard 1* (n 1), [19]. Also, [76]–[77], [94], [96], [101]. Cost was also noted by one of the medical experts instructed by the parents in *Evans 1* (n 9), [42].

[49] Note the establishment of 'Charlie's Army' and 'Alfie's Army' as public groups on Facebook www.facebook.com/groups/265101867249571/ and www.facebook.com/groups/alfiesarmy/, respectively. Also, the language of battle can be seen in, eg, *Evans 2* (n 26), [37] (King LJ).

[50] Note that in its statement of 24 July 2017, Great Ormond Street Hospital stated that Professor Hirano said in court that he 'retains a financial interest in some of the NBT [nucleoside treatment] compounds he proposed to use': GOSH's Position Statement, Hearing on 24 July 2017, [10], www.gosh.nhs.uk/news/latest-press-releases/gosh-position-statement-issued-high-court-24-july-2017.

[51] *Haastrup* (n 9), [69] (MacDonald J). Also, *MB* (n 9), [16 x)] (Holman J).

[52] J Brierley and V Larcher, 'Compassionate and Innovative Treatments in Children: A Proposal for an Ethical Framework' (2009) 94 *Archives of Disease in Childhood* 651, 655.

[53] *Gard 1* (n 1), [108], [112]. Similarly, see *Haastrup* (n 9), [59]–[62].

treated,[54] but that '[w]e truly believe that these medicines will work. … A chance to keep fighting, he deserves that chance.'[55] Although these may be understandable responses when living with and caring for an ill child, 'trust can breakdown because the parents believe the doctors don't value their child or want the best for them. Parental perception is as crucial as clinician's competence in maintaining trust.'[56] It is because of such responses that health professionals must 'avoid giving false hope'[57] and remember their obligation 'to protect the weak and vulnerable from interventions that are unlikely to achieve their intended benefits'.[58] Breakdown in trust can lead to avoidance behaviour (for example, not attending meetings or not discussing the issues), repetitive discussions or arguments leading to entrenched positions, and families micromanaging care.[59] These behaviours add further support to the argument that the court has an important role in the decision-making process when parents and treating teams cannot agree about providing experimental treatments.

D. Religious-Based Faith, Hope and Trust Working Together

It should be clear from the above that religious-based faith, hope and trust may work together (in various combinations) in such a way as to make it reasonable to question whether when experimental treatments may be a possibility, parents are able to decide whether to proceed with such treatment. Parents may cling to their religious-based faith or hope that an experimental treatment might work, and this makes it harder for them to appraise the treatments and they may be more likely to want to pursue these possibilities at all costs. A framework is thus required for dealing with these situations because of the complex issues involved in cases featuring experimental treatment. Such a framework should strike an appropriate balance between the positions, and I now explore the frameworks that currently exist and how they have been used.

3. The Role of the Court: Providing Clarity and Assuming Decision-Making Responsibility

Resort to the court when parents and treating teams disagree as to the use of experimental treatment should, as it is now, be a last resort. Before considering

[54] *Gard 1* (n 1), [110].

[55] ibid. See also *Gard 2* (n 1), [30]. Similarly, *Evans 1* (n 9), [10].

[56] A Gallagher, 'What Can We Learn from the Case of Charlie Gard? Perspectives from an Inter-Disciplinary Panel Discussion' (2017) 24 *Nursing Ethics* 775, 776.

[57] Editorial, 'Charlie Gard and the Limits of Medicine' (2017) 390 *Lancet* 531, 531.

[58] Brierley and Larcher (n 52), 651.

[59] L Forbat, B Teuten and S Barclay, 'Conflict Escalation in Paediatric Services: Findings from a Qualitative Study' (2015) 100 *Archives of Disease in Childhood* 769, 771.

the role of the court in such cases, it is first necessary to set out how experimental treatment is currently understood and the legal and ethical frameworks that regulate its use.

A. Defining Experimental Treatment

There is no one agreed definition of the term 'experimental treatment' and, as the Nuffield Council on Bioethics has recently noted: 'There is a spectrum of treatments that might be considered to be experimental, from those which have never been used in humans, to those which are used routinely but are not licensed for the condition in question.'[60] Examples of definitions include those provided by Joe Brierley and Vic Larcher, who have defined 'innovative treatment' as 'any newly introduced treatment, or a new modification to an existing therapy with unproven efficacy and side effect profile, which is being used in the best interests of a patient, often on an experimental and/or compassionate basis'.[61] Similarly, the New Zealand Ministry of Health has defined 'innovative practice' as 'the provision of a clinical intervention (diagnostic, therapeutic or prophylactic), be it a therapeutic drug, medical device or clinical procedure, that is untested, untried or not in common use and therefore poses its own set of characteristics and issues'.[62] Combined, these provide a sound definition of experimental treatment, as the fact that the treatment concerned has not yet been tried on a human being, or it has not yet been tried on a human being with the particular condition that the patient concerned has, should be included in any definition. Applying these definitions to the treatment offered in Charlie Gard's case, for example, nucleoside therapy would be deemed to be experimental treatment because it had not been used in human or non-human animals with the RRM2B mutation that Charlie had,[63] rather than 'pioneering treatment' as Francis J noted it had been called in some reports.[64] Although this may appear to be nothing more than a lawyer's semantics, language is important and using the word 'experiment' or 'experimental' in relation to such treatment correctly highlights the fact that it is not yet known whether the proposed treatment will benefit patients with a particular condition.[65]

[60] Nuffield Council on Bioethics, 'Patient Access to Experimental Treatments' (2018) *Bioethics Briefing Note* 1, 2.

[61] Brierley and Larcher (n 52), 651.

[62] Ministry of Health, *Operational Standard for Ethics Committees* (Wellington, Ministry of Health, 2006), [116], [117]–[135].

[63] *Gard 1* (n 1), [74], [52].

[64] *Gard 1* (n 1), [16].

[65] For further discussion, see S Fovargue, *Xenotransplantation and Risk: Regulating a Developing Biotechnology* (Cambridge, Cambridge University Press, 2012) 62–70; S Fovargue, 'The (Ab)Use of Those with No Other Hope? Ethical and Legal Safeguards for Recipients of Experimental Procedures' (2013) 22 *Cambridge Quarterly of Healthcare Ethics* 181.

B. The Current Regulation of Experimental Treatment

As no one definition of experimental treatment currently exists, it is perhaps not surprising that not only is it not always easy to determine the boundaries between 'research', 'experiment', and 'novel' or 'innovative use', but also that there is no one regulatory (professional, ethical or legal) framework which applies to such treatment.[66] This means that it can be difficult for health professionals to know how to ensure that the use of the experimental treatment is legal and that it has been appropriately ethically reviewed, if this is required. This can be contrasted to the regulatory scheme which exists for clinical research, and it means that the same treatment may be differently regulated and/or reviewed (if at all) depending on whether or not it is provided within a clinical trial.[67] Given this, the trust placed in some of those who offer to use an experimental treatment may be questioned.

Experimental treatment is not specifically considered in the professional guidance provided in England and Wales by the General Medical Council (GMC), for example, bar the statements that doctors must 'give patients the information they want or need about … whether a proposed investigation or treatment is part of a research programme or is an innovative treatment designed specifically for their benefit',[68] and that written consent should be obtained from a patient if 'the treatment is part of a research programme or is an innovative treatment designed specifically for their benefit'.[69] More generally, in its *Good Medical Practice*, the GMC states that: 'In providing clinical care you must … provide effective treatments based on the best available evidence' – a point to which I return below.[70] With regard to ethical guidance, in relation to 'unproven interventions in clinical care', the Declaration of Helsinki states that:

> In the treatment of an individual patient, where proven interventions do not exist or other known interventions have been ineffective, the physician, after seeking expert advice, with informed consent from the patient or a legally authorised representative, may use an unproven intervention if in the physician's judgement it offers hope of saving life, re-establishing health or alleviating suffering. This intervention should subsequently be made the object of research, designed to evaluate its safety and

[66] The lack of a compassionate-use programme in the UK, as set out on Art 83 of Regulation (EC) No 726/2004, was recognised by Cohen J in *University College London Hospitals NHS Foundation Trust v KG* [2018] EWCOP 29, [23] (*KG*). There is, however, a 'Specials' exemption process which is overseen by the Medicines and Healthcare Products Regulatory Authority (MHRA): MHRA, *The Supply of Unlicensed Medicinal Products ('Specials')*, MHRA Guidance Note 14 (London, MHRA, 2014).

[67] See also: E Jackson, *Medical Law: Text, Cases and Materials*, 4th edn (Oxford, Oxford University Press, 2016) ch 9.

[68] General Medical Council (GMC), *Consent: Patients and Doctors Making Decisions Together* (London, GMC, 2008) [9]. Note that experimental treatment is not addressed in GMC, *0–18 Years: Guidance for all Doctors* (London, GMC, 2018).

[69] GMC, *Consent* (n 68), 49.

[70] GMC, *Good Medical Practice* (London, GMC, 2013, updated 2014) [16].

> efficacy. In all cases, new information must be recorded and, where appropriate, made publicly available.[71]

The provision of experimental treatment in the form of medicines, medical devices and implants, and advance therapies is variously legally regulated in England and Wales,[72] and the use of experimental treatment has been judicially considered. In *Simms v Simms*, for example, the court was asked to consider whether such treatment (which had not yet been tested on human beings) could be provided to an 18 year old and a 16 year old with probable variant Creutzfeldt – Jakob disease (vCJD).[73] Dame Elizabeth Butler-Sloss said that there were four matters (which she framed as questions) that she should have regard to in considering the case: (i) does the patient have the capacity to decide for herself?, (ii) does the proposed treatment come within the *Bolam* test?,[74] (iii) is it in the patient's best interests to have the proposed treatment?, and (iv) if (ii) and (iii) are answered in the affirmative, can the proposed treatment be carried out within the NHS?[75] Furthermore:

> Where there is no alternative treatment available and the disease is progressive and fatal, it seems to me to be reasonable to consider experimental treatment with unknown benefits and risks, but without significant risks of increased suffering to the patient, in cases where there is some chance of benefit to the patient.[76]

Following the decision in *Simms*, it might have been thought that the use of experimental treatment was to be determined by the *Bolam* test, and that test was applied in subsequent cases involving patients with vCJD.[77] It was not, however, cited in *Gard*, nor has it been cited in any other reported case on experimental treatment. Its applicability to such treatment is thus unclear, particularly given the comments of Cohen J in *University College London Hospitals NHS Foundation Trust v KG*, that '*Simms* is a case that pre-dated the Mental Capacity Act, and I do not think it is helpful to layer an additional level of test on top of those which are set out in the Mental Capacity Act'.[78] I discuss this further below.

[71] *World Medical Association Declaration of Helsinki – Ethical Principles for Medical Research Involving Human Subjects*, adopted by the 18th WMA General Assembly, Helsinki, Finland, June 1964 and amended by the 64th WMA General Assembly, Fortaleza, Brazil, October 2013, para 37.

[72] See Nuffield Council (n 60), 2–3.

[73] *Simms* (n 33).

[74] Under the *Bolam* test, a doctor is not guilty of negligence if she has 'acted in accordance with a practice accepted as proper by a responsible body of medical men skilled in that particular art': *Bolam v Friern Hospital Management Committee* [1957] 1 WLR 582, 587.

[75] *Simms* (n 33).

[76] *Simms* (n 33), [57]. See also *An NHS Trust v HM* [2004] Lloyd's Law Reports 207, [8] (*HM*); *EP v Trusts A, B & C* [2004] Lloyd's Law Reports 211, [14] (*EP*). Note that the paragraph from *Simms* is replicated in the Department of Health's (DH), *Reference Guide to Consent for Examination or Treatment*, 2nd edn (DH, 2009) ch 1, [41]. Experimental treatment is also mentioned in ch 1, [40] and ch 3, [23], [29].

[77] *HM* (n 76), [4]; *EP* (n 76), [9].

[78] *KG* (n 76), [33].

C. The Role of the Court in Requests for Experimental Treatment

In the light of the uncertainties and lacunae in the professional, ethical and legal regulatory frameworks highlighted above, where parents and treating teams disagree about the use of experimental treatment, the court, as the ultimate arbiter, should determine whether the parents are making a 'fair request' for experimental treatment that is a viable alternative to other options. This may be one of the sites where parents and treating teams disagree; indeed, as Bridgeman has argued, the disagreement in *Gard* was not so much about what was *best* for Charlie, but whether nucleoside therapy *was* a viable therapeutic option for him.[79] However, as this was not directly considered, the case proceeded when it could, perhaps, have been stayed if not stopped. And in terms of decision-making, the focus may be on best interests rather than the question of whether the experimental treatment *is* a viable alternative; yet it is vital that *before* best interests are considered the latter is established.

The matter of a viable alternative was considered by the Court of Appeal in *Gard*, in the context of Charlie's parents' grounds of appeal concerning the jurisdiction of the court where there are two viable treatment options.[80] It was argued that in law there are two different categories of cases relating to the medical treatment of children, and that Category 1 cases were those where there was no other treatment option available.[81] Such cases were to be determined according to the best interests test, as now. In contrast, for a Category 2 case, where there is a viable alternative treatment option proposed by the parents and the court must choose between the options, then the parents' position must be respected unless 'it is established that the pursuit of that option is likely to cause the child to suffer "significant harm"'.[82] After setting out both parties' arguments, the Court did not provide an explicit definition of a viable alternative treatment but McFarlane LJ said that Francis J had:

> made clear findings that going to America for treatment would be futile, would have no benefit and would simply prolong the awful existence that he found was the current state of Charlie's life, he was fully entitled, on the basis of those findings to conclude as he did. The consequences of that conclusion is that the proposal for nucleoside therapy was not a viable option before the court.[83]

[79] J Bridgeman, 'Innovative Therapy and the Law: The Novel Issues Raised by the Case of Charlie Gard' (2018) 34 *Professional Negligence* 5.

[80] *Gard 2* (n 1), [36].

[81] ibid, [56]–[60].

[82] ibid, [58]. For further discussion of 'significant harm' as the test in medical treatment cases involving children, see D Wilkinson, 'In Defence of a Conditional Harm Threshold for Paediatric Decision Making', chapter 5 above.

[83] *Gard 2* (n 1), [97].

This suggests that for an alternative treatment to be viable, it must offer (some? how much?) benefit and not just prolong the existing state of affairs. Without such, 'There is no viable, alternative treatment for poor Charlie. That is the incontrovertible consequence of the judge's findings.'[84] Given this, 'the question of whether, as a matter of law, there is a group of cases to be labelled "Category 2", simply and most sadly does not arise for Charlie'.[85] It is thus not yet clear how the court should approach matters where there are viable treatment options, as the question of whether a different test should be applied to Category 2 cases, if such categories exist, was not considered by the Court.

The idea of an experimental treatment as a viable alternative is inherently connected to another matter that falls within the remit of the court – to determine whether the request for experimental treatment is a 'fair request'. The concept of a fair request in this sense draws on and adapts the concept of a 'fair offer' from the Nuffield Council on Bioethics' 2015 report on *Children and Clinical Research*. The Working Group recommended that when considering clinical research with children and young people, a number of questions should be asked, including whether the proposed study represented 'a fair offer to prospective participants',[86] in that 'the value of the research and its likely risks, burdens, and benefits have been carefully weighed up'.[87] In the research context, a fair offer of participating in research recognises that people respond differently to such an invitation, will have different views about what is an acceptable burden or risk for themselves or others, and will 'respond in diverse ways to the "offer"'.[88] Importantly, it 'emphasises that there is also a proper role for a layer of professional scrutiny, to provide the assurance to those subsequently receiving that "offer" or invitation that it is "fair" and can be trusted'.[89]

The concept of a 'fair offer' should be applied to the experimental treatment context because of what is involved and what is being asked here, and it should be phrased in terms of a 'fair request' meaning that a parental request for experimental treatment should be scrutinised to ensure that it is a request for a medically appropriate treatment – a viable alternative. Adapting the Working Group's clarification of the meaning of a 'fair offer', the role of the court is thus to:

> ensure that [a request for experimental treatment] would constitute a ['fair request'] … where the value of the [experimental treatment] and its likely risks, burdens and benefits have been carefully weighed up. This concept of [experimental treatment] as a ['fair request'] emphasises that it remains the ultimate responsibility of [the court] to make independent judgments about acceptable levels of risk and burden, and how these may be balanced against any possible benefits.[90]

[84] ibid, [113].

[85] ibid, [113].

[86] Nuffield Council on Bioethics, *Children and Clinical Research: Ethical Issues* (Nuffield Council on Bioethics, 2015) xxxvii. I was a member of this Working Group.

[87] ibid, 128.

[88] K Wright, 'Are Children Vulnerable in Research?' (2015) 7 *Asian Bioethics Review* 201, 209.

[89] ibid.

[90] Nuffield Council (n 86), [5.28].

Once the court has determined that an experimental treatment *is* a viable alternative because it has weighed up 'the likely risks, burdens and benefits', *then* the question becomes 'is it in X's best interests to receive this treatment?' If this approach had been adopted in *Gard*, for example, then once the court had determined that nucleoside therapy was not a viable alternative, that would have been in the end of the matter, as it cannot be thought to be in someone's best interests to receive a treatment that is deemed not to be medically viable.

In setting out the role of the court in requests for experimental treatment cases, my aim is not to introduce or suggest the use of a framework to unnecessarily limit and/or prevent medical advances; however, an 'anything goes' system should also not be tolerated. A request for experimental treatment should not automatically be treated as a fair request for a viable alternative, nor should it be sufficient for there to be a health professional who is willing to provide such treatment and/or for there to be patients or parents who are willing to pay for it.[91] Without an appropriate framework *and* court involvement where there is disagreement between parents and the treating team, we may too easily move to a situation where parents *demand* non-beneficial treatments for their children 'simply by claiming that they are paying out-of-pocket'.[92] Thus, decision-making frameworks, such as those noted in the preceding section, are important tools for the court because:

> While the most trustworthy advances come through the performance of well-designed trials, sometimes experimental treatments based on theoretical considerations alone may lead to major breakthroughs. But such successes are rare, and to be worth trying they must meet a threshold of scientific plausibility that transcends theoretical possibility.[93]

In determining whether the proposed experimental treatment is a viable alternative and that a fair request is being made for its use, the four questions set out by Dame Butler-Sloss in *Simms* are pertinent, with the second question being particularly relevant: does the proposed treatment come within the *Bolam* test?[94] As this is essentially a question of whether the experimental treatment can be viewed as a viable alternative, it applies to the determination of whether the request for experimental treatment is fair. Although it might be thought that adopting the *Bolam* test, along with the provisions in *Bolitho*,[95] would result in experimental treatment not being approved by the court, because the very nature of such treatment is likely to preclude the possibility of a responsible body of medical opinion supporting that request (especially where the treatment has not yet been tried on human beings), Dame Butler-Sloss expressly cautioned against this. She said that

[91] The converse is similarly unacceptable – where a family cannot pay but there is medical support for the experimental treatment. The rationing and limited resources aspects of experimental treatments are noteworthy but are outside the scope of this chapter.

[92] Truog (n 43), 1002.

[93] ibid.

[94] *Simms* (n 33).

[95] *Bolitho v City and Hackney HA* [1997] 3 WLR 1151, HL.

'the *Bolam* test ought not to be allowed to inhibit medical progress' because if that test was to be complied with 'to the fullest extent' then 'no innovative work such as the use of penicillin or performing heart surgery would ever be attempted'.[96] Thus, an experimental treatment could, as it did in *Simms* itself, meet the *Bolam* test.

Simms was cited in *Gard*, in the context of whether the proposed therapy was beneficial,[97] but the four questions asked by Dame Butler-Sloss were not suggested as a framework or an approach to experimental treatment. This is surprising given that, as Bridgeman rightly argues, what was required in *Gard* was an 'explicit assessment of the question whether there was a competent body of professional opinion which supported the trial of innovative therapy'.[98] Without such, the decisions in *Gard* do not, as noted above, 'provide any guidance for those who may in the future be faced with disagreement about what is medically possible'.[99] Given this, Bridgeman suggests that the answer lies in the *Simms* framework, and involves:

> considering professional duties of care in the determination of a competent and reasonable body of professional opinion, determination of the best interests of the child informed by parental knowledge and expertise gained as they care for their child, and good medical practice guidance and processes to ensure that the child is given the best possible care but is not exposed to harm by pioneering, novel, experimental, or innovative therapy.[100]

However, as I noted above, in *KG* the High Court held, in a case involving the administration of 'a novel treatment'[101] to an adult patient with sporadic CJD, that the first question was whether the patient had the capacity to decide for themselves and, given that it was determined that they did not, the best interests test was then to be applied.[102] Thus, Dame Butler-Sloss's questions (i) and (iii) in *Simms* were utilised by Cohen J,[103] but the Official Solicitor's argument that the *Bolam* test should be applied was dismissed and question (ii) was deemed to be unnecessary in a post-Mental Capacity Act 2005 case.[104] No further explanation was provided for this. Without more, I respectfully disagree with this conclusion, and Dame Butler-Sloss's four questions remain, for me, applicable to experimental treatment cases.

Additionally, and while not an experimental treatment case, Bodey J's comments in *An NHS Trust v SR* are also relevant to determining whether there has been a fair request for an experimental treatment. In this case, Bodey J set

[96] *Simms* (n 33), [48].
[97] *Gard 1* (n 1), [125].
[98] Bridgeman (n 79), 20.
[99] ibid.
[100] ibid.
[101] *KG* (n 66), [19].
[102] ibid, [16]–[17].
[103] *Simms* (n 33).
[104] *KG* (n 66), [32]–[33].

out what the court would require 'for there to be any realistic prospect of the court's preferring some complementary alternative to the standard mainstream treatment', including the identification of a clinician who was willing and able to take over the care and medical responsibility of the patient, with experience of treating similarly aged patients with the same condition, and with access to the necessary equipment and infrastructure.[105] Furthermore:

> The treatment proposed by any such clinician would have to be (or should preferably be) properly studied, tested, reported on and peer-reviewed. To have any realistic prospect of becoming selected by the court … the proposed plan would have to have a prognosis as to probable survival rate not much less than (and preferably equal to) the sort of survival rate achievable through the use of the orthodox treatment universally applied at present by oncologists in this country.[106]

And alongside the legal tests set out in *Simms* and in *SR*, a decade ago Brierley and Larcher proposed an eight-point ethical framework for reviewing requests to use innovative treatments in children:

- There should be a clear clinical need for this particular child.
- There is a realistic and reasonable scientific basis for what is proposed, which may be verified by an independent second opinion or review.
- There is realistic expectation that the child is likely to benefit from the intervention …
- There is consensus in the team that what is proposed is in the child's best interests and that there are no other reasonable or feasible or safer alternatives that might achieve the same result.
- The child's family, and the child if competent or able to understand, actually does understand that the procedure is experimental and what its possible risks, benefits and alternatives are …
- Allowing for the pressures produced by the child's clinical condition, there should be no coercion, and the family should be free to withdraw at any time.
- The resources utilised by offering the treatment must be justified against likely success.
- The results of the use must be reported, whatever the outcome.[107]

This framework has been in operation at Great Ormond Street Hospital for nearly a decade,[108] and Larcher and colleagues argue that it 'permits assessment of proposed innovative therapy according to sound ethical and legal principles'.[109]

Such a framework could be transposed into law, and used alongside the framework set out in *Simms* and the crucial points made in *SR*. Although it would be the court that would be ultimately using such frameworks to determine whether a fair request for a viable alternative has been made, treating teams and parents could also use them *before* a case reaches court – and using them may, in fact, prevent cases

[105] *SR* (n 34), [25].
[106] ibid.
[107] Brierley and Larcher (n 52), 652–53.
[108] Larcher and colleagues reported on the use of their framework between 2011 and 2016: Larcher et al (n 6).
[109] ibid, 42.

reaching court. My hope is that if frameworks were clearly set out and applied to experimental treatment requests, then this could strengthen the faith which could be placed in such a request, as well as in the actual treatment itself.

D. A Reminder as to why the Court should be the Ultimate Decision-Maker where Parents and Treating Teams Disagree about Using Experimental Treatment

Holmes J, in a very different context, famously commented that 'parents may be free to become martyrs themselves but it does not follow they are free, in identical circumstances, to make martyrs of their children'.[110] Although a child receiving experimental treatment is not (or may not be) a martyr as such, it is the idea that there are some things that we are able to do or decide for ourselves but that we cannot do the same for our children that is of interest to me here. Similar sentiments have been expressed in cases in this jurisdiction concerning children's medical treatment. So, for example, in *SR* there was disagreement between the parents as to the treatment N (the son) should receive (conventional treatment – the father and health professionals; or complementary and alternative treatment – the mother). The court was asked to determine which treatment was in N's best interests.[111] The treating team dismissed using complementary or alternative medicine, and it was said that: 'The case of an adult is different, as he or she can weigh risks and take his or her own decision as to his or her preferred treatment.'[112] It is not clear from the case report whether this was a comment from one of the treating team or the judge, nevertheless, it is, I suggest, correct. Indeed, when explaining what would be needed for a court to select complementary medicine as opposed to standard treatment, Bodey J said 'and I repeat that this is not a decision to be made by an adult for himself, but for a child'.[113] Finally, when discussing N's mother's attitude to sickness medication, which she was against, he said:

> That's a perfectly fair enough as a belief for herself; but it can't be in N's interests that the treating clinicians have to face the potential of being blocked as regards treatments which they would normally carry out in the interests of the welfare of their patient.[114]

So, there is a sense that there are some things that it is acceptable for us to believe and to accept for ourselves, but which cannot/should not be imposed upon or

[110] *Prince v Massachusetts* 321 US 158, 165 (1944) (US Supreme Court). Repeated by Ward J in *Re E (A minor) (Wardship: Medical Treatment)* [1993] 1 FLR 386, 391 (*Re E*).
[111] *SR* (n 34).
[112] ibid, [13].
[113] Ibid, [25].
[114] ibid, [27] (Bodey J).

transferred to others. We can think, too, of the Jehovah's Witness cases involving minors.[115]

There is something fundamentally different between saying 'I accept this risk for myself' and 'I accept this risk for someone else to take',[116] because the former can be seen as an expression of our autonomy whereas the latter cannot. On what basis, then, would we tolerate taking risks for another where their health is concerned? Is it (or should it be) enough to say that this decision falls within the remit of parental responsibility? The law permits parents to make medical decisions for their children, including whether they undergo some types of surgery, are vaccinated, or are circumcised. In consenting to such procedures, they are consenting to certain risks to which their child will be exposed. Surgery, for example, always carries with it the certain risks associated with anaesthesia; however, when we are dealing with experimental treatment things are different because of the nature and status of that treatment, and the fact that what is at issue is both experimental and medical.

Where an experimental treatment exists, all concerned must be aware that its efficacy is, as yet, unproven and that the 'best available evidence' may only relate to use on no human animals or on non-human animals only, and/or on other human beings with similar but different conditions. This important message may, however, get lost because of the faith that exists in the medical profession's ability to cure all, and the fact that the *possibility* that an experimental treatment raises may further engender religious-based faith and hope. Moreover, understandings of 'scientific plausibility' and 'theoretical possibility' are critically important when experimental treatment may be available,[117] because of the inherent uncertainty involved in such treatment. However, as I have already noted, drawing *and understanding* the boundary between established and experimental treatment is difficult but can be crucial, particularly where there is disagreement between the parents and the treating team.

Additionally, parents are likely to be asked to consent to experimental treatment for their child at a time when they will be under enormous stress and strain.[118] There may thus be legitimate questions as to their ability to reason, such that these may be situations where an external voice is required precisely because of the inherent difficulty that parents face in making decisions.[119] With experimental treatment we are dealing with uncertainty in terms of, for example, knowledge, risks and benefits, and parental decision-making is likely to be influenced by possibilities, faith and hope. Such uncertainty might be manageable when we are asked

[115] See, eg, *Re S (A minor) (medical treatment)* [1993] 1 FLR 376; *Re E* (n 110); *Re O (A minor) (medical treatment)* [1993] 2 FLR 149; *Re R (A minor) (blood transfusion)* [1993] 2 FLR 757.

[116] Shilling and Young make a similar point in relation to parents deciding whether their child should participate in a clinical trial: Shilling and Young (n 22), 1–2.

[117] Truog (n 43).

[118] Making this point in relation to paediatric clinical trials, see Shilling and Young (n 22), 2.

[119] See also Harrop (n 7); Shilling and Young (n 22), 4.

to consent to experimental treatment for ourselves, but it is different when we are being asked to agree to it for our child. Therefore, concerns about the request for an experimental treatment may be more acute when children are involved. This was recognised by Bodey J in *SR* where, talking about N's mother, he said:

> I'm worried that her judgement has gone awry as to the extent of the seriousness of the threat which N currently faces. … It concerns me that she may have become somewhat overwhelmed by the process whilst this case has been in court.[120]

Similarly, in *Re JM*, J's parents explained to their paediatric oncologist why they did not consent to an operation to remove a facial tumour, preferring Chinese medicine. The oncologist told the court that the parents:

> have not heard that the prospect of him growing up is completely remote, completely impossible, if they do not have surgery. … It's not that I have not tried to say that, and I have been very explicit, but *there is a difference between hearing the words and processing the words. … That is one of their issues. I think that they have struggled with the consent process* [emphasis added].[121]

This is not surprising, and in *Haastrup* MacDonald J said that Isaiah's parents' views were 'heavily influenced by the flattering voice of hope',[122] such that their evidence was not deemed to be reliable.[123] Could the same be said about parental decision-making in relation to experimental treatment?

Brierley and Larcher have raised this possibility and asked:

> How can the clinicians who propose using [innovative] therapy to the parents of a seriously ill child resolve the obvious problems in obtaining consent? Can parents really understand what is being proposed? How can they rationally consider the balance between the risks and benefits of a treatment when little is known of these risks and benefits? Does not the fact that this treatment may be the last possible curative option for the child produce extreme coercion?[124]

These questions deserve careful consideration, and concerns about parental decision-making capacity may be intensified:

> if there are concerns that the family's justifiable worry about their child's condition and their desperation might impair their ability or competence to understand what is being proposed. … The extent to which the family might feel that they must accept any treatment, which might prolong their child's life, could potentially reduce the voluntariness of the choices they make and should be sensitively explored.[125]

Such concerns have been raised in the context of parents consenting to their children being involved in research, and it has been noted that consent for paediatric

[120] *SR* (n 34), [22].
[121] *Re JM (A child)* [2015] EWHC 2832 (Fam), [10].
[122] This phrase was also used by MacDonald J in *Y and MH* (n 37), [45]: 'the father cannot quite bring himself to quiet the flattering voice of hope'.
[123] *Haastrup* (n 9), [92].
[124] Brierley and Larcher (n 52), 653.
[125] ibid.

oncology research, for example, 'is often required shortly after families have received the child's cancer diagnosis, while they are still in shock and disbelief and time to make a decision is limited [reference omitted]'.[126] This may be the case for experimental treatment too. Consent to treatment and research is one of the fundamental principles in healthcare law and ethics; however, Simon Woods and colleagues have argued that the requirements for consent to be valid (provided voluntarily by a person with capacity who is appropriately informed) do not 'leave room for other factors such as the possible false or irrational beliefs held in parallel by the individual, or the role that hope may play in the interpretation of facts and reasons'.[127] They suggest that '[t]hese other factors grow in significance when the person consenting is not the person who will be the bearer of the risk such as when parents are consenting for their child'.[128] Although parents may be free from external coercion, the question is whether their consent is legally valid because their hope and desperation to try anything for their child is overruling all other considerations. This might also be the case with regard to decisions we make about ourselves, but that is a different matter as I have argued above. Nevertheless, in the latter situation, David Price has suggested that:

> Rational decision-making may sometimes be compromised as a result of the vulnerability of the individual. … In particular, suffering and need may cause one to move toward a decision out of desperation rather than deliberateness and adherence to personal values and life choices which serve their core/critical interests.[129]

If this holds true when we are making decision for ourselves, there is no reason for it not to do so when we are called to make decisions for others, especially our children. Indeed, David Locke has said that:

> It is not for no reason that … the sanctions for serious criminality are not determined by the victims of the crime, or their families. The obligation to take an objective position, in a situation which is by definition so personally emotive, is realistically impossible. It is the same unavoidable, yet understandable subjectivity in the determination of the best interests of a sick child which means families cannot be the final arbiters. Any attempt to argue the contrary is no doubt an interesting philosophical exercise, but it certainly does not reflect a workable reality.[130]

Having said that, Woods and colleagues' suggestion could also be criticised on the basis that '[t]o attempt an examination of a participant's motives, or those of

[126] SAAS Dekking, R van der Graaf and JJM van Delden, 'Voluntary Informed Consent in Paediatric Oncology' (2016) 30 *Bioethics* 440, 442. Also, Shilling and Young (n 22).

[127] Woods et al (n 22), 15.

[128] ibid.

[129] D Price, 'Exploitation, Akrasia, and Goldilocks: How Many Pounds for Flesh for Medical Uses?' (2013) 21 *Medical Law Review* 519, 550–51.

[130] D Locke, 'A Common Purpose, a Common Humanity – Lessons from the Charlie Gard Case', *New Law Journal* (27 July 2017), www.newlawjournal.co.uk/content/common-purpose-common-humanity-lessons-charlie-gard-case.

their proxy, could even be seen as overly paternalistic and intrusive'.[131] Although this might be the case, it is also true that civil courts regularly consider questions of motivation, such as in cases regarding misfeasance in a public office, abuse of process, or malicious prosecution.[132] Furthermore, it is also true that:

> If a valid consent requires that the person consenting meets certain conditions, voluntariness and freedom from relevant constraints, appropriately informed, and able to use this information so as to weigh the risks and benefits of participation, then it matters that each component is satisfied to the relevant degree.[133]

In the light of all of the above, when there is disagreement between parents and the treating team as to experimental treatment the court should be responsible for authorising it. In such an intense and emotionally charged situation, it is not reasonable, responsible or appropriate to ask parents to decide whether experimental treatment should be provided to their child. Their hope that such treatment will work intensifies the situation they are in, and there is a risk that they will feel obliged to agree to experimental treatment in order not to be seen to be giving up on their child.[134] Although not an experimental treatment case, Hayden J noted in *Evans* that Alfie's father's 'primary position is that "no stone should be left unturned"', and that that caused a 'core dilemma, from which he struggles to escape', because while he 'recognises and understands fully that the weight of the evidence spells out the futility of Alfie's situation *he is, as a father, unable to relinquish hope* [emphasis added]'.[135] This sense of obligation or pressure may be further intensified if 'supporters' and other activists or organisations are also involved in a case, and there could be a subconscious desire not to disappoint or 'let them down' too.

Such pressures should, as far as possible, be removed from parents,[136] and the possibility of stress and distress minimised by transferring the authorisation of experimental treatment to the court. Although some may view this as an inappropriate infringement of parental responsibilities, it may well be welcomed by (or at least be a relief for) others. Indeed, some parents may not want to make what could be seen as the final decision about experimental treatment *because of* what is being asked of them and what a negative response to the request for it might

[131] Woods et al (n 22), 15.

[132] My thanks to John Murphy for this point.

[133] Woods et al (n 22), 15.

[134] Shilling and Young (n 22).

[135] *Evans 1* (n 9), [37].

[136] Note that McHaffie and colleagues reported that some health professionals believed that this was the appropriate response regarding the decision to withhold treatment from babies, 'which was too weighty a burden for parents to bear alone'. In that study, only 3% of doctors and 6% of nurses (of 176 in total) thought that parents should ultimately make the decision: HE McHaffie et al, 'Deciding for Imperilled Newborns: Medical Authority or Parental Autonomy?' (2001) 27 *Journal of Medical Ethics* 104, 105. Doctors' concern about the impact of sharing life or death decisions on families was also noted in G Birchley et al, 'Best Interests' in Paediatric Intensive Care: An Empirical Ethics Study' (2017) 102 *Archives of Disease in Childhood* 930, 932.

mean. As John Paris and colleagues note in the context of withdrawal of treatment from neonates:

> A parental decision to terminate treatment on a child is not the rational calculus of balancing burdens and benefits proposed by philosophers. Nor is it simply the logical conclusion of legal precedents cited by lawyers. These decisions are tormented situations, situations fraught with anguish, ambiguity and doubt. Such situations – overlaid with feelings of guilt, rage and inadequacy – are not readily subjected to rational analysis. Nor are they perceived as an opportunity to exercise personal choice. They are, at best, an awful and unwelcomed burden.[137]

The idea of *not* wanting to be responsible for the final decision was recognised in *Y and MH*, a case involving withholding treatment, and MacDonald J noted that:

> [T]he Father now adopts a position whereby he no longer actively contests the application brought by the Trust for the declarations. *He however cannot bring himself to agree to the declarations. He invites the Court to make a declaration in the best interests of his daughter* [emphasis added].[138]

As parents may, understandably, not want to be the ones to say 'no' when there are no other options available, transferring that decision to the court should reassure parents that they did all they could, and that if their child dies, it is not their fault.[139] It should also reassure the treating team that their opposition to the experimental treatment was reasonable, rational, appropriate. Although this proposal could be challenged as inappropriate for parents who *do* want to make the final decision, the position that parents are in when they are asked to make a decision about experimental treatment, and they and the treating team cannot agree, requires, as I have shown in the above, an external body to make the final decision.

4. Concluding Thoughts

None of this means experimental treatment cannot and should not be provided to those who cannot consent for themselves, but there are compelling reasons for saying that it should fall to a court to decide whether to proceed with such treatment where there is disagreement between the parents and the treating team. As Emma Cave and Emma Nottingham have argued, 'controls over access to innovative medicine are important to protect patients vulnerable to unsubstantiated

[137] JJ Paris, N Graham, MD Schreiber and M Goodwin, 'Approaches to End-of-Life Decision-Making in the NICU: Insights from Dostoevsky's *The Grand Inquisitor*' (2006) 26 *Journal of Perinatology* 389, 390.

[138] See, eg, *Y and MH* (n 37) [31]. Also [33], [44]–[46].

[139] eg, it was reported that the parents of a seriously ill 11-month-old 'could not make the decision to let their daughter die', but 'wanted a judge to take that responsibility': 'Judge Rules to Allow Severely Ill 11-Month Old to "Die Peacefully"', *The Guardian* (13 December 2018), www.theguardian.com/society/2018/dec/13/judge-rules-to-allow-severely-ill-11-month-old-to-die-peacefully.

promises of hope'.[140] It is such controls, if they are clearly set out and explained, which would help to preserve the therapeutic alliance and build trust, and not a blind concession to parental requests as Gold contends.

Where the treating team and parents agree that an experimental treatment should be provided, it may be sufficient for parents to consent to its provision. However, where there is disagreement, and as a last resort, the court, as an independent, impartial body, should be the ultimate decision-maker. This is because, as Arthur Caplan and Kelly McBride Folkers suggest in relation to *Gard*, 'Charlie's doctors, the courts, and the regulatory system have an appropriate role to play in ensuring that children like Charlie are not subjected to just anything anyone with a medical degree says might help'.[141] And in determining the matter, the court must first decide that there *is* a viable alternative available and that the request for it is fair, *before* considering whether it is in the child's best interests to receive the experimental treatment.

In endorsing a role for the court, I am not advocating an adversarial approach when parents and treating teams disagree about experimental treatment; nor am I ignoring parents' responsibilities to make decisions about their child's healthcare. Rather, these are situations where we should recognise that 'there is no need to compound the suffering … of the parents by insisting they must make a decision'.[142] Indeed, as Bridgeman suggests, 'Some parents may accept the ruling of the court as an authoritative determination with which they must comply, as a final decision meaning they have done all they can for their child'.[143] Although declaratory relief is currently appropriate in relation to experimental treatment where parents and the treating team disagree, if legal and ethical frameworks regarding such treatment are adopted and utilised, then the need for court involvement could (should?) diminish. Unfortunately, we are not yet close to that point. Until then, it is imperative that we endorse 'a commitment to upholding the integrity of medical practice by refusing to provide treatments that fail to meet a reasonable threshold of scientific justification'.[144] I hope that my proposal will help to move us in the right direction.

[140] E Cave and E Nottingham, 'Who Knows Best (Interests)? The Case of Charlie Gard' (2018) 26 *Medical Law Review* 500, 503.

[141] A Caplan and K McBride Folkers, 'Charlie Gard and the Limits of Parental Authority' (2017) 47 *Hastings Center Report* 15, 16.

[142] Paris et al (n 137), 391.

[143] J Bridgeman, '*Gard and Yates v GOSH*, the Guardian and the United Kingdom: Reflections on the Legal Process and the Legal Principles' (2017) 17 *Medical Law International* 285, 291.

[144] Truog (n 43), 1002.

9

Futility

CRESSIDA AUCKLAND

1. Introduction

This chapter will explore the way in which the courts are using the concept of 'futility' in cases involving the decision to treat or to withdraw treatment from a seriously ill child. It will argue that the courts have employed different understandings of the concept in different contexts, with futility being used interchangeably to refer both to a treatment being incapable of working or achieving a certain outcome, and to it being 'pointless', or unable to provide an 'effective benefit'. Understood in the former way, it is an objective and binary assessment: either the treatment is futile, or it is not. Taken in the latter sense, however, as it was in the Charlie Gard and Alfie Evans cases, it inevitably involves a value-laden assessment of what constitutes a meaningful 'benefit' or advantage to the child, and whether or not the chance of achieving this is worth undergoing the treatment in question. The effect of conflating the two is to obscure this, couching a value judgement about what constitutes worthwhile life as an objective fact about the likelihood of the treatment being successful. The result is that the courts often fail to confront honestly and openly the real question at the heart of many of the disputes brought before them: whether or not the treatment can achieve a quality of life that justifies its application.

2. The Value of 'Futility'

The concept of treatment being futile in some cases is not new: as far back as 400 BC Hippocrates was reputed to have said that physicians should not treat patients who were 'overmastered by their disease'.[1] However, it was not until the early 1990s that the concept became prevalent in the medical and ethical literature,[2]

[1] M Whitmer, S Hurst, M Prins et al, 'Medical Futility: A Paradigm as Old as Hippocrates' (2009) *Dimensions of Critical Care Nursing* 28, 67.

[2] For further discussion of this, see D Wilkinson and J Savulescu, 'Knowing When to Stop: Futility in the Intensive Care Unit' (2011) 24 *Current Opinion in Anaesthesiology* 160, 161.

as a means of resolving (or at least avoiding) disputes where the patient's family disagree with the doctors over whether or not further treatment ought to be provided. It was also at this time that the concept was first used by the courts as a justification for withdrawing life-sustaining treatment. In 1993 in the case of Tony Bland, an 18-year-old who had been left in a persistent vegetative state following the Hillsborough disaster, Lord Goff observed that:

> I cannot see that medical treatment is appropriate or requisite simply to prolong a patient's life, when such treatment has *no therapeutic purpose of any kind*, as where it is *futile* because the patient is unconscious and *there is no prospect of any improvement in his condition* [emphasis added].[3]

The effect of deeming the treatment futile in this case was therefore to relieve the doctors of the obligation to provide it. Futility thus triggers a shift in the doctors' ethical and legal obligations towards the patient, justifying the withdrawal (or withholding) of life-sustaining treatment. This was reiterated by Dame Elizabeth Butler-Sloss in *Re L*, who noted that: 'There is a strong presumption in favour of preserving life, but not where treatment would be futile, and there is no obligation on the medical profession to give treatment which would be futile.'[4]

Since the doctor is no longer under any obligation to offer the treatment to the patient, however, there is also no longer the same legal imperative to involve the patient in that decision. Charles Weijer and Carl Elliott have thus described futility as an 'ethical trump card', permitting (even requiring in some cases) doctors to withhold or withdraw care deemed inappropriate without subjecting the decision to patient approval.[5] John Lantos et al meanwhile, have argued that a finding of futility lessens the physician's obligation to discuss therapies or treatment with the patient, thus reducing patient participation in the decision.[6] There are some limits on this: although doctors are not generally legally obliged to discuss treatment that is not clinically indicated, in *Tracey v Cambridge University Hospitals NHS Foundation Trust & Ors*,[7] the Court of Appeal nonetheless unanimously held that the fact that cardiopulmonary resuscitation would be futile does not remove the need for the doctor to consult with the patient and their family about the decision to put a "do not attempt cardiopulmonary resuscitation" (DNACPR) order in place. Giving the leading judgment, Lord Dyson MR gave two reasons for this, both of which may be applicable outside of the DNACPR context:

> First, a decision to deprive the patient of potentially life-saving treatment is of a different order of significance for the patient from a decision to deprive him or her of other

[3] *Airedale NHS Trust v Bland* [1993] AC 789, 869 (*Airedale*).

[4] *Re L (Medical Treatment: Benefit)* [2005] 1 FLR 491, [12].

[5] C Weijer and C Elliott, 'Pulling the Plug on Futility: Futility Is Not the Ethical Trump Card that Some Would Like It to Be' (1995) 310 *British Medical Journal* 683, 683.

[6] J Lantos et al, 'The Illusion of Futility in Clinical Practice' (1989) 87 *American Journal of Medicine* 81.

[7] *Tracey v Cambridge University Hospitals NHS Foundation Trust & Ors* [2014] EWCA Civ 822.

> kinds of treatment. It calls for particularly convincing justification. Prima facie, the patient is entitled to know that such an important clinical decision has been taken. The fact that the clinician considers that CPR will not work means that the patient cannot require him to provide it. It does not, however, mean that the patient is not entitled to know that the clinical decision has been taken. Secondly, if the patient is not told that the clinician has made a DNACPR decision, he will be deprived of the opportunity of seeking a second opinion.[8]

Thus far, this decision has only been applied in the context of DNACPR orders and it is yet to be seen whether the principle will be applied to other life-sustaining treatments. Nonetheless it is clear that although the patient must be consulted in such cases, once a doctor has deemed the treatment to be futile, they are under no obligation either to provide the treatment *or* to involve the patient in that decision, beyond informing them that the decision has been taken. It is clear therefore that a finding that a treatment is futile is legally and ethically hugely significant. This is especially true given evidence that most deaths in emergency departments and intensive care units result from the withholding or withdrawal of treatment.[9] If futility operates as the justification in these cases for a failure to provide further treatment to the person, it is imperative that there is a clear understanding of what the concept means and when it is applied – both clinically, and in the courts. Unfortunately, this is severely lacking.

3. Differing Conceptions of Futility

Evidence suggests there is no shared understanding of futility, either in the way that it is being referred to in the ethical literature, or in how it is being applied by doctors and by judges. Julian Savulescu and Dominic Wilkinson, for example, highlight five different definitions of the concept that have been used in the ethical literature:

- **Physiological futility**: Treatment that cannot achieve its physiological aim
- **Quantitative futility**: Treatment that has <1% chance of succeeding
- **Qualitative futility**: Treatment that cannot achieve an acceptable quality of life; treatment that merely preserves unconsciousness or fails to relieve total dependence on intensive medical care
- **Imminent demise futility**: An intervention that will not change the fact that the patient will die in the near future.
- **Lethal condition futility**: The patient has an underlying condition that will not be affected by the intervention and which will lead to death within weeks to months.[10]

It is not necessary to draw out the differences between these conceptualisations in detail. Suffice to say, however, that deeming treatment futile because it cannot

[8] ibid, [55].
[9] Wilkinson and Savulescu (n 2).
[10] ibid, 161.

succeed or achieve a certain physiological aim is markedly different from deeming it so because it cannot achieve a quality of life that the doctor deems minimally acceptable. Both of the former involve objective assessments about the efficacy of the treatment in question; the latter meanwhile, entails a value-laden assessment about what constitutes a worthwhile, or minimally acceptable, quality of life, and whether this is capable of being achieved.

This inconsistency has also afflicted the case-law, where judges have varied between talking about the likelihood of a given treatment working (physiological or quantitative futility above) and whether or not it can achieve a quality of life that is thought to be worth sustaining (qualitative futility); as well as talking interchangeably about the *treatment* as futile, the patient's *situation* as futile and, perhaps most concerningly, the patient's *life* as futile. These differing uses of the term will be explored in the following section. Given that the most extensive discussion of the concept of 'futility' has taken place in the context of adult treatment decisions and it is on this which the judgments in cases such as *Gard* rely, this section will briefly consider the development of the concept more broadly, before turning to consider how it has been applied in the specific context of very young children.

A. The Development of Futility in the Case-Law

As noted above, the notion of futility originates in the case-law in the decision in *Bland*.[11] In the quote from the case given above, Lord Goff frames futility in absolute terms, using it to denote treatments that have '*no* therapeutic purpose *of any kind*',[12] because there is '*no* prospect of *any* improvement in [the patient's] condition'.[13] Certainly this is how it has been subsequently interpreted: in *Aintree v James* for example,[14] Lady Hale read this passage as suggesting that futility applied where a treatment can have '*no* benefit *at all* to the patient [emphasis added]'.[15] That the concept should be framed in such limited terms is unsurprising on the facts: Tony Bland was in a persistent vegetative state, and so the treatment in question was completely unable to improve his condition. The cases that follow, however, demonstrate a substantial broadening out of the meaning of futility, well beyond the narrow confines of *Bland*.

Pivotal to the legal conception of futility is the case of *Aintree v James*, where disagreement arose between the appellate courts over the meaning of the concept, and how it ought to be applied on the facts of that case. Mr James was a man in a minimally conscious state, who had been in intensive care for seven months when

[11] *Airedale* (n 3).
[12] ibid, 869.
[13] ibid.
[14] *Aintree University Hospitals NHS Foundation Trust v James* [2013] UKSC 67 (*James*).
[15] ibid, [38].

his treating clinicians applied to the Court of Protection for a declaration that it would be lawful to withhold further invasive treatment and CPR. At first instance, Mr Justice Peter Jackson was 'unpersuaded' that further treatment for Mr James was 'futile', explaining that:

> (a) In Mr James's case, the treatments in question cannot be said to be futile, based upon the evidence of their effect so far. (b) Nor can they be said to be futile in the sense that they could only return Mr James to a quality of life that is not worth living.[16]

Echoing the quantitative/qualitative futility distinction above, this implies that futility may be taken to have two different meanings. The first is that the treatment is *incapable of working* (and so, as there was evidence of it providing some positive therapeutic benefit to Mr James in this case, this could not be established). The second is that the *quality of life* that it achieves for the patient is not one worth pursuing, thus explicitly recognising a role for value judgements about what constitutes a worthwhile life in determinations that treatment is futile. This would seem to be a significant broadening out of the conception from that put forward by Lord Goff in *Bland.* Although it will often be the case that these two different understandings will coexist in a patient, there is a clear conceptual difference between saying a treatment provides *no* prospect of improvement to the patient, and saying it will not achieve a quality of life that the doctor regards as meaningful. Indeed it was precisely the value-laden nature of this formulation that was the subject of criticism by Sir Alan Ward in the Court of Appeal, who considered Mr Peter Jackson to have erred in his finding about futility.[17] He observed that:

> To answer the question whether the proposed treatment would be futile one had to ask what result the treatment sought to produce. Futility was an ethically controversial concept because what was worthwhile could only be assessed relative to its goal. Thus the crucial question was to determine what the proper goal was for life-sustaining treatment.

Accordingly, he went on to suggest various goals that could be identified for life-sustaining treatment. These included:

> (i) to prevent the patient's imminent death from the particular ailment which the treatment was designed to overcome;
> (ii) having prevented imminent death, to prolong life even though it was recognised that it would be for a relatively brief time only;
> (iii) to delay death even though it would not result in any significant alleviation of the patient's suffering;
> (iv) to provide for the patient a minimum quality of life for the remainder of his life;
> (v) to allow the patient to achieve the goal (or the wish) he had set for himself;
> (vi) to secure therapeutic benefit for the patient, that is the treatment, standing alone or with other medical care, had to have the real prospect of curing or at least palliating the life-threatening disease or illness from which the patient was suffering.[18]

[16] *An NHS Trust v DJ* [2012] EWHC 3524 (COP), [2012] MHLO 138, [84].
[17] *James* (n 14), [34].
[18] ibid, [35].

Having concluded that futility could not be judged simply by the ability to provide (i)–(iii), as there was no duty to prolong or maintain life at all costs,[19] he went on to say that:

> As for goal (iv), it was difficult to deny that there was *implicit in every judgement about whether treatment was futile or worthwhile a judgement about the quality of life the patient would have with or without that treatment*. Like it or not, lurking within the question, or perhaps behind it, was the ethically controversial question: was it worthwhile keeping this patient alive? [emphasis added][20]

Having noted the existence of this 'ethically controversial question', however, he did not seek to address or discuss it in any great detail. Instead he concluded that futility ought to be judged by reference purely to criterion (vi), that is, whether or not the treatment has a real prospect of 'curing or at least palliating the life-threatening disease or illness'. Although it is arguable that criterion (vi) may be under-inclusive (as will be explored later, there may be interventions which neither 'cure' nor 'palliate' a life-threatening illness but which nonetheless provide a therapeutic benefit to the patient), importantly, this definition of futility looked *only* at whether or not the treatment would bring a therapeutic benefit to the patient, not at the quality of life the patient, thus placing the problem firmly in the medical field, and avoiding the value judgements inherent in Mr Justice Peter Jackson's conception. Separating out the question of medical efficacy from assessments of quality of life also helped to distinguish those questions that doctors might be better placed to determine, from those that others (the patient and their family) may be just as well placed to decide.

Sir Alan Ward's attempt to confine futility to assessments of clinical efficacy was, however, short lived. In the Supreme Court, it was Mr Justice Peter Jackson's conception of futility that found favour with Lady Hale. Disagreeing with the findings of the Court of Appeal, she suggested that Mr Justice Peter Jackson had been 'correct to consider whether the proposed treatments would be futile in the sense of being ineffective or *being of no benefit to the patient*',[21] thus reintroducing the notion of whether or not the treatment could be regarded as 'beneficial' to the patient. In doing so, Lady Hale explicitly rejected the views of both the Intensive Care Society and the Faculty of Intensive Medicine, who intervened in the case, both of which favoured Sir Alan Ward's conception, which they felt better reflected the clinical understanding of the term – that the patient will not survive from the treatment.

While accepting the twofold test for futility put forward by Justice Peter Jackson, however, she also went some way towards addressing the concerns expressed by Sir Alan Ward about doctors or the courts becoming the arbiters

[19] ibid, [36].
[20] ibid.
[21] *James* (n 14), [40].

of whether or not a life is worthwhile. When considering what was meant by 'beneficial' in this context, she explained that:

> [W]here a patient is suffering from an incurable illness, disease or disability, it is not very helpful to talk of recovering a state of 'good health'. The patient's life may still be very well worth living. Resuming a quality of life which the *patient would regard as worthwhile* is more readily applicable, particularly in the case of a patient with permanent disabilities. As was emphasised in *re J [1991] Fam 33*, it is not for others to say that a life which the patient would regard as worthwhile is not worth living. [emphasis added][22]

'Benefit' to the patient was not therefore to be judged by whether or not the person's quality of life was one that the doctor or court considered acceptable. Rather it was a subjective assessment: would the person regard their quality of life in that situation as acceptable?

Although this overcomes some of the difficulties Sir Alan Ward identified, clearly ascertaining what quality of life would have been acceptable to the person will not always be simple, even for adults. This may be because the person has not given any prior thought to this issue, or even if they have, they may not have discussed this with others. Even if they have expressed opinions in the past, it may not be clear whether or not they would still stand by these views in the event that these circumstances eventuate. Relying on studies from psychology, Neil Levy, for example, has found that humans typically discount the future, overestimate the effects of events and changes in circumstances on their level of well-being, and underappreciate their ability to adapt to new circumstances, making them unreliable at predicting how future events will make them feel.[23] There is certainly much anecdotal evidence to support this. Many consider the prospect of life in a wheelchair intolerable, yet evidence suggests that many people who are paralysed frequently adapt and find meaning in their lives,[24] while the reality for people suffering from dementia does not always bear out the fears that many have of developing this disease.[25] It is possible, therefore, that a quality of life which a person might previously have regarded as intolerable does, in the event, provide them with meaning.

Clearly, however, this formulation is even more difficult to apply in the context of very young children. In cases such as that of Charlie Gard and Alfie Evans, both involving profoundly brain-damaged babies, it is meaningless to talk about what they would have wanted or considered to be an acceptable quality of life. To the extent that the courts or doctors attempt to do so, the result is either an assessment

[22] ibid, [44].

[23] N Levy, 'Forced to Be Free? Increasing Patient Autonomy by Constraining It' (2014) 40 *Journal of Medical Ethics* 293.

[24] LC Vogel et al, 'Long-Term Outcomes and Life Satisfaction of Adults Who Had Pediatric Spinal Cord Injuries' (1998) 79 *Archives of Physical Medicine and Rehabilitation* 1496.

[25] D Gilbert, *Stumbling on Happiness* (London, Vintage, 2005) 1.

of what the *decision-maker* generally considers to be an acceptable quality of life, or an assessment of what the *parents* regard as acceptable.

This is readily apparent from the case of *Re A (Withdrawal of Medical Treatment)*,[26] which involved a decision about whether or not it was lawful to remove ventilation from a two-year-old child who, following a road traffic accident, was left in a minimally conscious state, tetraplegic and blind. Lady Justice King cited with approval the trial judge's finding that treatment was futile, 'save simply to keep him alive',[27] with only a 'faint prospect' of any 'measurable benefit'.[28] In line with Lady Hale's understanding of futility in *Aintree*, she accepted the judge's conclusion that she did not think that 'A would want this life for himself'.[29] However, given the position of the child's parents in this case – that it *was* in A's interests to continue ventilation – it is difficult to see on what basis the judge could have reached this conclusion except through applying her own value judgement about what constitutes a worthwhile or minimally acceptable quality of life.

This highlights the difficulty with relying on *this* conception of futility in cases concerning children. Given that these disputes often arise in contexts where the child's parents fundamentally disagree with the treating clinicians over whether or not the quality of life hoped to be achieved through the treatment is worthwhile, it is difficult to see how futility (at least understood in this way) is capable of resolving such disputes. Where the parents regard the child's quality of life with the treatment as worthwhile and the doctors disagree, futility serves only to reframe the dispute, but it does not provide resolution to it.[30] Given this, it is necessary to consider more broadly how the concept of futility has been applied in cases concerning children.

B. The Use of Futility in Treatment Decisions Involving Children

Perhaps for the reasons identified above, in recent cases the courts have moved away from explicitly framing the test of futility in terms of what the child would want. It is clear, however, that underpinning the judgments is still an assessment about whether or not the treatment in question would enable the child to have

[26] *Re A (A Child)* [2016] EWCA Civ 759.

[27] ibid, [58].

[28] ibid.

[29] ibid.

[30] This is not to suggest that the concept of futility could not serve a purpose: as noted above, if understood in a clinical sense (as Sir Alan Ward did), futility may be useful in separating out the question of medical efficacy (which doctors are best placed to determine, and to which medical defences ought to apply) from that of what constitutes an acceptable quality of life (which the parents of the child may be just as well placed to assess).

a quality of life that the judge deems acceptable. In *Gard*, for example,[31] Charlie Gard suffered from an inherited mitochondrial condition, which left him substantially brain damaged, and unable to move or to breathe unaided. Great Ormond Street Hospital (GOSH) sought a declaration that artificial ventilation could be withdrawn from him, a position challenged by his parents who wished to take him to the United States to trial an experimental treatment called nucleoside therapy, which they hoped would improve his quality of life.

In the High Court, Mr Justice Francis ruled that nucleoside therapy would be futile. In doing so, he clarified that 'for the avoidance of any doubt, the word "futile" in this context means pointless or of no effective benefit'.[32] Once again, this leaves open the question of what constitutes an 'effective benefit' or an appropriate purpose. Whether or not something can be deemed 'pointless' depends entirely on what the 'point' of the treatment is deemed to be – which, as Sir Alan Ward cautioned in *Aintree*, may be subject to disagreement. Although, for many people, the point of a treatment will be to achieve a quality of life for the patient that they consider to be acceptable, for others, merely keeping the person alive and physiologically stable might be sufficient to justify it. In the Charlie Gard case itself, an important element of the disagreement between the parents and the doctors was the likely outcome that was going to be achieved if the treatment was successful. For Charlie's parents, the low chance of the treatment working was worth it, given the potential for it to extend his life by a few years and provide for some improvement in his condition. For his doctors, and ultimately the judge, the highest point of evidence was that he might live for a few more years, in a position where he was still profoundly brain-damaged, deaf and unable to move much. To characterise the treatment as futile in this case on the basis that it was 'pointless' for Charlie therefore presupposes that achieving a certain quality of life ought to be the 'point' of such treatment, and that prolonged life in a heavily disabled state is not the 'correct' or appropriate point or goal. The concept therefore does little to help resolve disputes in which the very nature of the disagreement is over what the goal is that ought to be pursued through the treatment: one cannot say something is pointless or is unable to achieve its goal when there is no shared commitment as to what that goal or point is.

Charlie Gard's parents went on to challenge this definition of futility in the Court of Appeal.[33] Drawing on the *Aintree v James* case, they argued that there was a distinction between the medical and legal definitions of futility. In medical terms, treatment that was futile was that which did not have 'a real prospect of curing or at least palliating the life-threatening disease or illness from which the patient is suffering'.[34] This was different from futility in legal terms, which, they

[31] *Great Ormond Street Hospital v Yates and others* [2017] EWHC 972 (Fam) (*Yates*).
[32] ibid, [93].
[33] *Yates & Anor v Great Ormond Street Hospital for Children NHS Foundation Trust & Anor* [2017] EWCA Civ 410, [2017] WLR(D) 391.
[34] ibid, [44].

argued, was a lower standard. Quoting from Lady Hale in *Aintree*, they suggested that medical futility might set the goal too high in cases where treatment 'may bring some benefit to the patient even though it has no effect on the underlying disease or disability'.[35] Accordingly whether treatment was futile for Charlie ought to be judged not by reference to whether it could cure him, but following *Aintree*, by whether it could bring *some* benefit to him, which his parents argued it could.

Giving judgment, Lord Justice Macfarlane did not dispute the existence of this distinction, but felt nonetheless that this was a 'difference without distinction' in the present case, as the trial judge had considered the benefit of nucleoside therapy to be 'zero' and therefore further treatment was 'pointless, or of no effective benefit'.[36] In fact, the trial judge had said that the prospect of the therapy having any benefit was 'as close to zero as makes no difference'.[37] Even if one accepts this as being effectively a 'zero chance' of producing any improvement in Charlie, importantly, however, neither the trial judge, nor Lord Justice Macfarlane, were explicit about why exactly it was that Charlie was expected to gain *no* benefit from the treatment.

One possible interpretation of this is that Lord Justice Macfarlane meant that the treatment had 'zero' chance of being successful. Understood in this way, the distinction proposed would not have made any difference in this case: offering the treatment would be pointless, not because the end sought to be achieved was pointless, but because it was *incapable* of achieving any benefit whatsoever – it simply would not work. Futility thus understood is an objective clinical fact, albeit not one that will always be easy to ascertain in practice.

If futility is understood in this way, however, then Lord Justice Macfarlane's suggestion that this was a 'difference without distinction' holds true only to the extent that one accepts that the chance of the nucleoside therapy working in this case was effectively zero – a conclusion that is certainly open to challenge on the evidence presented in *Gard*. The distinction will, however, be of huge importance in any case where the chance of treatment working is not quite so low. If the parents' submission is correct, and something ought not to be treated as futile if it may provide *some* therapeutic benefit to the person, then it follows that providing treatment is not *incapable* of working, it cannot be said to be futile at all.

Alternatively, Lord Justice Macfarlane may have meant that even in the event that the treatment was successful, the benefit to Charlie would be zero – that is, it would not result in any *meaningful* improvement to his condition. Although not made explicit in *Gard*, it seems that at the heart of this case was a concern that even if the nucleoside therapy was successful, the benefits it produced (in terms of prolonged life and minor physical improvements) were not sufficient to justify the

[35] ibid.
[36] ibid.
[37] *Yates* (n 31), [119].

risks and potential harms involved in trialling a highly experimental treatment. The issue, then, was not that nucleoside therapy was *incapable* of working – albeit extremely unlikely – but that it simply was not 'worth it', given the very limited improvements Charlie was likely to experience. Mr Justice Francis noted for example, that

> even if the treatment was to enter Charlie's brain and have a therapeutic effect, *the highest point of the evidence* (Dr I) was that if Charlie's seizures were controlled he would presumably be able to interact with others, to smile, to look at objects and to use his hands to grab objects [emphasis added].[38]

The implication of this is that this quality of life was not sufficient to warrant the treatment, and outweigh the potential risks of pain or mutations. Further evidence for this can be found in the fact that GOSH was initially willing to trial the nucleoside therapy, before Charlie suffered from a series of epileptic seizures that caused irreversible brain damage. Although the chances of nucleoside therapy working before had also been slim, the doctors had been willing to give this very small chance a go, if it could provide a meaningful quality of life for Charlie. What changed was not that it could no longer work, but that as it would not be possible to reverse the structural brain damage he had suffered, the treatment was no longer worth it. The quality of life that Charlie was expected to have – even if the treatment did work – was no longer one that justified its application.

By relying on the concept of futility in this case, the court thus avoided engaging in the real question: was the extremely small chance of improvement in his condition worth the potential pain and discomfort he might experience through having the treatment, given that his quality of life will remain significantly impaired? This is, as Julian Savulescu argues, 'not an "objective fact" but a value judgement';[39] and one that considers not just treatment efficacy but the quality of life that the child may expect if the treatment is successful. The language of futility therefore obscures the value judgement at the heart of the decision, by placing the emphasis on the treatment alone, and not on the foreseeable quality of life of the child. In doing so, an assessment of what constitutes an acceptable or meaningful quality of life is masked as an objective and purely medical assessment of whether or not a given treatment will work.

In fact, this is precisely the difficulty that Sir Alan Ward noted in *Aintree* when he advocated sticking to a purely medical and objective understanding of futility. If an assessment about whether or not the quality of life of a child is deemed to be minimally acceptable is to be made, it is imperative that it be made openly and transparently, not obscured by medical probabilities and statistics, and insulated from potential challenge by the parents. This is especially so given that it is a judgement over which people may (as the Gards did) legitimately disagree. The effect

[38] ibid, [120].

[39] J Savulescu, 'Is It in Charlie Gard's Best Interest to Die?' (2017) 389 *Lancet* 1868, 1868.

is also to place the parents on the back foot: if the decision is framed as being one about the clinical efficacy of a given treatment, then absent evidence from other medical professionals who disagree with the treating clinicians, it remains almost impossible for parents to challenge a finding of 'futility'. Given that an assessment about whether the foreseeable quality of life of a child justifies a treatment course is not a purely clinical decision, nor one over which doctors – or indeed judges – are necessarily any better placed to decide than parents, it is wholly inappropriate to contain it within the clinical domain.

It may well be that in the case of Charlie Gard, the quality of life he would achieve was sufficiently low that the court were right to regard treatment as not in his best interests. But the very small chance of it succeeding in this case should be one of many factors or interests that are considered in the round when deciding if the treatment is in his best interests test, not a trump card that outweighs all other considerations. After all, as Julian Savulescu has argued:

> [I]f [the odds] are not zero, why not have a trial of treatment for several months, or a year, under strict pain control (which we are told is so effective in palliative care)? The parents seemed to accept that Charlie's current state was not one which was worth prolonging and if no progress was made, one could stipulate that treatment must be withdrawn. … Is a month or year of experimental treatment that offers a slim chance of improvement clearly against his interests?[40]

In this respect, the judgment in the subsequent case of Isaiah Hastruup is preferable.[41] Mr Justice MacDonald did not invoke the concept of futility at all in his judgment that further treatment would not be in Isaiah's best interests. Rather he was explicit that 'to continue life-sustaining treatment for Isaiah will not result in his recovery and will condemn him to a life of profoundly limited quality'.[42] In this case, the parents of Isaiah wanted a tracheotomy to be performed on him and for artificial ventilation to be continued at home, in the hope of extending his life. The approach of the judge would therefore seem correct – the treatment in question could not rightly be described futile, since ventilation via a tracheotomy undoubtedly *would* achieve its aim of sustaining his life for a little longer. The disagreement was not then over the efficacy of the treatment, but over whether such treatment was sustainable, given that Isaiah's condition would not improve.

It is notable that in the Alfie Evans case,[43] which involved essentially the same question as *Hastruup* (his parents also wished for him to have a tracheotomy and further ventilation), the concept of futility was relied upon on multiple occasions by the trial judge. The very fact that futility was invoked at all in *Evans* would seem

[40] J Savulescu, 'Debate: The Fiction of an Interest in Death? Justice for Charlie Gard', *Journal of Medical Ethics Blog* (26 April 2017), blogs.bmj.com/medical-ethics/2017/04/26/debate-the-fiction-of-an-interest-in-death-justice-for-charlie-gard/.

[41] *Kings College Hospital NHS Foundation Trust v Ms Thomas, Haastrup and Haastrup* [2018] EWHC 127 (Fam).

[42] ibid, [110].

[43] *Alder Hey Children's NHS Foundation Trust v Mr Thomas Evans, Ms Kate James, Alfie Evans (A Child by his Guardian CAFCASS Legal)* [2018] EWHC 308 (Fam).

to lend support for the suggestion that the courts are using the concept to apply not only to the question of whether a treatment is capable of working, but also to whether the perceived outcomes of it are thought desirable. In this case, the treatment proposed was only ever likely to prolong Alfie's life, never to cure him – it was not seriously in dispute that his prognosis was ultimately terminal. To talk of the treatment being futile here is therefore unhelpful. Performing the tracheotomy, providing artificial feeding and continued ventilation, may well have prolonged his life. What it could not do was restore his life to a quality that the doctors and the judge considered to be acceptable or worthwhile. It was this, not whether or not the treatment would work, which was the subject of disagreement.

It is perhaps this lack of clarity about whether the decision relates to the efficacy of the treatment or the quality of life of the patient that has led to confusion in some of the case law about whether the term 'futility' ought to be applied to the treatment, or to the life of the patient. In the *Evans* case for example, Mr Justice Hayden switched between talking about the *treatment* being futile, Alfie's *situation* being futile, and his *life* being futile, not only within judgments but also, when asked to reconsider the case, between judgments. In the original judgment for example, he concluded that:

> I have on the parents' behalf taken very great care to evaluate the quality of Alfie's present circumstances, even though I accept entirely the conclusion of the medical evidence *that treatment for Alfie is futile*. It does not follow axiomatically that *the futility of Alfie's situation* leads to the immediate withdrawal of ventilation. Life itself has intrinsic value, however tenuous or vestigial its hold [emphasis added].[44]

Later in the same judgment, he went on to say 'the continued provision of ventilation, *in circumstances which I am persuaded is futile*, now compromises Alfie's future dignity and fails to respect his autonomy',[45] referring to the situation, rather than the treatment per se. In his two later judgments meanwhile, he stated first that in the original hearing he 'came to the conclusion, that Alfie's brain had been so corroded by neurodegenerative disease that his *life* was futile';[46] and later that he had concluded 'that Alfie's *situation* is now futile'.[47]

Saying that further treatment is futile is a wholly different claim from suggesting the child's life is futile. Imprecision in the use of language thus exacerbates the problems identified earlier of conflating the chances of the treatment working, with assessments about whether or not the child will have a worthwhile life. Given the focus of the disagreement was over whether a prolonged life in Alfie's current state was in his best interests, the use of futility does nothing to help resolve the dispute over whether or not his quality of life is acceptable. Relying on it here

[44] ibid, [51].

[45] ibid, [66].

[46] *Alder Hey Children's NHS Foundation Trust v Mr Thomas Evans, Ms Kate James, Alfie Evans (A Child by his Guardian CAFCASS Legal)* [2018] EWHC 818 (Fam).

[47] *Alder Hey Children's NHS Foundation Trust v Mr Thomas Evans, Ms Kate James, Alfie Evans (A Child by his Guardian CAFCASS Legal)* [2018] EWHC 953 (Fam).

therefore serves only to distract and confuse, enabling the courts to fail to confront honestly and openly the value judgement that lies at the heart of their decision.

4. Conclusions

The way that the courts have used the concept of futility in recent cases gives us cause for concern. By using 'futility' to denote both that a treatment is incapable of working, and that it is unable to provide a worthwhile outcome, the courts are able to obscure what are in fact value judgements about whether a child is likely to have a quality of life that they deem to be minimally acceptable as objective facts about the likelihood of the treatment being successful. Given the enormity of a decision that further treatment ought not to be offered to a child because they are not capable of experiencing a life that we regard as meaningful – especially when this is vehemently opposed by their parents – it is imperative that such assessments are made transparently, in a way which is susceptible to scrutiny and challenge, rather than being concealed behind the language of statistics and medical fact.

10

Vulnerability and Medical Decisions Concerning Children

JONATHAN HERRING

1. Introduction

This chapter will use universal vulnerability theory to explore the issues raised by the Charlie Gard and Alfie Evans cases. Universal vulnerability theory claims that everyone is in their nature vulnerable, but this is not recognised in public and legal discourse. The chapter will start by offering a brief summary of universal vulnerability theory and then us it to explore the vulnerabilities of the children, parents, medical staff and judiciary in these cases. Universal vulnerability theory, it will be claimed, offers some insights into the public and legal reaction to these cases.

2. Universal Vulnerability Theory

In this section the universal vulnerability theory will be explained.[1] I will explore its core claim; discuss the sources of vulnerability; and then explain the goods of vulnerability. Once these themes have been covered they will be used to examine the vulnerabilities in the Charlie Gard and Alfie Evans cases.

A. The Core Claim

Universal vulnerability theory is based on the claim that all people are in their nature profoundly vulnerable. Wendy Rogers, Catriona Mackenzie and Susan Dodds summarise the claim of universal vulnerability when they write: '[A]ll human life is conditioned by vulnerability, as a result of our embodied, finite, and

[1] For a more detailed discussion, see J Herring, *Vulnerable Adults and the Law* (Oxford, Oxford University Press, 2016).

socially contingent existence.'[2] Everyone is at constant risk of harm and lacks in themselves the resources to avoid and/or respond to those risks.

It is important to appreciate that universal vulnerability rejects the common approach of identifying vulnerable populations (eg the elderly, children or single parents). Rather it argues that being vulnerable is in the nature of all people. Martha Fineman, the leading proponent of the theory, explains it in this way:

> The vulnerability approach recognises that individuals are anchored at each end of their lives by dependency and the absence of capacity. Of course, between these ends, loss of capacity and dependence may also occur, temporarily for many and permanently for some as a result of disability or illness. Constant and variable throughout life, individual vulnerability encompasses not only damage that has been done in the past and speculative harms of the distant future, but also the possibility of immediate harm. We are beings who live with the ever-present possibility that our needs and circumstances will change. On an individual level, the concept of vulnerability (unlike that of liberal autonomy) captures this present potential for each of us to become dependent based upon our persistent susceptibility to misfortune and catastrophe.[3]

There is some disagreement among vulnerability theorists about how to respond to the fact that even though we may be all inherently vulnerable, this is experienced to a different extent by different people in different contexts. Martha Fineman accepts that in a typical lifespan there will be times of different capacities and strengths. But the typical 'adult liberal subject' focuses on just one part of that life span (middle age) and essentialises this as the standard. That means the base vulnerable state all are in is disguised. She argues:

> Throughout our lives we may be subject to external and internal negative, potentially devastating, events over which we have little control – disease, pandemics, environmental and climate deterioration, terrorism and crime, crumbling infrastructure, failing institutions, recession, corruption, decay, and decline. We are situated beings who live with the ever-present possibility of changing needs and circumstances in our individual and collective lives. We are also accumulative beings and have different qualities and quantities of resources with which to meet these needs of circumstances, both over the course of our lifetime and as measured at the time of crisis or opportunity.[4]

Other writers have suggested that we are equally vulnerable throughout our lives and it is the provision of social resources which grant some people greater resilience to their vulnerability than others. Hence, I have argued, taking this line:

> It is true that at different times and in different circumstances we may be more overtly in use of societal resources but that should not disguise the fact that we are in need of communal and relational support for all our lives. We may be differently positioned

[2] W Rogers, C Mackenzie and S Dodds, 'Why Bioethics Needs a Concept of Vulnerability' (2012) 5 *International Journal of Feminist Approaches to Bioethics* 11, 12.

[3] M Fineman, 'The Vulnerable Subject: Anchoring Equality in the Human Condition' (2008) 20 *Yale Journal of Law & Feminism* 1, 2.

[4] M Fineman, 'Feminism, Masculinities and Multiple Identities' (2013) 13 *Nevada Law Review* 616, 637.

> within a web of economic and social relationships and this will impact on our experience of vulnerability and the resources at our disposal.[5]

This is not the place to seek to resolve that debate and there is no need to for this particular chapter.

B. The Source of the Vulnerability

In this section I will highlight several innate features of humanity which reveal our vulnerable nature.

First, we are corporeal beings. But this corporality creates vulnerability. Our bodies are frail. They are constantly open to sickness, illness and accidents. Our bodies naturally wear down, tire, flake away and ultimately die.[6] Our bodies are dependent for their survival on non-human organisms, other human bodies and the wider environment. Hence the profound vulnerability of our bodies.

Second, our identity and sense of self is constituted in terms of relationships.[7] We define ourselves and relate to the world to a very large extent by how we relate to others and how they relate to us. From our birth we sought to interpret the world around us and develop a sense of self through interactions with those caring for us. The language we use, the way we interpret the world, and the sense of self in the world is generated through these early relationships and develops and changes through subsequent relationships. This highly relational understanding of the self explains our vulnerability. It means we are in constant danger of our self being challenged by others rejecting us, not accepting us as members of a group, not providing the support we expect or using relationships to harm us. As Jo Bridgeman puts it: 'Humans are vulnerable … because we care, love, are intimately connected to others.'[8]

Third, we are all vulnerable because we depend on others for our physical and mental well-being. It is interesting how we overlook our dependence on others. A student recently suggested to me that adults were far less vulnerable than children because children needed someone to bring them food whereas adults did not. I pointed out that nearly all adults depend on farmers, suppliers and shops to bring them food. Our society has built up a wide range of structures and forms of assistance that disguise our vulnerability. Whether we look at public transport, sewerage, shops, provision of electricity – we all depend on a huge range of resources. Few of us could, and fewer seek to, live utterly independent lives. Yet with interdependence comes vulnerability. Others might let us down in the provision of what we need, we might let others down and fail to provide them with what they need.

[5] J Herring, *Vulnerability, Childhood and the Law* (New York, Springer, 2018) 32.

[6] P-L Chau and J Herring, 'My Body, Your Body, Our Bodies' (2007) 15 *Medical Law Review* 34.

[7] J Herring, *Law and the Relational Self* (Cambridge, Cambridge University Press, 2019).

[8] J Bridgeman 'Vulnerabilities, Care and Family Law' in J Wallbank and J Herring (eds), *Vulnerabilities, Care and Family Law* (London, Routledge, 2014) 201.

C. The Good of Vulnerability

One of the most significant aspects of vulnerability theory is that it rejects the popular perception that vulnerability is a characteristic to avoid and to be overcome.[9] Instead it is an inevitable part of our nature that can be welcomed. It certainly has some benefits. Our mutual vulnerability requires us to reach out to others to offer and receive help from them. The virtues of beneficence and compassion are encouraged and necessary. We have to become open to others and our own and other's needs. It creates intimacy and trust. It compels us to focus on interactive, co-operative solutions to the issues we address. As Carseputs it: 'Our vulnerability is inextricably tied to our capacity to give of ourselves to others, to treasure and aspire, to commit to endeavours, to care about justice and about our own and other's dignity.'[10] Our vulnerability requires us to meet out to others to meet their needs and to have our needs met. Our very vulnerability provides us with the seeds for our growth through relationships with others.

I will now turn to the cases of Alfie Evans and Charlie Gard and examine them in light of the universal vulnerability theory.

3. Vulnerably of Alfie and Charlie

Much of the discussions of these cases have revolved around the vulnerability of Alfie and Charlie.[11] Ranjana Das, researching the social media discussion of the cases, explains:

> Analysis reveals that the Twitter presence of the support campaign showed a heavy and sustained use of single words, repeatedly, all of which conjure up an image of violence and devastation inflicted on a vulnerable individual by an unknowable, strange powerful hospital.[12]

And looking at social media general show she writes how the broader picture of the powerful elite against the vulnerable babies and 'ordinary people':

> [T]he discussions show clear moral distinctions between in and out-groups, producing 'the Establishment' (state healthcare systems, doctors, nurses, the judiciary and most politicians) as evil and damaging – the out-group; and 'ordinary' people as the wronged and vulnerable in-group whose voices must be heard, often terming GOSH

[9] D Bedford and J Herring (eds), *Embracing Vulnerability: The Implications and Challenges for Law* (London, Routledge, forthcoming).

[10] A Carse, 'Vulnerability, Agency and Human Flourishing' in Carol Taylor and Alberto Dell'Oro (eds), *Health and Human Flourishing* (Washington, Georgetown University Press, 2006) 48.

[11] Indeed, the very fact they tend to be referred by reference to simply their forenames plays a role in highlighting that.

[12] R Das, 'The Charlie Gard Twitterstorm: A Violent and Negative Impact', blogs.lse.ac.uk/polis/2017/08/04/the-charlie-gard-twitterstorm-a-violent-and-negative-impact-new-research/.

> as Great Ormond Street Hell, rather than hospital. There have been frequent cries that the out-group (GOSH and the judiciary) are 'holding Charlie hostage', or condoning the 'disposing of the disabled'.[13]

It was also a theme that was commonly referred to by the pressure groups who were seeking to influence the outcome of the case. For example, the Family Research Council stated:

> We urge the British government, the courts, and the hospital to release Charlie. You are holding him hostage. This is a case about parental rights coming into conflict with socialised medicine. We must protect the rights of parents to make decisions for their children's health – decisions that are based with best interests in mind. We must protect Charlie, *the most vulnerable person among us* [emphasis added].[14]

The pictures of Alife and Charlie used in the media were carefully selected. They commonly showed the children surrounded by a cuddly toy and apparently asleep. The small size of the children was emphasised by angling the camera to indicate the large size of the bed or by putting them beside adults. Inevitably these images stirred in anyone a wish to protect and the idea that a decision might be taken to end the lives of such a sweet baby horrific. They are designed to promote an instinctive human reaction to wish to protect 'vulnerable' babies. Andrew McGee has written of the profound instinct against killing babies:

> [O]ur maternal or paternal instincts and our consequent emotional make-up are background conditions which have served as the basis for the erection of moral norms, such as the norm that we ought not to kill our offspring. Our lives are defined in large part in terms of our relationships with our loved ones and, especially, our offspring. The value we afford to human life therefore stems from the central role our loved ones play in our lives, and the meaning they give to them.[15]

This profound instinct, he argues, creates a powerful intuition that someone who is seeking to kill a baby is doing something wrong. No doubt, he would not see what the doctors were doing in these cases as killing. But it is this deep intuition which is drawn on by the opposition to the hospital's response to these cases.

In fact, the description of Charlie and Alife as being the 'most vulnerable' people is somewhat misleading. First, they were receiving extremely high-quality care at hospitals with international reputations. In fact, it is hard to imagine a better place for them to be protected from possible harms. Second, their cases were discussed extensively within the medical and legal profession and the wider media. Many of the country's top minds were contributing to debates about what would be in their well-being. They could not have had a better set of protections from harm. Third, they were not in a position to suffer great harm because their capacity

[13] R Das, 'Social media and Charlie Gard: Populism versus Public Services?', blogs.lse.ac.uk/polis/2017/07/26/social-media-and-charlie-gard-populism-versus-public-services-guest-blog/.

[14] Family Research Council, 'Release Charlie Gard' (FRC, 2017).

[15] A McGee, 'The Moral Status of Babies' (2013) 39 *Journal of Medical Ethics* 345.

for understanding their situation and emotional distress was limited. In the case of Alfie Evans, Hayden J explained that the 'terrible reality' was that 'almost the entirety of Alfie's brain [has] been eroded leaving only water and cerebral spinal fluid'.[16] For Charlie it was said: 'The Great Ormond Street Team believe that Charlie can probably experience pain, but is unable to react to it in a meaningful way.'[17]

I would suggest that to some extent what we were seeing in the discussions of the particular vulnerability of Charlie and Alfie are the projection by adults of their fears. Tom Shakespeare has written of the way that non-disabled people 'project their fear of death, their unease at their physicality and mortality onto disabled people, who represent all these difficult aspects of human existence'. I think adults do the same with sick children. Shelley Day Sclater and Christine Piper explain:

> 'Projection' refers to an unconscious process whereby painful feelings are expelled from inside the self and located in another person. The subject can then deal with those feelings, as it were, at one step removed, as though they were characteristics of another. At its simplest, projection is happening when a part of the self is perceived in someone else, and we are therefore assisted, by a psychological defence mechanism, to avoid deeply painful emotions. It must be emphasised, however, that psychological mechanisms like projection are ordinary processes and are not indicative of pathology; projection is actually commonplace and ordinary.[18]

The response to the Gard and Evans cases reflects the orthodox distinction between childhood and adulthood being based on the idea of children being vulnerable and therefore in need of protection, whereas adults are able to look after themselves.[19] Childhood is at the same time a precarious time: the child is seen as at risk to wide range of dangers; but also a precious one: the child is learning skills and having experiences that will have a profound impact on their adult life. Children are unaware of the risks they face and therefore cannot avoid them. Further, they lack the physical, emotional and social resources to respond effectively to harms if they suffer them. Adults can see the dangers and have the job of protecting children from these dangers.

However, I have argued that this image of childhood as a time of particular vulnerability is a false one.[20] This is not for the reasons given by the child liberationists who have long claimed that we underestimate the capacities of children and need to recognise that they can be as competent and able as adults.[21] I argue the opposite. Children are vulnerable, as is everyone. In children we adults see our own vulnerability and are terrified of it. We need to recognise the vulnerabilities of adults. Part of our pretence to this idealised autonomous self is to claim that children

[16] *Evans v Alderhay Children's NHS Foundation Trust* [2018] EWCA Civ 805, [10].
[17] *Great Ormond Street Hospital v Yates and others* [2017] EWHC 972 (Fam), [22].
[18] C Piper and S Day Sclater, 'Social Exclusion and the Welfare of the Child' (2001) 28 *Journal of Law and Society* 409, 409.
[19] Herring (n 5).
[20] ibid.
[21] J Holt, *Escape from Childhood* (Holt Associates, 1996).

are completely different from adults. As Chris Jenks[22] once perceptively stated: 'The child cannot be imagined without considering the idea of "adult" just as it is impossible to picture the adult and society without positing "the child".'

The construction of childhood as different from adulthood allows adults to deny their own vulnerability by projecting their vulnerabilities onto children. This is particularly true of children where the fears of adults that our control over our children and their welfare is highly limited causes us to project a dialogue of children needing protection because of their particular vulnerability. A good example is a report in the *Independent* newspaper despairing for our children and alluding to the 'toxic climate' of dieting, pornography and school stress that our children face.[23] As if dieting, pornography and stress are not issues for adults. Indeed, these concerns about children may reflect the same fears of adults about themselves.

The language of 'saving' Alfie and Charlie drew on our identifying role as adults of being protectors of children. The idea that a child might be beyond adult protection and that adults might be powerless to improve the situation challenges the norm of the vulnerable child and the all-powerful adult which plays such an important role in our society in maintaining the adult/child distinction. Indeed, the cases show that however we might wish to disguise the vulnerability of us all, sometimes its reality cannot be avoided.

4. Vulnerability of Parents

One of the ironies of use of vulnerability as marking the child/adult divide, as described in the previous section, is that it creates vulnerabilities for adults. If adults are expected to look after children, this is particularly so for parents in relation to their children. Parents will go to extraordinary lengths to look after children because 'that is what parents do'. It is no doubt why new parents are willing to go through the sleeplessness, toils and strains of the early years of parenthood. Yet, that renders parents themselves vulnerable. The parents of Charlie and Alife were facing a direct challenge to the image of protective powerful parents that the law, government and media reinforce.

In order to comprehend the vulnerability of the parents in these cases, I want to capture the vulnerability of parents more generally. There has been a growth in recent years of the literature exploring the insecurities of parents. Certainly, the pressure on parents to keep children safe and ensure they succeed in life is perceived to be growing. It is not difficult to find examples of increased concern among parents about children's safety, be that worries about online dangers,

[22] C Jenks, *Childhood* (London, Routledge, 1996) 87.

[23] I Johnson, 'Mental Health Risk to Children Trapped in Toxic Climate of Dieting, Pornography and School Stress', *Independent* (20 January 2014).

increased use of home schooling, anxiety about the safety of children in public spaces, increased use of electronic surveillance of children (through wearable alarms, GPS trackers, etc). Yet all these actions taken to protect children expose vulnerabilities for the parents in terms of time, emotional energy and money spent.[24]

This insecurity felt by parents is influenced by the message reinforced by public bodies, including the government, about the significant impact of decisions of parents on children's welfare. This message that parents are core to their children's welfare generates considerable pressure on parents. Where things go wrong, it is parents towards whom the blame is directed. Here are some newspaper headlines capturing this message that parents are responsible for what happens to their children:

Parents Blamed Over Gang Culture[25]

Gordon Brown Says Parents to Blame for Teenage Knife Crime[26]

Parents Blamed for Rise in Bad Behaviour[27]

Parents of Obese Children Are 'Normalising Obesity' Say NHS boss[28]

Pupils Are More Badly Behaved than Ever and it's their Parents Fault, Say Teachers[29]

Mothers Who Can't Teach Basic Life Skills Are Failing Not Just Their Own Children, but Everyone Else's Too[30]

Parenting Is a Major 'Public Health Issue'[31]

A symptom of the vulnerability felt by parents is that there is a burgeoning literature of classes and books designed to help people be a parent.

- *Better Parent: No Matter how Badly your Children Behave or How Busy You Are*[32]
- *Calm Parents, Happy Kids: The Secrets of Stress-Free Parenting*[33]

[24] J Herring, 'Parental Responsibility, Hyper-Parenting, and the Role of Technology' in R Brownsword, E Scotford and K Yeung (eds), *Oxford Handbook of Law, Regulation and Technology* (Oxford, Oxford University Press, 2017).

[25] 'Parents Blamed over Gang Culture', *BBC News* (9 May 2008), news.bbc.co.uk/2/hi/uk_news/7393466.stm.

[26] J Kirkup, 'Gordon Brown Says Parents to Blame for Teenage Knife Crime', *Daily Telegraph* (21 July 2008).

[27] P Riddell, 'Parents Blamed for Rise in Bad Behaviour', *The Times* (5 September 2007).

[28] 'Health: Parents of Obese Children Are "Normalising Obesity" Say NHS Boss', *Western Daily Press* (19 May 2015).

[29] 'Pupils Are More Badly Behaved than Ever and it's their Parents' Fault, Say Teachers', *Daily Mail* (24 March 2013).

[30] 'Mothers Who Can't Teach Basic Life Skills Are Failing not Just their Own Children, but Everyone Else's Too', *Daily Mail* (15 February 2012).

[31] E Dermott and M Pomati, '"Good" Parenting Practices: How Important Are Poverty, Education and Time Pressure?' (2016) 50 *Sociology* 125.

[32] C Jardine, *How to Be a Better Parent: No Matter How Badly Your Children Behave or How Busy You Are* (London, Vermilion, 2003).

[33] Laura Markham, *Calm Parents, Happy Kids: The Secrets of Stress-Free Parenting* (London, Vermilion, 2014).

- *How to Raise an Amazing Child the Montessori Way*[34]
- *How to Be a Good Parent: 323 Great Tips for Better Parenting*[35]
- *Calmer, Easier, Happier Parenting: The Revolutionary Programme that Transforms Family Life*[36]

Although this title might resonate best with parents:

- *Go the F**k to Sleep*[37]

As these titles indicate, parents are clearly feeling under pressure to 'succeed' as a parent, interpreted as producing well-rounded, well-educated, high-achieving children. This has all contributed to parents feeling that parenting involves acquiring and following the advice of experts. As Frank Furedi puts it: 'Getting advice – and, more importantly, following the script that has been authored by experts – is seen as proof of "responsible parenting".'[38]

This is also reflected in the increased attention to hyper-parenting where parents are going to excessive lengths to make the child the best possible child. Alvin Rosenfeld and Nicole Wise explain: 'This is happening because many contemporary parents see a parent's fundamental job as designing a perfect upbringing for their offspring, from conception to college. … That is why the most competitive adult sport is no longer golf. It is parenting.'[39]

Jo Bridgeman has written particularly powerfully of the responsibilities parents feel towards their children and how this impacts on their engagements with healthcare professionals. She writes of the power of these caring responsibilities.[40] This itself creates vulnerabilities for parents as they struggle to negotiate the demands of professionals, their grief and children. The pain of the children generates pain, sometimes great pain in the adults. The vulnerability of child constitutes vulnerability in the adult. Also, and there is not space to develop this here, parental responsibility for children's well-being and behaviour can be highly gendered.[41]

These broader concerns about modern parenthood provide some insights into the Gard and Evans cases. First, the perception of children is based on a premise that adults/parents are competent, self-sufficient and independent, whereas children are dependent passive and require the support of parents for survival. The parents in these cases understandably saw it as their responsibility to fight for

[34] T Seldin, *How to Raise an Amazing Child the Montessori Way* (New York, DK Publishing, 2017).

[35] A Colton, *How to Be A Good Parent: 323 Great Tips for Better Parenting* (Liraz Publishing, 2017).

[36] N Janis-Norton, *Calmer, Easier, Happier Parenting: The Revolutionary Programme that Transforms Family Life* (London, Hodder & Stoughton, 2012).

[37] A Mansbach and R Cortes, *Go the F**k to Sleep* (New York, Cannongate Books, 2011).

[38] F Furedi, 'It's Time to Expel the "Experts" from Family Life', *Spiked* (12 September 2011), www.spiked-online.com/newsite/article/11067#.Vqg1IiorLIU.

[39] A Rosenfeld and N Wise, *The Over-Scheduled Child: Avoiding the Hyper-Parenting Trap* (New York, St Martin's Press, 2001).

[40] J Bridgeman, *Parental Responsibility, Young Children and Healthcare Law* (Cambridge, Cambridge University Press, 2007).

[41] ibid, 418.

their children. It was their responsibility to lead the fight and use every possible argument to protect them. Indeed, they went to quite extraordinary lengths to do everything they could that they thought might save their children's lives. This, I suggest, is a dramatic example of the lengths many parents feel expected to go to promote their child's welfare. It is worth noting that in Alfie Evans's case the parents were 18 and 19 when Alfie was born and his health issues developed not long after. The father had left school at 16 and served as an apprentice as a plasterer. It is clear he went to remarkable lengths to prepare for and present his case. Hayden J stated:

> F's presentation of his case was extraordinarily impressive. His knowledge of the paperwork and the medical records was prodigious. His understanding of the functioning of the brain and his exploration of competing hypotheses was remarkable. … It says much about his commitment to his son and the time and energy he has directed to this case that he has absorbed the issues so completely and intelligently.[42]

His determination and fortitude was astonishing. His efforts (not without success) to live up to the image of the powerful parent protecting the vulnerable child show the powerful hold over parents that the responsibility agenda has over them. Yet, it reflects the model of modern parenting, presented above, as requiring the parents to go to extraordinary lengths to protect their child from harmful societal influences and strive for their success.

Second, we see in much of the literature on contemporary parenting a merging of the identities of adult and child. The parents' success is measured by how well the child performs by standard measures. The concept of childhood agency or responsibility is lost. The powerlessness of parenthood gets no look in. We can see here Alfie and Charlie's parents tying their identities to the outcome for the children. The language of 'Charlie's army' and suggestions that the success of the parents is tied by how well they protect their children was a motivating factor behind what is done.

Third, we can see the privatisation of responsibility for children. The use of parental orders and contracts in criminal cases where children misbehave; government guidance on parenting; and the public rhetoric around parental responsibility, discussed above, all reinforce the message that where children behave badly or bad things happen to children, this must be the fault of the parents, rather than the lack of public resources, government policies or just the brute bad luck of nature. This easily translates into a message that you cannot rely on the government or the state to protect your child. You are responsible for your child and you must ensure your child is protected. This we may have witnessed in the Gard and Evans litigation. The parents were simply fulfilling their responsibilities as the government and media commonly presents them: as being ultimately responsible for the good or bad things that happen to their

[42] *Alder Hey Children's NHS Foundation Trust v Evans & Anor* [2018] EWHC 308 (Fam), [36].

child; and not to rely on the state to do this. This overemphasis on parental responsibility may be reflected in these cases.

Fourth, the model of parenting that is commonly presented in the contemporary dialogue is of parents controlling, protecting and shaping their child. The parental orders mentioned earlier put forward an image of a parent being able to control how their children behave. We can see this also with the blame attached to mothers who do not compel their children to visit fathers on contact sessions.[43] In the Gard and Evans cases we see the parents seeking desperately to control and manage what was happening to their children, as parents seem to be compelled to do in contemporary society.

This contemporary understanding of parenthood is, I have argued, based on a misunderstanding of the job of parents:

> Children care, mould, control, discipline, and cajole their parents, just as parents do their children. The misdeed of a parent seeking to genetically engineer or hyper-parent their child is not just that the parent is seeking to impose a particular view of what is a good life on their child, although that is wrong. It is the error of failing to be open to change as an adult; failing to learn from children, failing to see that the things you thought were important are, in fact, not. It is failing to find the wonder, fear, loneliness, anxiety, spontaneity, and joy of children, and to refine them for oneself.[44]

Perhaps, then, one response to the cases of Charlie and Alfie is to re-examine what it means to be a parent. To acknowledge that the job of parenting is interactive and co-operative – with the child and with a wide range of members of society. We should not see parents as alone having the responsibility of shaping their children.

Finally, there is the very obvious point that despite all the talk of 'Charlie's army' and the like, these parents were in deep grief. Hayden J wrote of the Evans's case.

> F [the father]'s case is not entirely easy to state. His core dilemma, from which he struggles to escape, is that whilst he recognises and understands fully that the weight of the evidence spells out the futility of Alfie's situation he is, as a father, unable to relinquish hope. This is to my mind entirely understandable. It is a facet of F's grief.[45]

He goes on to write of 'a father whose grief is unbounded and whose sadness, as I have witnessed in this court, has an almost primal quality to it'.[46]

The emotional turmoil of the parents is intense. It is notable that this grief manifests itself in different ways. Hayden J notes the contrasts with Alfie's parents:

> He is entirely besotted with his son. M, both parents agree, is far less involved in Alfie's practical care and less confident. Her contribution, in my assessment, is of an entirely different complexion. She has, if I may say so, a zany and delightful sense of humour entirely free from self-regard or pomposity. Her love for her partner and her son

[43] *Re B-H* [2015] EWCA Civ 389.

[44] Herring (n 24), 421.

[45] *Alder Hey Children's NHS Foundation Trust v Evans and Anor* [2018] EWHC 308 (Fam) (*Evans*), [37].

[46] *Alder Hey Children's NHS Foundation Trust v Evans and others* [2018] EWHC 953 (Fam), [2].

> was obvious. The atmosphere around Alfie was peaceful, dignified and though some might find it surprising for me to say so, very happy. The primary engine for all this is Alfie's mum.[47]

This requires us to be alert to the emotional expression involved in this litigation. Some of the academic critique has viewed this as a matter of balancing the parents' rights to make family decisions and the state.[48] Considerable sophistication has been used to develop models of how such decisions might be classified.[49] That is all helpful, but it must be remembered at the end of the day we are dealing with emotionally distraught litigation. There is no solution the courts, or perhaps anyone, could provide that would be 'right' solution. It could not be fair, or at least will never be seen by parents to be fair, because childhood illness simply is unfair.

These are parents who are driven by grief and a desperation to find a message of hope.[50] It is notable, how in many of these cases the parents turn to religious faith as offering some possibility of finding the outcome they wish. Hayden J noted in the Evans case: 'I have formed the view that F understands entirely what the significance of these scans is. Time and again in his evidence he avoided confronting them.'[51] This again indicates a rational evidence-based approach is not what the father could fully engage with. This highlights the limits of a court-based response to the issue. We must recognise that the court system based on rational evidence-based arguments will in many such cases not be engaging with the real issues. That is not necessarily an argument against courts being used at all, but we should do so with open eyes that benefit is more in terms of abstract justice than meeting the needs of parents of being able to engage with them. For that, mediation, discussion and counselling, if anything, are more likely to be effective.

5. Vulnerability of Staff

It is common to imagine that these cases involve the might of the legal and medical profession. But these cases reveal the vulnerability of the medical professionals. There is the obvious concern about the abuse of staff. In the Gard litigation this was acknowledged, where having spoken of the worldwide reputation of excellent in the hospital's care of sick children, Francis J goes on to note:

> It has sadly come into the public domain recently that some of the staff at that hospital have been subjected to serious threats and abuse. … Each and every man and woman working at Great Ormond Street Hospital is dedicated to the treatment of sick, very often desperately sick, children. These surgeons, physicians, doctors, nurses, ancillary

[47] ibid, [54].

[48] J Savulescu and D Wilkinson, *Ethics, Conflict and Medical Treatment for Children* (Edinburgh, Elsevier, 2019).

[49] C Auckland and I Goold, 'Defining the Limits of Parental Authority: Charlie Gard, Best Interests and the Significant Risk of Harm Threshold' (2018) 134 *Law Quarterly Review* 3.

[50] *King's College NHS Foundation Trust v Haastrup* [2018] EWHC 127 (Fam).

[51] *Evans* (n 43), [38].

> staff, technicians and all others working there are dedicated to the pursuit of excellence in the treatment of sick children and it is in my judgement a disgrace that they should have been subjected to any form of abuse whatsoever and it is to be condemned.[52]

As well as the vulnerability caused by the threats, perhaps the greater risk was the emotional harm. Professional guidance is clear that staff should keep an emotional distance from patients. The GMC makes it clear that a 'professional boundary' should be kept between doctors and patients.[53] Kathy Oxtoby writes:

> During their day to day work clinicians are regularly faced with the challenge of having to strike a delicate balance between maintaining a professional distance and not seeming so distant that they appear uncaring. Not knowing where to draw that line between being a professional delivering care and being overly caring can cause problems for clinicians.

But she acknowledges that:

> Doctors may find themselves worrying so much about patients outside working hours that it causes them anxiety and affects their home life, and even that of their colleagues. One doctor recalls a colleague who, concerned about a case, woke up the practice manager in the middle of the night to obtain the contact details and then visited the patient's home unannounced at the weekend to check that the patient was alright.[54]

But this pressure to maintain professionalism and distance can clash with the natural human feeling of emotion.

It is not sufficiently acknowledged that part of a medical professionals job is 'emotional labour',[55] as Kerasidou and Horn write:

> Empathy requires a level of emotional involvement from the side of the physician but the emotional resources required and the skills necessary for empathy are not always available to doctors. The medical profession is an emotionally challenging environment, which favours the image of the emotionally detached doctor. Often, in practice, the open expression of feelings is perceived as weakness, an attitude that leaves little room for the active pursuit of emotional wellbeing. Physicians are constantly faced with distressing situations, which can lead to depression, burnout, and subsequently loss of the ability to empathise. In order for empathy to flourish in the medical profession, doctors should feel able to deal with their emotions without the fear of being criticised or stigmatised as weak.

They conclude:

> The ability for empathy, namely the joining into someone else's feelings and emotions, presupposes a high level of self-awareness of one's own emotions. Physicians are

[52] ibid, [16].

[53] General Medical Council, *Maintaining a Professional Boundary Between You and Your Patient* (GMC, 2018).

[54] K Oxtoby, 'Where to Draw the Line in Relationships with Patients' (2013) 346 *British Medical Journal* 2848.

[55] A Kerasidou and R Horn, 'Making Space for Empathy: Supporting Doctors in the Emotional Labour of Clinical Care' (2016) 17 *BioMed Central Medical Ethics* 8.

> routinely trained to remain detached from their own as well as their patients' emotions, perpetuating the ideal of the skilled and cool-minded professional.

Yet these ideals may not match the reality. As an NHS palliative care doctor writing about these cases states:

> Yet giving up hope can be unbearably painful. I shall never forget a paediatric oncology colleague describing, blinded by his tears, how the mother of one of his young patients had thrown herself from the hospital roof, unable to endure the knowledge that her child's cancer was terminal. I have held fathers as they collapse in my arms, seen a mother biting her own arm in her grief, and wondered, over and over, at the vastness of the pain this world can inflict on its youngest, most undeserving and innocent.[56]

As these comments indicate the guidance about a professional distance is unrealistic in the case of such scenarios and is perhaps even harmful. An anonymous healthcare professional involved in the care of Charlie Gard wrote:

> I've been part of a team of 200 nurses, doctors and consultants who cared for Charlie Gard, not just doing all the medical interventions he required but also washing him, cuddling him, propping up his toys around his cot.
>
> Like all of the staff who work in our unit, I loved this child to bits. But it got to the point where there was nothing more we could do. I know everyone working in intensive care would agree with me when I say that every child who comes through this unit is loved, but there are a few who take a piece of your heart with them when they leave. We miss breaks, we stay late, we spend our days off researching and studying so that we can be better at what we do. We cry on the tube when we're not winning. We dream of nothing else.[57]

They go on to describe the pain of being presented in the media as wanting to harm or kill Charlie when that was the very opposite of what they were doing.

It is interesting that this emotional investment of the staff in Charlie's care gets no mention in the legal judgment (unlike the emotional states of the parents). Yet the staff at the hospital, particularly the nursing staff, will have got to know Charlie very well. They will have formed close bonds with him. If a grounding in parental rights claims is based on the parental investment in the child and being in a position to know the child deeply and so be in a good position to know what will, or will not, promote the welfare of the child, then the nursing staff will be well placed to make a similar kind of claim. Yet, the mask of professional detachment mentioned earlier means that arguments based on their emotional investment and the dedication of their care work get underplayed in the legal system. I am not suggesting the nursing staff in these cases should supplant the parents as decision-makers in these kinds of cases, but the depth of their caring relationship with the children gives them a legitimate voice in the legal decision-making process.[58]

[56] R Clarke, 'I Say: Let Alfie Evans Die with Dignity', *The Guardian* (26 April 2018).

[57] 'It Was our Agonising Job as Charlie Gard's Care Team to Say: Enough', *The Guardian* (4 August 2017).

[58] For further discussion, see J Herring, *Caring and the Law* (Oxford, Hart Publishing, 2013) ch 6.

6. Vulnerability of Judges

Finally, we must recall the vulnerability of judges. It is interesting how little is written on the emotional aspects of being judge or its emotional toll. It is hard to imagine that any of the judges in these cases did not find them emotionally draining, particularly given the pressure of media attention. In the *Evans* case Hayden J reports on his visit to Alfie:

> As I had promised the family, I attended the PICU at Alder Hey to meet Alfie. I was greeted not merely with courtesy by the parents and a number of aunts and uncles but with a sincere and genuine warmth. I was and remain grateful to them. Alfie's pod in the unit is large, comfortable and he is surrounded by some of the world's most up-to-date technology. … The atmosphere around Alfie was peaceful, dignified and though some might find it surprising for me to say so, very happy. The primary engine for all this is Alfie's mum.
>
> Alfie's bed is festooned with toys. His walls are plastered with photographs and his many supporters have delivered a variety of football shirts to him. One, in particular, was signed by the entire Everton squad specifically for him.

The willingness of the judge to visit Alife and the parents at his bedside was clearly an intense moment and the judgment captures, in appropriately judicial language, the significance to the judge of the moment. There is, of course, no discussion of the impact of this meeting on the judge himself, but one can only speculate.

Traditionally judging has been seen as a task of rational, detached thinking. Emotions are seen as a danger for judges in derailing an objective assessment of the facts and application of the law. However, this model is under challenge.[59] Madame Justice L'Heureux Dubé[60] of the Canadian Supreme Court, Judge Mary Schroeder[61] of the US Court of Appeals for the Ninth Circuit, and Judge Eldergill,[62] a former judge of the English Court of Protection, have all written of the importance of including compassion and other emotions in their judgments. Judge Eldergill writes: 'The notion that judicial objectivity requires being dispassionate and that objective decision-making is contaminated by empathy, sympathy and compassion is impossible to support.'[63]

Indeed, he goes on to claim that compassion is an important judicial quality that is needed to inform the other judicial responsibility. Procedural matters require empathy in understanding how witnesses and parties will be best placed to present evidence. In relation to substantive law the assessment of a person's best interests or a child's welfare requires the judge to make the assessment from an

[59] S Bandes and J Blumenthal, 'Emotions and the Law' (2012) 8 *Annual Review of Law and Social Science* 161.
[60] C L'Heureux Dubé, 'Making a Difference: The Pursuit of a Compassionate Justice' (1997) 13 *UBC Law Review* 1.
[61] M Schroeder, 'Compassion on Appeal' (1990) 22 *Arizona State Law Journal* 45,
[62] A Eldergill, 'Compassion and the Law: A Judicial Perspective' (2015) 3 *Elder Law Journal* 268.
[63] ibid, 276.

individual's point of view.'[64] If compassion and empathy is required and expected as a judicial quality, then this requires greater openness to the vulnerability of judges.[65] Judges can feel conflicted between their empathy and emotional reaction and the need to express judgments that are 'in accordance with the law'. Permitting, even encouraging, judges to be open about these tensions may produce a human law and even increase public acceptance of the judicial role. That may also require changes to substantive law to create space for the significance of emotions. Clearly there is much more to discuss on this topic,[66] but the cases of Alfie and Charlie require us to reconsider the role of emotion in judging and the law more generally.

7. Conclusion

This discussion has used the lens of universal vulnerability theory to explore the issues here. Academic discussion of the cases in the media has looked at issues of state power and parental authority, medical paternalism, and children's rights. Yet in this chapter I have sought to highlight the vulnerabilities of all of the parties. The chapter has explored the vulnerabilities of the parents in light of the broader social and legal pressures on parents to see themselves as responsible for their children's welfare and safety. It has also examined the way that medical professionals and even judges must struggle to balance 'professional detachment' with deep emotions, in a way that is not really appreciated sufficiently. It has also suggested that while the legal case is resolved in terms of rational objective arguments, this is no response to the emotional turmoil and weakness all the parties have. Indeed, this chapter has sought to highlight that underpinning the troubles surrounding these cases have been deeper issues about the responsibilities of parents, the roles of professionals and nature of judging.

[64] *Aintree University Hospitals Trust v James* [2013] UKSC 67, 45.

[65] D Feenan, D Bedford and J Herring, 'Judicial Compassion' (2015) *Elder Law Journal* 392.

[66] See: D Feenan, 'Law and Compassion' (2017) 5 *International Journal of Law in Context* 121; S Bandes, 'Compassion and the Rule of Law) (2017) 13 *International Journal of Law in Context* 184; J Herring, 'Compassion, Ethics of Care and Legal Rights' (2017) 13 *International Journal of Law in Context* 158.

11

Resolving Disagreements about the Care of Critically Ill Children: Evaluating Existing Processes and Setting the Research Agenda*

LOUISE AUSTIN AND RICHARD HUXTABLE

1. Introduction

In the mid-2000s, the English courts adjudicated on the high-profile case of Charlotte Wyatt, a critically ill child. Charlotte's parents wanted their daughter to receive potentially life-sustaining treatment (including ventilation), but her doctors believed that such treatment was not in the child's best interests.[1] This intractable dispute came before the courts on no fewer than 11 occasions.[2] Commenting on the dispute, Margaret Brazier noted: 'There is no right answer to the dilemma in *Re Wyatt*. Resolution in the courts may indeed exacerbate a tragedy nature created. But is there any alternative?'[3]

Brazier's question has become particularly pressing in recent years, with the courts confronting more difficult cases of this sort, such as *Gard*, and the attendant dilemmas playing out across the world's (social) media.[4] In this chapter, we survey and assess the main processes and mechanisms available for seeking to prevent, reduce or resolve disputes about the treatment (and non-treatment) of critically

* RH's work on this chapter was supported by a 'Balancing Best Interests in Health Care, Ethics and Law (BABEL)' Collaborative Award from the Wellcome Trust (209841/Z/17/Z). The chapter draws on a review, led by LA, which was undertaken for the Nuffield Council on Bioethics. We are grateful to the Council for permission to develop the review here and we are also grateful to our colleagues, Neera Bhatia, Giles Birchley and Jonathan Ives, for their input into that review. Responsibility for the chapter lies with the authors.

[1] *Portsmouth Hospital Trust v Wyatt* [2004] EWHC 2247 (Fam).

[2] J Bridgeman, 'Editorial: Critically Ill Children and Best Interests' (2010) 5 *Clinical Ethics*, 184, 187.

[3] M Brazier, 'An Intractable Dispute: When Parents and Professionals Disagree' (2005) 13 *Medical Law Review* 412, 418.

[4] N Bhatia, 'Disagreements in the Care of Critically Ill Children: Emerging Issues in a Changing Landscape' (2018) *Nuffield Council on Bioethics* 7, nuffieldbioethics.org/wp-content/uploads/Bhatia-N-2018-Disagreements-in-care-of-critically-ill-children-emerging-issues.pdf.

ill children. Our focus is on the UK (and England in particular)[5] and our analysis was informed by a 'rapid review' of available sources,[6] which was undertaken for the Nuffield Council on Bioethics.[7]

The review revealed five key processes for resolving disagreements about the care of critically ill children: discussions between families and clinicians; second-opinion experts; clinical ethics committees; mediation; and court proceedings. We found that the majority of these disputes appear to be addressed and resolved through discussion between the main stakeholders, primarily the parents and the healthcare team, with second opinions sometimes also being sought. Alternative processes – and the courts in particular – appeared to be viewed by stakeholders as options of last resort. Court proceedings had (at least) the benefit of securing resolution, but such resolution came at a cost, since it could exacerbate the damage already caused to the relationship of trust between these protagonists. Alternative processes such as mediation and clinical ethics consultation showed some promise, but data about these processes and their respective pros and cons appear to be lacking.

Our findings therefore indicate various areas in which further research is warranted. First, further research is needed into what the current situation actually *is*, which would usefully explore when, why, how and the extent to which these different mechanisms are used, and how they serve to secure resolution. Second, research is also needed into what the situation *should be*: how (if at all) should existing mechanisms be amended and, ultimately, which process (or processes) should be used in these cases of conflict?

2. Critically Ill Infants in (and Beyond) the Courts

Although cases of conflict have become particularly prominent in recent years, the treatment/non-treatment of critically ill children has long generated dilemmas and disagreement. As these dilemmas typically involve life-or-death questions, legal questions inevitably arise, and English law has a long history of seeking to resolve these sorts of disputes. The law in this jurisdiction has generally viewed these sorts of cases through three sets of lenses, which derive from criminal law, civil (family) law and human rights law.[8]

[5] Different legal systems operate within the United Kingdom.

[6] Rapid reviews involve 'a type of knowledge synthesis in which components of the systematic review process are simplified or omitted to produce information in a short period of time': AC Tricco, J Antony, W Zarin, L Strifler, M Ghassemi, J Ivory, L Perrier, B Hutton, D Moher, and SE Straus, 'A Scoping Review of Rapid Review Methods' (2015) 13 *BioMed Central Medicine* 224.

[7] L Austin, 'UK Processes for the Resolution of Disagreements About the Care of Critically Ill Children' (2018) *Nuffield Council on Bioethics*, nuffieldbioethics.org/wp-content/uploads/Austin-L-2018-UK-processes-for-resolution-of-disagreements-in-care-of-critically-ill-children.pdf.

[8] This section expands on points first made in R Huxtable, 'Clinic, Courtroom or (Specialist) Committee: In the Best of Interests of the Critically Ill Child?' (2017) 44 *Journal of Medical Ethics* 471.

In terms of priority and chronology, the *criminal* law comes first in this selective retrospective (or, to borrow a phrase that has fallen into desuetude, 'selective non-treatment' retrospective).[9] Failing to meet a duty to care for a dependant, which results in that dependant's death, can amount to murder or manslaughter, depending on the accused's intention or knowledge.[10] The last such trial involving a doctor occurred in 1981, when Dr Arthur, a paediatrician, was acquitted of attempting to murder John Pearson. After the mother rejected the new-born, who had Down's syndrome, Dr Arthur prescribed a painkiller and ordered 'nursing care only'. The child died 69 hours later.[11] In his direction to the jury, Farquharson J noted there was no 'special law' protecting doctors,[12] but he also pointed to the lawfulness of some omissions and of symptom relief, plus the good character and motives of the defendant, who had allegedly been following accepted practice.

Farquharson J's direction indicated his discomfort with examining Arthur's behaviour through the criminal law lens – indeed, the defendant was described in respectful terms, while the child was referred to as 'it'.[13] A different legal lens was already available, based in the civil – and specifically *family* – law, and it had been deployed in a ruling passed down only weeks before Farquharson J's direction, although he did not cite it. Contrary to the decision in *Arthur*, in *Re B*, the Court of Appeal authorised the provision of life-saving surgery in the 'best interests' of another new-born with Down's syndrome, as the court found it was not the case that 'the life of this child is demonstrably going to be so awful that in effect the child must be condemned to die'.[14] Like *Arthur*, that decision also had unfortunate aspects, since the appellate judges referred to the possibility that the child might be a 'cabbage'.[15]

Hopefully the more troubling features of these two decisions can be consigned to legal history,[16] but *Re B*'s central focus on the 'best interests' or – following the Children Act 1989 – the 'welfare' of the child otherwise continues to lead the way in these decisions. Using these tests, which are to be considered synonymous,[17] the courts have decided on numerous occasions that life-sustaining treatment is not indicated.[18] Neither concept has been defined but five key elements of the legal

[9] ibid, 471.

[10] *Gibbins v Proctor* [1918] 12 Cr App Rep 134; *R v Stone and Dobinson* [1977] QB 354.

[11] *R v Arthur* [1981] 12 BMLR 1.

[12] ibid, [5].

[13] ibid.

[14] *Re B (a minor) (wardship: medical treatment)* [1990] 3 All ER 927, 929 (*Re B*).

[15] ibid, 1423.

[16] However, the troubling term 'vegetative state' continues to be used, although there are calls for its abandonment, eg: S Laureys, GG Celesia, F Cohado, J Lavrijsen, J León-Carrión, G Sannita, L Sazbon, E Schmutzhard, KR von Wild, A Zeman, G Dolce and the European Task Force on Disorders of Consciousness, 'Unresponsive Wakefulness Syndrome: A New Name for the Vegetative State or Apallic Syndrome' (2010) 8 *BioMed Central Medicine* 68.

[17] *Re B (a minor) (wardship: sterilisation)* [1987] 2 WLR 1213, 1217.

[18] See, eg, *Re C (a minor) (wardship: medical treatment)* [1990] Fam 26; *Re J (a minor) (wardship: medical treatment)* [1991] 1 FLR 366; *Re J (a minor) (wardship: medical treatment)* [1992] 2 FLR 165;

position emerge from the 1989 Act and subsequent rulings.[19] First, as the 1989 Act states, 'the child's welfare shall be the court's paramount consideration'.[20] This remains the test and, in the aforementioned *Wyatt*, the Court of Appeal took pains to emphasise that references to an 'intolerably' poor quality of life,[21] which might be considered – in *Re B*'s words – 'demonstrably … awful',[22] are not to be treated as supplementary tests.[23] Second, 'the judge must look at the question from the assumed point of view of the patient'.[24] Third, there is a strong presumption in favour of prolonging life, but this presumption can be rebutted.[25] Fourth, 'best interests' is a broad, pluralistic concept, which 'encompasses medical, emotional, and all other welfare issues'.[26] Rather than offering a definition, the Act only provides a checklist of factors to consider, which includes the needs and 'ascertainable wishes and feelings of the child', and any harm he or she might suffer.[27] Finally, according to the Court of Appeal, 'The court must conduct a balancing exercise in which all the relevant factors are weighed and a helpful way of undertaking this exercise is to draw up a balance sheet'.[28]

By the time of *Wyatt*, the family law lens had been supplemented by a third, *human rights*, lens, which was provided by the Human Rights Act 1998. That Act, which came into force in 2000, essentially brought the European Convention on Human Rights directly into English law. There were soon challenges to the rulings in this area, based (inter alia) on Article 2, the right to life.[29] The English courts nevertheless confirmed that there would be no violation of the 1998 Act if a decision not to offer life-supporting treatment was made in the best interests of the child.[30] The European Court of Human Rights did, however, find against doctors, following the complaint in *Glass* in 2004, in which the relationship between the

Re C (a baby) [1996] 2 FLR 43; *Re T (a minor) (wardship: medical treatment)* [1997] 1 All ER 966; *Re C (medical treatment)* [1998] 1 FLR 384; *Royal Wolverhampton Hospitals NHS Trust v B* [2000] 2 FCR 76; *A National Health Service Trust v D* [2000] 2 FLR 677; *Re L (a child) (medical treatment: benefit)* [2004] EWHC 2713; *NHS Trust v A (a child)* [2007] EWHC 1696; *Re K (a child) (withdrawal of treatment)* [2006] EWHC 1007; *Re B (a child) (medical treatment)* [2008] EWHC 1996; *Re OT* [2009] EWHC 633. For a full discussion of these cases, see R Huxtable, *Law, Ethics and Compromise at the Limits of Life: To Treat or Not to Treat?* (London, Routledge, 2012), 39–49.

[19] See especially *Portsmouth Hospitals NHS Trust v Wyatt* [2005] EWCA Civ 1181 (*Wyatt*).

[20] Children Act 1989 s 1(1).

[21] *Wyatt* (n 19), [91].

[22] *Re B* (n 14), 929.

[23] ibid, [91]. Foster, however, has argued that in *Re A (male sterilisation)* [2000] 1 FLR 549, 'intolerability' returned through the 'balance sheet' approach advocated in *Wyatt* (n 19). Foster notes that in *Re A* it was held that the detriments of continuing life would have to significantly outweigh its benefits in order for the presumption in favour of continuing life to be overturned. Foster describes this as 'intolerability by another name': C Foster, *Choosing Life, Choosing Death: The Tyranny of Autonomy in Medical Ethics and Law* (Oxford, Hart Publishing, 2009) 160.

[24] *Wyatt* (n 19), [87].

[25] ibid.

[26] ibid.

[27] Children Act 1989 s 1(3).

[28] *Wyatt* (n 19), 87.

[29] *A National Health Service Trust v D* [2000] 2 FLR 677.

[30] ibid.

child's family and his doctors had deteriorated significantly, leading to fistfights on the ward.[31] The European Court found there to be a violation of Article 8, the right to respect for private and family life, since the mother's right to consent to treatment had not been respected. The court further emphasised the importance of resolving disputes promptly.[32]

Against the backdrop of cases such as *Wyatt* and *Glass*, professional organisations sought to issue guidance on how future cases should be addressed. Generic guidance – applying to patients young and old – was available from the General Medical Council and British Medical Association.[33] However, more specific guidance was issued by the Royal College of Paediatrics and Child Health, first in 1997,[34] which was updated in 2004,[35] and then again in 2015.[36] The latest guidance refers to the permissibility of withdrawing or withholding life-sustaining treatment where the child's life is limited in *quantity* (since the child is brain-stem dead, imminently dying, or his or her death is inevitable and treatment confers no overall benefit) or limited in *quality* (with reference to the burdens of treatment or the child's underlying condition, or the child's inability to benefit).[37] Like its predecessors, the 2015 guidance recommends that efforts be taken to resolve disputes.[38] Dispute resolution was also considered by a working party of the Nuffield Council on Bioethics, which issued its report in 2006.[39] The report found (inter alia) that existing 'legal principles centred on seeking agreement between parents and professionals as to the best interests of the baby are, in principle, appropriate and sufficient',[40] although it did recommend that 'all neonatal intensive care units have rapid access to a clinical ethics committee for advice'[41] and that further research be undertaken into 'the possible merits' of mediation in this context.[42]

Despite these various efforts to prevent or address disputes, the latter part of the 2010s brought a series of high-profile legal cases, of which we will briefly mention four. The first, in 2014, involved five-year-old Ashya King, who had

[31] *Glass v UK* [2004] 1 FCR 553.

[32] ibid, [79]–[81].

[33] General Medical Council, 'Withholding and Withdrawing – Guidance for Doctors' (2002) www.gmc-uk.org/-/media/documents/withholding-or-withdrawing-life-prolonging-treatments-2002---2010-55677704.pdf; British Medical Association, *Withholding and Withdrawing Life-Prolonging Medical Treatment* (BMA, 1999).

[34] Royal College of Paediatrics and Child Health, *Withholding or Withdrawing Life-Saving Treatment in Children: A Framework for Practice* (RCPCH, 1997).

[35] Royal College of Paediatrics and Child Health, *Withholding or Withdrawing Life-Sustaining Treatment in Children: A Framework for Practice* [1997] (RCPCH, 2004).

[36] Royal College of Paediatrics and Child Health, *Making Decisions to Limit Treatment in Life-Limiting and Life-Threatening Conditions in Children: A Framework for Practice* [1997] (RCPCH, 2014).

[37] ibid, 4–5.

[38] ibid, 12.

[39] Nuffield Council on Bioethics, *Critical Care Decisions in Foetal and Neonatal Medicine: Ethical Issues* (2006), nuffieldbioethics.org/wp-content/uploads/2014/07/CCD-web-version-22-June-07-updated.pdf.

[40] ibid, [37].

[41] ibid, [40].

[42] ibid, [41].

undergone surgical removal of a brain tumour. His doctors thereafter proposed chemotherapy and radiotherapy, but his parents favoured proton beam therapy (PBT). NHS funding for PBT was refused but Ashya's parents had identified a willing centre in Prague and had the requisite funding available. Believing the hospital would seek a Child Protection Order to prevent this (which the hospital denied), Ashya's parents removed him from the hospital and took him to Spain. Ashya was subsequently made a ward of court and a court hearing convened to determine whether he was at risk of significant harm from the plan to take him to Prague for PBT. Drawing on the medical evidence, Baker J concluded that the proposed treatment was reasonable, in Ashya's best interests and Ashya was not at risk of harm, so he could be transferred to the unit in Prague, at which point he would no longer be a ward of court.[43]

Although Ashya's case generated headlines, the second, involving Charlie Gard in 2017, appeared to have even wider, international reach. Charlie, who was eight months old, had a form of mitochondrial DNA depletion syndrome and was being treated in Great Ormond Street Hospital (GOSH). His treating clinicians judged his quality of life to be poor, with no hope of recovery, such that continued ventilation would be futile. His parents opposed withdrawal of ventilation on the basis that an experimental treatment was available in the United States, which might help their son. The hospital was initially prepared to consider such treatment but, following Charlie's deterioration, his treating clinicians concluded that this too would be futile. Charlie's parents maintained that he should be transferred to the United States.[44]

In the first substantive ruling, Francis J looked particularly to the (UK) medical evidence, deciding that mechanical ventilation was not in Charlie's best interests.[45] The Court of Appeal permitted an appeal on certain grounds,[46] but the Supreme Court refused permission to appeal, finding there was no arguable point of law.[47] The European Court of Human Rights also declared inadmissible the parents' attempt to have the case heard in Strasbourg.[48] The case did, however, return to the High Court, on the basis (inter alia) of new evidence from a US clinician. However, during this hearing, the US clinician met with the treating clinicians and reviewed up-to-date scans, which led him to conclude that there was no possibility of the nucleoside therapy having any effect. Charlie's parents thereafter withdrew their opposition to the proposal to withdraw ventilation and Francis J confirmed

[43] *Portsmouth City Council v Nagmeh King, Brett King, Southampton Hospital Trust, Ashya King (by his Children's Guardian)* [2014] EWHC 2964 (Fam).

[44] *Great Ormond Street Hospital v Constance Yates, Chris Gard, Charles Gard (a Child by his Guardian Ad Litem)* [2017] EWHC 972 (Fam).

[45] ibid.

[46] *Constance Yates, Christopher Gard v Great Ormond Street Hospital for Children NHS Foundation Trust Charles Gard (a Child, by his Guardian)* [2017] EWCA Civ 410.

[47] *In the matter of Charlie Gard* (8 June 2017), www.supremecourt.uk/news/permission-to-appeal-hearing-in-the-matter-of-charlie-gard.html.

[48] *Gard and Others v UK* (app no 39793-17) [2017] ECHR.

his earlier declaration, adding that Charlie would continue to be treated at GOSH, before being transferred to an agreed hospice.[49]

Two prominent cases were then brought in 2018. The first, involving 11-month-old Isaiah Haastrup, concerned whether ventilation should be withdrawn on the grounds of 'futility'.[50] Isaiah had been born by emergency caesarean section due to uterus rupture, which led to him sustaining severe hypoxic ischaemic brain injury. The circumstances of his birth reportedly led to a breakdown in trust between the parents and the hospital, which worsened when, shortly after his birth, Isaiah's parents were advised he was unlikely to recover and the possibility of palliative care was raised, following which Isaiah appeared to become more responsive. Various other doctors – including from other units – reviewed Isaiah, but they all concluded that further treatment was futile and ventilation should be withdrawn. Given the breakdown in trust, the treating hospital had sought to move Isaiah to another unit, but no willing unit could be found, given the perceived futility of further treatment. The court granted Isaiah's parents permission to obtain independent expert evidence from two further experts, but they too concurred with the treating clinicians; MacDonald J authorised the withdrawal of treatment from Isaiah.

The second case also concerned the withdrawal of ventilation.[51] Alfie Evans, who was nearly two at the time of the hearing, had been found (at six months) to have developmental delay and had been admitted to Alder Hey Hospital with seizures. The seizures persisted and Alfie was noted to have little response to different types of stimulation. No one was able to provide a definitive diagnosis of Alfie's underlying neurological condition but his condition had caused such significant brain damage that there was judged to be no prospect of recovery, so the hospital wished to withdraw ventilation. Alfie's parents contested this and wanted their son transferred to a hospital in Italy for further investigations and the continuation of life support. In light of the medical consensus as to the futility of further treatment, Hayden J concluded that treatment was not in Alfie's best interests. The parents unsuccessfully appealed,[52] and subsequently brought further proceedings, seeking the same outcome on different legal grounds,[53] including a failed attempt to initiate a murder prosecution against some of the clinicians.[54] None of the appeals succeeded.

Each of these cases appeared to involve intractable disputes, which suggests that they inevitably and understandably ended up before the courts. However,

[49] *Great Ormond Street Hospital for Children NHS Foundation Trust v Yates and Others* [2017] EWHC 1909.

[50] *King's College Hospital NHS Foundation Trust v Thomas, Haastrup and Haastrup* [2018] EWHC 127 (Fam) (*Haastrup*).

[51] *Alder Hey Children's NHS Foundation Trust v Mr Thomas Evans, Ms Kate James, Alfie Evans (a Child by his Guardian CAFCASS Legal)* [2018] EWHC 308 (Fam)

[52] *E (a child)* [2018] EWCA Civ 550; *Evans v UK* 14238/18 [2018] ECHR 297.

[53] *Alder Hey Children's NHS Foundation Trust v Evans* [2018] EWHC 818; *Evans v Alder Hey Children's NHS Foundation Trust* [2018] EWCA Civ 805; *Evans v UK* (app no 18770/18) [2018] ECHR 357; *Alder Hey Children's NHS Foundation Trust v Evans* [2018] EWHC 953; Evans v *Alder Hey Children's NHS Foundation Trust* [2018] EWCA Civ 984.

[54] *Alder Hey Children's NHS Foundation Trust v Evans* [2018] EWHC 953, [14].

prior to that point, each had involved recourse to a variety of methods by which the dispute might have been resolved. In the following sections, we review and assess some of the main methods, starting with discussions between families and clinicians.

3. Discussions between Families and Clinicians

As the aforementioned cases indicate, it is typical for clinicians and families (in particular, parents) to meet to discuss the child's condition, prognosis and treatment/non-treatment options. The process appears initially to involve discussions between the treating team, before a discussion (or discussions) is then held with the family.

The aim of such discussions is apparently to achieve consensus through 'shared decision-making'.[55] There is, however, no fixed definition of the latter concept,[56] nor agreement on whether it is entirely suited to paediatric decision-making.[57] Drawing on qualitative research with key participants in such decisions, some researchers have suggested that, in practice, these discussions might amount to no more than a *consultation* of the parents' views, with the true aim being to secure their *acquiescence* to the care plan proposed by the clinical team.[58] Efforts at persuasion appeared to feature in the cases just outlined. There is a risk, however, that such efforts will cause parents to feel they have no real choice in decision-making,[59] thus cultivating a fear of bad faith.[60]

Other research nevertheless suggests that a positive consensus can be reached through appropriate discussions. In a study of their unit at GOSH over three years, Brierley et al found that, following initial discussions, 186 out of 203 cases resulted in parents agreeing with clinicians that continued treatment was not in the child's best interests.[61] Six of the remaining 17 cases were resolved following further discussions with the families. In this study, discussions between the

[55] G Birchley and R Huxtable, 'Critical Decisions for Critically Ill Infants', in C Stanton, S Devaney, A-M Farrell and A Mullock (eds), *Pioneering Healthcare Law: Essays in Honour of Margaret Brazier* (London, Routledge, 2016) 120.

[56] C Charles, A Gafni and T Whelan, 'Shared Decision-Making in the Medical Encounter: What Does it Mean? (or it Takes at Least Two to Tango)' (1997) 44 *Social Science and Medicine* 681; C Munthe, L Sandman and D Cutas, 'Person Centred Care and Shared Decision-Making: Implications for Ethics, Public Health and Research' (2012) 20 *Health Care Analysis* 231.

[57] G Birchley, 'Deciding Together? Best Interests and Shared Decision-Making in Paediatric Intensive Care' (2014) 22 *Health Care Analysis* 203.

[58] Birchley and Huxtable (n 55), 121.

[59] G Birchley, R Gooberman-Hill, Z Deans, J Fraser and R Huxtable, '"Best Interests" in Paediatric Intensive Care: An Empirical Ethics Study' (2017) 102 *Archives of Disease in Childhood* 930, 932.

[60] C Shaw, E Stokoe, K Gallagher, N Aladangady and N Marlow, 'Parental Involvement in Neonatal Critical Care Decision-Making' (2016) 38 *Sociology of Health & Illness* 1217.

[61] J Brierley, J Linthicum and A Petros, 'Should Religious Beliefs Be Allowed to Stonewall a Secular Approach to Withdrawing and Withholding Treatment in Children?' (2013) 39 *Journal of Medical Ethics* 573, 573.

team and the family therefore generated consensus about treatment withdrawal in 94.58 per cent of the cases.

Gard demonstrates that discussions in GOSH do not always lead to consensus, but its reputation as a world-renowned specialist hospital and the expertise of its staff might explain its success in achieving consensus in many cases. The literature further reveals the importance of good communication to reaching resolution. Communication, of course, is a two-way process, and Richards suggests that a key component of good communication is that clinicians not only talk, but also *listen to* families and explore their views, including those about alternative treatment options.[62] As for what clinicians *say to* families, Birchley et al's study reveals that clinicians will sometimes need to reframe conversations in terms more acceptable to families,[63] with Waldman and Frader cautioning that words like 'futile', 'harm' and 'suffering' might cause parents to feel they are being accused of not doing what is best for their child.[64]

Communication evidently matters and Forbat et al have found communication breakdown to be the most common cause of conflict between families and healthcare professionals in children's healthcare.[65] Amongst the reasons for such breakdown are, first, *pejorative labelling* by clinicians of those parents who disagree with them. Forbat et al refer to this as a factor in the escalation of conflict in paediatric healthcare disputes.[66] In this vein, one might refer to a clinician's email, which described the parents in *Gard* as a 'spanner in the works'.[67]

Second, clinicians and parents will sometimes have *different understandings* of key terms or information. Forbat et al refer to divergent interpretations of terms such as 'futility' or prognostic information.[68] Such differences can arise, suggest Fassier and Azoulay, because families weigh the clinician's prognostic information against factors such as their own perception of the patient's strength of character and will to live, and the patient's history of illness and survival.[69] *Evans* exemplifies this, with the trial judge noting that the parents, having been told early on in their son's treatment to prepare for 'the real possibility that [he] might not recover',[70]

[62] T Richards, 'When Doctors and Patients Disagree' (2014) *British Medical Journal Online*, www-bmj-com.bris.idm.oclc.org/content/bmj/349/bmj.g5567.full.pdf.

[63] Birchley et al (n 59), 932.

[64] E Waldman and J Frader, 'Charlie Gard: How Did Things Go Wrong?' (2018) 6 *Current Paediatric Reports* 173, 174; see also: R Taylor, 'Parental Decisions and Court Jurisdiction: Best Interests or Significant Harm?', chapter 3 above. One reason Taylor gives for rejecting the application of the 'significant harm' test to such disputes 'is that it would be unnecessarily cruel and combative to require loving and sincere parents to defend themselves against a test based on harm' (p 61).

[65] L Forbat, C Sayer, P McNamee, E Menson and S Barclay, 'Conflict in a Paediatric Hospital: A Prospective Mixed Method Study' (2016) 101 *Archives of Disease in Childhood* 23, 25.

[66] L Forbat, B Teuten and S Barclay, 'Conflict Escalation in Paediatric Services: Findings from a Qualitative Study' (2015) *Archives of Disease in Childhood* 1, 3.

[67] *Gard* (n 44), [84].

[68] Forbat et al (n 65), 24.

[69] T Fassier and E Azoulay, 'Conflicts and Communication Gaps in the Intensive Care Unit' (2010) 16 *Current Opinion in Critical Care* 654, 661.

[70] *Evans* (n 51), [10].

viewed his initial recovery as 'indicative of his potential for more general recovery'.[71] *Haastrup* is another example of parents rejecting medical views in favour of their own. The judge recorded that 'neither parent is able to accept the consensus medical view' that Isaiah's condition was caused by his severe brain injury. Instead, the parents believed the inability to wean their son from the ventilator was due to the medication he was receiving.[72]

Third, clinicians and families will sometimes differ in their views about *decisional authority*. According to Forbat et al, many families believe that decisions about withdrawal or withholding of treatment should be made jointly between themselves and the clinical team, but a minority believe this should be a matter for the parents alone to decide.[73] Other studies support the latter point: essentially, some parents maintain that life-or-death decisions about their offspring are theirs to make.[74]

Even where the parties disagree about these (or other) matters, it is not necessarily the case that disagreement will develop into an intractable conflict.[75] Such escalation might even be avoided – and consensus potentially achieved – if discussions can enable the parties to identify areas of disagreement and clinicians are trained to recognise and manage conflict at an early stage.[76] But ongoing discussion can also impose costs, and not only on the parents and clinicians. First, ongoing discussion can exacerbate, rather than resolve, a dispute. If there is a breakdown in communication and trust that is not resolved, this can lead to both sides becoming entrenched in their positions,[77] rendering third-party intervention necessary.[78] However, as we will see, clinicians can be reluctant to seek such intervention, and particularly court proceedings, for fear of costs, negative publicity, inconsistent decisions or being seen as a failure by colleagues.[79] Such reluctance might incline clinicians to continue a discursive process, which is nevertheless failing to progress towards resolution. But quite *when* discussions should be deemed to have failed, and third-party intervention sought, is (as yet) unclear.[80] Second, ongoing discussion might be contrary to the interests of the child. In the absence of agreement about non-treatment/treatment, the status quo is likely to be maintained,

[71] ibid.

[72] *Haastrup* (n 50), [59]

[73] Forbat et al (n 65), 23.

[74] L Gillam and J Sullivan, 'Ethics at the End of Life: Who Should Make Decisions about Treatment Limitation for Young Children with Life-Threatening or Life-Limiting Conditions?' (2011) 47 *Journal of Paediatrics and Child Health* 594; Birchley et al (n 60), 932.

[75] D Wilkinson, S Barclay and J Savulescu, 'Disagreement, Mediation, Arbitration: Resolving Disputes about Medical Treatment' (2018) 391 *Lancet* 2302, 2304.

[76] Fassier and Azoulay (n 69), 661; Forbat et al (n 67), 4; S Barclay, 'Recognising and Managing Conflict Between Patients, Parents and Health Professionals' (2016) 26 *Paediatrics and Child Health* 314, 314.

[77] Forbat et al (n 66), 3.

[78] ibid; RD William Hain, 'Voices of Moral Authority: Parents, Doctors and What Will Actually Help' (2018) 44 *Journal of Medical Ethics* 458, 460; Wilkinson et al (n 75), 2304.

[79] Brierley et al (n 61), 576; Birchley et al (n 59), 932.

[80] Birchley and Huxtable (n 55), 121.

meaning the child will continue to receive the contested treatment. This may not be in the child's best interests – and might even be harmful.[81] In addition to the child, there are also the interests of the disputants to consider. Research suggests, for example, that healthcare professionals can experience moral distress as a consequence of being asked to treat a child contrary to what they feel is in the child's best interests.[82]

These observations suggest that communication and ongoing discussions between the stakeholders are important, but they also reveal at least two questions, which future research might usefully explore. First, at what point should clinicians (or, indeed, other parties) recognise that discussion is no longer effective and third-party intervention should be sought? Second, which form(s) of third-party intervention are indicated, and in which circumstances? We will start to explore the latter question in the following sections, beginning with the use of second medical opinions.

4. Second Opinion Experts

If discussions between the team and family have not resulted in agreement, then further clinical opinions might be sought. This, however, appears to be an under-researched phenomenon in this context. It is apparent that second (or third or more) opinions will sometimes be sought by clinicians and sometimes by families.[83] Such consultation might occur within or without the context of court proceedings, and, indeed, might even be ordered by a court. Those consulted can come from within the institution or from elsewhere, including from overseas; indeed, in all of the recent legal cases, both UK and non-UK experts were instructed.

Beyond these indications, however, there appears to be a lack of research into when and how second opinions are sought, who determines which expert is instructed, and any role they might play in addressing or resolving conflict. Some suspect that such additional opinions can prove useful, for example if the family's interpretation of the medical facts differs from those of the treating clinicians.[84] Families will also sometimes disagree with the clinicians about the treatment to be given, with Forbat et al noting that this is the second most common cause of conflict.[85] In such cases, an independent view might prove helpful.

The utility of such opinions is not, however, established in the literature. In their study, Brierley et al noted that second opinions were sought in six of the 203 cases in which withdrawal of treatment was recommended. However, in none of

[81] Brierley et al (n 61), 576.

[82] ibid; G Morley, C Bradbury-Jones and J Ives, 'Moral Distress in End-of-Life Care' forthcoming, 6.

[83] Brierley et al (n 61), 576; S Meller and S Barclay, 'Mediation: An Approach to Intractable Disputes Between Parents and Paediatricians' (2011) 96 *Archives of Disease in Childhood* 619, 619.

[84] Wilkinson et al (n 75), 2304.

[85] Forbat et al (n 65), 25.

those six cases did resolution result from the provision of the additional opinion. The authors suggested that this was due to the intractable religious views held by the parents in those cases,[86] and the study does not provide evidence that second opinions, in general, are ineffective.

But other authors do express concerns about the gathering of such opinions. First, the second opinion might lack – or be perceived to lack – the requisite *independence*. Meller and Barclay note this as a risk when the treating team, rather than the family, select the expert. To avoid that risk, they propose that families select the expert.[87] However, the family's satisfaction will also depend on what the expert *says*: in *Haastrup*, the father instructed his own expert, but he viewed that expert as colluding with the NHS when the expert took the same view as the treating clinicians.[88] Meller and Barclay also raise the concern that allowing families to select the expert will lead to families 'doctor-shopping' for those experts likely to share their view.[89] For example, in *Gard*, the mother's Internet research revealed the possibility of an experimental treatment, which led to the instruction of an expert from the United States.[90] Such cherry-picking can then lead to a second potential area of difficulty, if the expert departs from the view of the treating clinicians and this *exacerbates the conflict*.[91] This appears to be what happened in *Gard*, as the expert's views did indeed differ from those of the responsible team.[92]

These are, however, only indications and further research appears to be needed. Such research could, in particular, explore how often second opinions are sought, how the process works, and its effectiveness, or otherwise, in resolving disputes.

5. Clinical Ethics Consultation

Clinical ethics support services are another source of external input to the clinicians (and, occasionally, patients and their families). Such services take different forms internationally but, in the UK, a clinical ethics committee (CEC) model dominates. Unlike their research-facing counterparts, CECs are not legally mandatory or even regulated as such. During the passage of the Mental Capacity (Amendment) Bill through the House of Lords, an amendment was tabled that would have required all NHS bodies to have access to CECs.[93] However, the proposed

[86] Brierley et al (n 61), 574.

[87] Meller and Barclay (n 83), 619.

[88] *Haastrup* (n 50), [46].

[89] Meller and Barclay (n 83), 619.

[90] *Gard* (n 44), [71]–[72].

[91] C Wallis, 'When Paediatricians and Families Can't Agree' (2018) 103 *Archives of Disease in Childhood* 413, 413.

[92] In the court hearings, the US expert acknowledged that the treatment was unlikely to work, although he felt, if the parents wanted to try it, then it should be provided, given the lack of other treatment options: *Gard* (n 44), [18]–[19].

[93] The proposed amendment also included provision for regulations to be made as to their membership, funding and constitution. See publications.parliament.uk/pa/bills/lbill/2017-2019/0117/18117-I(a).

amendment was subsequently withdrawn in favour of discussions with the minister instead.[94] Pending any such change in the law, the UK Clinical Ethics Network (UKCEN) provides leadership, by seeking to promote clinical ethics support and facilitate communication between UK CECs.[95] It describes CECs as 'multidisciplinary groups, including health professionals and lay members that aim to provide support for decision-making on ethical issues arising from the provision of patient care within NHS Trusts and other health care institutions'.[96] Committees therefore tend to include health professionals, lay members, legal members and 'ethicists', but they have no fixed structure, function or membership criteria, and their constitution varies between settings.[97] The number of UK committees (voluntarily) registered with UKCEN waxes and wanes, from 20 in 2000, to 85 in 2009,[98] to 77 in 2018.[99] Where they exist, CECs tend to be involved in education and policy, as well as – of most relevance here – case consultation.

CECs tend to have an *advisory* remit: they issue advice on request, rather than making decisions about (for example) ethically contentious cases. There are, however, many questions surrounding UK committees, including about the extent to which their advice is sought. The literature suggests that CECs are infrequently utilised as a mechanism for dispute resolution,[100] with most UK committees advising on 1–10 cases a year.[101] As many CECs are based in large NHS Trusts, the referrals they receive will span a variety of patients and specialties. However, even in paediatric settings, referrals appear to be low, with Brierley et al noting that only six of the 186 contested cases in their study were referred for ethical review.[102] The relative scarcity of ethical review also appears to be borne out in the recent legal cases: only in *Gard* is reference made to CEC input.[103]

They may appear to be relatively under-utilised, but commentators nevertheless believe that CECs have the potential to contribute positively to the resolution of difficult cases. Three groups of reasons tend to be given. First, 'CECs seek to

pdf. Parental access to CECs in the case of disagreements about the care of critically ill children is being sought by Charlie Gard's parents as part of the proposed 'Charlie's Law', Charlie Gard Foundation, 'Charlie's Law', www.thecharliegardfoundation.org/charlies-law/.

[94] Hansard HL vol 793 cols 387–88 (15 October 2018).

[95] UK Clinical Ethics Network, 'About the Network', www.ukcen.net/main/about.

[96] UK Clinical Ethics Network, 'Clinical Ethics Committees' www.ukcen.net/committees/introduction.

[97] Birchley and Huxtable (n 55), 123; UK Clinical Ethics Network (n 96).

[98] V Larcher, 'The Development and Function of Clinical Ethics Committees (CECs) in the United Kingdom' (2009) 22 *Diametros* 47, 48.

[99] UK Clinical Ethics Network, 'CEC Member List', www.ukcen.net/committees/member_list.

[100] A Fiester, 'The Failure of the Consult Model: Why "Mediation" Should Replace "Consultation"' (2007) 7 *American Journal of Bioethics* 31, 32.

[101] AM Slowther, L McClimans and C Price, 'Development of Clinical Ethics Services in the UK: A National Survey' (2012) 38 *Journal of Medical Ethics* 210, 212–13.

[102] Brierley et al (n 61), 574. The CEC's advice did not lead to resolution in those six cases, which the authors attribute to the parents' decisions being driven by fundamentalist religious beliefs that they were not prepared to discuss.

[103] *Gard* (n 44), [17] and [59]. It should be noted, however, that some CECs do not offer formal advice and will only act to help the clinical team work through the presenting problem.

provide practical advice, thus neither amounting to a mere "talking shop", nor posing a threat to clinical autonomy'.[104] Second, CECs explicitly focus on the ethical dimensions of the case before them, which suggests they might be well equipped to advise on values-based disputes. For example, as was the case in *Haastrup*,[105] a clinician might believe that treatment should stop, but a family with particular religious beliefs – such as in the sanctity of life – might want treatment to continue.[106] In such cases, a CEC could help to identify and elucidate the underlying ethical values, and point to areas of commonality or in which a compromise might be achieved, through which efforts resolution might then be reached.[107] Moreover, CECs appear to have the experience (and perhaps even some form of expertise) in addressing dilemmas such as those considered here, since they notably tend to be consulted about such issues as withdrawing or withholding life-supporting treatment.[108] Indeed, some CECs exist in specialist settings – like GOSH's committee[109] – which implies they will have a specialist body of experience (and, again, perhaps also specialist expertise).[110] Third, CECs are intended to be supportive and as such they may have advantages over their competitors. For example, relative to the courts, CECs are able to pool diverse, pertinent expertise and they are less formal and costly (in both financial and emotional terms).[111] Although data is lacking, not only about how often CECs are used, but also about whether their advice is accepted,[112] some parties do record high satisfaction rates.[113]

The news is not all good, however. Amongst the 'unresolved issues' noted by Weise and Daly are 'questions about qualifications for clinical ethicists, required competencies, the appropriateness of formal certification or licensure, and metrics for evaluation'.[114] The main concerns can be gathered into three groups. First, there are problems of *orientation*. UK CECs are typically there to support clinicians, which raises questions about their availability and commitment to patients and their families,[115] their accountability,[116] and their independence from the

[104] Huxtable (n 8), 473.

[105] *Haastrup* (n 50), [54].

[106] Brierley et al (n 51), 576.

[107] Wilkinson et al (n 75), 2304; Huxtable (n 18), 156–57.

[108] Slowther et al (n 101) 212; KM Swetz, ME Crowley, C Hook and PS Mueller, 'Report of 255 Clinical Ethics Consultations and Review of the Literature' (2007) 82 *Mayo Clinic Proceedings* 686, 686.

[109] Great Ormond Street Hospital, 'About the Clinical Ethics Service', www.gosh.nhs.uk/wards-and-departments/departments/clinical-specialties/clinical-ethics-service-information-health-professionals/about-clinical-ethics-service.

[110] Huxtable (n 8), 474.

[111] ibid, 473.

[112] Fiester (n 100), 31.

[113] Fassier and Azoulay (n 69), 662.

[114] KL Weise and BJ Daly, 'Exploring Accountability of Clinical Ethics Consultants: Practice and Training Implications' (2014) 14 *American Journal of Bioethics* 34, 34.

[115] AJ Newson, 'The Role of Patients in Clinical Ethics Support: A Snapshot of Practices and Attitudes in the United Kingdom' (2009) 4 *Clinical Ethics* 139; V Fournier, E Rari, R Forde, G Neitzke, R Pegoraro, AJ Newson, 'Clinical Ethics Consultation in Europe: A Comparative and Ethical Review of the Role of Patients' (2009) 4 *Clinical Ethics* 131.

[116] Weise and Daly (n 114).

healthcare setting.[117] The parents and nurses interviewed by Birchley were supportive of CEC involvement in paediatric disputes, although those participants did not have direct experience of CECs.[118] Others' concerns about bias and the like might nevertheless be assuaged if, for example, parents and nurses are permitted to *bring* referrals;[119] indeed, as we noted, Charlie Gard's parents have proposed legislation that would ensure such access.[120] As for those *receiving* the referrals as members of the committee, it is also possible – as GOSH's CEC evinces – to include in the membership those who have direct ('lay') experience of care in the relevant setting.[121]

Second, there are questions of *operation and process*, which McLean pithily captures when she refers to CECs as a 'due process wasteland',[122] and asks: '[W]hat and who are clinical ethics committees for?'[123] The relative informality of CECs may appear to be a strength but, as Weise and Daly noted, there are concerns about the qualifications, certification and competencies of CEC members, and about the ethical deliberation frameworks that CECs use to reach their advice.[124] As things stand, there are no formal requirements for the expertise or training required to sit on such committees,[125] and Birchley's study noted that one of the criticisms paediatric clinicians had of CECs was their lack of paediatric experience.[126] Fiester has argued that lack of training and expertise may bring into question CECs' right to be involved in decisions that affect the lives of others.[127] Having the 'wrong' sort of expertise or focus can be problematic: some of Birchley's clinicians felt that CECs have too great a legal focus,[128] but legal scholars (eg McLean) have conversely queried whether CECs sufficiently attend to legal concerns, such as those associated with due process, transparency and consistency.[129] But quite what the requisite expertise should be remains an open – and vexed – question.[130]

[117] M Magelssen, R Pedersen, R Førde, 'Sources of Bias in Clinical Ethics Case Deliberation' (2014) 40 *Journal of Medical Ethics* 678.

[118] Birchley and Huxtable (n 55), 124.

[119] ibid, 124, 127; R Forde, T Linja, '"It Scares Me to Know that We Might Not Have Been There!": A Qualitative Study into the Experiences of Parents of Seriously Ill Children Participating in Ethical Case Discussions' (2015) 16 *BioMed Central Medical Ethics* 40.

[120] Charlie Gard Foundation (n 93).

[121] *Great Ormond Street Hospital* (n 109); E Updale, 'The Challenge of Lay Membership of Clinical Ethics Committees' (2006) 1 *Clinical Ethics* 60.

[122] S McLean, 'Clinical Ethics Committees: A Due Process Wasteland?' (2008) 3 *Clinical Ethics* 99.

[123] S McLean, 'What and Who Are Clinical Ethics Committees For?' (2007) 33 *Journal of Medical Ethics* 49.

[124] V Larcher, AM Slowther and AR Watson, 'Core Competencies for Clinical Ethics Committees' (2010) 10 *Clinical Medicine* 30; AM Slowther, L McClimans and C Price, 'Development of Clinical Ethics Services in the UK: A National Survey' (2012) 38 *Journal of Medical Ethics* 210.

[125] Huxtable (n 18), 159.

[126] Birchley and Huxtable (n 55), 125.

[127] Fiester (n 100), 31.

[128] Birchley and Huxtable (n 55), 125.

[129] McLean (n 122), 101–03; Huxtable (n 18), 166–72.

[130] Huxtable (n 18), 172–76.

Another vexed question is whether a CEC is even the best model for providing clinical ethics support. Other models exist, such as clinical ethics consultants, although these tend to be rare in the UK.[131] Of course, what counts as the 'best' (or even just an 'appropriate') model remains to be seen, and this leads onto a third area of difficulty, concerning the *impact and evaluation* of clinical ethics support. The impact of CECs is questionable, not least because they lack the ability formally to resolve disputes by determining the outcome: they only offer advice to clinicians, which the clinicians are free to reject.[132] But, again, quite what is to count as impact in this context, and how it is to be evaluated, merits further research.[133]

CECs therefore show promise but also appear to have their pitfalls. Amongst the many proposals for improving CECs are: ensuring that committees are pluralistically composed and that members have training in (for example) communication and conflict management;[134] having specialist committees with subject-specific expertise;[135] and formalising committees, including through the creation of an appeals process and auditing and evaluation of decision-making.[136] Further research is nevertheless needed into CECs and these proposals, including those for alternative types of clinical ethics services.

6. Mediation

One alternative to CECs, which is beginning to be explored in this context, is mediation. Mediation is a flexible, confidential process which involves a neutral third party helping the parties in dispute towards a negotiated resolution, where the parties have the final say as to whether agreement is reached and, if so, on what terms.[137] Already familiar in some other contexts, there is growing interest in mediation as a method for resolving paediatric healthcare disputes, following the establishment of the Medical Mediation Foundation in 2010.[138]

[131] For a discussion of the benefits that clinical ethics consultations can offer clinical ethics support services, see: E DeRenzo, N Mokwunye and JJ Lynch, 'Rounding: How Everyday Ethics Can Invigorate a Hospital's Ethics Committee' (2006) 18 *HEC Forum* 319; E DeRenzo, J Vinicky, B Redman, JJ Lynch, P Panzarella and S Rizk, 'Rounding: A Model for Consultation and Training Whose Time Has Come' (2006) 15 *Cambridge Quarterly of Healthcare Ethics* 207.

[132] Birchley and Huxtable (n 55), 126.

[133] E Fox and RM Arnold, 'Evaluating Outcomes in Ethics Consultation Research' (1996) 7 *Journal of Clinical Ethics* 127; J Schildmann, B Molewijk, L Benaroyo, R Forde and G Neitzke, 'Evaluation of Clinical Ethics Support Services and its Normativity' (2013) 39 *Journal of Medical Ethics* 681.

[134] Fassier and Azoulay (n 69), 662; Huxtable (n 18), 169.

[135] Birchley and Huxtable (n 55), 127; Huxtable (n 8), 473. This is arguably already the case with GOSH's CEC.

[136] Huxtable (n 18), 160, 170, 171.

[137] Centre for Effective Dispute Resolution, 'Glossary of Terms', https://www.cedr.com/about_us/library/glossary.php.

[138] Meller and Barclay (n 83), 620.

The use of mediation in this context has attracted support including, in *Gard*, from Francis J.[139] Mediation is said to have various benefits. First, the method allows for – indeed, requires – open discussion, which might help to rebuild relationships and restore trust.[140] The method can therefore be contrasted with more adversarial mechanisms, such as recourse to law. Second, and again in contrast to court proceedings, the timing is flexible: Wilkinson et al note that mediation can be attempted at any stage of a dispute.[141] There is also, third, flexibility over who can be involved in the process – unlike, again, court proceedings.[142] Input beyond that of the disputing clinicians and parents can prove beneficial: Brierley et al, for example, found that involving religious leaders in discussions of end-of-life care aided resolution of disputes.[143]

Despite these advantages, mediation also has its drawbacks and uncertainties. First, the process requires voluntary engagement and a willingness on the part of the disputants to move beyond their initial positions.[144] Not every disputant will be so inclined. Indeed, according to the Trust's legal counsel, mediation failed in *Evans* because the family and their advisors did not genuinely engage with the process.[145] It is not only families who might fail to engage, however. Second, research by Forbat et al found that healthcare staff see mediation as a mechanism of last resort.[146] Yet, as *Evans* arguably illustrates, such a waiting game might doom mediation to fail because, by the time it is attempted, relationships have broken down and the parties have become entrenched in their positions.

[139] *Gard* (n 44), [130]. The legislation Charlie Gard's parents are seeking (n 95) also provides for access to medical mediation when disputes as to the care of critically ill children arise.

[140] T Allen, 'A New Way to Settle Old Disputes: Mediation and Healthcare' (2005) 73 *Medico-Legal Journal* 93, 98; Meller and Barclay (n 83), 620; Huxtable (n 8), 473.

[141] Wilkinson et al (n 75), 2304.

[142] Meller and Barclay (n 83), 620. Whilst third parties can intervene in court proceedings, this is restricted to the provision of written or oral submissions and only applies to third parties who have some 'knowledge or particular point of view [that enables them to provide the court] with a more rounded picture than it would otherwise obtain' (*Re E (A Child) (AP) (Appellant) (Northern Ireland)* [2008] UKHL 66, [3]).

[143] Brierley et al (n 61), 573. Whilst there is scope for others besides the parties to a dispute to intervene in proceedings (eg religious leaders), it is at the court's discretion whether to accept such submissions and, if they do, the weight they will be given. In addition, whilst the intervention can support one of the parties, the interveners must raise issues of principle beyond those raised by the parties: A Samuels, 'The Intervener Is Here to Stay' (2017) *New Law Journal* 17.

[144] Allen (n 140), 99.

[145] M Mylonas QC, 28 April 2018: '[1/2] In Alfie's case the first mediation in July 2017 with 2 trained mediators (one medical) was useless when family turned up very late allowing only 90 minutes rather than full day. Second was hijacked days before when Giuristi per La Vita said no to [2/2] mediation and family wanted only a "meeting". 3rd in Jan failed after start was delayed for 5 hours (with whole Alder Hey team waiting) while pro-life activist Broesamle argued with family's advisors. Mediation will not work unless families are properly advised', tweets: twitter.com/mmpolista/status/990472258853441537 and twitter.com/mmpolista/status/990478302866563078.

[146] L Forbat, J Simons, C Sayer, M Davies and S Barclay, 'Training Paediatric Healthcare Staff in Recognising, Understanding and Managing Conflict with Patients and Families: Findings from a Survey on Immediate and 6-Month Impact' (2017) 102 *Archives of Disease in Childhood* 250, 253.

Even if the parties do sincerely engage, third, there is the risk that important elements of the dispute might be missed. Disputes in this context appear often to rest on conflicting ethical positions, which mediation might fail to draw out or seek to resolve.[147] To address such a concern, scholars suggest that mediation should be underpinned by an ethical framework and be directed towards the goal of achieving an ethical outcome.[148] Proponents of mediation, such as Meller and Barclay, agree that effective mediation in this context requires mediators to be equipped with knowledge of medical law and medical ethics, an understanding of paediatric issues, and access to independent expert advice.[149]

These latter proposals suggest that CECs and mediation might usefully be brought together, since they apparently offer different ways of fulfilling the same, or at least similar, functions. CECs can provide the requisite ethical reflection, whilst mediation brings an impartiality and independence that CECs might lack. Whether the two can and should be brought together looks like a promising line of research. Research into mediation in this context is certainly needed, in order to ascertain when and how it is used and its effectiveness.[150] In Brierley et al's study of dispute resolution, there was no reference made to mediation being used.[151] Research is now underway, primarily through the Medical Mediation Foundation's Evelina Resolution Project, which offers mediation services as well as conflict recognition and management training.[152] However, its data to date has focused upon conflict management training, rather than on mediation.[153] Allen has suggested that the lack of data on the success (or otherwise) of mediation is due to mediation being confidential.[154] However, data on the extent of mediation and whether this has led to resolution could be gathered and reported (subject to the parties' agreement) without breaching confidentiality. In sum, mediation, like clinical ethics support, looks promising, but more research is needed to ascertain the advantages and disadvantages that this approach to paediatric disputes offers.

7. Courts

Finally, the courts are available to make decisions in contested cases. Proceedings may be brought under the Children Act 1989, according to which the 'welfare of

[147] Huxtable (n 8), 473.

[148] Wilkinson et al (n 75), 2304.

[149] Meller and Barclay (n 83), 620.

[150] The Nuffield Council on Bioethics had previously recommended the benefits of medical mediation be explored: Nuffield Council on Bioethics (n 39), [8.62].

[151] Brierley et al (n 61).

[152] Medical Mediation Foundation, 'Evelina Resolution Project', www.medicalmediation.org.uk/evelina-resolution-project/.

[153] See: Wilkinson et al (n 75); Forbat et al (n 65); Forbat et al (n 146); L Forbat and S Barclay, 'Reducing Healthcare Conflict: Outcomes from Using the Conflict Management Framework' (2018) *Archives of Disease in Childhood* 1.

[154] Allen (n 140), 95.

the child' shall be the court's 'paramount consideration',[155] or under the inherent jurisdiction, where the focus is on the 'best interests' of the child. Although there are procedural differences,[156] the courts have confirmed that welfare and best interests are to be treated as synonymous.[157] Since the early 1980s, the courts have adjudicated on numerous cases involving critically ill infants.[158]

There are various reasons why courts might be considered appropriate and effective fora for resolving such disputes, three of which we will mention here. First, unlike the other mechanisms we have considered, courts provide authoritative judgments about what treatment (or care) may – perhaps must – be given.[159] In short, courts can decide and thereby settle a dispute. Second, in apparent contrast to some of the preceding alternatives, the legal process is rigorous. Judges are, for example, able to evaluate a variety of evidence,[160] and, whilst it is undoubtedly subject to criticism, the legal process aspires to impartiality and does enjoy some credibility as a means of decisively settling disputes. Third, and despite its procedural rigour, the legal process also allows for some flexibility, including in the sorts of evidence to be considered. Judges can, for example, engage with the ethical dimensions of the cases before them – as indeed has occurred in paediatric disputes.[161]

Despite these apparent advantages, recourse to the courts appears to be relatively rare. Although not every ruling is reported, there annually appear to be only two or three such cases coming before the courts.[162] The literature nevertheless indicates that there are many more disputes occurring in paediatric healthcare settings. Brierley et al's study supports this impression, wherein only one of the disputed cases was litigated.[163] Infrequent recourse to the courts might be attributable to their perceived disadvantages, five of which we will note.

First, the legal process is *adversarial*, which generates the impression that there are winners and losers.[164] This is not necessarily an appropriate framing, particularly in an ethically sensitive context such as the present one, which does not necessarily encompass ethical blacks and whites but might instead be replete with ethical shades of grey.[165] Furthermore, and contrary to the earlier observation,

[155] Children Act 1989 s 1.

[156] See, eg, R George, 'The Legal Basis of the Court's Jurisdiction to Authorise Medical Treatment of Children', chapter 4 above.

[157] *Re B* (n 17).

[158] Cited within this chapter and discussed in Huxtable (nn 8, 18).

[159] Courts resist the idea that they *order* doctors, but that is arguably the practical import of their decisions. However, the courts will not always *decide*: for example, in *R v Portsmouth Hospital NHS Trust ex parté Glass* [1999] 2 FLR 905, the court refused to make an order as to the course the doctors should take in the event of future disagreements over treatment. Failure to issue a decision appears rare but, even where (as is usual) decisions are made, these will not always *settle* the dispute: for example, Bridgeman (n 2) notes that the *Wyatt* case came to court at least 11 times.

[160] Wilkinson et al (n 75), 2304.

[161] Huxtable (n 18), 145–46.

[162] Birchley (n 57), 207.

[163] Brierley et al (n 61), 574.

[164] Huxtable (n 18), 147; Birchley and Huxtable (n 55), 122; Huxtable (n 8), 472; Wallis (n 91), 413.

[165] Meller and Barclay (n 83), 620.

the courts will not always be willing or equipped to attend to these complex ethical dimensions.[166]

Second, an adversarial framing can have *adverse effects* on the protagonists and, indeed, on the (already compromised) relationship between them. Fassier and Azoulay noted concerns expressed by ICU staff that court action could amplify the feelings of frustration and grief in such disputes,[167] resulting in the proceedings escalating the conflict and entrenchment of different views, as the focus shifts to the conflict itself, rather than the child.[168] This could then lead to a complete loss of trust between the family and healthcare staff,[169] with the involvement of the media and social media further contributing to a climate of fear and distrust.[170] Brierley et al noted that fear of negative publicity was one reason why healthcare professionals are reluctant to utilise court proceedings.[171] There are also suggestions that, when judicial decisions *are* sought, relationships can suffer – regardless of who 'wins' or 'loses'. If the judge decides that treatment should be withdrawn contrary to the parents' wishes, then the parents will obviously feel that their assessment of the welfare of their child has been overruled.[172] But even the 'winning' clinicians need not be entirely satisfied, since the decision will signal that, whilst they had been seeking resolution, they had been treating the child against his or her best interests.[173] Alternatively, if the judge decides that treatment should be provided, then this might further erode the parents' trust in the clinicians and create a conflict for the clinicians between honouring the legal ruling and acting in what they perceive to be the best interests of the child. In short, an adversarial process can impose costs on the parties, including, of course, on the child.[174]

Third, the costs are not only emotional or relational, but also *financial*.[175] There will be the costs associated with providing ongoing treatment to the child until the judicial decision is issued (and that decision, of course, might be that treatment should not be given).[176] There are also the costs of the legal proceedings themselves. Such costs will often be borne by Trusts, but one might wonder whether this is a good use of the limited NHS budget, when cheaper, potentially less divisive mechanisms exist. If, instead, parents must fund the proceedings, then there is a paucity of legal aid funding, but even where this is available, it will not

[166] Huxtable (n 18), 152–53.
[167] Fassier and Azoulay (n 69), 662.
[168] Meller and Barclay (n 83), 619; Forbat et al (n 66), 3.
[169] Waldman and Frader (n 64), 175.
[170] Fassier and Azoulay (n 69), 662.
[171] Brierley et al (n 61), 576.
[172] J Bridgeman, 'Gard v Yates v GOSH, the Guardian and the United Kingdom: Reflections on the Legal Process and the Legal Principles' (2017) 17 *Medical Law International* 285, 292.
[173] Waldman and Frader (n 64), 176; D Wilkinson and J Savulesca, 'Hard Lessons: Learning from the Charlie Gard Case' (2018) 44 *Journal of Medical Ethics* 438, 440.
[174] Morley et al (n 82), 6.
[175] ibid; Forbat et al (n 66), 2; Birchley and Huxtable (n 55), 122, 123.
[176] Huxtable (n 8), 472. This might imply that treatment should not *have been* given.

always cover the entire costs.[177] The parents in *Gard* managed to secure pro bono representation, but this will not be available to all parents; the judge in *Gard* understandably expressed the view that, in such cases, legal aid should be available.[178] Turning to the child, the state will also meet the costs of the Children's Guardian, who will appear to represent the child. This appears to be legitimate expenditure, since the Guardian represents the interests of the child independent of the views of his or her parents or doctors; however, Meller and Barclay have queried whether the Guardian is truly independent, given the apparent frequency with which the Guardian concurs with medical opinion.[179]

Fourth, the courts' *reasoning* about the best interests of the child can appear inconsistent, opaque and unpredictable. The parties to a case will receive a determinate outcome but the judgments arguably fail to issue guidance that is sufficient to inform future decision-makers. The Children Act only enumerates some of the factors to be considered,[180] with the judges enjoying a great deal of discretion in the interpretation of a child's best interests.[181] The factors – and the weight accorded to them – that inform best interests decisions appear to vary between cases.[182] Close et al have called on the courts to be clearer in their written judgments about the factors that influenced their decision, the weight given to those factors and the reasons for this.[183] The language used can also add confusion; for example, there may be references to treatment being 'futile', without judges explaining how that has been interpreted in a particular case.[184] The perceived lack of clarity might explain Brierley et al and Birchley et al's findings that healthcare professionals were reluctant to seek court orders because of uncertainty as to the likely outcome.[185] Such findings raise the concern that clinicians will only seek court hearings if they are confident that the court will support their decision about treatment (a concern which echoes that of parents 'cherry-picking' second-opinion experts). Further research could usefully explore whether there are better alternatives to the best interests standard, such as the 'harm standard' (which featured in *Gard*),[186]

[177] ibid.

[178] *Great Ormond Street Hospital for Children NHS Foundation Trust v Yates and Others* [2017] EWHC 1909, [17].

[179] Meller and Barclay (n 83), 619. See, eg, *Gard* (n 44), [117]; *Haastrup* (n 50), [67]; *Evans* (n 51), [54].

[180] C Lim, MC Dunn and JJ Chin, 'Clarifying the Best Interests Standard: The Elaborative and Enumerative Strategies in Public Policy-Making' (2016) 42 *Journal of Medical Ethics* 542.

[181] M Hedley, *The Modern Judge: Power, Responsibility and Society's Expectations* (Bristol, Jordans, 2016).

[182] Huxtable (n 18), 146; Huxtable (n 8), 472.

[183] E Close, L Wilmott and BP White, 'Charlie Gard: In Defence of Law' (2018) 44 *Journal of Medical Ethics* 476, 478.

[184] See, eg, *Evans* (n 51), [24], [25], [35], [37], [51] and [66]. In contrast, in *Gard* (n 45), the judge explained his interpretation of 'futile' as 'pointless or of no effective benefit' [93]. We highlighted in section 2 of this chapter the potentially damaging effect that terms such as 'futile' can have in the context of such disputes. C Auckland, 'Futility', chapter 9 above.

[185] Brierley et al (n 61), 576; Birchley and Huxtable (n 55), 122.

[186] *Gard* (n 46), [113]. See, eg, Birchley et al (n 59), 933; Taylor (n 64); I Goold, 'Evaluating Best Interests as a Threshold for Judicial Intervention', chapter 2 above.

or whether there might be better approaches to the interpretation and operationalisation of the existing standard.

The final drawback of legal proceedings is that these entail *delay*.[187] Proceedings that make it to court can be time consuming. Bridgeman has noted that, despite being fast-tracked, the proceedings in *Gard* lasted for five months, including the appeals.[188] As already noted, during this time, the healthcare team are continuing to treat the child, potentially contrary to what they consider to be in the child's best interests. This was recognised by the Supreme Court in *Gard* when they considered whether to continue to stay proceedings whilst the parents pursued the appeals:

> The hospital finds itself in an acutely difficult ethical dilemma: although the stays have made it lawful to continue to provide him with AVNH [artificial ventilation, nutrition and hydration], it considers it professionally wrong for it to have continued for over two months to act otherwise than in his best interests.[189]

Similar timescales were seen in *Haastrup* (three months) and *Evans* (five months), although in *Haastrup* there was no substantive appeal hearing. Some cases are quicker: *King* was dealt with within two weeks, but the key difference there was that the Trust did not oppose the parents' desire for alternative treatment. The courts need to balance procedural fairness with expediency,[190] but the prospect of delays can deter clinicians from seeking judicial resolution.[191] Yet, this is not the only reported reason for clinicians' reluctance. Birchley et al found that some clinicians saw the avoidance of court as a measure of personal and professional success.[192] This implies that courts are used only as a last resort, and Wallis notes that paediatricians are usually advised only to seek a judgment when the dispute has become entrenched and reached an impasse.[193] However, waiting for this impasse could further undermine the trusting relationship and encourage an adversarial approach towards proceedings, thus further contributing to the sense that courts are not appropriate mechanisms for resolving paediatric healthcare disputes.

In summary, the courts have their benefits – not least in issuing authoritative decisions that settle disputes – but they also have various drawbacks. In addition to investigating alternatives to the courts, future research could usefully explore how legal processes, approaches and the best interests standard might be amended to address these problems, as we presume there will always remain some role for the courts to play, particularly in intractable disputes.

[187] Celia Kitzinger and Jenny Kitzinger have written about the difficulty of delays in court proceedings in the context of withdrawing/withholding life-sustaining treatment from adults: C Kitzinger and J Kitzinger, 'Court Applications for Withdrawal of Artificial Nutrition and Hydration from Patients in a Permanent Vegetative State: Family Experiences' (2016) 42 *Journal of Medical Ethics* 11.

[188] Bridgeman (n 172), 299.

[189] *In the matter of Charlie Gard* [2017] UKSC 94, [15].

[190] Close et al (n 183), 479.

[191] Fassier and Azoulay (n 69), 662.

[192] Birchley et al (n 59), 932.

[193] Wallis (n 91), 413.

8. Conclusion

Commenting on a high-profile ruling back in 2005, Margaret Brazier asked whether there are alternatives to court proceedings, when disputes about a child's healthcare become intractable or threaten to do so.[194] Alternatives certainly exist, including discussions between families and healthcare professionals, as well as recourse to other parties, such as second-opinion experts, CECs and mediators. However, despite the benefits they may bring, each of these alternatives has their own problems and there appears to be a reluctance amongst healthcare professionals to seeking external input when such disputes arise, with such recourse being seen to be a 'last resort'. Discussions between the parties appear, overwhelmingly, to be the preferred method of dispute resolution but, as we have seen, such discussion might have the effect of exacerbating the conflict, as well as potentially being contrary to the child's interests. Further research is needed, however, to identify the point at which clinicians (or, indeed, other parties) should recognise that discussion is no longer effective and third-party intervention should be sought. The question then becomes: which form(s) of third-party intervention are indicated, and in which circumstances?

Second-opinion experts may be beneficial in demonstrating to the family that the clinicians' proposed course of action is the 'right' one. Yet, the cases of *Gard*,[195] *Haastrup*[196] and *Evans*[197] are stark reminders that a second (or even third) opinion might not resolve the dispute if the parties are unwilling to accept an opinion that differs from their own. This is, however, an under-researched means to resolution and further research could explore how often second opinions are sought, how the process works, and whether it is effective at resolving disputes.

Clinical ethics support services also have the potential to resolve such disputes and, in light of the Charlie Gard Foundation's campaign for access to CECs as part of 'Charlie's law',[198] there may be growing public support for this mechanism. Access alone, however, is not enough, and to ensure this is an effective resolution mechanism, further research is needed to understand how often CECs are used and the extent to which their advice is accepted and/or resolves disputes. There are also questions to be addressed around the nature of their composition, expertise, training, impact, evaluation and so on, and whether CECs offer the best model of ethics support or whether there are (in some sense) better alternatives.

There is also growing support, including amongst judges, for mediation as a means of resolving disputes about the healthcare of children.[199] The creation of the Medical Mediation Foundation means that mediators are available in these

[194] Brazier (n 32).
[195] *Gard* (n 44).
[196] *Haastrup* (n 50).
[197] *Evans* (n 51).
[198] Charlie Gard Foundation (n 93).
[199] *Gard* (n 44).

cases. However, more data is needed on how often mediation is used and when it is 'successful'. The Evelina Resolution Project is collecting data, which should provide some answers to these questions in due course. But further research might usefully explore whether mediation could be combined with ethics support, so as to enable the impartial and independent steering of negotiations, where those negotiations are alert to their ethical dimensions.

Finally, whilst courts are used infrequently and as a last resort for resolving such disputes, it is likely their input will continue to be necessary in those cases that are truly intractable. The courts therefore should not be absent from future research agendas. Pertinent research questions include when recourse to court (as opposed to some other mechanism) is necessary and how the court should approach the best interests standard. The latter standard underpins decisions in this context, but is this the right standard, understood and operationalised in appropriate ways, or are adjustments or alternatives required? Work to address questions around the best interests standard is underway in the Balancing Best Interests in Health Care, Ethics and Law (BABEL) project, a five-year programme of work funded by the Wellcome Trust. The project asks how the best interests of incapacitated patients should be understood: which factors and values should be considered, who should be involved, and indeed is 'best interests' the best approach?[200]

In sum, further work is needed to understand, in the context of resolving child healthcare disputes, what the current situation actually *is* and what the situation *should be*. Such research could explore: when, why, how and the extent to which the different resolution mechanisms are used; how they serve to secure resolution; how (if at all) existing mechanisms should be amended; and, ultimately, which process (or processes) should be used in these cases of conflict? Some progress towards answering these questions has been made since Brazier's inquiry in 2005, but the recent suite of widely discussed rulings suggests that more work is needed in this area.

[200] *Balancing Best Interests in Health Care, Ethics and Law*, https://www.bristol.ac.uk/population-health-sciences/centres/ethics/research/babel/.

INDEX

NB–page locators in **bold** indicate information in tables and page locators in *italics* indicate information in figures

advance care planning, 8, 15, *17*, 18, 20–21, 26
  NICE guidelines, 16, 19–20
***Aintree University Hospitals NHS Foundation Trust v James* [2013],** 180–83, 185
***Airedale NHS Trust v Bland* [1993],** 178, 180–81
***Alder Hey NHS Foundation Trust v Evans* [2018],** 2, 148, 213, 215–16, 228
  best interests as the threshold, 29–30, 31, 38–39
  conflict and conflict management, 21, 213
  futility concept, 183–84, 188–90
  harm threshold test, 85, 86, 102–3, 105
  media portrayals of Alfie and family, 194–96
  mediation, 223
  no significant harm argument, 102–3
  professional conscience and professional judgement, 148
  religious-based faith, 155, 157
  vulnerabilities, 194–97
    vulnerability of judges, 205
    vulnerability of parents, 199–202
    vulnerability of staff, 204
alternative treatments:
  parents' right to request, 153–54
  parents' right to seek, 50
  right to be transferred to another hospital, 36, 38
  see also experimental treatments

best interests approach, 1, 22, 31–32, 50–51, 87, *89*, 216–17, 227–28
  Alfie Evans case, 213–14
  Ashya King case, 63, 211–12
  assessment of best interests, 46, 85, 125–26
  balancing parental autonomy, 39–40, 91–92
  Charlie Gard case, 35–39, 42, 86–87, 188, 212–13
  Children Act 1989, 55, 57–58, 63, 65, 110–11, 209–10, 224–25
    courts application of, 51–52, 55–56, 72–73, 81, 82–83, 224–25, 227
  court intervention, 55–57
  declarations of unlawfulness, 79
  experimental treatments, 162, 164, 165
  going beyond best interests, 137–38
    see also professional conscience; professional judgement
  harm threshold compared, 8, 29–30, 85, 107–9, 209–11
    arguments in favour of harm threshold, 45–47
    Charlie Gard case, 86–87, 188
    no difference between harm and best interest approach, 93–95
    objections to harm threshold, 39–44
  indeterminate nature, 96–97
  inherent jurisdiction, 60–61, 224–25
  Mental Capacity Act 2005, 81–82
  moral uncertainty, 88–91
  parental disputes, 54–55, 62–64
  parental responsibility, 51, 65
    welfare standard, 56–57
  quality of life, 210
  third-party intervention, 55–57, 62–64
  threshold for judicial intervention, 1–2, 33–35
    Charlie Gard case, 35–39, 42
bioethical arguments for harm threshold, 107–8
  Diekema, Douglas, 112–13
  language of "best interests" and "harm", 115
  major thresholds for (non)treatment, **118**, 121–22
    best for child, 120–21
    best for family, 121
    pain and suffering threshold, 119
    quasi-quality of life threshold, 119–20
  Mill, John Stuart, 111–12
  minor thresholds for (non)treatment, **118**
    child's potential to be happy, 117
    child's will, 116
    economic reasons, 117
    life at any cost, 117
  parental autonomy, 112–14

***Bolam* test,** 37, 164, 167–68
British Medical Association (BMA) guidance, 211

capacity:
competent children, *see* competent children
consent, 173
deprivation of liberty, 80–81, 82–83
experimental treatments, 164, 168
minors, 79
inherent jurisdiction, 68
Mental Capacity Act 2005, 81–82, 82–83, 164, 168
Mental Capacity (Amendment) Bill, 111, 218–19
parents, 172
sterilisation in adults lacking capacity, 75
vulnerable individuals, 192, 194, 195–96
category 2 cases:
definition, 1
experimental treatments, 165–66
risk of significant harm threshold, 37, 93
child protection orders, 53–54, 212
childhood mortality rate, 13
Children Act 1989, 3–4, 72–73
deprivation of liberty issues, 81–82, 83
inherent jurisdiction and, 70–72
local authority decisions, 59–60, 61
medical cases, scope of Act in, 74–76, 82
parental responsibility, 51, 57–58, 72–73
prohibited steps orders, 73, 74, 76, 82
removal of children from parents, 59–60, 61, 86
secure accommodation orders, 81
specific issue orders, 73, 74, 76, 82
harm threshold criteria, 1, 37, 110–11
rejection of, 61
significant harm, 87, 96
welfare principle, 55, 57–58, 63, 65, 110–11, 209–10, 224–25
courts application of, 51–52, 55–56, 72–73, 81, 82–83, 224–25, 227
children in care, 63–64, 67–68, 77–78
choice of medical team/hospital, 37
choice of treatments, 1, 37–38
clinical ethics committees, 208, 218–19, 229
accountability, 220
advisory remit, 219
ethical focus, 220
independence, 220–21
operation and process, 221
practical advice, 220
qualifications and competence, 220
supportive role, 220
clinical ethics consultants, 208, 222
clinician-parent relationship, 22, 25, *26*, 151, 159–60, 208, 210–11, 226
mediation, role of, 223
collective responsibility for children, 53–54
communication, *see* **conflict management; information sharing and communication**
competent children, 3, 67, 68, 79, 80
conditional harm threshold, 105
default best interest threshold, 98, **99**
prolonged unconsciousness, 102
no significant harm, 102–3
significant harm, 103–4
relevant situation:
parents demanding a treatment, 100–2
parents refusing a treatment, 99–100
conflicts, 21–23
conflict management, 26, 106–7
advance care planning, *26*
Alfie Evans case, 213
Ashya King case, 211–12
Charlie Gard case, 212–13
clinical ethics committees, 208, 218–21, 229
clinical ethics consultants, 222
court proceedings, 208, 224–28, 230
discussions between clinician and family, 208, 214–15, 229
Charlie Gard case, 215
decisional authority, 216
primacy of communication, 217
understanding information, 215–16
information sharing, *26*
Isaiah Haastrup case, 213
mediation, 208, 222–24, 229–30
second opinions, 23, 208, 217, 218, 229
training, lack of, 23
consent, 35–36, 67–68, 75
deprivation of liberty and, 80–81
experimental treatment, 163, 171–74, 176
Court of Protection, 82–83, 180–81
court proceedings, 208, 224–25, 230
advantages, 225
impartiality, 225
disadvantages, 225–28
adversarial nature, 225–26
cost, 226–27
delay, 228
discretion, 225, 227–28
when appropriate, 225

decision-making:
clinician-parent relationship, 22, 25, *26*, 151, 159–60, 208, 210–11, 226
mediation, role of, 223
guidance, 16
law reform, 27
spinal muscular atrophy, 14–15
withholding treatment, 9–12
active decision-making, 13
declarations of unlawfulness, 36
inherent jurisdiction, 69–70, 78–79
deprivation of liberty, 80–83
deprivation of liberty, *see* **right to liberty and security liberty (ECHR Art. 5)**

ending life-sustaining treatments, *see* **withdrawing treatment**
European Convention on Human Rights (ECHR):
right to liberty and security liberty (art. 5), 80–83
right to respect for private and family life (art. 8), 39, 64
experimental treatments, 4, 7, 175–76
conflict between parties, 161–62
courts' role, 165–70
why courts should make final decision, 170–75
consent, 163, 171–74, 176
current regulation, 163–64
definition, 162
hope, 156–57
nucleoside therapy, 36–37, 49–50, 109–10, 148–49, 159, 162, 165–67, 185, 186–87
religious-based faith and rejection of medical advice, 155–56
right to request, 153–54
trust/mistrust, 158–61
see also alternative treatments

faith, 161
hope, 156–57
doctor shopping, 156
religious-based faith and rejection of medical advice
blood transfusion cases, 155
parental decision-making, 156
refusal of treatment, 156
requests for experimental treatment, 156
withdrawal of treatment cases, 155
trust/mistrust, 158–61
futility concept, 4, 177–78
case law:
Bland case, 178, 180
James case, 180–83
"do not attempt cardiopulmonary resuscitation", 178–79
imminent demise futility, 179–80
lethal condition futility, 179–80
physiological futility, 179–80
qualitative futility, 179–80
quantitative futility, 179–80
treatment decisions involving children, 184–85
Alfie Evans case, 183–84, 188–90
Charlie Gard case, 183–84, 185–88

General Medical Council (GMC) guidance, 16
***Gillick* competence,** 3, 34–35, 51–52, 80
***Gillick v West Norfolk and Wisbech Area Health Authority*,** 34–35, 51–52
***Glass v UK* [2004],** 210–11
***Great Ormond Street Hospital v Gard* [2017],** 1
background, 109–10
best interests approach, 31–38, 110–11, 188, 212–13
harm threshold compared, 86–87, 188
threshold for judicial intervention, 35–39, 42
challenge to, 35–36
choice of medical team/hospital, 37
choice of treatment, 37–38, 49–50, 59
conflict management, 212–13, 215
futility concept, 183–84, 185–88
harm threshold, 132
when courts may override parents, 86
judicial intervention threshold, 1–2
best interests as the threshold, 31–38
justifications for law reform, 32–33
medical mediation, 223
parental responsibility, 51, 65
inherent jurisdiction, 58, 59–61
third-party intervention, 62
welfare standard, 56–57
professional conscience, 148–50
public opinion, 32, 229
right to be transferred to another hospital, 36, 38
qualitative futility, 184–89, 212
vulnerability, 206
media portrayals of Alfie Evans and Charlie Gard, 194–96
whether courts' right to intervene, 31–32

guidance:
British Medical Association, 211
General Medical Council, 16, 211
key points, 19–20, 25
National Institute for Health and Care Excellence, 16, 19
Nuffield Council on Bioethics, 211
Royal College of Paediatrics and Child Health, 16, 211

harm threshold, 2–3, 39–41, 108, 132–33
applicability:
when not applicable, **99**
arguments in favour of harm threshold, 44–47, 87–93, 107–8, 122–32
best interests threshold compared, 85, 122–23
bioethical arguments for harm threshold, 111–15
major thresholds, **118**, 118–22
minor thresholds, 116–18, **118**
see also bioethical arguments for harm threshold
Charlie Gard case, 109–11, 132
when courts may override parents, 86
compromising child's best interest in favour of parents/family, 95–96
conditional harm threshold, *see* conditional harm threshold
conflict reduction, 129–30
consistency argument, 92–93
ethical arguments, 87–93
harm is always an issue, 41–43, 93–95
harm threshold test defined, 87, *90*
indeterminate nature of harm, 96–97
insufficient consideration of parents' views, 39–40
medical decisions, 86–87, 127–29
moral uncertainty argument, 88–91
non-medical parental decisions, 86
social welfare decisions, 127
objections to harm threshold, 40–44, 93–97
parental freedom argument, 91
parents as prima facie decision-makers, 44–45
privileging parental views, 43–44, 95–96
reflecting current practice, 46
resource limitations, 130–31
risks of adopting harm threshold, 131
significant risk of harm, 40–41
tolerance and value decisions, 46–47
treatment against better judgement of professionals, 97–98
hope, 156–57
Human Rights Act 1998, 3–4, 210–11

immunisation of children, *see* **vaccinations**
information-sharing and communication:
advance care planning, 8, 15, *17, 18*, 20–21
conflict management, *26*
NICE guidelines, 16, 19–20
inherent jurisdiction, 59–61, 83
capacity, 68
children in care, 77–78
declarations of unlawfulness, 69–70, 78–79
deprivation of liberty, 80–83
exercising jurisdiction, 69
judicial intervention threshold
inherent jurisdiction, 59–61
legal aid, 78
source of power to make orders, 69
declarations of unlawfulness, 69–70
injunctive relief, 70
parens patriae jurisdiction, 70
injunctions:
injunctive relief, 70
non-removal injunctions, 81
prevention of travel abroad for alternative treatment, 38

joint action by parents:
education decisions, 55
court intervention, 55–57
best interests test, 63, 65
judicial intervention threshold, 1–3, 4
best interests as the threshold, 29–31
attempts at law reform, 32–33
Alfie Evans case, 31, 38–39
Charlie Gard case, 31–38
Isaiah Haastrup case, 31
justifications for law reform, 32–33
whether courts' right to intervene, 31–32
Children Act 1989, 57–58
challenges to, 35–36
Alfie Evans case, 31, 38–39
Charlie Gard case, 31–38
right to be transferred to another hospital, 36
inherent jurisdiction, 59–61
legal history, 33–35
parental responsibility, 64
when courts intervene, 2, 31–32

***Kings College Hospital NHS Foundation Trust v Ms Thomas, Haastrup and Haastrup* [2018],** 2, 7, 31, 157–59, 172, 188–89, 213, 216, 218, 220, 228

legal aid, 78, 111, 226–27
local authorities holding parental responsibility, 63–64, 67–68, 77–78
long-term ventilation, 13–14
spinal muscular atrophy, 14–15
see also Great Ormond Street Hospital v Gard [2017]; mechanical ventilation

meaningful cure, 7, 186–87
mechanical ventilation, 7, 13–15, 103–4, 140, 144–45, 148–49, 212–13
medical mediation, 8, 22, 23–24, 202
advantages, 222–23, 229–30
Charlie Gard case, 223
Charlie's Law, 111
conflict management, *26*, 32, 208
drawbacks, 223–24
general features, **23**
Medical Mediation Foundation, 12, 229–30
Mental Capacity Act 2005, 81–82, 164, 168
Mental Capacity (Amendment) Bill, 111, 218–19
moral uncertainty regarding a course of action:
assessment of best interests, 88–89
competing views of best interest, 89–90, **90–91**

National Institute for Health and Care Excellence (NICE) guidance, 16, 19
advance care planning guidelines, 16, 19–20
non-*Gillick* competent children, 3
non-treatment of critically ill children, *see* **treatment/non-treatment of critically ill children**
novel therapies, *see* **experimental treatments**
nucleoside therapy, 36–37, 49–50, 109–10, 148–49, 159, 162, 165–67, 185, 186–87
see also experimental treatments; *Great Ormond Street Hospital v Gard* [2017]
Nuffield Council on Bioethics, 162, 166, 207–8, 211

***parens patriae* jurisdiction,** 33–34, 70–71, 83
limitations, 71–72
parental authority, 2, 35, 49, 51–54, 202, 206
parental autonomy, 113–14
special cases, 74–75, 94–95
see also parental responsibility
parental autonomy:
advance care planning, 20–21
balancing, 39–40, 124, 129, 138
best interests test, 125–26
harm threshold and, 108, 112, 113–14, 122, 132–33
Mill, J.S., 112, 131
parental decision-making, 9–12, 85
clinician-parent relationship, 22, 25, *26*, 151, 159–60, 208, 210–11, 226
mediation, role of, 223
religious-based faith, 155–56
parental discretion, 1, 3
best interests test
lack of clarity, 113
clinicians' latitude, 123–24
courts' interference with, 34–35, 39, 62
harm threshold and, 126
limitations, 47, 53–54, 126
education, 54–55
moral uncertainty and, 102
parental disputes:
best interests test principle, 54–57
section 8 orders, 59
education, 54–56
vaccinations, 63
parental responsibility, 51–52, 139, 149, 200–1
care orders, 63–64
Children Act 1989, 51, 57–59, 72–74
medical cases, 74–76
section 8 orders, 57–58, 76–78
deprivation of liberty, 80–81
inherent jurisdiction, 59–61, 70
limits of parental responsibility, 51–54
local authorities holding parental responsibility, 67–68
care orders, 63–64
section 8 orders, 77–78
nature of concept, 51–54
parental autonomy, 34–35, 49–50, 171
parental disputes, 54–57
responsibility for the child lies with parents, 52–53
scope, 67–68
UN Convention on the Rights of the Child, 51

Patient Advice and Liaison Services (PALS), 8, 16
primacy of parental role, 53, 56, 57–58
  parental freedom, 91–92
  section 8 orders, 58–59
    restrictions, 73
professional conscience, 137–38, 139–40
  Charlie Gard case, 148–50
  medical treatment of a child, 141–43, 150–52
    withdrawing treatment, 143–48
  professional judgment compared, 138–40
  Re Wyatt, 141–42
  significance, 150–52
professional judgement, 137–38, 138–39
  medical treatment of a child, 139
  professional conscience compared, 138–40
prohibited steps order, 73, 74, 82
  limitations, 74
  sterilisation of a child, 74, 76
public opinion, 2–3, 200–1
  Alfie Evans case, 30
  Charlie Gard case, 32, 229
  harm threshold, 129–31

quality of life, 7, 12, 13–15, 156
  best interests test, 210
  moral uncertainty, 88–89
  qualitative futility, 179–80, 181–84, 190
    Alfie Evans case, 189–90
    Charlie Gard case, 184–89, 212
  quasi-quality of life thresholds, **118**, 119–21

***Re Ashya King* [2014],** 37, 57, 63, 158, 211–12. 228
***Re JM (A Child) (Medical Treatment)* [2015],** 74–76, 172
  declarations of unlawfulness, 78–79
  section 8 orders, 58–59, 76–78
***Re Wyatt* [2005],** 86, 137–38, 141–43, 144–45, 151–52, 207–8, 210–11
religious-based faith:
  rejection of medical advice:
    blood transfusion cases, 155
    parental decision-making, 156
    refusal of treatment, 156
    requests for experimental treatment, 156
    withdrawal of treatment cases, 155
right to liberty and security (ECHR Art. 5), 80–83
right to respect for private and family life (ECHR Art. 8), 39, 64
Royal College of Paediatrics and Child Health (RCPCH) guidance, 16, 26–27

second opinions, 8, 16, 32, 138, 143
  Charlie's Law, 111
  "cherry-picking", 227
  conflict management, 23–24, 208, 217–18, 229
  independence of second opinion, 149, 169, 218
section 8 orders, 58–59
  children in care, 77–78
  limitations, 76–77
    children in care, 77–78
  parental disputes, 59
  parental responsibility, 57–58, 76–77
    local authorities holding parental responsibility, 77–78
  primacy of parental role, 58–59
  prohibited steps order, 73, 74, 82
    limitations, 74
    sterilisation of a child, 74, 76
  Re JM (A Child) (Medical Treatment) [2015], 58–59, 76–78
  restrictions, 73
  specific issue order, 73, 74, 82
    limitations, 74
    sterilisation of a child, 74, 76
  sterilisation of a child, 74, 76
significant harm, 8, 37
  arguments in favour of harm threshold:
    parents as prima facie decision-makers, 44–45
    reflecting current practice, 46
    tolerance and value decisions, 46–47
  child protection, 53–54
  inherent jurisdiction, 61
  objections to harm threshold:
    blaming parents for causing harm, 41
    excluding vexatious claims, 39, 40
    harm is always an issue, 41–43
    insufficient consideration of parents' views, 39–40
    privileging parental views, 43–44
    significant risk of harm, 40–41
specific issue order, 73, 74, 82
  limitations, 74
  sterilisation of a child, 74, 76
spinal muscular atrophy, 14–15
sterilisation of a child, 60, 74–76, 154

treatment/non-treatment of critically ill children, 118
  Children Act 1989, 209–10
  civil law, 209–10
  criminal law, 208–9

guidance, 211
Human Rights Act 1998, 210–11
human rights law, 210–11
trust/mistrust, 158–61

UN Convention on the Rights of the Child, 51, 53
universal vulnerability theory, 4, 191–93, 206
benefits of vulnerability, 194
sources of vulnerability, 193

vaccinations, 63–64, 73, 93, 94–95, 127, 171
vexatious claims, 39, 40, 65
vulnerability, 206
adult construction of vulnerability, 196–97, 199–200
children's outcome tied to parents' identity, 200
exploitation of parental insecurities, 197–99
judges' vulnerabilities, 205–6
media portrayals of Alfie Evans and Charlie Gard, 194–96
parents as protectors, 199–200
parents' vulnerabilities, 197–204
privatisation of responsibility for children, 200–1
see also universal vulnerability theory

welfare of the child, *see* **best interests approach**
withdrawing and withholding treatment, 9–12, 143–48
active decision-making, 13
declarations of unlawfulness, 79, 146
delay of, 124
futility, 4, 177–79, 184–86
guidance, 16, 211
indeterminate nature of "best interest" and "harm", 96–97
judicial intervention, 31–32, 86
mechanical ventilation, 7, 13, 212–13
professional conscience, 148–50
professional judgment, 103, 137–38, 140
second opinions, 217–18
whether hospital can withdraw treatment, 36, 49

www.ingramcontent.com/pod-product-compliance
Lightning Source LLC
LaVergne TN
LVHW052308200926
848481LV00002B/499